RALEGH AND THE THROCKMORTONS

RALEGH AND HIS SON WALTER

RALEGH
AND THE
THROCKMORTONS

BY
A. L. ROWSE

THE REPRINT SOCIETY LONDON

PREFACE

SIR WALTER RALEGH has not ceased to compel the imagination of the English public, indeed of English-speaking people across the world, in America as much as in Britain. But the curious thing is that there is no satisfactory modern biography of him. The best are still two Victorian works: Edwards's *Life* (Macmillan, 1868) which, though published almost a century ago, is admirable for its steady good judgment and still indispensable, for it contains the *Letters*; and Stebbing's *Biography* (Oxford: Clarendon Press, 1899), excellent for its intelligence and perception. But time has rendered these works inadequate: so much more material has come to light since Edwards wrote, while Stebbing is oddly full of misprints and small errors.

The numerous literary biographies that have appeared, and still appear, are useless to the serious student of the period or of Ralegh — worse than useless in that they perpetuate old mistakes already cleared up by scholars. Their authors for the most part have no idea that Ralegh is the most difficult of all the Elizabethans to get right — the most enigmatical or at least self-contradictory, a combination of qualities calculated both to attract and repel. For the most part, beglamoured, they romanticise him and see everything through his eyes: everything he did was right, his opponents always wrong. This is very ingenuous and the truth was far otherwise. Then, too, the subject is surrounded by pitfalls, both of technical historical scholarship and of political, as well as personal, interpretation. Only a seasoned Elizabethan scholar can hope to get Ralegh right.

My aim has not been to add yet another to the tale of full-length, repetitive biographies, but to do something, I hope, more original and something new: to place him, and make him more intelligible, in the perspective of his family and the still more remarkable family into which he married, the Throckmortons. The whole accent of this book, then, is on the personal and the family background — I have had my say in other books on Ralegh's maritime and colonial ventures — and what better perspective is there for the understanding of a man? For many years I have ruminated about him without feeling satisfied that

v

I had grasped the problematical, essential nature of this so difficult man. At last I feel, though I know well one is not supposed to say such things, that I have *got* him.

The discovery of the fullest Elizabethan diary I know, that of Ralegh's brother-in-law, Sir Arthur Throckmorton, has thrown new light on the missing centrepiece of Ralegh's life : his secret marriage with Elizabeth Throckmorton, and the birth of a child hitherto unknown, sponsored at baptism by (of all people) the man who was to become his mortal enemy, Essex. One could hardly get nearer than that — while the chances of finding anything new about an Elizabethan so famous as Ralegh are extremely exiguous.

I have made the undreamed-of good fortune of the Diary my setting for Ralegh's life : all one needs know for a biography is here, with the accent on person and family, tracing the latter down to its end with Sir Walter's grandson. In addition there are the Throckmortons, who offer their own excitements. Here is the first account at any length of Sir Nicholas Throckmorton, foremost of Elizabethan diplomats and chief rival of William Cecil. The Diary of his son Arthur offers us other interests and accents : his youthful record of war in the Netherlands ; the fullest account we have of the continental tour of a young English aristocrat of the age ; his life at Court, with new glimpses of familiar personalities, its rewards and dangers ; then the quieter and more reflective pursuits of a country gentleman nursing his estates, building his house, bringing up his family, all the coming and going of society in London and the country, in the age and countryside of Shakespeare.

For my first acquaintance with the Diary I am indebted to Mr. A. B. Emden, former Principal of St. Edmund Hall ; for arranging for me to study it conveniently over a long period at Oxford, to my friend of many years, Canon F. J. Shirley of Canterbury ; and for help both practical and scholarly, to Mr. W. Urry, archivist and librarian of the Chapter there. I am obliged to the President, Fellows and Librarian of Magdalen College for allowing me to study Sir Arthur Throckmorton's books, and in particular to my friend K. B. McFarlane, who had the foresight to collect them all conveniently together nearly twenty years before I had need to study them. Together, too, equipped with eighteenth-century topographies and county histories we have explored Throckmorton countryside, churches and tombs. I have been greatly helped by Sir Robert Throckmorton, not only for kindness at Coughton but for the loan of the late Lady Throckmorton's valuable notes on the history of the family. Mr. John Stoye kindly corrected my chapter on the continental tour.

In Northamptonshire my debts are agreeably most numerous. Miss Joan Wake has helped me generously from her immense store of local knowledge, and vetted those chapters. The Rector of Paulerspury, the Rev. J. T. Lewis, has been most co-operative and hospitable, has put up with many visits and enquiries, and helped me with the parish registers and its history. To Lady Hesketh, of Easton Neston, I am obliged for encouragement and hospitality and for driving me around her beautiful countryside in the rain. Over the years I have received much friendly hospitality and kindness in Northamptonshire, from the Duke and Duchess of Buccleuch at Boughton, Earl and Countess Spencer at Althorp, Sir Gyles Isham at Lamport, Mr. and Mrs. Brudenell at Deene, Mr. and Mrs. Stopford Sackville at Drayton : all of which has helped me to appreciate and understand better a county so remote and different from my own. Dr. P. A. J. Pettit allowed me to read his unpublished thesis on the Forests of Northamptonshire.

The Marquis of Salisbury was generous, as always, with hospitality at Hatfield and with permission to explore his archives for Ralegh material. I am indebted to his librarian for help with this, and to my friend Miss N. O'Farrell for constant aid from the Public Record Office, the British Museum and Somerset House. In Kent Miss Alison Clark showed me over Boughton Place, of the Wottons, and the church of Boughton Malherbe where they are buried. At Oxford the Warden of All Souls was constantly helpful in answering literary enquiries and encouraging the work; so, too, Mr. John Buxton of New College, and Mr. Howard Colvin of St. John's with architectural information.

From the West Country I cannot refrain from paying tribute to the life-work of an admirable Victorian antiquary, Dr. T. N. Brushfield of Plymouth, to whom we owe far more new information in his day about Ralegh than to many other, and more celebrated, scholars. Mr. Charles Woolf, of Newquay, came all the way from Cornwall to photograph the tomb of the author of the Diary at Paulerspury. The book's revision was made under the hospitable roof of Christabel, Lady Aberconway, at lovely Maenan.

A. L. ROWSE

ALL SOULS
Sunday, 11 June 1961

TO
SIR JOHN NEALE
MOST GENEROUS OF SCHOLARS
AND CONSTANT FRIEND

CONTENTS

ILLUSTRATIONS

xi

CHAPTER I

THE THROCKMORTONS

T HE Throckmortons spring from a place of that name in the parish of Fladbury in Worcestershire, between Evesham and Pershore, in that delectable country of meadows and orchards dominated by Bredon Hill. The parish is mostly contained within a loop of the Warwickshire Avon; but between the water-meads of Fladbury and the moated grange of Throckmorton comes the ridge of Craycombe Hill — wood and pasture and fruit-orchards — rising above the meandering medieval lanes. Here the Throckmortons were established in the later Middle Ages, were certainly to be found in the thirteenth century, cultivating their fields, making their marriages, being gathered to their fathers in the churches of Throckmorton and Fladbury.

When John Leland, the King's antiquary, rode about the country in the dark days of the fall of the monasteries and the rise of the gentry — as I drive round in the time of the destruction of their houses and all that made England beautiful — he noted that 'John Throckmorton was the first setter-up of his name to any worship in Throckmorton village, the which was at that time neither of his inheritance nor purchase, but as a thing taken of the see of Worcester in farm, because he bare the name of the lordship and village'.[1] The Throckmortons, then, got their name from the place; it is indeed descriptive of its physical features.[2]

The family got its first rise from this rich low-lying country of streams and meadows in the service of the Beauchamp Earls of Warwick, the grandees of these parts, at the turn of the fourteenth into the fifteenth century. John's father Thomas was a

[1] *The Itinerary of John Leland*, ed. L. Toulmin Smith, II. 14.
[2] A. Mawer and F. M. Stenton, *The Place-Names of Worcestershire* (*English Place-Name Society*, IV.), 169-70, suggest that the name may mean the farm by the 'throc'-mere, 'throc' being connected with a dialect word meaning 'drain'. Considering the frequency of the pronunciation, and spelling, 'frogmorton', is there any objection to the obvious meaning that suggests itself to the inexpert, the farm by the frog-marsh ?

retainer of the Earl, and so was promoted constable of Elmley castle in Henry IV's reign.[1] His son John was forked into the more promising office of chamberlain of the exchequer, often called that of under-treasurer of England — a place to which the most celebrated of his descendants, the Edwardian Sir Nicholas Throckmorton, succeeded more than a century later. This John was the first of his family to be knighted; better still, he married the heiress of the Spineys, with whom came Coughton in Warwickshire, where the Throckmortons still are. Sir John and his wife were buried in the old parish church at Fladbury, where may be seen their admirable brasses upon their Purbeck marble tomb under the tower.

This couple had a son, Sir Thomas, who married the heiress of Robert Olney and thus brought in to the Throckmorton inheritance the charming village of Weston Underwood in Buckinghamshire, where the poet Cowper became friendly with members of the family in the eighteenth century. Sir Thomas was succeeded by his son Sir Robert, who may be said to have initiated the marked vein of Catholic piety in the house of Coughton, since he died in Italy in 1519 on pilgrimage to the Holy Land. But not before he had erected a fine monument for himself in the church at Coughton; so we may presume that it was with him that the family executed its definitive move to those still more promising prospects. For Coughton lies not far from Alcester, royal Kenilworth and Stratford-on-Avon, the highway to London.

The pious Sir Robert achieved nothing much, except a good match with a daughter of a Lord Mayor of London, and a mass of children. We find him serving quietly, as we should expect, in the commission of the peace for Warwickshire. Sir Robert was to be justified, or at least distinguished, by his sons. With the eldest, George, who early became an esquire for the body to Henry VIII, the family resumed its official station with a still more promising position in the royal household. It was this that led to its rapid ascent to power and influence, the opportunities and dangers, of the Reformation decades. Sir George had a narrow squeak at the hands of his acquaintance Cromwell. His brother Michael, the devoted servant of Cardinal Pole, whose long exile he shared, was attainted of high treason along with him: one of several members of the family to attain that distinction in the ups and downs of the sixteenth century.

---

[1] T. Nash, *History of Worcestershire* (ed. 1799), Throckmorton Pedigree, I. 452.

Young George got the rewards of attendance upon the king in beneficial leases for long periods without fine, in stewardships, keeperships and such advantageous grants. In 1511 he got a lease for forty years of the Crown manors of Tanworth-in-Arden and Sheriff's Lench, in the Throckmorton country, the borders of Warwickshire and Worcestershire.[1] Next year he became chief steward of the lordship of Yardly, the year after keeper of the park of Claredon for life. In 1513 he was drawing £60 : 16 : 8 a year from his post — as much as the rector of a fat parsonage. Ten years later, in April 1528, Sir George was thought to be dying : it was reported at the supper-table of Wolsey's Dean of Christ Church that he was 'sore sick of a disease in his back and in his huckbones, and his physicians and surgeons think he cannot live'.[2] So far from this, Sir George was on the threshold of the most interesting, acquisitive and dangerous portion of his life. In July he wrote to Cardinal Wolsey asking for various offices : he would like to be sheriff of Worcestershire and *custos rotulorum* of Warwickshire, also steward of the see of Worcester and under-treasurer of England. If Wolsey would help him, he would contribute to the building of the Cardinal's college at Oxford. We find the younger generation of King and Cardinal's servants intimate : cousin George sends the Cardinal's right-hand man, Cromwell, a greyhound and asks him for some sturgeon and quails. A few years later there was much correspondence with Cromwell, now become the all-powerful minister, about buying and selling lands, for these years of the Dissolution were the classic period in the building up of estates.

In 1529 the epoch-making Reformation Parliament met, and Sir George was returned as a knight of the shire for Warwickshire.[3] True to the Catholic tradition of his family Sir George took a line in opposition to the whole policy of the government — Henry's divorce from Catherine of Aragon, his marriage with Anne Boleyn, the Acts withholding payment of Annates and ending all appeals to Rome, the Act of Supremacy. It is not surprising that it brought him in danger; it cost Bishop Fisher and Sir Thomas More their heads. We have a letter describing Sir George's conduct in these years; it is extraordinary for the vividness of the scenes it describes, arguments with the King about *his* conduct, discussions with opponents of the King, like

[1] *Letters and Papers of Henry VIII*, I, pt. 1, grants 924 (12), 1083 (4) ; pt. 2, grant 2137 (10) ; II, pt. 2, grants 1460, 1222.
[2] *Ibid. Addenda*, I, pt. 1, 193, 396 ; *ibid.* IV, pt. 2, 1961–2.
[3] *Members of Parliament* (Return of 1878), I. 370.

Friar Peto and Bishop Fisher, the encouragement Sir George received from the sainted More himself.[1] It is no less important as a revelation of how far opposition to Henry VIII could go — salutary for those who think that Henry's rule was just a personal despotism.

Sir George made one of a group of Parliament men who used to foregather for dinner and supper at the 'Queen's Head' during the divorce proceedings, and here he incautiously boasted of an interview he had had with his redoubtable sovereign. Henry sent for him as an opponent and confided that his conscience was troubled at having married his brother Prince Arthur's wife. Sir George, nothing loth, told the King that if he married the Lady Anne 'your conscience would be more troubled at length, for ye have meddled both with the mother and the sister'. This seems going pretty far, but all the King said was, 'Never with the mother'. At this Cromwell, who was standing by, put in, 'Nor never with the sister either, and therefore put that out of your mind'. The inwardness of this was that Mary Boleyn had been Henry's mistress, and that constituted a canonical bar then to marrying the sister.

Early in 1533 Henry married Anne Boleyn in secrecy. This was followed by the Act of Appeals, the cardinal step in the breach with Rome, for it forbade any appeal to any authority outside the country, temporal or spiritual. Henceforth England followed its own rule, acknowledging no superior to itself; everything else flowed from that. So clear and definite a break with the long medieval past — though it had the bulk of the country with it, for nothing was more unpopular than the papal claims in England — naturally evoked some opposition. Sir Thomas Dingley commented to Sir George that he wondered the Act should pass so lightly. Sir George replied provocatively that few would care to displease the Lord Privy Seal, *i.e.* Cromwell.

Sir George's kinsmen were still more outspoken and obstinate. His cousin, Friar Peto, preached an Easter day sermon before the King at Greenwich denouncing the divorce, and told him that he could have no other wife than Catherine, unless he could prove carnal knowledge between Prince Arthur and her — and this was impossible, for she had received the sacrament to the contrary. Prince Arthur's word that he had been in the midst of Spain was probably but a naughty joke.

Sir George continued determinedly on his course and made

---

[1] *L.P.* XII, pt. 2, 332 foll.

a speech in Parliament against the Act of Appeals. For this Sir Thomas More, the intellectual leader of the Opposition, sent for him to give him encouragement. They met in the Parliament chamber, 'where, as I do remember me, stood an altar, or a thing like an altar, whereupon he did lean'. Sir Thomas More said he was glad Sir George was so good a Catholic, and if he continued he would deserve great reward of God and, he thought, at length from the King. (Here the saint was wrong — it would at length have cost Throckmorton his head, as it did his own.)

Puffed up with this encouragement Sir George went on to discuss the Acts of Appeals, Annates and Supremacy with Bishop Fisher. From this edifying conversation he went on to Father Reynolds, the well-known confessor at Syon, to whom he opened his conscience on these matters. Father Reynolds advised him to stick to his opinion to the death, or else he would surely be damned, and not to hold his peace in Parliament even if he thought his speaking could not prevail. This was contrary to Bishop Fisher's view, but Reynolds assured Sir George he could not tell how many others he might encourage in the House to do the same. (Father Reynolds received his 'great reward' shortly after, when he was executed in 1535.)

It is not surprising that after so prolonged a course of opposition Sir George found himself in trouble; it is more surprising that after so much good advice from such excellent people he should have escaped with his life. Already in the autumn of 1533 he received a warning from Cromwell, to which Sir George replied that he would follow his advice to live at home and meddle little.[1] But this was what most Throckmortons were incapable of. In the year 1535, when More and Fisher were brought to the block, in spite of their wise refusal to utter any words against the Act of Supremacy, we hear that the King was displeased with Sir George — and that was apt to be ominous.

In 1536 Pole exploded his long prepared time-bomb against Henry. Pole was a much favoured cousin of the King's, of Yorkist royal blood, whom Henry had supported for years abroad as the King's scholar, so generously that he could draw a cultivated circle of virtuous young men around him in whose company he delighted.[2] Henry now needed his moral support. Pole long kept silence, and then launched a formidable indictment of all Henry's proceedings, a full-length Latin treatise

---

[1] *Ibid.* VI. 543; VIII. 9.
[2] For this circle *v.* W. G. Zeeveld, *Foundations of Tudor Policy.*

addressed to the public opinion of Europe, concluding with an open incitement to the people of England to depose their King. What made this personally unforgivable was that it came with the crisis of Henry's reign, the Pilgrimage of Grace when much of the North lay in open revolt, to the purposes of which Pole lent himself when he accepted the Pope's legateship and moved towards England. This was treason, and in those terrible years Henry would have had Pole murdered if he could. The delayed-action time-bomb of a Latin treatise was entrusted to Michael Throckmorton to hand personally to the King. It is a matter for some surprise that he ever got safely out of the country again ; it is said that he promised Cromwell to return to Pole as a spy on him — which he had no intention of doing. He threw in his lot with the newly made Cardinal, became his steward and passed the days of their long exile together with him.

At the first tremor of the risings that convulsed the year 1536, the peasants' movement in Lincolnshire, Sir George Throckmorton led three hundred men to the King's standard at Ampthill. In the autumn Yorkshire broke out and the rebels under Aske moved southwards. Sir George was ordered to raise two hundred men from his county and join the king's forces.[1] On his return to London in November he made himself too free in discussing Aske's demands. One night at supper at the 'Queen's Head' by Temple Bar he lent Sir William Essex a printed tract of the rebels' demands and this was copied by a servant of Sir William's. By the time Sir George rode down into Berkshire to stop the night with his brother-in-law at Englefield, the rumour of this and copies of the Pilgrims' Articles had preceded him to Reading. On learning this, Sir George burnt this inflammable material there. However, it was bruited about that it had come from him. At another supper-table, when the subject of the rebel demands was raised, 'and every man looked upon another, and no man would make answer', Sir George had not hesitated to say what he thought. All this called for a personal explanation to the King: we have his confession subscribed, 'By your true faithful humble subject and servant, with the heaviest heart that ever had living man'.

When the Pilgrimage of Grace had been broken, the crisis surmounted, there were many reckonings to be made. In October 1537 Lady Throckmorton wrote urgently to Sir William Parr, 'Good brother, Mr. Throckmorton is in trouble, as I think you

---

[1] *L.P.* XI. 233, 557-9.

know. Come up here immediately on the coming of my son to
you. . . . Not that I desire you to speak to my Lord Privy Seal
[Cromwell] for him, but to give me your best counsel what to
do for the help of him and myself.' Now Sir George had to
account to the King for the whole course he had followed in the
past four or five years, dissociate himself from his brother in
exile and make an absolute submission. He wrote the King an
account of the successive stages of his opposition, putting it down
to vainglory and evil counsels. As for his 'unthrifty and unnatural brother', the last he had heard of him was from a neighbour who had seen him at mass in a chapel in Antwerp, to which
news Sir George had replied that he would he had never been
born. He now besought the King's pardon, having been blinded
so long by the above counsels and having now perceived his
error by reading the *New Testament* and *The Institution of a Christian
Man*.

The tradition in the family was that Sir George very narrowly
escaped :

> My father's foes clapped him through cankered hate
>   In Tower fast, and gaped to joint his neck.
> They were in hope for to obtain a mate
>   Who heretofore had laboured for a check.
> Yea, Grevilles grieved him ill without a cause,
> Who hurt not then nor yet the Prince's laws.[1]

However, to submit, with Henry, was usually to be forgiven;
and, after making a clean breast of everything, Sir George
shortly began to receive the rewards for thinking better of it.
When the monastery of Bordesley in Worcestershire was plucked
down in 1538, it was suggested that the glass, stone, etc. should
be given to him.[2] In 1540 Sir George received a lease of the
titles of Church Honibourne and the manor of Middle Littleton,
with the grain rents of certain farms, all late of Evesham priory
in Worcestershire. Another George in the family got a lease of
the cell of Deerhurst, with several of its manors and rectories in
Gloucestershire, parcel of the possessions of Tewkesbury abbey.
All very convenient.

That spring Henry callously sacrificed Cromwell to the

---

[1] *The Legend of Sir Nicholas Throckmorton*, ed. J. G. Nichols (Roxburghe Club), 5.
All quotations are from this edition. But there is no reason to accept the editor's
suggestion that the poem was written at Chastleton, when it specifically gives Littleton
(near Evesham). A note at Coughton says that it was written by Thomas Throckmorton of Coughton, 1533-1615.

[2] *L.P.* XIII, pt. 1, 556; XIV, pt. 2, 202; XV. 6, 563, 564.

exigencies of his foreign policy, to his resentment at Cromwell's entangling him in the marriage with Anne of Cleves — the 'Flanders mare', as he called her — to Cromwell's general unpopularity, who had no other support but the King. Henry was an able politician, and his sense of the temporary Catholic reaction coincided with his wayward fancy alighting upon young Catherine Howard. Sir George Throckmorton had long had a score against Cromwell, and to this was added the grievance of Cromwell's getting possession of the manor of Oversley, which lay conveniently near to Coughton. Now came Sir George's turn. He and the odious Rich — whose convictions were as Catholic as Sir George's — turned King's evidence against Cromwell, and witnessed that the minister had betrayed his master's confidence before them in regard to his secret matter, *i.e.* the marriage.[1] It is impossible now to discover what it was, but the fearful doctrine of constructive treason covered it, and it was enough. In one of his last appeals for mercy, to a King without mercy, Cromwell wrote that to his remembrance he 'never spake with the Chancellor of the Augmentations and Throckmorton together at one time. But if I did I am sure I spake never of any such matter, and your Grace knoweth what manner of man Throckmorton hath ever been towards your Grace and your proceedings.' Cromwell's fall disgorged Oversley, and the Throckmortons were able to pick it up, paying a good price for it.[2]

In 1542–3 Sir George at last got his sheriffwick of Worcester, and with it a lease of the manor of Beauchamp's Court in Warwickshire, late of Alcester priory, and the tithes of Oversley.[3] Next year he was sheriff of the counties of Warwick and Leicester, and was able to purchase the manor of Tanworth outright for £630 : 17 : 2. Such were the rewards of submission and sense. They were by no means all; other members of the family continued to pick up desirable bits and pieces that fell from the royal table in the general feast; Sir George had a numerous brood of his own to provide for. Then came an unexpected stroke of luck from Henry's last move into the marriage-mart, whence earlier there had threatened so much danger. It may seem paradoxical that the best help yet for this Catholic family should come from Henry's marriage to a woman of Protestant leanings, Catherine Parr; but this was a question of family interest, which is sometimes more important than religious differences.

[1] R. B. Merriman, *Life and Letters of Thomas Cromwell*, I. 296; II. 265.
[2] *L.P.* XVI. 427.   [3] *Ibid.* XVI. 427; XVII. 696.

Sir George had married Catherine, daughter of Lord Vaux of Harrowden, whose mother was the widow of Sir William Parr. Sir William was the grandfather of Queen Catherine; Lady Throckmorton always regarded Catherine as her niece, and when she became Queen the Throckmortons were not likely to let her forget it.[1] Not that she wished to, for she was a kind, good woman, who at the same time as she assuaged the royal tyrant's ulcerated leg did her best to assuage people's ulcerated convictions and damp down the Catholic persecution of Protestants under the ferocious Act of Six Articles.

Sir George and Catherine Vaux made a fruitful, philo-progenitive couple; as a result of their activities there was a large family to provide for — seven sons and eleven daughters. One by-product of the Catholic strain was that among their descendants were four, and the wife of a fifth, of the Gunpowder Plot conspirators, while two more grandchildren, Francis and Thomas Throckmorton, were traitors under Elizabeth, the former executed for conspiracy. The cleverest boy of the family was the fourth son, Nicholas, who became the most celebrated of the Throckmortons — a member of the inner governing circle at the beginning of Elizabeth's reign, ambassador to France and Scotland, a militant, forward Protestant.

In the generation after Sir Nicholas, his nephew, Thomas Throckmorton, wrote an informative poem about the exciting ups and downs of his uncle's public, and well-publicised, life. It is in the manner of the popular *Mirror for Magistrates*, and has come down to us haphazardly in various manuscripts from the family; but the poem incorporates authentic details from the family tradition, and is in general corroborated by the historical documents that remain.

From this we learn that as a boy Nicholas was placed a page in the household of Henry's bastard son, the Duke of Richmond.[2]

> A brother fourth, and far from hope of land,
>> By parents' hest, I servèd as a page
> To Richmond's Duke, and waited, still at hand
>> For fear of blows, which happened in his rage.
> In France with him I lived most carelessly,
> And learned the tongue, though nothing readily.

[1] She was really a half-cousin, with one grandparent in common.
[2] From 1540 Nicholas was in receipt of an annuity from Pipewell monastery, *L.P.* XVI. 28.

9

This would have been in 1532–3; but in 1536 the Duke died, and young Nicholas was out of a place at the time when his father's troubles were at their worst:

> Our sun eclipsed a long time did not shine;
> No joys approached near unto Coughton house . . .

In this situation Lady Throckmorton had resort to her 'brother', Sir William Parr, who on his niece's later elevation became Lord Parr of Horton.

> So with her brother I was safely placed.
> Of alms, he kept me in extremity.

When Catherine Parr became Queen the Throckmortons were in clover, so long as it lasted — 'pourvu que ça dure', as Madame Mère used to say of Napoleon's astonishing luck.

> Lo! then my brethren, Clement, George and I
> Did seek, as youth do still, in Court to be :
> Each other state as base we did defy,
> Compared with Court, the nurse of dignity.
> 'Tis truly said, No fishing to the sea's,
> No serving to a king's — if you can please.

> First in the Court my brother Clement served,
> A fee he had the Queen her cup to bring.
> And some suppose that I right well deserved
> When server they saw me chosen unto the King.
> My brother George in youth by valour rare
> A pension got and gallant halberd bare.

This is borne out by the documents, though naturally the chronology of the poem, written a generation later, is not always in order. Clement became cup-bearer to the Queen, Nicholas a server in waiting; they both ate in the Queen's chamber — this was what kinship could do.

When Henry got himself involved in his last French war, four of the brothers served — while their cousin Catherine acted as Queen Regent — in France at the siege of Boulogne:

> There three of us did serve in royal band,
> The fourth did wait upon Northumberland :

that is, John Dudley, then Viscount Lisle. We find Nicholas being paid as captain of a hundred light horsemen, Northern staves; George, advancing impetuously into the enemy lines, was taken prisoner, and for him the French asked a very high ransom.

> A thousand pounds our brother George redeemed,
>   Yet then an hundred pounds and he were wide :
> With golden weights they prized him, as it seemed,
>   For that he was unto the King allied. . . .
>
> Then none of us did unrewarded go ;
>   I had a gift yearly worth fifty pound.

This is certainly borne out by the documents, so far as Nicholas is concerned. In June 1546 he received a gift, shortly after a lease of tithes in Coughton, and then, for services, a grant of the manors of Benjowe and Panshanger, late of the Marchioness of Exeter who had been attainted with her husband.[1]

Nicholas's uncle Michael had been attainted along with them — they were of the old Catholic grouping allied to Cardinal Pole in exile abroad and looking to the Princess Mary for better days. Before the breach one finds Michael writing home from Venice to his friend Thomas Starkey, glad to hear of 'the towardness of my nephews', thanking him for his 'furtherance of the young fry'.[2] But Nicholas and his nearer brothers, Clement, Kellam and George, were affected by the Reforming tendencies of the Queen's circle; they all went forward as Protestants, while the eldest and youngest brothers, Robert and John, remained Catholics. Three of them exposed themselves by their marked sympathy for Anne Askew, a woman of good family whose shocking persecution under the Act of Six Articles made the worst impression and whose burning certainly helped on the reaction against these ghastly acts-of-faith with Edward's reign. Even Henry had been forced — perhaps under Catherine's gentle pressure — to make an appeal to Parliament for more Christian charity in the execution of the Act. It is always said that the three Throckmortons attended Anne Askew to her execution, when she had to be carried to Smithfield in a chair, since she could not stand from the racking she had endured in the Tower at the hands of Wriothesley and Rich, both Catholics. Certainly the three Throckmortons paid her and her fellow prisoners a charitable visit, for an unknown man called out, 'Ye are all marked that come to them; take heed to your lives'.[3] But the Throckmortons were not wanting in courage.

---

[1] *L.P.* XIX. 307; XX, pt. 2, 549; XXI, pt. 1, 780, 566, 575.
[2] *Ibid.* VIII. 203.
[3] *Narratives of the Reformation*, ed. J. G. Nichols (Camden Soc.), 42.

Moreover, they were protected by their high favour with the Queen and her kin, the Parrs and Pembrokes.

> Then Pembroke and his wife, who sister was
> Unto the Queen, their kinsfolk friended much;
> And Parr, their brother, did them both surpass:
> Who, for to pleasure us, did never grutch . . .
>
> In many suits their help did us avail;
> Few things, or none, that time with us sped ill . . .

This blissful state of affairs was brought to a sudden stop by Henry's death:

> Death did surprise
> Our King, yea then when most we looked to rise.

On Henry's death Catherine felt free to marry her former suitor, Protector Somerset's brother, Lord Admiral Seymour, with whom she had been in love before her marriage to the King, when she had been 'overruled by a higher power'. Young Nicholas continued in the household of the Queen dowager, where he saw a good deal of Princess Elizabeth, who was made much of by her stepmother and still more by her ambitious husband. The poem has a convincing portrait of the demure Princess as she was at this time, Edward's 'sweet sister Temperance', rising hope of the stern unbending Protestants.

> If some of us that waited near the Queen
> Did aught for her,[1] she passed in thankfulness.
> I wondered at her answers, which have been
> So fitly placed with speedy readiness.
> She was disposed to mirth in company,
> Yet still regarding civil modesty.

Henry had bequeathed a war with Scotland to his successor, and we find Nicholas and Kellam, serving under Lord Parr, taking part in the raiding and burning on the Scottish Borders.[2] Then came the battle of Pinkie, where the Protector won a resounding victory: the Scots deserted an impregnable position and laid themselves open to a bloody defeat with the loss of many hundreds of lives. Nicholas must have been present, for he was given the honour, with the attendant chances, of carrying the news to the young King. This was the beginning of his high favour with the boy, who was much taken with him, and rewarded him with an annuity of £100, and other things too. In

---

[1] *I.e.* Princess Elizabeth.   [2] *L.P.* XVIII, pt. 2, 166.

the course of the next year Queen Catherine died in child-bed, and her husband was executed for conspiracy against his brother. The Protector arranged for Nicholas to be transferred to serve the King in the Privy Chamber. This was very agreeable to both parties; Edward took a fancy to the young man, who became a prime favourite.

> Let Sidney, Neville and the rest that were
>   In Privy Chamber then but tell a truth
> If they have seen his liking anywhere
>   Such as to me, who never felt his wrath.
> I lived in so great favour that my could
> Was well nigh joinèd then with what I would.

The poem tells an amusing story of Nicholas's irregular knighting by the spirited boy-King:

> And on a time when knighted I should be
>   The King said, 'Kneel'. Yet then I went my way.
> But straight forth himself ran and spièd me
>   Behind a chest in lobby where I lay;
> And there against my will he dubbed me knight:
> Which was an eye-sore unto some men's sight.

Even this is negatively borne out by the documents, for there is no other record of his knighting; they positively corroborate other favours received. About this time Nicholas married a wife, Anne, daughter of Sir Nicholas Carew of Beddington in Surrey. The Carews were an official Court family, like the Throckmortons. Sir Nicholas had been in high favour with Henry VIII and was his Master of the Horse; his fall from grace was all the more sudden and cruel. He had had the temerity to express his sympathy with the Poles and Courtenays and the unwisdom to engage in a compromising correspondence with them. So he was attainted and executed in 1539. The attainder had not yet been reversed, and his lands were still in the possession of the Crown. So Anne cannot have been much of a catch, nor was young Throckmorton in much of a position to marry: all was in prospect. Their situation is described in the poem: how, when Nicholas brought his wife to Court to present to the King, Edward noticed how poorly clad she was, and asked the young husband—

> Dost thou want, and blush to crave?
> But we are well contented for to give
>   Something of profit, which thou shalt espy.

A Throckmorton needed no further invitation : Nicholas spied
out the job of under-treasurer of the Mint, which brought in 200
marks a year, besides his 100 marks as gentleman of the Privy
Chamber.[1] Better still, the attainder of the Carews was reversed
about this time and their lands restored ; perhaps this came as a
wedding-present for the young couple : if so it would give us a
date for the marriage, 1549–50.

In December 1551 Nicholas was given a profitable exchange
with the Crown : he surrendered his £100 annuity for the
manors of Paulerspury, Cosgrove, Silverstone, Tiffield and the
park of Paulerspury in Northamptonshire ; the priory of Luffield
with its lands in Oxfordshire and Buckinghamshire ; the manor
of Baddesley near Romsey in Hampshire, with the advowsons
and rectories dependent on them.[2] All this to be held of the
honour of Grafton, paying the Crown rents, but without any
fine. It made a munificent grant : enough to bring up a family
on. The main clutch of these estates lay near Towcester, on
either side of Watling Street, the highway Nicholas was accustomed to follow between his home at Coughton and the Court at
Westminster.

Equipped with a wife and with these excellent prospects
opening out before him, Sir Nicholas got leave to absent himself
from Court to go back along that road and show himself at
Coughton. To his surprise he found himself not at all welcome
to the old patriarch, his father. Sir George treated him civilly
enough in public during their stay, but privately he upbraided
him with a good deal of bitterness. The poem says nothing
whatever on the subject of their different religious sympathies,
though that may have been an element of friction ; and indeed
later we do not find much contact, or any evidence of affection,
between the junior branches of the house making their way up
with the new deal, and the senior line remaining Catholic in
the old home. The old man was clearly jealous of the young
people's success at Court, his country fare was not good enough
for them, he suspected their disdain, etc. — one sees the situation.
At last a definite grievance was expressed : Sir George felt himself insulted that a younger son had been knighted before his
eldest son. (The eldest son, a person of no particular importance, remained mostly at Coughton, transmitting his father's
conservative views to his posterity. They have survived, where
the clever Protestant lines have died out. So much for the

[1] *Cal. Patent Rolls, Edward VI*, III. 137.
[2] *Ibid.* IV. 104.

supposed intolerance of Protestant England.)

When Sir Nicholas went back to Court he dutifully set himself
to remedy this state of affairs.

> To Court my eldest brother then and I
>> Did come; yet would I no man should disdain
> That by my means he knighted home did hie:
>> Whereby my father pleasèd was again.
> My brother John too, let it no man scorn,
> By furtherance mine King Edward's man was sworn.

Nor was this by any means the tale of the perquisites of royal
favour in those days. Brother George had the yearly rent of his
manor of Alne, across the fields from Coughton, and leased from
the Crown, abated £20 as a reward for good service.[1] Brother
Clement obtained the surveyorship of the woods of the Duchy of
Lancaster. Youngest brother John, trained to the law, had a
post in the Court of Requests. In January 1553 Sir Nicholas
gave up his tiresome job as under-treasurer of the Mint in the
Tower in return for an annuity of £100 for life. In May he
was granted a licence to retain twenty-five persons. A retinue — a
figure of importance, though still a young man: he had certainly
arrived.

During these years Sir Nicholas could preen himself in the
sun of royal favour:

> The King me fancied daily more and more,
> For as his years so did my favour grow . . .
>
> When some with false reports did me accuse
>> And yet could not enforce his Majesty
> His settled fancy thereby to refuse,
>> In childish cradle of security
> I rocked myself asleep, devoid of care:
> For why? I was the King's familiar.

The one source of disquiet was Northumberland's suspicion, his
jealousy of Throckmorton's intimacy with Edward:

> He much misliked our secret conference,
>> The privy whisperings that the King did use;
> He thought they little made for his defence,
>> And that alone the King I did abuse
> With tales. But sure of me he did misdeem,
> Who thought I drew not yokèd in his team.

[1] *Acts of the Privy Council, 1550–2*, 119, 325; *C.P.R.* V. 9, 92.

These middle years of the century saw the family as such at its apogee:

> When all of us at years, when two made knights,
> When five of us had been of Parliament:
> All forward in the world: when all these sights
> Our father saw, then summoned hence he went.

The family representation in Parliament speaks for itself.[1] In Edward's last Parliament, that of 1552–3, half the representation of Warwickshire was held by the family, three seats out of six; Sir Nicholas sat for Northamptonshire; there may have been one or two more, since the returns are not complete. In Mary's first Parliament, 1553, two Throckmortons sat for Warwickshire, Sir Nicholas and young John for Old Sarum, cousin John for Wootton Basset. In Elizabeth's first Parliament there may have been five or six; the returns for Warwickshire are missing, for which there may have sat two or three of the family; Sir Nicholas for Lyme Regis, Simon of the Huntingdonshire branch for that county, Kellam for Sudbury in Suffolk where he was setting up. Sir Nicholas, as the busy politician of the family, had the fullest experience of Parliament: he sat in five, from that of 1544 when he represented Maldon, to that of 1562–3 when he sat for Tavistock. There were other members of the family, from other branches, who sat in other Parliaments too.

Old Sir George could well say his *Nunc dimittis*; he had reason to be well satisfied, all things considered. He had planted out his sons and married off most of his daughters. It is said that before he died the old patriarch could count descendants to the number of a hundred and sixteen living. Sometime in these last years he built the fine gatehouse with its tall octagonal turrets, which still dominates the entrance to Coughton — 'that stately castle-like gate-house', Dugdale calls it, where, tradition says, the women of the Gunpowder Plot conspirators waited for news of their men-folk.

Leland describes the country hereabouts as it was in Sir George's last years. 'I rode from Stratford by champion ground, fruitful of corn and grass, a five miles to a ford and a small wood bridge, where I passed over Alne brook, that came down, as I marked, from the north. I passed at Coughton by a wood bridge over the Arrow river. The parish church of Coughton is very fair, exceedingly well glazed and adorned, partly made by Sir George Throckmorton's father, partly by Sir George himself.

---

[1] Cf. *Members of Parliament*, 380 foll.

There is a goodly tomb in the body of the church, made by Sir George's father that died in peregrination going to Jerusalem. From Coughton to Alcester two miles by enclosed ground. I remarked the country about Coughton and Alcester to be meetly well wooded. Part of the forest of Feckenham in Worcestershire is within three miles of Coughton.'[1]

Some time in 1553 Sir George died, and was buried with his wife beneath a table-tomb in the chancel, with their brasses and the inscription, *Of your charity pray for their souls*; for by the time it was made Mary was Queen.

[1] Leland, *ed. cit.* II. 50.

CHAPTER II

SIR NICHOLAS THROCKMORTON

THE death of Edward VI was a disaster for young Sir Nicholas on the threshold of a brilliantly promising career; a personal favourite with the boy-king, he was certainly not so with his sister Mary or even, as we shall see, with Elizabeth. The princess Mary knew him as the bearer of unpleasant messages from her brother putting pressure on her to conform to the laws of the country with regard to religion.[1] (She had no intention of doing so.) The intimate circle surrounding Edward were taken by surprise by the strength of the reaction in favour of Mary — not of her Catholicism, but of her right to the crown : she was the legitimate heir. And they were swept off their feet by the rapidity of events.

This may account for what seems a discrepancy between the account of Sir Nicholas's conduct as given in the Poem and what we learn from the documents ; or there may quite well have been some confusion in his actions, or possibly an astute reinsurance. Perhaps, again, the family tradition was not clear about what exactly happened at this critical turning-point for everybody. On Edward's death the Poem states that the Throckmortons sent a secret message to warn Mary — she might otherwise have fallen into the power of Northumberland :

> Wherefore from four of us the news was sent
> How that her brother he was dead and gone.
> In post her goldsmith then from London went,
> By whom the message was dispatched anon.
> She asked if we knew it certainly ?
> Who said, Sir Nicholas knew it verily.
>
> The author bred the errand's great mistrust :
> She feared a train to lead her to a trap.
> She said, If Robert had been there she durst
> Have gauged her life and hazarded the hap.

[1] *Cal. S.P. Spanish, 1550–52,* 212.

Her letters made, she knew not what to do :
She sent them out, but not subscribed thereto.[1]

This must represent something of what happened.

Meanwhile, Lady Jane Grey was being proclaimed Queen by the Edwardian ruling circle and was now holding state in the Tower of London. The child of one of the Throckmorton's Warwickshire cousins, Edward Underhill, a Protestant, was christened in the church on Tower hill, very grandly with the Duke of Suffolk, the Earl of Pembroke and Queen Jane as gossips — Sir Nicholas's wife standing deputy for the last. Immediately after the christening Queen Mary was proclaimed in Cheapside and, when Lady Throckmorton came into the Tower, already 'the cloth of estate was taken down . . . she would have gone forth, but could not be suffered'.[2] A few days after Clement Throckmorton posted from Coventry to the Tower to report to poor Lady Jane that her father the Duke of Suffolk was a prisoner.

While the women remained in London their men-folk were about the country. At Northampton on 18 July 1553, when Sir Thomas Tresham proclaimed Queen Mary, 'Sir Nicholas Throckmorton being present, withstanding him to his power, was driven for safety of his life to take to a house, and so being borne amongst divers gentlemen escaped with much ado ; the inhabitants would have killed him very fain'.[3] Such was the magic of the Crown in sixteenth-century England that there was a landslide in favour of the rightful Queen, Catholic or no. Within the week Sir Nicholas was fain to do a quick about-turn, for by the 24th he was ready with his cousin Tresham, with their men on horseback in red and white, to guard the Queen to London.

Sir Nicholas did not suffer in any way from his misadventure — or the Queen remembered in his favour the warning message the brothers had sent. For that autumn they were rewarded. In September Sir Nicholas, as 'the Queen's servant', got a grant for life of the keepership of the royal parks at Brigstock, vacant by the attainder of his kinsman Parr, Marquis of Northampton, temporarily laid low by the turn of fortune.[4] In October Nicholas and Clement received formal pardons, while their younger brother Anthony, also 'the Queen's servant', got a grant for life of the keepership of the park of Haseley in Warwickshire.

---

[1] *The Legend of Sir Nicholas Throckmorton*, 29.
[2] *Narratives of the Reformation*, ed. J. G. Nichols, 151, 163.
[3] *The Chronicle of Queen Jane and Queen Mary*, ed. J. G. Nichols, 12, 13.
[4] *Cal. Pat. Rolls, Philip and Mary*, I. 206, 440, 200.

At this moment a more questionable figure was clamouring at the gates for admission : their uncle Michael, whose attainder had never been reversed. The Queen, who had to feel her way carefully, wrote asking the private advice of Renard, the Emperor's ambassador, as to what she should do.[1] Michael had been waiting a month at Louvain seeking admission on the plea of visiting relatives. (Clearly he was being sent on behalf of Pole to see how the land lay.) The Queen asked whether the recent pardon might not cover him. Renard reported to Charles V that he had replied that Throckmorton must not be permitted, both on account of Parliament 'and the papal authority which the English loathe more than ever'. More important to these high politicians, Renard feared he might do mischief where the projected match with Philip was concerned. Already Mary's advisers were breaking into two parties : those who favoured the Spanish marriage, and those who were against.

Before the marriage took place Michael Throckmorton was allowed in, for in June 1554 he got 'for service' a considerable grant of lands in Warwickshire, the manors of Winterton, Honeyley and Blackwell, Ullenhall and other monastic lands, with the reversion to Haseley.[2] He did not stay long in the inclement country ; no doubt after his long exile he was now more Italian than English. Next year he went back to his home in Mantua, where he died in the same month as Queen Mary. Before leaving England he made over Haseley to his nephew Clement, and that became the home of Clement's son Job Throckmorton, the celebrated Puritan and Martin Marprelate pamphleteer, and of that Puritan branch of the family : there they lie buried.[3] Such are the turns of the Throckmorton kaleidoscope; but it serves to bring home something in the family temperament — its extremism. With the Throckmortons it was either one thing or the other : either wholly Catholic, involved in recusancy, exile, sometimes treason, or else left-wing Protestant, militant and aggressive, becoming Puritan in Elizabeth's reign, Parliamentarian under the Stuarts. No middle course was good enough for them, no moderation in their temperament; impetuous and ardent, they all inclined to that 'busy-ness' old Lady Throckmorton had had reason to deplore in Sir George.

This was never more evident than in Nicholas's next venture, which brought him within a fraction of the block; indeed his escape from it was unprecedented and made history.

[1] *Cal. S.P. Spanish, 1553*, 316, 323.
[2] *Cal. Pat. Rolls, Philip and Mary*, I. 401,   [3] *Ibid.* II. 209.

Immediately upon Mary's announcement in January 1554 of her intended marriage with Philip, Wyatt's rebellion broke out in Kent. The Spanish marriage was universally unpopular; Mary had gone forward with it against the bulk of her councillors, the wishes of Parliament and the nation. There was a rebellious feeling in many parts of the country, especially in the West, where the Earl of Devon, rejected suitor of the Queen, was expected to take the lead. He refused to go west, and remained in London, hoping to profit if things went well. So did Sir Nicholas. There can be little doubt that he was aware of Wyatt's plans, and he remained in London as a link between the movements in Kent and in the West. But he was too fly to commit himself on paper or to take overt action. Wyatt's rebellion brought many people in danger, and its failure — as is always the way with such enterprises — brought about the reaction that enabled Mary to go the whole way, restoration of Catholicism, reconciliation with Rome, burnings, alienation of the country, her own ruin. The Duke of Suffolk, Lady Jane Grey and her husband were at once executed; Princess Elizabeth and the Earl of Devon were imprisoned in the Tower. So was Sir Nicholas Throckmorton, with others like Sir Gawen Carew, his wife's cousin. (Sir Peter Carew escaped overseas in a vessel belonging to Walter Ralegh, father of Sir Walter.) This was the chance of the reactionaries to hit back at the Edwardians.

Sir Nicholas was kept prisoner in the Tower for nearly two months before he was arraigned at Guildhall on 17 April. Persons arraigned of high treason by the state in sixteenth-century England were never acquitted; there was no reason to suppose that Sir Nicholas would be.[1] His case, and his defence of himself, made such an impression at the time that we have practically a verbatim account of it.[2] He conducted his case with far greater skill than the Crown lawyers conducted theirs — though that would not have saved him. What saved him was that in Parliament that autumn the Henrician statutes governing treason cases had been repealed; the law lapsed back to the famous statute of Edward III governing the matter, and Throckmorton's case could not be brought under its provisions. This is its importance in the constitutional text-books; while 'the trial was memorable as affording an almost unprecedented example of the independence of a jury at the trial of one who was charged

---

[1] For the state of the law of treason at this time cf. Sir William Holdsworth, *History of English Law*, IV. 496 foll.

[2] Cf. *Holinshed's Chronicles* (ed. 1808), IV. 31 foll.

by the Crown with treason'.[1] Mary's government, immediately
after, remedied this by tightening up the law once more; but
meanwhile Throckmorton had escaped them, squeezed through
by this very narrow aperture.

The judges were obviously out to get him, though they did
not vilify him as Coke did Ralegh at his trial precisely half a
century later. The jury were a body of London citizens, and the
sympathies of Londoners were almost wholly Protestant. At the
beginning of the trial Sir Nicholas intercepted a move from
the bench to interfere with the jury and pack them against him.
He did most of the talking, and throughout the day addressed his
appeal skilfully to them, and to those on the bench who had been
in Parliament and were as much opposed to the Spanish marriage
as he was. 'I confess I did mislike the Queen's marriage with
Spain and also the coming of the Spaniards hither, and then
methought I had reason to do so; for I did learn the reasons of
my misliking of you, Master Hare, Master Southwell, and others
in the Parliament house: there I did see the whole consent of
the realm against it.'

The gravamen of the Attorney-General's charge was this:
'it is apparent that you lay at London as a factor, to give intelligence to them in the West as to Wyatt in Kent'. And this was
probably the case: Sir Nicholas did not deny that he had had
communications with Wyatt and the malcontents, for Wyatt's
lieutenant, Cuthbert Vaughan, turned Queen's evidence against
him. Sir Nicholas gave a convincing impression of candour and
force, admitting his contacts but proving his point that they did
not come within the compass of the treason law after the act of
repeal. He came back to this again and again, and ended with
an eloquent plea: 'to what purpose serveth the statute of repeal
the last Parliament, where I heard some of you here present and
divers other of the Queen's Council grievously inveigh against
the cruel and bloody laws of King Henry VIII . . . Some
termed them Draco's laws, which were written in blood; some
said they were more intolerable than any laws that Dionysius or
any other tyrant made. . . . And, moreover, the preface of the
same statute doth recite that for words only, many great personages and others of good behaviour have been most cruelly cast
away by these former sanguinolent thirsty laws, with many other
suggestions for the repeal of the same.'

There was no getting round Sir Nicholas's argument. Lord

[1] *Dict. Nat. Biog. sub.* Sir Nicholas Throckmorton.

Chief Justice Bromley upbraided the Queen's counsel for not being able to answer him. The fact was that Throckmorton had got up his case with characteristic thoroughness, stuck to it tenaciously, and expressed himself with all the eloquence and fire of his temperament. At five o'clock the jury returned a unanimous verdict of acquittal, 'whereat many people rejoiced'.[1]

Not so Queen Mary and her advisers. A week later the jury were had up before the Star Chamber, the two foremen sent to the Tower and the rest to the Fleet prison.[2] Nor was Sir Nicholas released: he went back to the Tower. Renard reported that, on Throckmorton's acquittal, the people showed their joy by shouting and throwing their caps in the air.[3] It so much angered the Queen that she was ill for three days together and was not yet herself. Attempts were being made to punish the judges, but 'the Queen has no authority, nor her Council, on account of the split'. When the jurymen were imprisoned, he thought that if there were more progress like this things might go better. Later, he reported that Michael Throckmorton was in the country, given the mission to present Cardinal Pole's congratulations on the marriage, but, the Pope had commanded, with all the discretion possible in the present condition of religious affairs. Evidently things did not look promising for Mary's absurd course, completely against the instincts of the nation — with which she was out of accord.

It was not until 18 January 1555, after nearly a year's imprisonment, that Sir Nicholas, Sir Gawen Carew, Sir James Croft, and others who were to become prominent in Elizabeth's service, were released from the Tower.[4] An act of clemency, for Mary was now expecting her child, to make sure her work for God. Solemn prayers were offered up in all the churches. The burnings, also for God, were begun.

Early next year Sir Nicholas was incriminated by the madcap enterprise of John Throckmorton, an obscure member of the clan, to rob the Exchequer for money with which to raise a rebellion. What gave this light-headed plan some seriousness was that it coincided with widespread disaffection among the Western gentry, many of whom were going overseas, and with the conspiracy of Henry Dudley and others against the Queen. The plain fact was that it was impossible for Mary to keep order

---

[1] *Chronicle of Queen Jane and Queen Mary,*/ 75.
[2] For the penalties these men suffered cf. Holinshed, *ed. cit.* IV. 74.
[3] *Cal. S.P. Spanish, 1554,* 221, 228, 308.
[4] *Diary of Henry Machyn,* ed. J. G. Nichols (Camden Soc.), 80.

in the country against its will. Sir Nicholas had been released upon a bond of £2000 for good conduct, Sir Gawen Carew upon £500, Edmund Tremayne £40.[1] Edmund Tremayne now fled across the Channel — to return and become clerk to Elizabeth's Privy Council. Sir Nicholas's name was brought in question, and, though he seems to have been guilty of nothing, the name itself was incriminating.[2] Wishing to take no more chances, at the end of June Sir Nicholas broke his bond and fled overseas.

On his way from St. Malo to Paris his horse fell on him and injured him.[3] He put himself dutifully in touch with Dr. Wotton, the English ambassador, to whom he swore that he would have nothing to do with the English rebels. Wotton therefore forwarded his letters to the Queen — in which he urged his innocence at his arraignment — to the Cardinal, the Chancellor and his kinsman Sir Francis Englefield, influential in Mary's immediate circle. Sir Nicholas lay low and avoided his fellow-exiles ; he continued to visit Wotton, who was assured of his loyalty and to whom he reported all he heard. He was hard put to it to live ; already in 1555 he had sold off the manors of Panshanger and Benjowe, no doubt to raise cash for his heavy bond.[4] In October his wife, who was making earnest suit for him, was allowed to send over some 'present relief . . . so that the same exceeded not the value of forty crowns'.[5] Yet in December his keepers were put out of the parks at Brigstock, on the charge of making spoil and waste there. In April, on the threshold of war, he was able to send Wotton information about the Admiral of France's practice to capture Guisnes, the preparations in French ports under Jean Ribault and Stafford's plan for a descent on England. In addition to his other gifts Throckmorton was the ablest intelligence-man of his time : a sphere in which he was succeeded by his follower Walsingham.

For these services Sir Nicholas procured a pardon for his flight, on condition of standing to his indictment.[6] The war broke out, into which Mary was dragged by her devotion to Philip and for which the country was ill-prepared. Sir Nicholas remained abroad, to take part in Philip's victory at St.-Quentin in August 1557. His services were sufficient to gain him a pardon, and he had intermediaries to plead for him, in particular his youngest brother John, Master in the Court of Requests, shortly

---

[1] *Acts of the Privy Council, 1554–6*, 90.   [2] *Cal. S.P. Dom. 1547–80*, 78.
[3] *Cal. S.P. Foreign, 1553–8*, 241, 293, 299.
[4] *Cal. Pat. Rolls, Philip and Mary*, II. 8, 12-13.   [5] *A.P.C. 1556–8*, 7, 29.
[6] *Cal. Pat. Rolls, Philip and Mary*, III. 476.

to be made Justice of Chester. A life-long Catholic, he seems to have been Mary's personal lawyer, in favour with her. So Sir Nicholas was free to return home. Early in 1558 Sir William Cecil, whom Mary would gladly have recruited to her government, was commissioned to restore Sir Nicholas to his keepership of the parks at Brigstock.[1] Were they not both now Northamptonshire men?

The Edwardian circle was coming together once more, to re-form around Elizabeth after the disastrous interlude of Mary's rule. Mary was giving up hope, though still plodding on her self-appointed course, with only Pole now by her side: masses, processions, burnings, the country glum with resentment at her pious rule, waiting for the end to come. Calais was lost, and in London people ceased to go to church; the war was a failure, everything was a failure. She made her will, still thinking herself to be with child — it had become a fixation in that fanatic mind; John Throckmorton witnessed the will.[2]

The very day after Mary's death Sir Nicholas was executing Elizabeth's commission to her nobles, taking measures to stay the passage of the ports and secure Cardinal Pole's house and goods — he had conveniently died within twelve hours of Mary — and conferring with Cecil to arrange the new Queen's state-entry into London.[3] Three days later Sir Nicholas went across to Lambeth, with Rutland and Sir Gawen Carew, to make an inventory of Pole's possessions and go through his papers. They selected from his plate what they thought meet for the Queen's service, paying its value to Signor Priuli, the head of that Italia-nate household. Among the papers they found a note of all those who had been frazzled for the faith.[4]

Some time during Sir Nicholas's absence abroad, it would seem upon a premature report of Mary's death, he hastened to press his advice upon Elizabeth as to the steps she should take upon her accession.[5] It was characteristic of him that he should do this unsolicited; she was already better advised by Cecil, whom she chose for her chief adviser, and most of Throckmorton's

---

[1] *A.P.C. 1556–8*, 282. [2] H.M.C. *App. to Fifth Report*, 309.
[3] *Cal. S.P. Dom. 1547–80*, 115. [4] *A.P.C. 1558–70*, 11; *Legend*, 37.
[5] Sir John Neale brought this paper to light in *E.H.R.*, January 1950, 91 foll. But it is clear that it must be dated earlier than Elizabeth's accession: 'the bruits which I hear consonant to some advertisements, the place where I am presently, so far from your presence, the faithful zeal which I owe to your Grace's honour, safety and happy government, which is to succeed happily through a discreet beginning' . . . all this is consistent with a rumour abroad of Mary's death.

personal recommendations were not taken up. Though he made no mention of himself, he did not hesitate to bring forward the names of two of his brothers, George and Kellam, for jobs. Though having to accept the idea of Cecil as Secretary, he was anxious that there should be a second appointed. 'It may please you to call Mr. Cecil to exercise the room of Secretary about your person forthwith and no other until I may speak with your Highness.' Perhaps he hoped he might be called in himself; but he was not appointed.

He had indeed reason to be disappointed when Elizabeth's accession came about: all measures were already in train on Cecil's advice, and not much place was left for Sir Nicholas or his recommendations. It provided the ground for the intense jealousy of Cecil that became the governing factor in Throckmorton's conduct. Soon another sphere was marked out for him, the diplomatic — away from the centre of power at Court.

However, by it began the most brilliantly illuminated period of Throckmorton's career, by which he is best known to history — his embassy to France. He was the first diplomatic envoy of his time, indispensable to Elizabeth's government in the complex diplomatic situation left by Mary's defeat and with a weak hand to play to begin with. We shall see him strengthening his hand with all his ability and impetuosity, taking advantage of every weakness in his opponents' situation, until in the end he overplayed his cards and brought about a defeat for his country and a humiliating experience for himself.

In May 1559 Throckmorton was sent as resident ambassador to France: a magnificent allowance of plate, 1685½ ounces, to make a good show, £3 : 6 : 8 a day for diets, but — never well off — he had to be lent £1000 to start with.[1] His instructions were to confirm the Treaty of Câteau-Cambrésis — which brought an end to the long conflict between Habsburg and Valois, with a private understanding between Philip II and Henri II to extirpate their Protestants. Here was a menace to England. The prime objectives of Elizabeth's government were to get the French out of Scotland and to get back Calais. In all three matters the Guise family — Mary Stuart's closest relations — were the enemy. They were responsible for their niece quartering the arms of England with hers, in those terms asserting her claim to the English throne, to Elizabeth's intense vexation. Throckmorton was instructed to know the Guises without

---

[1] *Cal. S.P. For. 1558–9*, 238, 240, 253.

their knowledge, 'if any harm be meant, it is to be learned thence, and therein ye may have most help of the Scots'. The situation in Scotland, where Mary Stuart's mother, Mary of Guise, was combating the Scottish Lords of the Congregation with the aid of French forces, dovetailed into that in France. Secretly Throckmorton was to arrange for the escape of the Earl of Arran from France: he was next heir to the Scottish throne, candidate of the Scots for Elizabeth's hand, and a most valuable hostage for the French to hold. It will be seen that Sir Nicholas had a ticklish and difficult assignment. It was not long before his energy made itself felt; with his finger on every pulse he became a well-known figure in Europe and ended up as Public Enemy Number One in France.

On his way to Paris that early summer he was royally entertained by the magnificent Constable Montmorency, a friend to England, in his sumptuous new Renaissance château: Maytime, *les amandiers en fleur* amid the woods and waters of Chantilly, the rich tapestries, the sculpture and stained glass of Écouen up on its hill, looking out over the Île-de-France. Sir Nicholas lost no time in reporting on young Mary Stuart, married to the Dauphin, heir to the French crown: 'the Scottish Queen, in mine opinion, looketh very ill on it, very pale and green, and therewithal short-breathed; and it is whispered here amongst them that she cannot live'.[1] Every appearance of this very important young woman was observed; in June, 'the Queen Dauphiness, being the said day at church, was very evil at ease, and to keep her from swooning, they were fain to bring her wine from the altar'. When he came to have an audience with her, however, he found that she was full of the Guise spirit and intelligence: 'the Queen took upon her to speak more than her husband' and, young as she was, gave Throckmorton all his answers. At one audience with her the self-possessed young woman sent away her ladies and, calling him to sit beside her, put her view of the disputed points between her and Elizabeth with force and passion.

Actually, militant Protestant as Throckmorton was, this was the beginning of an undoubted sympathy between him and Mary. They understood each other and did each other good services; Throckmorton always tried honestly to help her, in the end the last entanglements and troubles of his life, and his last imprisonment, were on her behalf.

Early in July the situation was transformed by the unexpected

---

[1] *Forbes's State Papers* (ed. 1740), I. 102, 144, 160.

death of Henri II, mortally wounded in a jousting tournament.
Throckmorton was present and gives us a vivid account of it —
his dispatches are more lively reading than anyone else's in the
age. At first the injury was thought not fatal: 'Marry, I saw a
splint taken out of a good bigness, and nothing else was done to
him upon the field; but I noted him to be very weak and to have
the sense of all his limbs benumbed; for being carried away, as
he lay along, nothing covered but his face, he moved neither
hand nor foot but lay as one amazed.'[1] The King lingered a few
days in agony and died. With his son Francis II as king, Mary
Stuart became Queen of France. At once all power came into
the hands of the Guises. They were determined to support their
sister and the French hold on Scotland; reinforcements were put
in hand, trained French troops fully equipped and sent there.
Throckmorton now had the able Cardinal of Lorraine to deal
with; we have from his pen fascinating close-ups of this powerful
ecclesiastic, with his way of putting his finger to his nose while
thinking up a sly point.

Throckmorton's reaction was that now was the time to recover Calais; he never ceased to urge aggressive forward action.
To the Council: 'the remedy is to take time as it serveth and
beat the iron while it is hot'.[2] Again, 'my lords, it is not mine
opinion alone, to have the Queen's Majesty to follow her opportunity while it is offered, but the discourse of all the world'.
Cecil used him to press the Queen to intervene decisively in
Scotland, while she, not yet sure, was reluctant to commit herself. Meanwhile, Throckmorton helped in the most effective
way he could: he spirited Arran out of the country, to the fury
of the Guises. He engaged Portinari, ablest of the Italian military engineers, for English service for whatever siege-operations
might be necessary — Leith? Edinburgh? Calais? He arranged for Melville, later Sir James Melville, to be got across
for service in Scotland; this was the beginning of a close friendship between these two statesmen. He did his best for John
Knox; he urged permission for him to return through England
and prevailed on him to write to the Queen, apologising for his
insulting *First Blast of the Trumpet against the Monstrous Regiment of
Women*. (With Mary Tudor and Elizabeth, Mary Stuart and
Catherine de Medici, women were too much to the fore for this
Old Testament fanatic.) John Knox's conception of an apology
was to write to the Queen that 'her displeasure was most un-

---

[1] *Forbes's State Papers* (ed. 1740), I. 151.   [2] *Ibid.* 318, 372.

SIR NICHOLAS THROCKMORTON

justly conceived', and ending up by 'praying that her heart may be moved to understand what is said, and discretion given her to rule herself and actions to the glory of God'.[1] The 'glory of God' meant, of course, what John Knox approved. It is not surprising that he was never admitted into Elizabeth's England.

In the intervals of all this Throckmorton had his private affairs to attend to. In August he wrote Cecil that the wife of his brother George, after many devilish devices, had sought his destruction by poison, and finally tried it on him.[2] He knew not what case his brother was in, but there could be no greater felicity than such a brother. If interest were made to colour the matter he hoped Cecil would not be too pitiful or remiss. He pointed out that civil law punished the offence by death, while canon law dissolved the matrimony. He wrote again trusting justice would be done — the only danger was that the woman's deeds were done before the Queen's accession and might have come under the general pardon. Here is a specimen of the Throckmorton temperament: the strength of family feeling, the passionate resentment.[3] George Throckmorton had been an exile, too, during Mary's reign; he had married the daughter of Lord Chandos.

Another of Throckmorton's relations, his cousin Henry Middlemore, was with him in France as his confidential servant. We find Middlemore carrying out missions on Sir Nicholas's behalf, and later, after some pressure, he managed to get him taken into the Queen's service.[4] He himself was looking out for a likely man for Cecil's vineyard. That Throckmorton had a virginal-player in his service we know, for the Guises managed to send him to the galleys — he was evidently a Protestant. We have other evidences of Sir Nicholas's tastes. The Queen herself entrusted him with commissions to buy her trinkets, jewels, a striking clock in Paris; we see her poring over a box of medals he sent home and rejecting them on the ground that the price was too high. We find Throckmorton asking Sir Thomas Challoner to send him 'two pair of parfumed gloves, parfumed with orange flowers and jasmine, th'one for my wife's hand, the other for mine own'.

---

[1] *Cal. S.P. For. 1558–9*, 398-9.   [2] *Ibid.* 500.

[3] And also of Sir Nicholas's feverish rushing to conclusions. For it seems that this was not a case of poisoning, but of a love-potion. Lady Chandos, mother of the accused wife, wrote Cecil that her daughter was given overmuch to palmistry, but not to poison, and that her aim had been to win her husband's love. Her innocence would be apparent 'if she has impartial judges'. *Cal. S.P. Dom.* 20 August 1559.

[4] *Forbes's State Papers*, II. 113; I. 115, 206; *Cal. S.P. For. 1561–2*, 333; H.M.C. *Salisbury MSS.* I. 266.

That Sir Nicholas was a man of taste we may infer from the fine portrait remaining from about this time. From a long chain hangs a Renaissance cameo with profile-portrait and a pendant pearl. More striking is the face: reddish hair and beard, sideways-looking, alert eyes, with more than a touch of irascibility in them; the personality a tense one, on the *qui vive*, ready to explode, one would say.

In October on account of his wife's suit, who was vexed with ague 'in more fear than danger we trust', the Queen gave Sir Nicholas licence to return to see her.[1] This naturally was interpreted as a preliminary to war. The Cardinal of Lorraine and the Duke of Guise said that his wife was in no such danger and his going was 'smally to their advantage'; if he had not come into France Arran had still remained there, yet they could not lay it home to him. Noailles in England thought the return a prognostic of war; the English were selling a large quantity of lead from the monastic houses for ammunition. The Spanish ambassador thought that the real reason for his return was to hurry up sending arms to the Isle of Wight and fitting out the fleet. Throckmorton did not return to his post until the very end of the year.

March 1560 saw the struggle openly engaged: the French forces in Scotland were besieged by the English in Leith. From Amboise Throckmorton wrote to Cecil, 'these men here have their hands full, and are so busied to provide for surety at home that they cannot intend to answer foreigners. If now you lose your time and advantage you lose your surety and reputation for ever.'[2] Cecil needed no pressing; the Queen did. This was the moment of the Tumult of Amboise, which hamstrung the French government: 'they do greatly suspect me to have been a doer in these troubles happened, whereby I am in much danger for mine own particular. And therefore I trust your Majesty will be pleased, with as much speed as may be, to have regard to my revocation.' Throckmorton had certainly been doing his bit; he was in touch with the Huguenot leaders against the Guises, Admiral Châtillon and the Prince of Condé. When Condé's brother, Antoine King of Navarre, came to Paris Throckmorton intercepted him for a secret interview; he was not able to persuade this poltroon to assume the leadership of his own cause and party.

In May the English forces were defeated in front of Leith.

[1] *Cal. S.P. For. 1559-60*, 31, 104, 122; *Cal. S.P. Spanish, 1558-67*, 114, 121.
[2] Forbes, I. 374-5, 379.

Cecil to Throckmorton: 'God trieth us with many difficulties. The Queen's Majesty never liketh this matter of Scotland. . . . And now, when we looked for best fortune, the worst came. . . . I have had such a torment herein with the Queen's Majesty as an ague hath not in five fits so much abated.'[1] The bad news rendered Throckmorton not merely diplomatically but physically ill: he took to his bed. Cecil, however, kept his nerve in the crisis: 'I think my lord of Norfolk shall enter in with a greater army . . . if we cannot compass our honest and reasonable desires, he shall or must do it. We only seek surety, which chiefly dependeth upon the liberty of Scotland, and yet upon a lawful liberty.' The naval blockade of the French was maintained, and Cecil went north to decide the issue: 'what will follow of my going towards Scotland, I know not, but I fear the success, *quia* the Queen's Majesty is so evil disposed to the matter, which troubleth us all.' English naval power turned the scale; by the Treaty of Edinburgh the French were turned out of Scotland for good and all. It was Cecil's greatest triumph, and a resounding defeat for the Guises.

Throckmorton's next commission was the agreeable one of getting Mary Stuart and her husband to ratify the Treaty. Elizabeth was in jubilant and giving mood; there were rewards all round. Cecil got a handsome grant of lands; Throckmorton was given the monastic manors of Alderminster in Warwickshire and Sheriff's Lench in Worcestershire.[2] He did not cease urging his recall, however. This was common form with sixteenth-century ambassadors, for on embassy they could not make but only lose money. Besides, there was the disadvantage of being away from the centre of power and favour. At the disposition of offices at Elizabeth's accession, Throckmorton was disappointed that only

> Chief Butlership reservèd was for me.
> Excepting that, all offices were gone:
> The fruits were pulled, and all the birds were flown.[3]

Later, a chamberlainship of the Exchequer was added to Throckmorton's share, an office held in his family more than a century before, when the Cecils were unheard of. Now William Cecil was immovably entrenched at the heart of power; it was more than Throckmorton could stand.

Cecil returned from his triumph to find everything jeopardised

[1] *Ibid.* I. 454.5, 460-1.
[2] Cf. my 'Alltyrynys and the Cecils', *E.H.R. 1960*, 69; *Cal. Pat. Rolls, Eliz. I.* I. 420.   [3] *Legend*, 37, 38.

by Lord Robert Dudley's ascendancy and the fear that the Queen would marry him. In September Amy Robsart was found dead at the foot of her staircase. There is not the remotest likelihood that she was murdered, but everybody hated Lord Robert so much that they were willing to believe anything of him. Henceforward he had this kind of thing to put up with all his life. His wife's funeral at Oxford was turned into a popular demonstration against him; Amy was buried in front of the altar in St. Mary's, where one sees her tablet.

Rumours ran all over Europe. Sir Nicholas wrote to his kinsman, the resuscitated Marquis of Northampton, in a passion, wishing he were dead rather than hear the scandalous reports of the Queen and having to bear the malicious joy of the French Court, with the princes promising themselves good success against England — speeches which 'every hair of my head stareth at and my ears glow to hear'.[1] (Sir Nicholas was every bit as virtuous and respectable as Cecil.) He was at his wit's end to know how to answer them; some laughed, others reviled or threatened with insults like 'What religion is this that a subject shall kill his wife and the Prince not only bear withal but marry with him?' (Actually just this situation came about within a few years, but in Scotland with a Catholic Queen.) Sir Nicholas went on that all English prestige had clean gone, if these slanders were not slaked it would be the subversion of the country. He prayed 'with weeping eyes . . . that God would not suffer her to become *opprobrium hominum et abjectio plebis*'. (This was precisely the fate reserved for her cousin Mary Stuart.)

To Lord Robert, Throckmorton wrote, more circumspectly, condoling with him on the death of his late bedfellow and thanking him for the present of a nag.[2] He hoped that Dudley would find means to bring him home to hunt and hawk in England — more meet than to be ambassador in France, as things had fallen out. Henry Killigrew wrote that he was not likely to get his recall that winter; all his friends, who were doing their best, said that 'there is but a woman only who is the cause of his stay'. (This was the Queen, who knew a good man when she saw one and was not letting him go.) Nothing could be more false than the lewd rumours, Killigrew assured him, though it was little marvel Throckmorton had heard them in France, when they were so common in England. All the same everybody would like to find an English husband for the Queen.

---

[1] *Cal. S.P. For. 1560–1*, 348.   [2] *Ibid.* 349, 355.

In December young Francis II died — a stroke of luck for Elizabeth, for Mary Stuart ceased to be Queen of France and the Guises were shortly removed from power. Throckmorton wrote Cecil that Queen Elizabeth had cause to thank God for all his mercies, and went on, 'but if her Majesty do so foully forget herself in her marriage as the bruit runneth here, never think to bring anything to pass, either here or elsewhere.'[1] ('Here' meant Calais.) He urged Cecil to do everything to prevent her marriage to Lord Robert, adding, with some superiority, 'remember your mistress is young, and subject to affections; you are her sworn councillor and in great credit with her . . . my duty to her, my good will to you, doth move me to speak plainly'. Cecil would never have spoken out plainly like that — that was the difference between him and Throckmorton — and fortunately it was not necessary.

In France Catherine de Medici now took control, sensible, unfanatical, compromising; with her the moderates came in, the *politiques*, who could not understand why fanatics should be so keen on killing each other for things that were in their nature uncertain. Throckmorton advised that the Earl of Bedford be sent over on an embassy of condolence, since he spoke Italian well and the Queen Mother took pleasure in her own tongue. The real purpose of his mission was to press the new French government not to take part in the renewed sessions of the Council of Trent; a free national council in France was suggested, to which the English would send representatives. Throckmorton was the intellectual leader in all this, very much to the fore in the discussions. Bedford thought him 'a very wise and expert man'. Throckmorton's superfluous candour about Lord Robert got him into bad odour with the Queen — understandably, though nothing was said. On his return Bedford wrote, 'the great matters whereof the world was wont to talk are now asleep, having had some fits both hot and cold'.[2] Cecil was now in greater credit than any other and did everything. The Queen would not make up her mind to Throckmorton's recall.

With Catherine de Medici in control there was no future for Mary Stuart in France; she was having to make up her mind to return to sombre Scotland. In April Throckmorton sent Elizabeth a discerning diagnosis of what her intentions were. He approved of her half-brother, Lord James, a Protestant and friendly to England. He could not resist improving the occasion to tell

[1] *Ibid.* 474.   [2] *Cal. S.P. For. 1561–2*, 23.

the Queen how Mary and her brother had talked with the
Cardinal of Lorraine, before setting off for the Coucil of Trent,
'and how they made their advantage of the cross and candles
in your chapel, saying you were not yet resolved of what religion
you should be'.[1] He embarked on a long argument with Elizabeth as to the advantages she now held — and, indeed, it was a
contrast with the situation at her accession, such a short time
before. The Constable of France said that 'the Queen of England
was the happiest Princess and her amity the best in Christendom'.
If she accepted the Romish religion she would recover the same
amity her sister bought to her cost — *i.e.* the Spanish alliance,
which lost England Calais. Elizabeth hardly needed to be told
this, and it was not the way to talk to the daughter of Henry
VIII. At home Cecil was 'forced to seek byways' with her;
this was more effective. Throckmorton remained in France and
in May his wife rejoined him.

He was now engaged in the awkward business of trying to
get a pass for Mary Stuart to return to her kingdom through
England. She had not withdrawn her claims to the English
throne, and Elizabeth was in no mood to grant her a safe-conduct.
In July Mary sent him word that she was minded to send her
horses through England and requiring a pass; Throckmorton
did not know what to say.[2] Mary much resented this, though
she did not vent her resentment on him: he had done his best.
Shortly after she took shipping and suddenly arrived in Scotland
without touching English soil. Randolph, the English envoy,
wrote a full account of her unexpected arrival to Throckmorton.
That autumn he sent her a copy of Beza's *Oration*, somewhat
hopefully. He was in correspondence with Calvin himself and
the leaders of the French Huguenots: they all looked to him for
protection, as the two extremes made civil war inevitable and
life unlivable for sensible people in the middle.

That autumn, 1561, Cecil's son and heir, Thomas, was
travelling in France with Thomas Windebank as bear-leader;
in the youth's sickness Throckmorton was 'a natural father' to
him.[3] When the boy recovered, Sir Nicholas advised him to see
all the notable places of France before his return. Later, Cecil
was much disturbed by his young hopeful's refractoriness and
reports of his dissolute conduct; he told Windebank to take the

[1] *Cal. S.P. For. 1561-2*, 85; for the advantage Elizabeth made of this cf. Maitland's
famous chapter in *Cambridge Modern History*, vol. II, c. xvi.
[2] *Cal. S.P. Scottish*, I. 539, 547, 560.
[3] *Cal. S.P. For. 1561-2*, 487, 514; *Cal. S.P. Dom. 1547-80*, 197, 200.

advice of Sir Nicholas how to proceed. The ambassador sagely advised that Windebank should remove his charge to a house seven leagues away from Paris. Though Cecil had no high opinion of his first-born, he grew up to take a very respectable place in society, Lord-Lieutenant of the county of Northampton, where Sir Nicholas's son and heir became one of his deputies.

Throckmorton sent an agent to London, who saw the Queen in a garden of the palace; she asked mischievously how Lady Throckmorton 'could away with France'.[1] The agent answered that Throckmorton was a man more subject to sickness than health. But the Queen would not grant his recall, because of the scarceness of able men. As for Lady Throckmorton, she so little liked the French that she excused herself from learning the language. In March 1562 she came back to England, where she proved herself so good a solicitor that Sir Thomas Smith was ordered to prepare himself to succeed Throckmorton as ambassador. In June she gave birth to a son, whom they expected to call Robert after his godfather Lord Robert; but Dudley would not have him Robert and named the boy Nicholas. Sir Henry Sidney was the other godfather. Sir Nicholas's agent moved the Queen for Throckmorton's bond in the Exchequer, but found cold comfort: she said he had asked it but as a loan. He had spoken on behalf of Middlemore, but got a dilatory answer, commending the man's parts but not accepting his person. Throckmorton was obviously no favourite for his unsolicited candour.

Lady Throckmorton busied herself forwarding money to her husband, though it was hard to obtain.[2] The Queen was set on going a progress to Sheffield to meet the Queen of Scots. Poor Lady Throckmorton had no means, but nothing would serve; the Queen told her to make ready as well as she could, and for the rest she would take order for her. He would know that these were only words: she looked for nothing else. Would he lend her his lackey to wait on her this progress? She trusted that his anger was appeased; his letters were so bitter, she was now afraid. A house next her brother's, Beddington, was to be sold: how convenient this would be for them, how many good neighbours he would have there!

But now Sir Nicholas was inextricably involved in the first of the French Wars of Religion which were to occupy France for the rest of the century with excitement, suffering, increasing

[1] *Cal. S.P. For. 1561–2*, 333, 514, 602; *Cal. S.P. For. 1562*, 80, 129.
[2] *Ibid.* 629.

degradation, murder and misery. The massacre of the Protestants at Vassy by Guise and his followers, succeeded by other massacres at Sens and elsewhere, precipitated civil war.[1] Throckmorton regarded Vassy as responsible for the outbreak of European war, when all parts of Christendon were in a good peace. The Huguenot party took to arms to defend themselves and concentrated on Orleans with their forces under Admiral Châtillon and Condé. On the way thither Throckmorton got suspiciously mixed up in a charge the Admiral made against opposing forces, in which the ambassador lost all the Queen's plate, and, as he reported, 'of mine own goods, besides that of your Majesty's, I lost above the value of six thousand crowns'.[2] This was more than unfortunate, it was very odd; was it a way of contributing by collusion to the Huguenot cause? For, of course, he was hand in glove with their leaders; it was only to be expected that they would be hand in pocket with him. And this was what was thought in England: it was believed he had given warning to the Admiral himself and that it was all a put-up job. His wife had received £200 for his diets, but could get no money from those to whom he had lent. She had had much ado to get Sir Thomas Smith on the move. Would Nicholas buy two partlets with sleeves in Paris, which she would give the Queen, and a piece of fine lawn?

Shortly Sir Nicholas was able to report to the Queen the return of her plate.

In the outbreak of civil war in France he saw a providential opportunity to get back Calais — the Treaty had stipulated in eight years and the French had given hostages for its return. Sir Nicholas wrote to Cecil, 'if in this matter you can go well to work, her Majesty shall be able through Christendom to be both arbiter and umpire' — instead of the King of Spain.[3] In pursuance of this the English government offered its mediation between the parties to the French; though it was rejected, what a change it showed since Throckmorton had arrived as ambassador! The possibilities of the situation went to his head, as nothing went to Elizabeth's or Cecil's. But they allowed themselves to be overborne by his pressure and the prospects opening out. In September they made the Treaty of Hampton Court with the Huguenot leaders, invoking common religion and the interest of Christ, promising subsidies and armed intervention. In October

[1] Cf. J. H. Mariéjol, *La Réforme et la Ligue*, in E. Lavisse, *Histoire de France*, VI, pt. i. 58 foll.   [2] Forbes, II. 37, 42; *Cal. S.P. For. 1562*, 309.
[3] Forbes, II. 15; cf. Mariéjol, 67 foll.

English troops took possession of Le Havre: it was simply a gauge for Calais.

Catherine de Medici was, not unnaturally, furious with Throckmorton. She refused him a safe-conduct to leave Orléans, where he was in league with the Huguenot leaders; he was in danger if he left it without. In these circumstances he sent Middlemore to the French Court for a safe-conduct, who received instead a severe reprimand, charging Throckmorton with ingratitude, considering that the French government had saved his life under Mary, and that 'the offices which I had done since I was your Majesty's ambassador here were not correspondent to the favour and kindness I had received here aforetime'.[1] There was no answering this. Meanwhile Sir Thomas Smith arrived as ambassador with the French king, while Throckmorton, unable to get a safe-conduct, remained in his equivocal position with the Huguenot leaders, helping to advance the cause in every way.

Châtillon and Condé called Throckmorton into consultation, and he did his best to commit the Queen further in the cause. He was present at the battle of Dreux in December, when the Huguenots were defeated, and was afterwards brought to the victorious Guise in camp, who wanted to know if he had borne arms in the battle and charged him with being a great author of their troubles. Nothing abashed, Throckmorton had long arguments about this, and to the Queen he put the issue concisely: if the civil war continued, the French would come to terms about Calais. This was a doubtful point, however; the Cardinal of Lorraine said the English were mad if they thought they would ever get back Calais. The assassination of Guise shortly after was no help; it worked out, as so often in politics, in just the opposite manner: it opened the way for an accommodation between the parties, leaving the English in isolation holding on to Le Havre.

The occupation enabled Throckmorton to cross the Channel, for in February he returned to Le Havre with a large sum, some £20,000, for the Admiral to pay his German *Reiters*.[2] Throckmorton had been able to send back a number of French mules as presents at Court. His wife wrote that Cecil had chosen a black mule with velvet saddle and gilt stirrups, Lord Admiral Clinton a black mule — he was desirous to have a French muleteer; Sir Ambrose Cave had chosen the dun mulet. She besought

---

[1] Forbes, II. 112.   [2] *Cal. S.P. For. 1563*, 97, 154.

him not to venture into Flanders; 'I take my leave of you, good frog'.

The Queen summoned up courage to tell the French ambassador that she would not restore Le Havre unless Calais were restored first.[1] In April Throckmorton told Châtillon that the English needed Calais as a mart for their wool and cloth; they now had no other place but Antwerp — and so were dependent on Philip's Netherlands. He had returned to Court at Easter; at a large and brilliant supper party at the Lord Chamberlain's, Throckmorton discounted Philip's ability to intervene, since he had no troops and was heavily in debt. If the French were united they could easily subdue the Netherlands. He gave no information, however, as to Châtillon's designs. At Court he was called on for his advice on how to treat the French emissaries arriving. He asked Lord Robert to get him a better lodging: at Richmond he had a chamber with garderobe and kitchen; this was too scant, he wanted a chamber to dine in. At the same time the young Earl of Hertford, who had been in the Tower for his secret marriage with Lady Jane Grey's sister, with her claims to the throne, wrote to thank him for his friendly dealing for his liberty.

The religious truce patched up in France under the liberal Edict of Amboise left the English out on a limb in the occupation of Le Havre, which was not really defensible. Throckmorton was very much behind this act of aggression; he had urged it, relying far too much on his own personal influence with the Huguenot leaders. Elizabeth and Cecil, now committed to a course they were doubtful about, had to take the consequences. It turned out to have been the worst miscalculation they ever made.[2] A slip of paper that survived among Throckmorton's *Nachlass* announced the plague at Le Havre in June: 'this evening Dr. Julio is fallen extremely sick in my Lord's house [the Earl of Warwick was in command], who hath removed thrice and hath already four dead out his chamber. God must now be our only physician.'[3] The outbreak was one of extreme virulence and rapidity among the English garrisons; hundreds died, the defence was completely undermined; the more reinforcements that were sent, the more died. On July 28 the town surrendered; the Lord Admiral told the French emissaries that 'the plague of deadly inflexion had done for them that I think

---

[1] *Cal. S.P. Spanish, 1558–67*, 299, 301, 319, 327; *Cal. S.P. For. 1563*, 378.
[2] Cf. A. F. Pollard, *History of England, 1547–1603*, 248.
[3] Forbes, II. 444, 499.

all the force of France could never a done'. The returning
soldiers spread the fearful infection over the whole south of
England, where the plague raged hot the rest of that year. The
intervention had ended in disaster.

In these circumstances, unfortunately for himself, Throckmorton arrived at Rouen, sent on a mission to *régler* matters with
the French Court.[1] It was very tactless on the part of the English
government to send *him*; Catherine de Medici was much offended
and, on the ground that he was still without a safe-conduct, she
had him arrested and kept him in confinement for the next ten
months until peace was made. Sir Thomas Smith, who was
Cecil's man, reported that Throckmorton was hated by both
sides, the Queen Mother regarding him as the chief doer of the
taking of Le Havre, and asked Elizabeth to revoke him. This
naturally created acute distrust between the two envoys; for
Throckmorton regarded himself as superior to a mere Smith, as
indeed he was, and also senior in rank. It is also clear to us
that where Smith was Cecil's man, Throckmorton was Dudley's:
the dichotomy in Elizabethan policy that became open later on
with Walsingham and Burghley announced itself thus early, for
Walsingham was Throckmorton's man and took his place when
he died.

The French now held all the trumps, and Throckmorton
himself became a prime issue in the diplomatic negotiations;
meanwhile his position was equivocal, humiliating, exasperating
— and he was not the most patient of men. He was taken under
guard to St.-Germain, where he was under lock and key in his
chamber for many months, though allowed to walk in the park
for an hour in the morning, and in the garden of an evening.
His spirit was as aggressive as ever, and he urged Elizabeth not
to make peace: 'those that put doubts into your heads of invasion do play with you as folks do with children when they tell
them of Robin Goodfellow'.[2] He asked that Smith might not
be allowed to negotiate without his concurrence; he would not
suffer the loss of credit. The Constable of France, when passing
by, took him out to dinner with him and assured him that,
whatever fair weather the English had in Scotland, the French
alliance there would not be dissolved. The English should be
contented with their isle; their acts of late had lost them Calais.
Between these friends there was a full and fascinating discussion;
the Constable had the better of the argument, or rather, of the facts.

---

[1] *Cal. S.P. For. 1563*, 477, 503.   [2] *Ibid.* 530.

Diplomatic discussions went to and fro over Throckmorton; the French ambassador in London was put under mild constraint, far too mild to suit Sir Nicholas who was kept close prisoner. Smith was negotiating on his behalf — not hard enough to please Throckmorton. From Scotland Mary Stuart wrote again and again to her Guise relations to procure his release — the year before he had been doing business for her with her uncles. It was all very complex. The Cardinal of Lorraine told his niece that Throckmorton would not be released so long as the state of war continued; and, though Throckmorton would not recognise it, this was the fact. The French government had him by the throat and were not letting go of so valuable a gauge. They demanded the return of the four French hostages for Calais before returning him. He was convinced that Cecil was making but lukewarm efforts on his behalf, but there was nothing more that he could do. In November he was taken to an interview with Catherine at Meaux, guarded like a prisoner. When he protested, he was answered that he had been taken as a prisoner of war. No agreement reached, he was taken back to St.-Germain. He now fell sick and wanted leave to go to Paris for medical treatment. There followed complicated interviews at the Louvre between both Throckmorton and Smith, and the Queen Mother. The English government were not giving way on any points of substance to procure Throckmorton's release. Back he went to St.-Germain, where the Queen Mother sent her own doctor to see him.

He wrote to Cecil that his ill-treatment kept pace with Cecil's courtesy towards the French — indirectly charging Cecil with the prolongation of his confinement.[1] Angry, humiliated and ill he now embarked on bitter recriminations against Smith as Cecil's man, threatening what he would do when he recovered his liberty. Again he was brought from St.-Germain to the Louvre for joint discussions with Smith and the French. In February Elizabeth committed the handling of the negotiations to Throckmorton alone — a surprising move which must represent a turn in favour of Lord Robert at home. The Queen, however, gave Throckmorton an impossible assignment, reserving her general rights and putting forward a number of bargaining points. So Throckmorton conducted the tough and intricate discussions that followed at Fontainebleau, wrangling with the Queen Mother and the French ministers, especially at meetings

Cal. S.P. For. 1564–5, 6, 17, 40.

with the Cardinal of Lorraine. Only Throckmorton could have kept track of it all and kept his end up as he did. The French stand now was that Elizabeth had sacrificed her rights under the Treaty, *i.e.* to Calais, by her intervention — or, rather, by its failure, we may add. In return for the Calais hostages the French offered an inadequate sum ; Throckmorton embarked on a course of bidding them up. They replied that he would not be liberated except in return for the hostages. Elizabeth conceded the point, but subsequently disapproved the negotiations at Fontainebleau. Back he went as prisoner to St.-Germain.

This turn Throckmorton considered he owed to Smith's representations and Cecil behind him ; for in the final negotiations at Troyes Smith was joind with him as an equal, while Throckmorton went as a prisoner, closely guarded throughout.[1] He wrote Dudley that the French understood Elizabeth's determination on peace so plainly that before they began to treat they said they had the peace in their hands.[2] And they had. In the course of the negotiations Throckmorton made a violent attack on Smith, drawing his dagger on him and threatening that if this had been King Henry VIII's time Smith should have lost his head. Smith reported it all at length to Cecil. After which they both accompanied the French king and the Queen Mother to a *Te Deum* at the cathedral. The Treaty said very little ; beyond settling the release of the French hostages in exchange for Throckmorton and 120,000 crowns, all rights were reserved on both sides. In fact, it was practically the end of English hopes for the return of Calais. At the conclusion of it all Charles IX presented Throckmorton with a splendid gold chain of 164 ounces, worth 1400 crowns — a fine courtesy. Before returning Throckmorton was commissioned by Elizabeth to buy her in Paris a sounding clock, a chain and a jewel to wear with her order of the Garter or as a pendant.

More important, he returned from his French experiences an open rival of Cecil, the closest confidant and political adviser of Lord Robert.

[1] *Ibid.* 101, 103, 121, 133.   [2] H.M.C. *Pepys MSS.* 17.

CHAPTER III

SIR NICHOLAS AND MARY STUART

THE remaining years of Sir Nicholas's life were dominated by the question of Mary Stuart and the problems she gave rise to, for herself and everyone connected with her:

The daughter of debate, that eke doth discord raise

— as Elizabeth wrote of her in her antique manner of versifying. As the result of his embassy in France he was well known to Mary, and we find presents and tokens being exchanged among members of this small exalted circle. In the summer of 1563 Lady Throckmorton sent a ring and a token by Captain Tremayne to Marie de Béthune, one of the four Maries, with her love and commendations to the Queen of Scots. Marie promised to send her a ring 'quhilk I vais accustumat to veir dayle', with remembrances to Sir Nicholas.[1]

On his return from France the rumour went round that he would be promoted to the Privy Council — Dudley's candidate, a counterweight to Cecil.[2] A project for Elizabeth's marriage with the Archduke of Austria now came forward, and, Cecil wrote to Smith, Throckmorton 'hath had some conference with her Majesty for the embassade to the Emperor, which at this present standeth thus. For my sickness, and the affairs at home, I am excused. Sir Nicholas will go with none but me.'[3] This was a peaceable way of saying that Throckmorton would not again leave the centre of power for any length of time to Cecil alone.

With Elizabeth unmarried, Mary's marriage became a matter of the first importance to English policy: she was, though undeclared, the obvious heiress to the English throne, and in default of children to Elizabeth, a child of Mary's had the best chance of succeeding to their joint thrones and bringing about the unity of the island. More immediately, upon Mary's mar-

---

[1] *Cal. S.P. Scottish*, II. 16.   [2] *Cal. S.P. Spanish*, *1558–67*, 377.
[3] T. Wright, *Queen Elizabeth and her Times*, I. 177.

riage depended the gains of the Treaty of Edinburgh, the Anglo-Scottish alliance, keeping the French out. To achieve all these purposes Elizabeth offered the best available candidate: her favourite — not, though people thought so, her lover — Lord Robert. To improve him as a candidate he was made Earl of Leicester in October 1564. Mary would have done well to marry him: it would have tied her firmly to the English alliance, and it would have saved a lot of trouble. Instead of that she was affronted; her royal blood boiled. And out of resentment and spite she determined on the marriage that was most of a menace to the Queen of England — that with Darnley, who had both Tudor and Stuart royal blood in his veins and came of Catholic stock. There rose up before Elizabeth the apparition she most dreaded: a crowned leader of the Catholic opposition, a young couple with an heir to her throne.

In April 1565 Throckmorton was given the assignment to go to Scotland and break, or at least delay, the Darnley marriage; to procure Mary's acceptance of Leicester or any foreign prince agreeable to the Anglo-Scottish alliance — that meant a Protestant, such as Condé.[1] Elizabeth's anxiety and embarrassment are revealed in her instructions to Throckmorton: he was to declare on behalf of Leicester that 'to add to his value we will yield to advance our sister's title, with him, as far forth as with one that were our natural brother and yet not inheritable to our crown, as it might be being our brother on our mother's side;[2] and without him we mean not nor can find in our heart to do the like with any other'. Further instructions pursued Throckmorton, that Elizabeth's grief at the Darnley marriage was not personal chagrin, but based on the good deliberation and advice of her council; only with Mary safely married to Leicester was she ready to pronounce on Mary's title.

Meanwhile, Mary was anxious to push through her marriage before Throckmorton arrived. At Berwick he learned that her resolve was indissoluble, 'but when I consider the foundation of the matter, which was despite and anger, I cannot assure myself that such qualities will bring forth and continue such fruits and effects as the love and usage that is bestowed on the Lord Darnley doth show'.[3] How right his forebodings were: it all ended in the horror of Kirk-o'-Field. In Edinburgh Throckmorton found the best brain among Mary's ministers, Maitland of Lethington,

[1] *Cal. S.P. Scottish*, II. 145, 150.
[2] One wonders at this reference to Anne Boleyn; it was hardly calculated to appeal to Mary.   [3] *Cal. S.P. Scottish*, II. 159.

disturbed. Throckmorton got a sight of Mary's own dispatch: 'you would have said there neither wanted eloquence, despite, anger, love nor passion'.

Throckmorton pursued Mary to Stirling, where the gate of the castle was shut against him; every step was taken to delay his access until Darnley's creation as duke announced the marriage as inevitable. The ambassador had to lodge in the town, whence he sent his cousin Middlemore to demand an audience. Immediately after Darnley's elevation, Throckmorton was given an audience, in which Mary argued her case with her accustomed eloquence, passion and lack of sense. Throckmorton concluded that she was 'so captived either by love or cunning (or rather, to say truly, by boasting or folly) that she is not able to keep promise with herself, and therefore not most able to keep promise with your Majesty in these matters'.[1] The same day he wrote to Leicester that he was well out of it: 'if solicitations of many . . . if persuasions and severe commandments of her Majesty from time to time, if evident presumptions and manifest assurances of your never enjoying her Majesty', if all this had prevailed on him to marry Mary he would have been an unhappy man.

Before his departure Mary made Throckmorton dine alone with her at her table, and sent Lethington after him with a gold chain, 50 ounces in weight. Throckmorton, however, thought that Elizabeth should use her power to break the marriage. The Guises preferred this match to any in England or Scotland; naturally, for it constituted a threat. On his way back Throckmorton spent a day or two inspecting the fortifications of Berwick. The marriage was carried through privately; the English envoy Randolph reported Mary's loss of control and respect in her kingdom.[2] At once the Hamiltons, next in succession, went into opposition and were pressing Throckmorton for his good offices with Leicester.

Henceforth most of the matters with which Sir Nicholas was concerned related to the dangerous subject of royal marriages and the succession to the throne. Early that spring the Earl of Hertford, who was a cousin, wrote to thank him for the support he had given him with Leicester in his troubles.[3] Hertford was still in confinement at Sir John Mason's; he hoped for help over the lamentable case of his marriage with Lady Catherine Grey.

As spring passed into high summer it was the more ticklish business of the Queen herself: would she marry the Archduke,

---

[1] *Cal. S.P. Scottish*, II. 161; H.M.C. *Pepys MSS.* 57.
[2] *Cal. S.P. Scottish*, II. 181.   [3] *Cal. S.P. Dom. Addenda, 1566–79*, 557.

or could Leicester win the prize? The Spanish ambassador regarded Leicester as entirely ruled by Sir Nicholas, who managed his affairs for him and was for ever coming to find out how the land lay with the Archduke.[1] Throckmorton advised Leicester to find out definitely if she would marry him and, if not, to go over to the Archduke's marriage in order to retain influence under his star. In order to find out, Throckmorton suggested a stratagem: to make up to another lady at Court and then ask for leave of absence. Leicester accordingly made up to the beautiful Lettice Knollys, the Queen's cousin and a favourite with her. (Lettice was married to the first Earl of Essex and became mother of the second Earl, the Queen's last favourite; years later she married Leicester and thus won Elizabeth's detestation.) Leicester thereupon asked leave to go. There followed a quarrel with the Queen and bitter words between them, upon which he sulked four days in his apartments. It fell to Cecil and the Lord Chamberlain to smooth things over. The upshot was that both the Queen and Leicester shed tears and made it up: *redintegratio amoris*, but still she did not marry him. Throckmorton's plan had not worked with her, but he certainly was a schemer.

Cecil, who was not moved by any passion, took a cool view of these matters. He was not disturbed by the renewed 'great means' made to have Throckmorton promoted to the Privy Council; he contented himself with thwarting that.[2] As for Throckmorton's influence over Leicester, Cecil wrote to Smith, 'I think my Lord well able to judge what is meet or unmeet, and doth use Master Throckmorton friendly because he doth show himself careful and devoted to his lordship. What is said of me I think I cannot know; but this I am assured of, that I have no affection to be of a party, but for the Queen's Majesty, and I will always travail to accord noblemen, and not to minister devices of discord.' He reaped the reward of virtue; in the Throckmorton family the tradition was that he was the effective obstacle.

In his position at the centre of things Sir Nicholas was a target for demands from his family and the innumerable tribe of his relations. His youngest brother Sir John was now Vice-President of the Council of Wales. Nicholas thought that John had an Anglo-Saxon New Testament which would do for Archbishop Parker, much interested in these antiquities. Sir John

[1] *Cal. S.P. Spanish, 1558–67*, 388, 438, 459, 472.
[2] Wright, *op. cit.* I. 199, 209.

replied that he never possessed one, but he had a house full of children and a wife with child again — and 'I am forced to wander up and down like an Egyptian in other men's houses for want of one of my own'.[1] Queen Mary had granted him the manor of Feckenham, but there was no house on it, and, intending to build in the park, he could find no water. He wanted the adjoining manor of Hanbury, where he could build, and Leicester's influence in getting it along with the patronage of the church. (Sir John was a Catholic, father of the subsequent traitors, Francis and Thomas.)

Sir Nicholas himself was this year thinking of buying Ashridge, where Elizabeth had resided as princess.[2] Putting it in order would be much less expensive than building a new house; there were the walls about it and plenty of wood for repairs and rebuilding. But he never did purchase a country house; he had to content himself with a house in the City, the 'principal place' with a large garden next St. Catherine Cree, which had belonged to the abbot of Evesham.[3] It would seem that Sir Nicholas and his wife used Beddington, her family home in Surrey, a good deal; it remained to their son and heir, Arthur, to build a house on their Northamptonshire estate.

In February 1566 Sir Nicholas was advising Leicester to delay coming to Court so as not to involve himself in the marriage embroglio with the Archduke — the Queen was making difficulties, the Archduke must promise secretly to alter his religion, and so on.[4] In May there was a reconciliation between Cecil and Throckmorton, effected by the latter's kinsman, the Earl of Pembroke.[5] Sir Nicholas asked Cecil, in front of Leicester, why he had deprived him of his friendship. Cecil replied frankly because Throckmorton was too fond of innovations in the state, which Cecil thought pernicious, and that Throckmorton was inclined to embroil matters. If he would act for the public good, he would be his friend; if not, otherwise. Sir Nicholas promised he would act well. The Spanish ambassador considered his disposition well known and very French. Cecil agreed.

Meanwhile in Scotland Mary's reign ran its pitiful, catastrophic course, to the tune of disasters that reverberated all over Europe and have left an imperishable record in the world's memory. There was the unforgivable murder of Rizzio in her presence, just before her child was about to be born, her dramatic

[1] *Cal. S.P. Dom. Addenda, 1547–65,* 574.
[2] *Cal. S.P. Dom. Addenda, 1566–79,* 16.   [3] *Cal. Pat. Rolls, Elizabeth,* II. 400.
[4] H.M.C. *Pepys MSS.* 78.   [5] *Cal. S.P. Spanish, 1558–67,* 554.

escape and revenge on the contemptible Darnley, her incrimination in his murder and marriage with Bothwell, chief among the murderers, the revolt of the Lords and of the capital against her, her imprisonment in Lochleven. All this presented a frightful problem for Elizabeth, with whom the authority of monarchs and the subjection of subjects was the strongest of beliefs, mitigated only by the overriding concern for the interests of her country. Hence the ambivalence of her attitude: she knew what *she* wanted, but was it what suited England best? After all, the Lords of the Congregation were England's allies against France.

Into this mill-race the only person to send was Throckmorton — he knew the situation, and the personalities involved in it, from A to Z. Already in April, after Darnley's murder, Throckmorton had commented to Leicester on the scandal of 'the parricide having the guard of the son . . . all the disfamed persons in this murder are now advanced and have charges committed to them'.[1] The instructions with which he went north were much altered in draft by Cecil — one descries the tug between him and the Queen. The object of Throckmorton's mission was to mediate between Mary and the Lords, to see what could be done and 'not suffer her, being by God's ordinance the prince and sovereign, to be in subjection to them, that by nature and law are subjected to her'.[2] Thus Elizabeth — and Throckmorton was to inform the nobles that 'her Majesty does not think this because herself is by God's order a prince, but because it is so ordained by God and received for a truth in doctrine in all good Christian governments'. Cecil and Bacon were in favour of having the young prince brought to England and brought up there. Throckmorton was under no illusion about the impossibilities of his task. Before leaving, he saw Darnley's parents, the Earl and Countess of Lennox: 'my lady wept bitterly, my lord sighed deeply'. Well they might — they had been very anxious for their son's promotion to Mary's bridal-bed.

On the way Throckmorton encountered the French envoy to Scotland. The French objective was to restore Mary to power without conditions; the English object must therefore be, Throckmorton considered, to attach weighty conditions to her restoration — the punishment of Darnley's murderers, security for the Lords. His fear was that Elizabeth would leave them 'in

[1] H.M.C. *Pepys MSS.* 101.   [2] *Cal. S.P. Scottish*, II. 339, 342.

the briars'; she would not come out fully in their support.[1]
She instructed him to assure Mary that the best course was to
let the prince be brought up in England as her own child. (That
would have been a solution to *her* marriage-problem!) Throckmorton replied with a very candid letter reporting the Scottish
Lords' complaints of her coldness to them. Mary would neither
prosecute Darnley's murderers nor give up Bothwell: 'if it were
put to her choice to relinquish her crown and kingdom, or the
Lord Bothwell, she would leave her kingdom and dignity to live
as a simple damsel with him'. The people were in a commotion
against Mary: 'the women be most furious and impudent
against the Queen, and yet the men be mad enough'. Lethington
told Throckmorton outright that this was no time to talk of
delivering their prince. Throckmorton was refused any access
to Mary in Lochleven — where she gave birth to Bothwell's
child. The Scots Lords meant to settle the issue themselves,
without any interference from England. 'I find she is in very
great danger.'

Elizabeth replied that she could in no respect allow the Queen's
captivity.[2] As for Mary's desire to come into England, she did
not know what to say. The Lords replied, truly enough, that
Mary could not be restored, or given her liberty — the feeling of
the nation was too strong. They meant to crown the prince and
govern in his name. Throckmorton was afraid that in these
circumstances the French would come out on top. Here the
cooler heads of Elizabeth and Cecil were better judges: since
there was no chance of that, she could afford to leave them to it
without paying them good English money for what they were
determined to do anyway. The Lords obtained Mary's abdi-
cation and her consent to James's coronation, at which they
required Throckmorton to assist. He asked Elizabeth for his
revocation. She threatened that she would come out openly
against the Lords if they proceeded against their Queen, and
forbade him to attend James's coronation. At the end of July
Throckmorton wrote to Leicester that 'though I could neither
get access to the Queen, nor procure her liberty, yet I have at
this time preserved her life — to what continuance I am uncertain'. He had at last succeeded in getting a message through
to her, that Elizabeth had sent him to relieve her by all means
possible, 'which I am sure the poor lady doth believe'. And
Mary managed to get a letter out, through his friend Melville,

[1] *Cal. S.P. Scottish*, II. 348-50. [2] *Ibid.* II. 357-8, 366, 368.

48

thanking him for his *bonne volonté* and Elizabeth's efforts on her behalf.[1]

In August the Spanish ambassador reported that because Mary's life was in danger, the Queen had ordered Throckmorton to stay on for the present, and that he had acted vigorously and earnestly in favour of Mary, 'as he has always been attached to her'.[2] He was an enemy of Cecil, whom the Queen believed to favour Lady Catherine Grey. (If so, he was too wise to say so.) After Throckmorton's recall Elizabeth had ordered a relation of his to stand by in Scotland. This was Middlemore, who sent him a report of James's coronation at Stirling by the Bishop of Orkney.[3] John Knox had preached on the crowning of Joas very young; some accustomed ceremonies were omitted, 'many retained'. There were great rejoicings in Edinburgh, dancings and acclamations of the people.

Still Throckmorton was put off having any access to the Lords, who delayed meeting him. Elizabeth directed that Middlemore be sent to them to declare her dissatisfaction, 'and as their usage and proceedings towards their sovereign lady and Queen overpasses all, she will consume no longer time' but revoke her ambassador, who is to demand his passport.[4] Throckmorton ascertained that the Lords had really wanted to put Mary to death, for, as long as she lived, a party would be maintained at her devotion. She would not divorce Bothwell, who was now in the Orkneys. Throckmorton summed up all he had been able to achieve to Leicester: 'I have so travailed with Lethington and others of estimation that I dare affirm to her Majesty that this woeful Queen shall not die any violent death, unless some new accident chance'. Lethington, who was friendly to England and Throckmorton, candidly wished him away; the Scots could not go back on what they had done, 'unless we should cast our king, our country and ourselves away'.

On 11 August Elizabeth revoked her ambassador in the sharpest terms, promising revenge upon the Lords for keeping Mary in prison or if they touched her life or person.[5] She made a very offensive speech to Cecil that nothing was thought of to revenge the Queen of Scots' imprisonment. Cecil saw through this tantrum as just re-insurance; 'the planet' that had moved her was a conference with the Spanish ambassador; her real motives were 'that she be not thought to the world partial

[1] *Lettres de Marie Stuart*, ed. Prince A. Labanoff, II. 63.
[2] *Cal. S.P. Spanish, 1558–67*, 672, 674.   [3] *Cal. S.P. Scottish*, II. 370.
[4] *Ibid.* II. 373, 374, 377.   [5] *Ibid.* II. 378, 384, 389, 392.

against the Queen' and 'that by this example none of her own be encouraged'. Throckmorton reported that the French envoys were quite willing to throw over Mary so long as the old alliance was revived. Before he left, Mary's half-brother, Murray, arrived from France, to accept the Regency. Throckmorton regarded his conduct as statesmanlike and honourable; he had no disposition to keep Mary in perpetual prison, but would exercise the government in proper obedience from all sections of the nation to King James. The Hamiltons, however, were conspiring to liberate Mary. Upon this Elizabeth declared to Throckmorton her sympathy with them! At his taking leave of the Lords, they led him into a little cabinet where, out of their paucity, they had prepared him a present of gilt plate of more than 200 marks value, as from the King. He refused anything but from their sovereign Queen.

Throckmorton remained closely *lié* with Leicester, who could do nothing without him. About this time Leicester got letters of incorporation for a body of Preachers of the Gospel in the county of Warwick — the plan seems to have taken a more permissible form with his hospital over the West gate there a little later.[1] He named as governors the Earls of Huntingdon and Warwick, Sir Nicholas and Clement Throckmorton, Sir Thomas Lucy and Sir Richard Knightley — all of them militant Protestants inclining to Puritanism. We have a long letter from Leicester showing how much he depended on Throckmorton.[2] The clue has been lost, but evidently Leicester had slipped from grace with the Queen. Leicester pleads, 'I never wilfully offended, nor did that thing that both fear and duty went not withal toward them, and so shall do as long as I live. Time has been when my doings should never have been worse taken than they were meant, nor my meaning so scanned as should stretch from an unwilling stepping aside to a wilful slipping away. . . . If many days' service and not a few years' proof have made trial of unremovable fidelity enough, without notable offences, what shall I think of all that past favour which in such unspeakable sort remained towards me, thus to take my first oversight as it were an utter casting off of all that was before?' We shall see the pattern repeated in similar words with Leicester's successor, Ralegh, in this exposed position later.

In the summer of 1568 Throckmorton was ill again, and

[1] *Cal. S.P. Dom. 1547–80*, 304.   [2] *Cal. S.P. Dom. Addenda, 1566–79*, 28.

Cecil showed himself attentive.[1] Sir Nicholas approved the
course he had taken with the French and proposed when better
to kill a buck of Cecil's in his park at Mortlake. In October
Leicester and Cecil sought his advice on how to receive Cardinal
Châtillon coming over, for he was a Protestant and moreover
married. 'I know assuredly her Majesty has a marvellous liking
for him, and one thing more than I looked for, which is her
liking to hear of his wife, and is very desirous to see her.'[2] A
Cardinal who was a Protestant, with a wife, was clearly something worth making an exception for.

Next year was a year of crisis, with the Rising of the Northern
Earls and the intrigue in Elizabeth's inner circle for marrying
Mary to the Duke of Norfolk. The project emanated from both
Catholics and Protestants who were hostile to Cecil; it was
designed to wrest power away from him and to settle the chronic
uncertainty with regard to the succession. It might have achieved
that, but Elizabeth said that within four months of the marriage
she herself would be inside the Tower. The party pushing forward the marriage consisted of Norfolk, Arundel, Pembroke,
Lumley and, out of jealousy of Cecil, Leicester and Throckmorton. The whole thing came into the open in September;
in October Norfolk was sent to the Tower and the others, except
Leicester, were placed under arrest.[3] We are only concerned
with Throckmorton, whom the Spanish ambassador described as
a heretic, but such an enemy of Cecil's that on this account he
belonged to the Queen of Scots' party. Camden throws retrospective light here on the coming together of all Cecil's enemies
and the solid support the Queen gave him: they saw this most
dangerous crisis of the reign through together, eye to eye. 'They
conspired therefore secretly to cast him into the Tower, Throckmorton, his emulator, suggesting to them that, if he were but
once imprisoned, means to undo him would not be far to seek.
But the Queen (by whose discovery I know not)[4] came to the
knowledge hereof in good time; and Cecil, through the magnanimous fortitude of his princess (who, coming upon them in the
very instant of time, restrained them by her beck) easily defeated
the plot that was laid against him.'[5] It was Sir Nicholas who
fetched up in the Tower for a bit.

Under examination Throckmorton said that he had not

[1] *Cal. S.P. Dom. 1547–80*, 315.　　[2] *Cal. S.P. Dom. Addenda, 1566–79*, 59.
[3] H.M.C. *Salisbury MSS.* I. 426; *Ca . S.P. Spanish, 1568–79*, 200, 201.
[4] It seems she learned it through her ladies.
[5] W. Camden, *History* (ed. 1675), 122.

moved the marriage, but that he had conferred in the matter with Norfolk, the Lord Steward and Leicester. Leicester's attitude was that 'he would not have her if he might', but 'if no better remedy could be for so dangerous a woman, it were good to make a virtue of necessity, so it might be allowed by her Majesty'.[1] He thereupon requested Throckmorton's advice, and their conclusions were that (1) the situation had greatly changed in Scotland, France and Spain; (2) Murray's position as Regent was insecure; (3) the Queen purposed such a restoration of Mary as she could not be sure of her; (4) good provision might be made by marrying Mary to Norfolk — the conditions should be such that Queen Elizabeth and her realm might profit. The Protestants involved had an idea of the conditions that would be necessary, but there was no guarantee, 'not with such a woman'.

When Edward Herbert had asked Throckmorton if he found the Queen's displeasure towards him appeased, he had answered that he found himself not in such case as he had any cause to retire; when the truth of his doings was known he trusted the Queen would become his good lady.[2] He admitted that he had spoken in anger against those who would advance other titles to serve their turn. This meant Cecil. He claimed that 'such as have meddled in this matter do mean as dutifully and truly to her Majesty as you do', and charged that others were not disinterested, wishing to advance Hertford's children.[3]

Jealousy of Cecil, along with a sick man's temperament, had warped Throckmorton's judgment. But his loyalty to Elizabeth was never in doubt, and shortly he was released. In spite of the Queen's prohibition, Norfolk continued on his way into conspiracy, the Ridolfi plot, and treason. One of his confessions throws a retrospective light on his conversations with Throckmorton.[4] One morning they were in a gallery together at Westminster when Throckmorton told him that Leicester was moving a marriage between the Duke and Mary — 'it seemed strange to me, knowing how desirous he [Leicester] once was of that marriage himself'. Throckmorton's idea seemed to be to marry Mary to Norfolk for religion's sake, since he was a Protestant, and to make her wholly dependent on Elizabeth. Throckmorton had been the go-between Leicester and Norfolk; his advice had been for Norfolk to seize an opportune time before broaching the matter to the Queen. Once she gave him a

---

[1] H.M.C. *Salisbury MSS.* I. 430.   [2] *State Papers*, ed. S. Haynes, 541-3.
[3] H.M.C. *Salisbury MSS.* I. 435.   [4] *Cal. S.P. Scottish*, IV. 32, foll.

deliberate opening, which he did not take ; and he missed another chance 'coming into the privy chamber one morning at Loseley, one of Master More's children singing to a lute, her Majesty sitting upon the threshold of the door, my lord of Leicester kneeling by her Highness'.

Thus Norfolk had stumbled forward to his execution. The Spanish ambassador thought that his word could be trusted, 'only that he is an Englishman, and the best of them are not to be trusted overmuch'.[1] In fact, Norfolk least. His execution, over which the Queen long hesitated, marked Cecil's victory for good and all.

Throckmorton did not live to witness this consummation. In February 1571 he was taken ill in Leicester's house, and after lingering some days, attended by the Queen's doctors, he died, and was buried in his parish church of St. Katherine Cree in Aldgate. There we see him on his Renaissance tomb : columns, triglyphs, the numerous quarterings of his family, an inscription reciting his virtues and achievements. What is peculiar to the monument is that his head lies on his helmet, tilted outwards to the spectator, giving a very much alive look. He has come through air-raids, bombs, rockets, vandals, wreckers, the burnings of the City, the immense destruction of our time.[2]

Camden has a character-portrait of him : 'a man of great experience, very ready wit and singular diligence who, busily attempting many things in Queen Mary's days, hardly saved his life by his eloquent wisdom ; and under Queen Elizabeth, having with indefatigable pains discharged many embassies with great commendation, yet could he rise but to small wealth and those slight dignities (though glorious in title) of Chief Butler of England and Chamberlain of the Exchequer, whilst he showed himself an antagonist against Cecil in favour of Leicester. In whose house as he was feeding hard at supper on salads, he was taken, as some report with an imposthume [burst abscess] of the lungs, as others say, with a violent catarrh and died (not without suspicion of poison) in a good time for himself and his, being in great danger of losing life and estate by his restless spirit'.[3]

Thus Camden ; it is a pity to have to repeat the imputation against Leicester, if only to show how absurd it is and the kind of thing he had to put up with all his life. Cecil wrote philosophically to Walsingham, Throckmorton's real successor : 'this

---

[1] *Cal. S.P. Spanish, 1568–79*, 50.
[2] *v. Royal Com. on Historical Monuments*, London, IV, plate 20.
[3] W. Camden, *History . . . of Elizabeth* (ed. 1675), 152.

afternoon God hath called to his mercy Sir Nicholas Throckmorton, having been sick not past six or seven days of a pleurisy, joined with a disease called periplen, he doth but lead the way to us, whereof I for my part have had sufficient schooling by my present sickness'.[1] In Paris the news gave grief to the ambassador Lord Buckhurst, to whom it came as a personal loss.[2] So it was to the Earl of Rutland, though he said that it did not grieve the French. Walsingham, whose first introduction to foreign affairs dates back to a couple of years before, when Throckmorton had been too ill for work, now wrote to Leicester on the loss of 'so dear a friend as Sir Nicholas was to me, whose lack, if it were private only to his friends were great, but if it be weighed generally in respect of her Majesty and our country, the want of him will then appear greater. For, be it spoken without offence to any, for council in peace and for conduct in war, he has not left of like sufficiency his successor that I know.'[3] Let this be his epitaph. He was in his fifty-sixth year, only five years older than his rival, Cecil, who had more than a quarter of a century of activity before him. His successor was already lined up. Such is the way of life, such the injustice in the nature of things.

[1] *The Compleat Ambassador*, ed. Dudley Digges, 45.
[2] *Cal. S.P. Foreign, 1569–71*, 407.
[3] Conyers Read, *Mr. Secretary Walsingham*, I. 27.

CHAPTER IV

THE YOUNG HEIR

SIR NICHOLAS THROCKMORTON left a young family of six sons and only one daughter, all of them under age. Of these the most important to our story are the second son Arthur and his sister Elizabeth, who became famous as Lady Ralegh. While Sir Nicholas and his wife were in France, their children were in other people's care. In May 1561 Francis Goldsmith, who had charge of them, expressed the opinion that 'they cannot, being well brought up, degenerate utterly from their fathers, whose service towards England I delight rather to consider than to report the same to you'.[1]

Now, ten years later, Sir Nicholas left his lands — mainly in Northamptonshire, Paulerspury, Cosgrove, Silverstone, Tiffield — to his widow for her life.[2] His eldest son, William, was nearly eighteen, born therefore in 1553. The second son Arthur was left the manors of Alderminster (near Stratford-on-Avon) and Sheriffs Lench. The house by St. Katherine Cree was to go to the fourth son Thomas, after his mother's death; Nicholas, Henry and Elizabeth were to have £500 each during their minorities.[3] His brothers Kellam and Clement owed him sums of money. To Kellam he left a remainder of £30, to Clement a 'russet satin gown furred with black fox, and a standing cup'; to his brother Anthony his best 'black damask gown, a dozen gold buttons, £20 and a gelding'; to his brother-in-law Francis Carew, 'my gilt harness for my body and my next best sword, girdle and dagger'; to his nephew Job, the later Puritan of the Marprelate Tracts, 'a coat, cloak and sword'.

Bequests were made to the supervisors of his will: to Leicester 'two bowls with rosemary branches', Sir Walter Mildmay 'my best standing gilt cup', the Master of the Rolls 'a standing cup with a cover', Sir John Throckmorton 'a pair of blue flagons garnished with silver and gilt, and a standing cup with a cover'.

---

[1] *Cal. S.P. Dom. Addenda 1547–65*, 511.
[2] Inq. Post Mortem, C 142/157/104.   [3] P.C.C. Daper 8.

His cousin the Marquis of Northampton, always a rather indigent man, got 'my gown of wrought velvet furred with sables, with parchment lace of gold'; his cousin Henry Mildmay a 'black damask gown, a dozen gold buttons, £20 and a gelding'. To William Killigrew, faithful groom of the chamber to the Queen all her days, he left 'my best coat and cloak that he will choose'; 'unto Mr. Secretary Cecil', it is pleasant to record, 'the two bowls of tortoise-shell garnished with silver and gilt'. To Lady Warwick, a favourite with the Queen, his diamond ring worth twenty marks; to Lady Stafford a piece of plate or a jewel of the same value. He left his lawyer William Hughes of the Inner Temple £20, and a standing cup and cover; to the faithful Francis Goldsmith a standing bowl with a cover; to Arthur Agard, the eminent antiquary and a kinsman, £10; various sums to menservants, small amounts to the French and Dutch churches, five marks each to the Puritan divines, Lever and Sampson; he asked that one of them should preach at his burial. These bequests reveal Sir Nicholas's religious sympathies as consistent to the last.

What is peculiar is that the eldest son William did not succeed to his father's estate; it came into the possession of the second son Arthur on attaining his majority, and he took the place of head of the family. Though there is no information on the subject we can only infer that William was *non compos mentis*, or at any rate not fully competent. For some years he continued to live with his mother; in 1583 he was living at Tiffield; in 1593 he made over two-thirds of the London house that came to him from brother Thomas to Arthur.[1] In return we find Arthur making payments for him, for polling him, providing hose, doublet and gown for him, or shirts and socks, or sending him silk mocado for his doublet. When Arthur came to make his will in 1623, William had been long dead and buried in the chapel on the north side of the chancel of Paulerspury, where Arthur was laid beside him.[2]

Of the rest of the family Henry died young; Robert went to Cambridge and we lose sight of him. In December 1587 Thomas went off in a huff without saying goodbye to Arthur; but in August 1588, after the Armada had passed by our shores, Arthur lay with his brother a night at the 'Limpet' at Mile End, where Thomas had a chamber. Two years later he was dead. The only brother to have as successful a life as Arthur's was the

---

[1] The material here and elsewhere comes from Arthur Throckmorton's Diary, unless otherwise stated. [2] P.C.C. Hele 106.

youngest, Nicholas. He was clearly intelligent; in June 1588 we find Arthur sending money to him in Italy, where he was educating himself by a continental tour. He was adopted by his uncle, Sir Francis Carew of Beddington, who had no children; he took the name of Carew along with the estates in Surrey and died there during the Civil War.

This leaves Elizabeth, who had been baptised at Beddington 16 April 1565, and was therefore almost certainly born there that month.[1] A child of six at her father's death, she was probably the youngest and lived with her mother until she became a maid-of-honour to the Queen. In February 1572 her mother lent her portion of £500 to the hard-up Earl of Huntingdon, and this debt was never recovered. Half a century later we find Ralegh's representatives pressing the Earl's heir for its repayment; so that Sir Walter married a portionless wife.[2] She inherited her share of the Throckmorton temperament, however.

It did not take Lady Throckmorton long to find a second husband, and indeed, with a family of young children, it was a necessary protection.[3] She found one without children of his own, a decided advantage: Adrian Stokes, the good-looking Welshman for whom Henry VIII's niece, the Duchess of Suffolk, had fallen. Immediately upon the Duke's execution she married him: one sees him red-headed, broad-shouldered and wide-awake beside the stout party, sixteen years his senior, in Hans Eworth's double portrait of them. When she died she left him comfortably provided with a fine estate at Beaumanor, with its park and wooded prospects, in Leicestershire, a town residence in the historic New Wark in Leicester.[4] Lady Throckmorton did well for herself by marrying him: he was generous to her and her children in his will. Being of superior rank she kept her name, under which we find gifts made to her in the Leicester town-accounts for 1574-5. She retained her house in the city of London and continued to visit her brother at Beddington. Of the house that he rebuilt there on a noble scale, and where he entertained the Queen in 1599, the great hall remains with parts of the garden and policies.[5] In consequence, with the family complicated by these relations, there were many goings to and fro

[1] Beddington Parish Register.
[2] Cf. P. Lefranc, 'La Date du mariage de Sir Walter Ralegh', *Études Anglaises*, 1956, 193 foll.
[3] Marriage licence granted by the Bishop of London, 10 April 1572, *Notes and Queries*, 1 Series, XII. 452.
[4] M. Bateson, *Records of the Borough of Leicester*, III. 139, 160, 161, 168, 228.
[5] W. E. Brayley, *History of Surrey*, III. 274 foll.

between these various residences. In addition there was the immense network of Throckmorton kin.

In the year of his father's death Arthur Throckmorton matriculated from Magdalen College, Oxford, at the age of fourteen — so he was born in 1556–7.[1] We know nothing more about his education, though it seems clear from references in his Diary that he followed the usual course for gentlemen of his class of proceeding to an Inn of Court. In his will he refers to Magdalen, 'where I was sometime a too much careless and negligent student', and made the college a very fine bequest of those of his books in foreign languages — tribute to his scholarly interests. So the young man succeeded in getting himself educated, in spite of the difficulties and intermissions of his family life. He became an accurate and conscientious diarist; the care and devotion with which he kept his Diary, the meticulousness of its details, are much to the credit of a youth left fatherless, with inadequate direction and the means to go to the bad if he chose. Instead of that, and in spite of his share of the Throckmorton temperament, impulsive and hot-blooded, he was a virtuous youth and man. Keeping his Diary became a mode of self-education, as with others similarly left on their own resources. He began by making careful observations of the world around him, especially on his sojourns abroad. But the Diary became a habit, as with all true diarists, and his is the fullest, the most extensive and revealing of all Elizabethan diaries that remain.

The Diary may once have covered the span of his life from his service in the Netherlands in 1578 to the the end of his days in 1626. What we have remaining is three volumes, the first two covering the eighteen years from 1578 to 1595. There is then a gap till 1609. The third volume covers the years 1609 to 1613, and then breaks off short, though it may have been continued. Arthur Throckmorton must have collected a mass of papers — all his father's diplomatic papers he handed over to Sir Henry Wotton for preservation, who gave them to Charles I for his state paper office. He was a collector of facts, especially about himself, the day's doings, his health and his wife's, travels, journeys and their observations; visits, the occupations and troubles of friends, his financial accounts and estate business, flocks and herds, his building and planting; the medicines he took, the books he purchased; his interests of mind, his career and progress, his setbacks, quarrels and troubles. His Diary, the

[1] J. Foster, *Alumni Oxonienses*, IV. 1483.

events and persons of which can be vetted and filled out from contemporary documents at every point, gives as full a picture as of any man of his age that I know.

The Diary has the further interest that, though Throckmorton was not a man of the first rank like his father, he moved in the same aristocratic society and had a more representative, though less exciting, life. Perhaps that is right for a diarist — he might not have been a diarist if it had been otherwise. The main interest of the Diary is social: it provides a clear and candid mirror of Elizabethan social life. The young man begins, as so many others of the time began, with the fighting in the Netherlands, an apprenticeship to war against the Spaniards. He next goes, in 1580–1 — precisely the same time that Montaigne was making his tour into Italy[1] — on the continental tour, down the Rhine across the Alps to Italy and back through France. This section of the Diary is the fullest of the first two volumes and is packed with interest. The German part, travelling down the Rhine, is descriptive and contains observations on the places they were passing through: an Elizabethan guide-book. The Italian part is most revealing of how a young Elizabethan settled down to learn the language and the arts of Renaissance Italy. There were the young men who accompanied him, or whom he met, engaged in polishing their northern barbarism at the fount of sixteenth-century culture: the Sidneys, Philip and Robert, Anthony Bacon, a Neville, Saville, Pelham, Mildmay, Spencer, the Catholic exile Sir Anthony Standen who forwarded intelligence to Walsingham. I know of no other such concrete and detailed account of the process.

On his return he is given a small post at court in attendance on the Queen, has his foot on that precarious ladder. In this period there appear in the mirror many of the famous figures of the time — Leicester, Walsingham, Sir Christopher Hatton, the Queen herself. Among the younger men are the Earl of Oxford, Philip Sidney, Essex, very much a friend, later on not so. The movements of the all-powerful Lord Treasurer register shadows on the glass; for the Cecils were no friends, they formed another grouping. It is the time of the Anjou marriage — Throckmorton has to receive Anjou's confidential envoy Simier, for whom the Queen conceived a comic affection, her '*singe*'; or he has to meet Duke Casimir of the Rhine, at the Queen's service with his *Reiters* for cash, under whom Throckmorton fought in the

---

[1] Cf. *The Diary of Montaigne's Journey to Italy in 1580 and 1581*, trans. E. J. Trechmann.

Netherlands, or to conduct to Oxford the Polish prince Laski.
Numbers of names well known in their day flit by — Mildmays,
Spencers, Paulets, Cavendishes, Hastings, Mordaunts, Darcys,
the ladies of the Court, Lady Warwick, always a favourite with
the Queen, the beautiful Lady Rich, Sidney's Stella.

The real affairs of life intervene. Throckmorton falls in love
and marries — it is a love-match. Life engages him in its ten-
tacles. We hear all about his wife's illnesses, her periods and
their symptoms — though this always appears in French, along
with their tiffs and reconciliations, and other awkward information of personal or family trouble, quarrels, imprisonments.
Very infrequently he uses a cipher. Children are born and
baptised; friends gather with their presents for a social occasion.
Life proceeds; people recur.

Then his sister comes to Court; the tall, dark shadow of
Ralegh appears. They are secretly married — though how they
could have supposed that they could keep it from the Queen
passes belief, when one of them was a prime favourite, the other
sworn to her service as a lady-in-waiting. Lady Ralegh takes
refuge in her brother's house for her lying-in; a child is born,
of whose existence no-one has known since that day, baptised
Damerei, by Throckmorton, his wife and, of all people, Essex.
The child is put out to nurse with a Throckmorton relation at
Enfield, is taken to Durham House to be shown to the father,
then disappears utterly from view. What might have been expected happens: Ralegh and his wife are imprisoned in the
Tower; he is released after a couple of months — for his services
are needed in connection with the *Madre de Dios* — Lady Ralegh
not until the end of the year. By the fatality of his Throckmorton
marriage Ralegh suffered a set-back from which he never fully
recovered, though he came back to Court after some five years'
exile; Lady Ralegh, for all that she pushed and intrigued to get
back, never.

Always and everywhere there is the background of the family
and its immense network of relations, particularly thick on the
ground in certain areas. Throckmorton's marriage into the
family of the Lucases of Colchester gave him connections round
Essex and the Thames estuary. His sister's marriage extended
his cousinage in the West Country. When he travelled down to
Devon, or to Sherborne to stay with his sister at the time Ralegh
was away in Guiana, or to Bath for the waters, he rarely needed
to stop at an inn; there were stopping-places at the houses of
his kin most of the way.

It is a pity that the Diary is wanting for the years 1596 to 1609; for that period includes the expedition to Cadiz, on which Throckmorton served. It also covers the Essex conspiracy and Ralegh's trial and imprisonment in the Tower. The Diary of 1609–13 is careful to say nothing of that dangerous connection. There are references to the most intriguing, and elusive, member of Ralegh's circle, Thomas Hariot.

We have indications that Throckmorton was mildly affected by the intellectual interests of the circle: he engaged the mathematician, Thomas Hood, to teach him geometry. But his interests of mind were, in general, orthodox. The Diary has nothing much about religion — in this like Shakespeare's plays; Throckmorton notes when he and his wife receive their Easter communion, for this was a matter of conformity with the law. There is the usual business about livings to fill, parsons who die or are to be presented. He bought books on theological subjects, in that showing the conventional taste of his day: the works of Luther, Calvin and Beza, Jewel's *Apology* and Harding's *Reply*. More interestingly, he bought occasional bundles of plays — if only *those* had survived! — and he never failed to purchase the infrequent publications of Donne, with whom he had been on the Cadiz voyage.[1] Characteristically Elizabethan, he had an intense interest in medicine, which one can only regard as deleterious when one considers the tortures he inflicted upon himself by the potions he took, the purgations and sweatings he underwent. But that too was conventional.

The last volume of the Diary is not the less interesting for being that of a quiet country gentleman no longer at the centre of things, who seldom goes away from home. Though getting older, he is certainly busy enough. There is the usual public work of a man of his station, as Justice of the Peace and Deputy-Lieutenant; having seen service abroad, it was a point of pride with him to take his part in organising the musters. As sheriff of the county in the year of Gunpowder Plot he took an active share in following up the tracks of the conspirators and rounding up recusants, showing himself the more zealous since many of them were his relations. Sometimes grandees from Court passed by along Watling Street, on his threshold at Paulerspury, and turned off the road at the mill to be hospitably entertained in the fine new house he built himself, with its pleasaunces and walks, on the western slope beneath the ancient church of the Paveleys,

---

[1] His brother Nicholas married the sister of Donne's wife.

where he himself now lies. Or King James would come to hunt in Grafton park, with its earlier memory of Edward IV and Elizabeth Woodville meeting under the great oak that survived for centuries. Or Lord Wotton came to stay, with a large following, to hunt the deer in Whittlewood Forest and the parks round about — an expensive visit, for there was all the neighbourhood to entertain day after day, and minstrels engaged to play at every meal. Queen Anne's players pay a visit; a dancer is engaged, who falls on trouble and has to be helped out of prison. There are the comings and goings of Northamptonshire neighbours: young Washington comes over from Sulgrave, the Wakes from Salcey Forest, Shakerley Marmion from Aynho, Treshams and Spencers, Lanes and Temples from Stowe, Fermors from Easton Neston just across Watling Street — the same people we still see upon their tombs in the churches today: Jerome Fermor upon his monument at Towcester, who lived 'in wedlock forty two years and attained to the honour of a great granduncle and after seventy fours years left this life for a better, 7 September 1602'; or Agnes Ogle under her pretty brass in gown, kirtle and brimmed hat, in the church of Potterspury, by the black-and-white monument to her husband, Cuthbert Ogle, Lieutenant of the Forest, whose bugle is heard in the rides of the Forest no more.

After Oxford and the Inns of Court a period abroad was the rule for a young man of high position expecting to enter his country's service. France was now in the full flood of the Wars of Religion, in which the Massacre of St. Bartholomew in 1572 made an indelible mark upon the minds of Protestants throughout Europe, especially those like Walsingham and Philip Sidney who witnessed it. To us it is the world of Dumas and Mérimée, of the Three Musketeers and the *Chronique du règne de Charles IX*, of the *Mignons*, of Joyeuse and d'Entragues and the murderous career of Bussy d'Amboise, which made such an impression on the Elizabethans. It was the world of Henry of Navarre and Marguerite de Valois, of the industrious Catherine de Medici for ever hard at work keeping things together, patching up pacifications which as soon broke down; the years of Jarnac and Moncontour, when young West Countrymen went to France to gain their apprenticeship in war, among them Walter Ralegh.

A few years later, in 1576-7, there was an interval of peace and the Queen kindly considered that this was the moment for young Throckmorton to go. Sir Amyas Paulet's embassy in September 1576 provided the chance: 'my ordinary train is no greater of necessity, being augmented by some young gentlemen, whereof one is Sir Nicholas Throckmorton's son, who was recommended to me by her Majesty and therefore I could not refuse him'.[1] We know nothing of him during his ten months in France other than what that sourpuss Paulet tells us, namely that he had now got the language well and by August 1577 was returning home, 'being hereunto required by his mother, who hath promised to get him licence to travel into Italy, because having now gotten the French tongue in good perfection, he cannot make any other profit by his abode in France. To be plain with you', Paulet continued, 'I think myself very happy that I am honestly delivered of him. He is a very young man, and hath his imperfections, which riper years and good counsel may remove from him. He may not go into Italy without the company of some honest and wise man, and so I have told him, and in many other things have dealt very plainly with him. I hear he hath been chargeable to his mother, which must be imputed to his folly, having had his meat and drink with me for himself and his man, and I have not only from his first coming to Paris provided him of a horse, but also have found his horse at my charges. His mother prayeth that his coming over may seem to proceed of his own request, because the Queen shall not be offended with it.'[2]

Young Throckmorton was not yet in a position to go on the continental tour to so-much-desired Italy; so in the summer of 1578, now about twenty-one, he went over to the Netherlands to fight in the English contingent under Black John Norris. The situation in the Netherlands was complex and confused as always; impossible to go into it here, except in so far as it illuminates Throckmorton's part in it. The year 1577 was that of the Pacification of Ghent; Spanish troops left the country and if only it had been able to hold together they need never have returned. This, however, was not the Spanish intention; at this moment Philip's Secretary, Escobedo, was writing that the Spaniards must get hold of Holland and Zealand: 'it is a more difficult job than England; but if the one falls into our hands the other will do so too'.[3] It is true that Philip had Escobedo murdered, but he did not necessarily disagree with the sentiment. The threat was sufficient to justify English intervention, and in 1577 Norris went

---

[1] *Cal. S.P. Dom. Addenda, 1566–79*, 504. Nicholas Hilliard, the painter, was a companion in Paulet's train at this time. E. Auerbach, *Nicholas Hilliard*, ii.

[2] *Copy-Book of Sir Amias Paulet's Letters*, ed. O. Ogle, (Roxburghe Club), 89-90.

[3] *Cal. S.P. For., 1577-8*, xii.

over with a regiment. In January 1578 Don John of Austria —
Philip's half-brother — who had been surreptitiously gathering
forces, suddenly launched them at the States' army and routed
them at Gemblours. This renewed the war. There was con-
sternation in England; the Queen, who was reluctant to send
forces, engaged Casimir with his German mercenaries. Casimir
was a Calvinist who distrusted all Frenchmen; he trusted the
Queen of England, so far as her cash went.

In June she sent over Lord Cobham and Walsingham to
explore the ground. Their real purpose was to prevent the States
from falling under French domination, an even greater danger
than Spanish. But William the Silent was bringing in Anjou to
his aid, and Elizabeth's marriage negotiations with the latter
were really meant to keep a check on him. The English ambassadors travelled about sounding opinion, from Antwerp to the
States' camp near Lierre. Casimir was in camp at Zutphen
when Anjou arrived at Mons. Anjou's dashing companion
Bussy d'Amboise captured Maubeuge from the Spaniards and
was besieging Beaumont, when Henri III sent his agent Bellièvre,
also to keep a check on Anjou. The States' army was now in
camp in a strong position at Rymenam near Mechlin. This is
where the Diary opens.

Throckmorton starts methodically with a list of all the com-
panies and commanders serving under Casimir — Maurice of
Saxony, Count Mansfeld, John Barnard of Wahlbrun; then the
French under theirs, and there were even 300 Hungarian horse.
It reads like a roll call from Macaulay's 'Ivry' or Rilke's *Cornett
Christoph Rilke*. We are more interested in the English regiment
under Henry Cavendish with its captains, three Binghams, a Lygon,
Cobham, Markham, Carew, Fuljambe. We observe how many of
them are sick this plague-stricken summer. With youthful pride
this volunteer notes, 'we have ten pieces of great ordnance in
our camp, the which are planted on our trenches, they are
guarded by the high Almain [German] footmen; whereof three
of them are discharged every night and every morning at the
setting and the discharging of the watch.' It must have been
great fun to the tiro; there follows a list of the different sorts of
guns from cannon downwards, youthful enthusiasm reflected in
the simple direct writing. He was, indeed, a straightforward,
rather naïve character — *naïveté* is usually endearing — who
liked information for its own sake and went about the world
jotting it down, with an instinct to record everything. Therein
lies his interest for us, therein lies his difference, for not many

people have that itch. For the rest, he was straight and dutiful, hot-tempered but kindly, with an ingenuousness that not only makes him the more likeable, but the more valuable as an historical source. There was no return upon himself, no fracture or frustration to poison him or make him dangerous. The Diary, however, must have fulfilled some obscure, unconscious need; perhaps loneliness, perhaps fatherlessness.

On 1 August took place the engagement in which the English troops were blooded and where they bore the brunt of the fighting with success. It was Lammas day, especially honoured by the Spaniards as the day of Lepanto, Churchyard tells us, and Don John proposed to celebrate it by a surprise attack on the camp at Rymenam.[1] Norris arrived only just in time to take part in the action — he had three horses killed under him that day. Of the three Bingham brothers two were slain. But, mainly owing to the good fighting qualities of the English regiment, the Spaniards were beaten back. Count Bossu, their commander, reported that 'the way the men did their duty could not have been better. Norris . . . and Bingham, who lost two brothers, behaved so that Caesars could have done no better.'[2] Davison, the English agent in the Netherlands, wrote proudly to Burghley of 'the value which our countrymen showed, notwithstanding that most of them were newly come to the camp'. The news administered a welcome fillip in England; the Spaniards had never yet been defeated in open field; evidently they were not invincible. Throckmorton reports it in the laconic way of Elizabethan diarists: 'we fought with the Spaniards from 8 o'clock before noon until 4 at night and we drove them to the flight, at which encounter were slain of English Captain Bingham, Captain Lygon *et al.*'.

English spirits rose. At home the Queen was willing to go farther than before in supporting the rebellious Netherlanders, whom for the rest she did not like. In the field Rowland Yorke, later a name that became infamous with Sir William Stanley for the betrayal of Deventer, 'made challenge against that French that made the letter that was sent to St. Aldegonde [the Prince of Orange's right-hand man] speaking in the dishonour of us Englishmen'. 7 August: 'we won Aerschot and spoiled it. I came from Antwerp with Mr. Norris to the camp.' There were further alarms of attack: 10 August: 'we stayed in arms all night looking for the enemy's coming, which should have given us a

---

[1] Thomas Churchyard, *A True Discourse of . . . the Netherlands*, (ed. 1602), 30 foll.   [2] *Cal. S.P. For. 1958–9*, 115.

camisado in white shirts crying, "Orange, Orange".' Next day
two trumpeters came from Don John, one to exchange prisoners,
'the other with a challenge to assail him if he durst or else that
we would but come lie out of our trenches, and he would soon
make a day of it and end one way or other the war'. A drum
was sent him with a suitable reply, and so the exchanges went
on. These were the days of a bastard chivalry:

> Don John of Austria is going to the war.

The realities of war were otherwise. 12 August: 'our men
brought in a booty of kine, mares and horses from the enemy;
five spies were taken and put to death in our camp'. Next day
three more spies; the day after '400 horse brought home a great
booty of cattle from the enemy'. Similarly on 15, 16 and 20
August. On St. Bartholomew's day, 23 August, 'Casimir with
the chiefest of his train came to our camp and dined with Count
Bossu. The enemy forsook the town of Aerschot and left it at
our devotion, out of the which our men brought home great
spoils.' The fact was that this rich country was being systemati-
cally plundered, the peasantry spoiled and reduced to the misery
of endemic war; shortly plague was to appear. The Germans,
having to evacuate Aerschot, set it on fire. 27 August: Throckmorton went there; on the way near Diest there was an action
in which thirty *Reiters* were taken by the Spaniards and the English
lost sixteen men; but Throckmorton returned 'with a booty'.

Other amenities were enjoyed: at a dinner for Casimir a
quarrel arose between M. de Bouy of his train and M. de Lagarde
of Count Bossu's, 'the which quarrel made a very great uproar
throughout all the company, by the means that the Viscount of
Ghent took the quarrel in hand and gave the lie to M. de Bouy,
the which told him that he was as good a gentleman as himself.
A quarrel fell out between the *Reiters* and the French that came
with Casimir, wherein four French were slain and three *Reiters*;
to the parting of which quarrel came our general Count Bossu,
where he had great ado to appease it. At which time one of the
Viscount of Ghent's gentlemen was thrust through the body by a
Frenchman. Captain Polmenier thrust through the body by
Captain Samson, being at dinner.' A good time was evidently
being had by all these young swordsmen *à la Dumas*.

Meanwhile more serious affairs, negotiations of extreme com-
plexity, were on foot. Bussy d'Amboise came and went on behalf
of Monsieur (Anjou); his activities were always noticed, for
Bussy's was a name, and not only a name, to play with. The

famous Huguenot commander La Noue, *Bras-de-fer*, came to offer his services to the States. English agents moved between the capital and the camp. The Archduke Matthias arrived to take over the governorship of a distracted, ungovernable country. The Prince of Orange was everywhere, ceaselessly negotiating, intriguing, trying to hold the country together; the Catholic nobility, inflamed with jealousy of him, as ceaselessly intrigued against him. On St. Bartholomew's day Cobham and Walsingham at last met Don John under a great oak outside Louvain and delivered him an ultimatum. The Puritan Secretary paid him a warm tribute in his letters home: 'surely I never saw a gentleman for personage, spirit, wit and entertainment comparable to him'.[1]

At the end of the month Anjou was proclaimed Protector of the Low Countries. The States' army advanced upon Louvain; on 10 September the English, French and Scots contingents skirmished before the walls and drove the Spaniards back into the town. In an assault upon a neighbouring castle Norris was wounded and sixteen English slain. The castle of Genappes surrendered without an assault; so also the town of Neuville. Monsieur was cannonading Binches, somewhat ineffectively. On 1 October the rumour ran through the English camp that Don John was dead; a few days later it was confirmed, and Throckmorton tells us that he died of the plague, 'having taken it of the Count of Rhens' daughter, with the which he had meddled with all the night before her death, having before gotten her with child'. The sedate Walsingham sent home the news that Don John had died of grief and melancholy, but 'partly of a disease they call *les brogues*, by which he was extremely tormented, but chiefly, as it is given out, of the French sickness, whereof in the opening he was found to be inwardly wasted and consumed'.[2]

So much for the hopes placed upon this romantic candidate for the hand of Mary Stuart.

On 7 October the town of Binches was at last battered into submission to Monsieur. The governor Don Diego was received at the breach in the walls by Bussy, but in despite of Bussy and the gentlemen the soldiers entered, sacked the town and set it on fire. Monsieur was satisfied with this achievement; the news that the Prince of Parma, a far greater soldier than Don John, was taking over the command gave Monsieur no satisfaction: the Protector of the Low Countries was set on returning to Paris

---

[1] *Cal. S.P. For. 1578-9*, xxiv.   [2] *Ibid.* 233.

for other pleasures. The States' army advanced towards Namur, and in the move Throckmorton was struck in the leg. Sick, he went to Brussels, to which his man Peter brought his stuff from Mechlin; his horse he sold to Captain Morgan for nearly 40 florins. The campaigning season was coming to an end, the armies taking to their winter quarters. The rumour went the rounds that peace would be made. During his sickness at Brussels Throckmorton spent 78 guilders; 1 November he went from Brussels to Antwerp, next day to Wynsches in Zealand, where he fell sick of a burning fever. After ten days the fever left him and he was able to make preparations for home, having a cloak made and sending a letter to his mother by Arthur Champernowne — a cousin of Ralegh's.

Throckmorton continued to jot down notes of public events until he left the Netherlands — the disposition of the armies, the extrusion of strangers from Antwerp, the efforts made by the Prince of Orange to bring about a reconciliation between the people of Ghent and the Walloons. Early in December his stuff was sent 'a ship board to Bennet's ship', while he went back to Brussels to take his leave of La Noue. By the time he went from Antwerp to Ghent the Prince had succeeded in effecting a peace between the quarrelling inhabitants of Ghent and the Walloons. From Ghent to Bruges, Nieuwpoort and Dunkirk, where Throckmorton went on board at one in the morning and landed at Broadstairs at five in the evening.

Stopping the night at Lord Cobham's on the way to London, on his arrival he at once went to Richmond to pay his respects at Court, in the usual manner for a man of his family and position returning from abroad. He received his Michaelmas rent from Alderminster, £13 : 6 : 8, and at once spent it on yards of tawny velvet and white satin, silk stockings and a tawny shirt; a New Year's gift from his uncle, Sir Francis Carew, went on silver lace and tinsel, silver for his hat, a ring and losses at dice and tennis — real tennis, of course; a present from his father's dependent, Arthur Agard, clerk in the Exchequer, went on a velvet hat and far too generous gifts to 'my man Swan'. Throckmorton had a room in London, where he occasionally supped, but whence he was more often paying visits to Court, to his uncle Sir John Throckmorton or Lord Mordaunt at Chelsea — a Northamptonshire neighbour at delightful Drayton, where he built the Elizabethan wing of that splendid house. Such was the round and such the equipment of a young courtier.

On Twelfth day he went to Court at Richmond, where

'Harry Brouncker drew upon Tom Perrot . . . having first given him the bastinado and thereupon were both committed prisoners to their chambers to the Marshal'.

The danger from Spain was now greatly increasing, with Parma in the Netherlands determined to conquer the northern provinces and the power to effect it — North and South had now broken apart — and with Philip on the threshold of succeeding to Portugal and its ocean-going fleet. It was becoming indispensable for Elizabeth to make sure of a French alliance, without — if possible — an open breach with Spain. The prime way to effect this was a marriage with Anjou, the one possible candidate, though small, dark, pock-marked and only half her age. Elizabeth herself was still the best marriage in her parish, as Walsingham put it, a spinster with a kingdom for her dowry. The French ambassador Mauvissière, better known as Castelnau, described her at this moment, with perhaps French gallantry: 'la Reine d'Angleterre ne fut jamais plus jolie ni plus belle. Il n'y a rien de vieil en son fait que les ans qui ont été ce jour d'hui de ce mois quarante six . . . Ceux qui naissent en ce signe ne sont jamais stériles et ne meurent guère sans héritiers.'[1] Anjou was sending his favourite Simier to reopen negotiations and, if possible, close the issue.

On 9 January 1579 Throckmorton was sent with Sir Edward Stafford to London to meet Simier and bring him to Court. Stafford was the son of Sir Nicholas's friend, Lady Stafford, and went on to make the diplomatic career Throckmorton did not make: he ended as ambassador to France. They duly met Simier with his train of gentlemen, took them to Syon house to lodge for the night and brought them to Richmond, where Simier had his first audience of the Queen. He supped with Leicester, who was at this time the strongest opponent of the marriage, to which Burghley and Sussex, the Lord Chamberlain, were for good political reasons inclined. Next day Simier had another audience and found himself personally gaining favour with the Queen. He was clever, and she liked clever men; he was amusing, and she needed to be amused. Camden describes him as 'a choice courtier, a man thoroughly versed in love-fancies, pleasant conceits, and Court-dalliances'.[2] This was the language that the spinster-sovereign delighted to hear and talked to her dying day — such a relief from, or at any rate a sweetening to, politics. Next day Simier had a long business audience with the

---

[1] Conyers Read, *Mr. Secretary Walsingham*, II. 19.
[2] W. Camden, *History*, 227.

Council, 'and afterwards went abroad walking in the garden
with her Majesty'. The day after 'the ambassador's gentlemen
came to Court and danced'.

On 17 January Duke Casimir landed at Dover on a mission
to extract more money out of the Queen. He was accompanied
by the eminent Huguenot scholar Languet, who nourished such
a tender feeling for Philip Sidney; and Sidney was appropriately
sent to meet them. The Court moved to Whitehall; Lady
Throckmorton came up to London to go to Court, while her
husband gave his stepson £5, which was spent on black velvet,
black satin and silk grogram, black taffeta and carnation cloth
of silver, with carnation silk stockings. The young man must
have made a suitable figure at the running between Sir Christopher Hatton and Mr. Sidney before the Queen, Casimir and
Simier. Next day, 2 February: 'the challenge between Mr.
Hatton and Mr. Sidney at tilt and tourney ended. Sir William
Drury's arm was broken at tourney by Mr. Ralph Bowes.'

The Diary notes that all the first week of February it snowed,
and Camden tells us that 'in a sharp and snowy winter' Casimir
had a warm and generous welcome from the City. 'He was most
honourably received and conducted with great pomp into London,
with torches lighted, by the Lord Mayor, the alderman and
citizens, and to the Court by the chief of the nobility; where he
was entertained with tilting, barriers, and costly banquets, and
honoured with the Order of St. George, the Queen herself buck-
ling on the garter about his leg.'[1] Throckmorton was well in on
the proceedings. 3 February: 'Casimir dined with my Lord
Mayor of London, where he received of the City in gifts to the
value of £500. I was at the Court. I supped at Somerset house
with Casimir. Wednesday the 4th: 'Casimir dined at the
Barbican with the Duchess of Suffolk, where I dined and after
dinner I went to the Court'.[2] Throckmorton was at Court when
Casimir was made a Knight of the Garter on Sunday the 8th;
three days later he took his leave of the Queen, paying a sightseeing visit to the Tower before being shipped back to the Netherlands. The German mercenary had done rather well out of his
visit — but not so well as he fancied; the Queen had reached
the conclusion that if Anjou would do her work in the Netherlands, Casimir could be dispensed with. The marriage negotia-

---

[1] W. Camden, *History*, 232.
[2] This was the Dowager Duchess of the Brandon line, who had married Richard
Bertie. She died 19 September 1580. The *Complete Peerage*, ed. G.E.C., XII, pt.
1. 460.

tions went on. This was not pleasing to more candid souls like Philip Sidney.

The Diary now sounds an ominous note in regard to Sir John Throckmorton and his son Francis, with whom Arthur was on terms of affection though they were Catholics: this was the beginning of their troubles. On 15 February Sir John and his son were had up before the Privy Council and committed to the keeping of the Dean of St. Paul's, the celebrated Alexander Nowell. Unfortunately this did not do them any good. Francis had been a student at Hart Hall from 1572, the year after Arthur went up to Magdalen;[1] when Magdalen under Laurence Humphrey had a decidedly Protestant inflexion, Hart Hall seems to have had a Catholic flavouring — for which reason Donne was sent there a decade later. Francis next was admitted to the Inner Temple in 1576 and married this very February in the midst of his troubles — evidently an imprudent youth.[2] While confined in the Deanery, he was to have conference with none but his trusty keeper — he had been hearing mass at various places in London.[3] On 21 February Arthur went to the Dean of St. Paul's to speak with his cousin; next day to Court to speak to Lord Dudley on his behalf, on the 24th again to plead for his cousin's deliverance. Next day Francis was freed, 'being bound to appear before the Council within twelve days after'. Perhaps he was released as an act of consideration in order to get married, for he got his licence to marry that day.

On 3 March Arthur took his sister to Court for the first time; they stopped the night there and returned next day. The Queen kindly spoke to him and 'commanded me to tell her excuse for her not coming to see my mother. My Lord of Huntingdon would have put me to her Majesty.' The Earl of Huntingdon, who combined Plantagenet ancestry with Puritanical inclinations, had an interest in his old friend's children. Arthur notes public events briefly in his Diary along with his private occupations: the death of Sir Nicholas Bacon, Lord Keeper, his burial in St. Paul's, the promotion of the Queen's solicitor, Sir Thomas Bromley, in his place. On 22 March Arthur was at Court when Anjou's Secretary arrived with Simier bringing the Duke's response to the conditions propounded for the marriage. Sunday the 29th Throckmorton's old President of Magdalen, Dr. Humphrey, preached before the Queen; 'Simier and Monsieur's Secretary were before the Council in my Lord Treasurer's

---

[1] J. Foster, *Alumni Oxonienses*, I. 1483.
[2] J. Foster, *London Marriage Licences*, 1340.　　　[3] *A.P.C. 1578–9*, 47.

chamber'. Next day similarly; again on 12 April: 'I went to
the Court. Simier with the Queen in the garden.'

By this time nobody knew what she meant to do next. Even
Leicester, who knew her as well as anyone, was perplexed; he
wrote to Davison, 'touching the other matter at home here for
Monsieur which you desire to understand of . . . I think none
but God can let you know yet. Only this I must say, outwardly
there is some appearance of good liking, for the messengers are
very well used and her Majesty's self doth seem to us all that she
will marry if she may like the person. And if the person adventure
without condition on assurance to come hither, if she then like
him it is like she will have him. His ministers say he will adventure his coming and stand upon that matter of liking, etc.
And this is all, I assure you, that can yet be said to you. As for
mine own opinion, if I should speak according to former dispositions, I should hardly believe it will take place. And yet if I
should say conjecturally by that I newly hear and find in her
deep consideration of her estate and that she is persuaded nothing
can more assure it than marriage, I may be of mind she will
marry if the party like her.'[1]

That, if one can follow the labyrinthine expression, was how
things stood with the Queen of England; in modern English:
if marriage were indispensable to her country's safety, she would
not exclude the possibility.

Easter time brought the scattered family together. Sister
Bess came up to stop with their Markham cousins at Chelsea,
and thence she went to pay her respects at Court. Lady Kitson
and her daughters from musical Hengrave came to visit Lady
Throckmorton in London. Young Robert joined them from
Cambridge, and on Saturday they received communion according to the statute. On Easter Monday Lady Throckmorton
went abroad grandly in her coach to Ratcliffe, and Arthur went
to Easton park in Essex to stay with uncle Kellam and sport
there — for which purpose kind Arthur Agard had bought him
a bow and arrows. Young Arthur had his troubles with his man
Swan, whom he put away and then took back again; then he
had to bail him out of the Counter for debt, and next write a
letter on his behalf to Lord Garrett. Meanwhile there was an
'uproar of the people against my Lord of Warwick for enclosures
he made at Northall. Master Hatton, Master Vice-Chamberlain,
went to appease them.' Throckmorton himself went into the

---

[1] *q.* Conyers Read, II. 11-12.

country to various weddings, and in May took a hand in such an affair himself: 'I moved Mistress A. Isham for my cousin F. C.' (This is probably a Catesby cousin.)

In May Arthur's private affairs and his uncle Sir John's public troubles came to a head. Sir John was ordered up to appear before the Privy Council; Arthur took the opportunity to use his uncle's advice in regulating his succession to his father's estate, in place of his simple brother William. On 4 May, Arthur was with his uncle, Lord Windsor, Mr. Talbot and Sir Edward Herbert. 7 May was the first day of Easter term; next day Arthur received the books from his father's study.[1] The next days he was with Sir John, for advice how to have the commission to succeed to his father's lands made over to him, going to Westminster Hall — the seat of the law-courts — about it, and accompanying him to the Star Chamber where the business was to be settled. In the intervals of this, on 11 May Arthur went with his cousin Francis Darcy to Lord Garrett and 'lay with my cousin F. D. all that night'. They were at Lord Garrett's next day; after supper Darcy and Throckmorton went to Court, where 'we both were commanded to avoid the Privy Chamber by Watt and Wingfield. My cousin F. D. and I lay together.' (This was common Elizabethan form.) On 14 May Arthur was 'with my cousin H. M. about Mr. W. A. going over with him into France' — this refers to Middlemore who would be in a position to aid William Ashby to go. Ashby at this time entered into bond to pay Throckmorton £110 at his coming into the country; he was a Midland neighbour who accompanied Arthur on his continental tour and later went on a diplomatic mission to Scotland. Towards the end of the month Throckmorton finished his affairs with his uncle Sir John, took leave of Lord Huntingdon and from Court, and journeyed into the Midlands to spend the summer with his mother and her relations.

Meanwhile Sir John's career was coming to a disagreeable end. Various complaints had been made against him in Wales during his years as Vice-President of the Council there.[2] Now the tenants within the forest of Feckenham were complaining of his enclosures, of his unlawful felling of timber and entering suits at common law against the inhabitants. Sir John was the brother-in-law of George Puttenham, who is usually considered to be the author of the primary work of Elizabethan literary

---

[1] Many of these now repose upon the shelves of the library at Magdalen.

[2] *A.P.C. 1558–70*, 375; *A.P.C. 1577–8*, 363, 375; *A.P.C. 1578–9*, 25, 98, 129, 189, 191.

criticism, the admirable *Art of English Poesy*.[1] Puttenham married the widowed Lady Windsor, who, after an unhappy life with her first husband, now complained that her second was defrauding her of her inheritance with the connivance of Sir John. Unfortunately there was something in the charge; Sir John seems to have helped to convey away the manor of Heriard from the poor lady to Puttenham. Perhaps this accounts for the laudatory appearance Sir John makes in the *Art of English Poesy*, which is otherwise unexpected and corroborates Puttenham's claim to the authorship.

The Privy Council thought less favourably of Sir John, sequestered him from the offices Queen Mary had conferred upon him for his orthodoxy and committed him to the Fleet prison.[2] His nephew heard the news in the country and entered in his Diary for 3 July: 'J. Th . . . found by the Council to be guilty of negligence and ignorance, or erasing or wrong certifying a record, in penance whereof he himself committed to the Fleet, his offices sequestered until her Majesty's pleasure and fined a £1000'. It is not likely that the fine was paid. After Sir John's release, the Council had to write to him inquiring why their order in the case had not been carried out and the sums of money agreed upon paid to Lady Windsor. The dispute over the forest was remitted to Sir Thomas Lucy — the Lucy whom the young Shakespeare, then fifteen, would know — 'their lordships being troubled with affairs of greater importance'.

Sir John was shortly beyond the reach of Privy Council warrants; within a few months he was dead and gathered to his fathers in the church at Coughton beneath a splendid canopied monument, whereon he is depicted holding his wife, Margery Puttenham, by the hand, where his offices are recited, 'sometime Master of the Requests unto Queen Mary of happy memory' — the churches must indeed be few where she is so described — and repeating the old formula as late as 1580, 'on whose souls God have mercy'.[3]

Arthur Throckmorton had an agreeable time in the country that summer with his kin. He began by staying at Beaumanor, whence he went to christen cousin Henry Cavendish's child as deputy for his stepfather and went on to the musters at Loughborough. His cousins Edward Winter and Job Throckmorton

---

[1] This has been, rather unnecessarily, questioned.
[2] *A.P.C. 1578–9*, 193, 299, 320.
[3] Puttenham cites an epitaph of his own making to Sir John in *The Art of English Poesy* (*Arber's English Reprints*), 189-90.

— one a Catholic, the other a Puritan — came to pay visits. With another cousin he went to stay with uncle Anthony at Chastleton, perched on the edge of the escarpment over the Vale of the Red Horse. All three went on to Sir Edward Boughton's in the forest of Wychwood to kill a buck. They next proceeded to Alderminster to view the manor, stopping at cousin Underhill's at Nether Ettington on the leafy slopes across that delightful Warwickshire road. They spent four days at the Gloucester Assizes where a case concerning a family property was being tried, and then came back to Chastleton. At the beginning of August he went from Beaumanor to Brigstock, where brother Robert visited him from Cambridge. There are still memorials of those years in that pleasant village, about the centre of Rockingham forest, on the steep slope down to Harper's brook with the ancient stone bridge : the pretty manor house with fragment of its former moat, above all the fine Elizabethan column with the royal arms, put up in 1586 in place of the medieval cross.

In August business interrupted Throckmorton's jollifications in the country : he had to go up to the Court for a settlement of his father's arrears in regard to his office as Chief Butler of England and to pursue the chance of a Court appointment for himself. The Council took order to enable him to pay off his father's arrears, and on 14 August, 'Mr. Secretary Walsingham spake with me about her Majesty's letters for myself'. The Court was at Greenwich ; Throckmorton's visit coincided with Anjou's private visit to the Queen, about which little is known. Elizabeth made it an indispensable condition to marriage that she must see the man ; Anjou was prepared to brave the venture. The Diary tells us that on the 15th the Lord Treasurer came to Court — the Queen would settle nothing without him. Two days later, 'Monsieur came to London to Mauvissière's house and lay that night at Greenwich in Mr. Light's house'. Throckmorton dined that day with a family friend, apt to be useful : Sir Owen Hopton, Lieutenant of the Tower. Anjou's visit was to all appearances a success with the Queen, though everything was kept private — dinners, dances, walks in the garden together, parties at night. Anjou became her pet 'Frog' ; he was spirited and lively, though a light-weight he came from the cultivated French Court, and — what weighed more than anything with the Queen of England — he was of royal birth, the only person to whom she could talk as an equal. It may be doubted whether, for all her freedom, she opened her heart to him ; a great deal was play-acting, more was politics, underneath everything was the woman who could not accept the fate that to her alone marriage was denied. After the junketings, the Diary records, 28 August: 'Monsieur returned towards France, the Queen having brought him on his way to my Lord Cobham's and from thence she went to Wanstead'. *There* — it was Leicester's great house in Essex — lived the man she loved.

Throckmorton's affairs in a promising way, he resumed his summer vacation in the country, passing through Epping forest to stay with uncle Kellam at Easton. He went on to Cambridge, where he supped with the Vice-Chancellor, Dr. Byng, presumably at Clare of which he was Master.[1] Thence to Beaumanor, where numerous visitors came and went. There were Thomas Wilkes — a Fellow of All Souls, now a professional diplomat, and Henry Cavendish, with whom Throckmorton had served in the Netherlands, eldest son of the redoubtable Bess of Hardwick. Lady Throckmorton and her husband went to stay at Gopsall, Sir George Hastings's house, and hunt in the fine park there. When they returned Lord and Lady Cromwell came with their daughter to Beaumanor, and they all 'went a hunting to Garradon park, my Lord of Bedford's, and killed a buck'. Robert came over from Cambridge and the brothers dined together at Quorn, while their parents were away, at Mrs. Katherine's. Arthur bought amber bracelets for 5s. We are the less surprised to read the entry, 'I received a letter from A. Agard about wenches' matters'. There are constant comings to and fro on the part of William Ashby of Lowesby: a friend of the family, who accompanied Arthur on his continental tour next year. In October Arthur paid a visit to his aunt, Job Throckmorton's mother, at Haseley. At the end of the month he fell out with his stepfather, a choleric type himself, and went off to Dalby — a place not much changed since, with its Elizabethan manor-house and church, a rarity. Writing on the way to his mother, sister and brother William, but not to Mr. Stokes, he returned to the Court at Greenwich.

There the marriage negotiations were entering their last phase. Public opinion had hardened against it. The Puritan Stubbes had come out with his pamphlet, *The Discovery of a Gaping Gulf in which England is like to be swallowed by another French Marriage* — and been made to suffer for it. Philip Sidney wrote his celebrated letter of protest to the Queen, for which he was not soon forgiven. The Council was now fairly united against

---

[1] C. H. and T. Cooper, *Athenae Cantabrigienses*, II. 279.

the marriage; Elizabeth wept hysterically at them — why was she of all women denied marriage? She expected them to go on their knees beseeching her to carry it through. Simier had earlier revenged Leicester's opposition by revealing his secret marriage to Lettice Knollys to the Queen — that lady, a favoured cousin, never recovered her favour again. Between one and the other of them the woman was driven beyond endurance — and yet had to remain Queen and do her duty, whatever that was.

The day Throckmorton arrived at Greenwich he wrote to his friend Simier; two days later he visited him at his lodging and went to Court with him. On 10 November the Queen announced her intention to marry to the assembled Council; she recalled Stafford who had been sent with a message to Anjou. But she could not get the Privy Council to assume the responsibility for inviting him over. Distraught, she ordered a committee of them to draw up the terms of a marriage contract; at the end of the month Simier left with it in his pocket. But it was really over: the country would not now allow her to marry. For Sunday, 29 November Throckmorton entered in his Diary:

> Quinti Evangelii libertas,
> Regni Anglicani calamitas,
> qui stet videat ne cadat.

The next Sunday his own good fortune was assured: 6 December, 'I was sworn squire for the Body by Mr. Wingfield' — he was following in the footsteps of his father and his grandfather; this was the way his family had made its fortunes. Next day he and Edward Hoby — Burghley's nephew, son of the formidable Lady Russell — were ordered to meet Sir Amias Paulet, returning from his embassy in France, at Rochester. The Queen removed from Greenwich to Whitehall, as usual, to spend Christmas, and on Christmas Eve Throckmorton took his chamber at Westminster. His friend Stafford came and went with messages for Monsieur — if he were not going to marry the Queen, he had to be pacified. On 16 January 1580, comes an ominous note: 'my lord H.[1] told me how my lord L[eicester], would speak to me for speaking ill against him'. The Anjou marriage negotiations had left a trail of partisanship and ill-feeling behind: Leicester and Walsingham, with Philip Sidney — nephew of one, soon to become son-in-law of the other —

---

[1] Probably Lord Huntingdon.

were on one side; Burghley and Sussex, the Lord Chamberlain, were on the other, and the gifted but scapegrace young Earl of Oxford was a partisan on that side. Young Throckmorton took up with Oxford, quite against his natural alignment with his father's friends, Leicester and Walsingham. This was the moment of the celebrated quarrel on the tennis-court between Oxford and Sidney. 27 January, 'my lord Oxford writ a challenge to Philip Sidney'. Next day, 'I supped with my lord Oxford. Friday the 29th, my lord Oxford, commanded to keep his chamber by the Queen.' A week later, 4 February, 'I writ to my lord of Leicester. Friday the 5th, I was commanded to my chamber by my lord Chamberlain. Saturday the 6, I writ a letter to my Lord Chamberlain.' On 10 February and again on Shrove Monday, he spoke with him; both Oxford and Throckmorton were released from confinement. He thereupon left the Court for London. It was not an auspicious beginning for a Court career.

Meanwhile there were his private and family affairs, his finances, his friends and avocations. Peter, whom he had had with him in the Low Countries, was his manservant at this time and seems to have managed his money and done his house-keeping. From the first Throckmorton was methodical in keeping accounts of his cash; though he spent it, he kept a record of what he spent. Occasionally he receives a pound or ten shillings from his mother or stepfather: it is always entered. He is very conscientious about writing to his family, especially to his mother and his sister; we find him writing impartially to Puritan Job and Catholic Francis, now farther advanced in trouble. That autumn he gave his sister his fan of feathers, latest of Italian fashions — one sees the Queen portrayed with one about this time. His sister stops with him in London and thence goes home to Beaumanor. He pays a visit to Reading with Lord Windsor and back to Court, where M. de Bourg arrives from France. The Queen pays a visit to the house of the French ambassador.

In April he went to Colchester with Lady Darcy and stayed at the Lucases' house there, St. John's abbey in the suburbs — to become his home for a time, on marrying into that family. Back in London for Easter term he received his half-year's rent for Alderminster, £19, whereof brother William received £6 : 13 : 4 and Agard £5, leaving himself £7 : 6 : 8, of which £5 : 10s. immediately went on cloth for liveries. His stepfather came to London for the trial of a law-suit, which he won; he exchanged several letters with Mr. Stokes. In June-July he was making preparations for going abroad. He cut off the entail on his lands by a fine; he received £100 and entered into a statute. He took his leave of Lord Stafford, Lord Mordaunt and his cousin Middlemore at Putney.

All was set for the tour he had so long desired.

CHAPTER V

CONTINENTAL TOUR, 1580–1582

A CONTINENTAL tour was almost as important in the education of a young Elizabethan aristocrat as it was again in the eighteenth century. But we are so much better informed about the latter. Here again is a further value of the Throckmorton Diary to us : there is no other account that lets us see so fully and so intimately what the tour did for these young Englishmen, not only their sightseeing, their adventures on the road, whom they met and the acquaintances they made, what they paid for things, but the actual process of their education, the lessons taken in Italian and music, with what tutors and with whom they lodged, the books bought, the difficulties met with. Throckmorton's meticulous conscientiousness, the detail of the Diary, stand us in good stead. What would we not give for a similar diary of Philip Sidney's travels on the Continent in the 1570's or Ralegh's unrecorded adventures in France !

In the well-known letter that Sir Philip Sidney wrote to instruct his younger brother, Robert, setting forth just before Throckmorton, we learn : 'your purpose is, being a gentleman born, to furnish yourself with the knowledge of such things as may be serviceable to your country'.[1] This meant taking note 'of all leagues betwixt prince and prince, the topographical description of each country, how the one lies by situation to hurt or help the other, how they are to the sea well-harboured or not, how stored with ships, how with revenue, how with fortifications and garrisons, how the people warlikely trained or kept under', etc. Lord Burghley's instructions to the young Earl of Rutland had been to the same point, and he added, characteristically, 'it is good that you make a book of paper wherein you may daily or at least weekly, insert all things occurrent to you'.[2] Evidently these counsels were the regular thing in that age; but we have no such thorough example of their being taken to heart and carried out as by the conscientious Throckmorton.

[1] Sidney's *Works*, ed. A. Feuillerat, III. 124–7.
[2] C. Howard, *English Travellers of the Renaissance*, 37, 39.

In a windless late July the party left London on the 26th by water for Gravesend, Arthur having bought himself a trunk for 8s. 10d. — one of those large trunks such as one sees in the Hilliard picture of young Mildmay at Cleveland, Ohio. On the 29th they sailed from Gravesend to the 'Land's end', but for lack of wind lay all night at Queenborough. After a further attempt they had to return there a couple of days later for want of wind. Throckmorton begins his guide-book for us with a note that the Isle of Sheppey is 21 miles about, with four villages and a castle, whereof Mr. Thomas Randolph had the keepership — a reward for diplomatic service. 'It stands up on corn and pasture and has upon the shore marl whereof brimstone is made, of the which Mr. Pepps hath the commodity.' 2 August, 'we sailed from Queenborough and rested all that night in the hole of the Spaniards on shipboard'. Next day they coasted along by Broadstairs and Margate, but were driven to cast anchor until the afternoon; then sailing all night, they reached Flushing at 2 p.m. Arthur delivered Ashby 3 crowns, and this gives the pattern of their relations on the tour: the young aristocrat held and provided the money, which he doled out to Ashby to pay expenses as they went. Their passage cost them 4 crowns, their victuals 8 shillings.

Next follows a description of the island of Walcheren and its towns. We learn that it stands upon corn, fishing, pasture, making of salt and portage of merchandise. It can set forty ships of war to sea and levy 20,000 men for service. 'The isle is wholly of the religion [*i.e.* Protestant], and wholly to be directed by the Prince of Orange', who has a trusty servant of his, a Walloon, as governor. Flushing has a Fleming as governor, with a garrison of 300; it lives chiefly by fishing, 'and receiveth great commodities by strangers passing by her', notably from pilotage dues. Middelburg was the staple for French wines, and had great fishing and much trade. It had no garrison but its own burghers and 'no other governor than the burghermaster. . . . This town hath no manner of profession of papistry.' Not far from Flushing was the fort of Rammekins — which became familiar to a whole generation of English troops, when Elizabeth came openly out in support of the Dutch five years later and Flushing was occupied as a 'cautionary town', a kind of pledge, with Philip Sidney as governor.

5 August they went by wagon to Armen and thence by hoy all night to Dordrecht, which was the staple for Rhenish wines, with no garrison but the burghers. The passage by water cost

23 stivers, 1 shilling for portage, 2 stivers for drink. Here their three meals cost 4 guilders, 3 stivers. Throckmorton's man Peter came to him from London and they met Mr. Browne — one of the Catholic Lord Montague's family — and Edward Morgan on their way from Cologne. On Monday, 8 August, they went by ship along the river Waal to Tiel in Gelderland, passing by Dorkum, which was 'wholly of the religion and endureth no papists'. Bommel was similarly free of them, had a garrison of 200, with Count John as governor of the island and of all Gelderland. (The little town of Tiel was shortly to distinguish itself for its resistance to the Spaniards.) Leaving Tiel at six in the morning they reached Nijmegen by noon; an hour afterwards an alarm was given to the town by malcontents — though 'it hath no profession of papistry yet there are many in it'. The chief town of Gelderland, it had at one end a strong castle upon a hill, built (of course) by Julius Caesar; within, a garrison of three ensigns of soldiers, with a Scot, Rudolph Foster, for captain.

10 August they went in a small boat to Emmerich in Cleveland and lay at the 'Cat'; their passage cost 20 stivers, their suppers 27 stivers. Emmerich was 'wholly of the Romish religion', with a garrison of 100 soldiers, a school and a residence of the Duke of Cleves. Thence they went by wagon south-east to Wesel, 'where we rested us a while and then hired us a wagon to carry us to Düsseldorf, wherein we rid to a village one mile from Wesel and were forced to rest there that night'. Wesel was an imperial town, but under the government of the Duke of Cleves 'it endureth papists, Lutherans and Calvinists, every one their profession', and with no garrison but the townsmen. It sounds a sensible place. Next day, leaving at 3 a.m., they arrived at Duisburg for breakfast — where the Duke and his Estates were assembled; after breakfasting they rode on through the forest, where there was great store of red deer, wild boars and horses running wild. Duisburg was a Lutheran town, without a garrison, standing in champion country environed with a forest. Düsseldorf, on the Rhine, was wholly Romish with a garrison of 100 soldiers; the town made linen and possessed a school. The river Düssel ran through the town and through the Duke's palace into the Rhine.

Rising at 5 a.m. on 13 August they went on foot to a village where they took boat for Cologne and arrived there at 6 p.m. to put up at the hostelry of the 'Holy Ghost'. Their passage cost two batts. Throckmorton describes Cologne in the form of a half-moon upon the Rhine, in champion country environed with hills. It had a garrison of 400 besides townsmen, a monastery and as many churches as days in a year. 'The three kings which came to the birth of Christ there died and lie buried in the Dom. St. Ursula and her virgins of England lie there also buried in a church of her name; therein lieth also buried a king of England.' We here enter the region of fable. They spent three days at Cologne, their fifteen meals costing 18 'whysphennynges' (rixpennies), 'a piece for every meal', their beds 24 of the same coins. Every other day or so Throckmorton hands over a crown to Ashby to be changed. The next few days they spent at Neuss and Düsseldorf, returning to Cologne on 20 August and sending Peter back to Nijmegen to fetch their baggage. That day they were set upon by thieves on the river, and six warships of the Prince of Orange passed down the Rhine. On St. Bartholomew's day, 24th, Peter arrived with their stuff — the carriage cost three dollars; Ashby wrote to Secretary Walsingham and Arthur, having laid in a stock of paper, wrote letters home before the next stage of their journey up the Rhine. For the journey he bought a petronel, a large horse-pistol, in addition to the smaller one he already possessed.

They left Cologne by boat at 9 a.m., and spent the night at a riverside village where they met with some gentlemen of the Marquis of Brandenburg and a servant of the Archduke Matthias. Day by day we follow their progress up the Rhine through Bonn, Andernach, Coblenz — all of them Catholic and belonging to prelates. Throckmorton breaks into Latin verses against monks in the margin —

> Quicquid agit mundus, monachus vult esse Secundus.
> Monachi vestri stomachi sunt amphora Bacchi
> Vos estis deus est testis turpissima pestis
> Certum ac ratum verum est probatum —

a recognisably English reaction abroad. He notes, however, that only a mile from Coblenz was Rhens, belonging to the landgrave of Hesse, Protestant with no profession of papistry. One sees the tesselated pavement of a happier Germany.[1]

On they proceeded, passing by St. Wert, which had belonged to the Prince of Orange, but which he engaged and lost to the landgrave of Hesse — now Lutheran; by Oberwesel, belonging to the archbishop of Mainz and so papist, to Bacherach, which

---

[1] The impression of Sir Edward Unton's companion on his tour in 1563 was that 'the people [along the Rhine] are very painful [*i.e.* live laborious lives], and not so painful as rude and sluttish'. Howard, 40.

belonged to the Palsgrave and was therefore wholly Protestant. He had a castle in the town, possessed the best tin-mines thereabout and received tolls of the river-traffic. They spent the night at the 'Angel', where their supper cost 13 batts. Of Bingen Throckmorton inevitably notes the Mäuse Turm, 'wherein a bishop was eaten with rats, having yet there retired himself from them'. And so to Mainz, passage from Cologne having cost 1 kaiser-royal, and on to Frankfurt, which they reached on 30 August, to stay at the sign of the 'Ox'. Arthur 'delivered 3 crowns, one kaiser-royal, 2 milreis to W. A. out of my purse' to meet expenses — one sees the medley of coins and currencies Elizabethan travel required.

They had arrived at Frankfurt in time for the autumn fair and there they stayed for a few days. Throckmorton describes it, a free town of the Emperor's, standing in champion country, with liberties a mile about, a watch tower in every quarter, the town ditch forty paces broad with plenty of fish, and with its double walls. They changed from their inn to Pierre Lybrère's house. 5 September was the first day of the Mart, and Arthur bought himself two brushes and a rubbing brush; two books of Latin and Dutch (*i.e.* German) cost two batts, a little Dutch-Latin-French dictionary, 10 rix-pennies, a Terence in Latin and Slavonish, 4 batts. 'Paid for my pistol to the shipper, 12 batts . . . soleing my horse, 5 batts . . . given away 8 batts.' In the margin he tries out his Italian, notes payments for washing shirts, for boot-hose, reckons up his money in the large and small purses, concluding that at Frankfurt he had spent 3 pistols, 4 batts.

Leaving Frankfurt on 7 September they reached Nuremberg after three days' journey by wagon, for which they paid 6 crowns, and stopped there at the 'Golden Goose' for some three weeks. For here they met with a group of young Englishmen similarly engaged in educating themselves by a continental tour: Robert Sidney — Philip's younger brother — Henry Neville, who became a diplomat and ambassador to France, but compromised himself in the Essex conspiracy, a Pelham, Carew, Harmer, Smyth and Savile. Letters from home were awaiting them, and Throckmorton was able to help Carew by changing his money for him. Careful as ever about money, Arthur notes down currency calculations which show how complicated it was, with so many currencies circulating. £60 sterling from London amounted to 318 guilders, 38 crychers; 'received of Mr. Ashby for my £10 sterling, 53 guilders, 6 crychers. 20 pieces of 3 crychers to a guilder, and so I have in my bag of canvas 8 guilders to 5 crowns French. A French crown, 24 batts. 15 batts to a guilder. 4 crychers to a batt. To a French crown 96 crychers; to a pistol 92 crychers. 1 October: taken out of my canvas bag 7 guilders, whereof 6 I turned into dollars, the 7th I put in my spending purse. I put 1 crown into my purse, of gold.' Let this be enough.

The appearance of a comet this autumn appealed to Throckmorton's growing interest in astronomy and astrology — the two were hardly separate in those days. From the beginning of his journey abroad he has astrological notes in his margins and these become regular as the Diary goes on. Now, 12 September: 'there appeared in the east at night a great blazing light'. On the way to Prague, 9 October: 'I saw the comet appear between (nearest to) Pegasus and Pisces. 10 October: I fell into the river by Altdorf Regnitz.' (Was he, perhaps, star-gazing?) 11 October: Johannes Pretorius came and read to me.[1] The comet by his natural course removed from Pegasus to Pisces's head. 12 October: now the comet is come over the first star in Aquarius's hand, which makes from his first motion hither 10 degrees . . . 20 October: the comet is between Dolphin and Aquila, south-east of the middle star in Aquila, 60 degrees; gone westward by his natural course since his first appearing near Pegasus and Pisces . . . 27 October: I saw Orion and Procyon rising out of the south at one after midnight, the moon rise in Gemini and then appeared above them at nine of the clock of the night. We may see' — and there follows a series of astrological signs. Before leaving Nuremberg he had equipped himself with Ptolemy's *Geography* and his *Almagesti*, Sacrobosco's standard work on the Sphere and Johannes Garceus's *De Tempore* — for which he paid the considerable sum of 4 guilders. Altogether he bought quite a lot of books on his travels, particularly in Italy: they were a major item of expense with him. Most of them have now come to rest on the shelves of the library at Magdalen.

Throckmorton spent the whole winter, from November to early April, in Prague. It was then, in the first years of the reign of Rudolf II, at its apogee: the Emperor made it his favourite residence and, a patron of the arts, collector of pictures and

---

[1] Pretorius, mathematician and astronomer, was born 1537. Educated at Wittenberg, he was called to Vienna to instruct the Emperor Maximilian II in mathematics. He became professor of mathematics at Wittenberg in 1571, and in 1576 he moved to Altdorf where he died in 1616. The author of a work *De Cometis*, 1578, and maker of astronomical calendars, he was an important precursor of Kepler.

statuary and botanical specimens, creator of gardens, he was engaged in embellishing the city. The Emperor was also a gifted linguist — he even knew some Czech — with a passion for Latin poetry and for history. To these he added an interest that became ever more absorbing — for astronomy and chemistry, with their attendant astrology and alchemy. Within the next few years he was to invite the English mathematician and astrologer, Dr. Dee, to Prague, and there followed the curious, chequered, comic episode of Dee and his medium Edward Kelly's residence there, 1584-6, until it was brought to an end by Mother Church. For, to these other passions, the Emperor, like so many of the figures at the head of European society, as the sixteenth century wore into the seventeenth, added that of homosexuality. He shared the tastes of the kings of France — Henri III and Louis XIII; of England — James I; and of Spain — Philip III; not to mention Count Maurice, the soldierly son of William the Silent. What accounts for such an exalted constellation at that time? Could it be anything to do with the stars?

Throckmorton and his companions boarded with Signor Scipioni of Ferrara, 'paying 20 dollars a month between us, $17\frac{1}{2}$ batts to the dollar'. We cannot be sure who his companions were, for at Nuremberg Ashby left him for a time and rejoined him later. Towards the end of their stay, in March, Arthur notes that they — R. S., H. N. and A. T. — jarred with their host; 'A. T. said to H. N. that etc.' This means that Henry Neville and probably Savile had accompanied him from Nuremberg. All was not well between him and Ashby. At the end of November Ashby wrote to Secretary Walsingham railing against Mary Queen of Scots — this would not be popular with Sir Nicholas's son. He took the opportunity to write next day to Leicester. Ashby was in correspondence with the Italian humanist and reformer Castelvetro, who had been driven to take refuge in England, with Horatio Palavicino, now rising to eminence in business and diplomacy, and with Dr. Willes, the English envoy to Venice. In December Arthur wrote Ashby 'a letter of Re: con: sil: ly: and received another of him'. But a winter together was too much for their good temper: at the end of it, 18 March, 'W. A. jarred'; a week later he was sick. Then, 27 March: 'W. A., A. T., unconstant, not secret, quarrelsome, flatterer, envious, etc.' They had evidently got on each other's nerves; it was not unlike the famous case of Horace Walpole and the poet Gray on their continental tour.

Nevertheless work and entertainments went forward that

winter. Arthur continued to buy books: Suetonius's *Lives of the Emperors* in three volumes for 24 batts, Euclid, Piccolomini on the Sphere, Vitruvius on Architecture, Horace with Lambini's Commentary, published at Frankfurt in 1577. In this last, now at Magdalen, he has written on the title-page, so like him—

> aequa in arduis, temperata in bonis,
> mens mea semper.
> est quoddam fatale malum per verba levare—

a rather touching reminder of what he wished to be like, with perhaps an expression of regret for their quarrels. And then, lower down, he has written:

> Ni aux légers la course,
> Ni aux forts la bataille.

The young man conscientiously noted down information about the Empire, the names of the Emperor's ministers, foreign envoys and ambassadors, their comings and goings, political events and news — all the things that would be helpful to him one day if he were to follow in his father's footsteps.

There were plenty of people to meet in Prague, a distinctly cosmopolitan society. Early on in their stay they were 'with Anna Strada, a Scotswoman married to a Spaniard'. There they met Father George Ware, an English Jesuit, who had been at Oriel College, Oxford.[1] The Jesuits were much to the fore at Prague, for though the Emperor's dominions were at this time dominantly Protestant, Rudolf was very Catholic. On 3 January Arthur was 'at the disputations at the Jesuits' college, where proceeded six bachelors of arts, having seven questions: two of metaphysics, three of physics, and two of logic, beginning at one in the afternoon. Georgius Warus an Englishman moderator and reader, in that house, of philosophy.' Next day he was at the Jesuits' again and 'saw a dialogue of the birth of our Lord Jesus Christ'. These were the educational methods with which the Jesuits were reconquering some of the ground lost by the Reformation. However, this Throckmorton escaped easily with a gift of a dollar to Father Robert the Jesuit; not so others.

In November they dined with Signor Scotti of Piacenza, where were also Monsieur Fabian, brother-in-law of the Polish prince Laski, whom Throckmorton was to meet on his visit to England, Captain Ricco of Florence, and Laski's bastard son

---

[1] Fellow of Oriel in 1569, shortly before Ralegh was a student there. J. Foster, *Alumni Oxonienses, 1500–1714*, IV. 1571.

Albertus. That month news came of the Queen of Spain's death; the Pope's legate returned to Rome; the snows came. On New Year's eve Arthur received a letter from his mother dated from Leicester, 8 November; and 'I cut my finger with the glass' — was he crystal-gazing or prognosticating? Next day, 'I was ready to sownd [faint] and felt myself very ill'. For the most part he got through the winter well in health; not until the end of February was he sick of a colic, and the next day, with decorative emphasis, 'I voided worms'. This is followed two days later by an unintelligible entry: 'uncovered the hideous herbs (sanguerea) of the winter'. It can only have meant something unpleasant, perhaps haemorrhoids.

In mid-January his cousin George Carew came on from Nuremberg to Prague. 3 February: 'we heard how my Lord of Arundel and others should conspire to kill her Majesty and other lords of the Council in a mask, by letters from Antwerp'. In March he sent home letters to the Queen, Lord Oxford, Lord Windsor, Lady Stafford, his uncle Carew, his mother and sister. As the time draws near for his departure to Italy, the Diary includes useful notes for his stay there, names of persons and currency reckonings: 5 April, 'for £30 sterling to receive at Venice 120 ducats. For 3 Vienna ells of Holland 84 batts, 28 batts an ell, the which I gave to my hostess Madonna Diana at my going from Prague towards Italy.' Writing to his agent Parvis for more money, and leaving Ashby in Prague, he set out on 8 April for Vienna.

The journey, some thirty-four German miles, took five and a half days and cost four dollars, 'but I gave him [the coachman] 3 French crowns'. Throckmorton stayed five weeks in Vienna stopping at Dr. Blotin's, where board and lodging cost two florins a week.[1] Dr. Blotin had married Ursula Ungulter — typically charming German name — but he had had 5000 florins with her. Later Dr. Blotin borrowed 10 pistols of him — the total charge for his keep during his stay. This was to celebrate the marriage of Dr. Blotin's man, Snyder, where dined Herr Strotpfennig, prefect of Archduke Maximilian's Court, Signor Good, Chancellor to Archduke Ernest, and others. Arthur contributed a French crown to the marriage. He dined at Court with Herr Rupert and Don Christofero de Guevara, with whom he played tennis. For the hot weather had come, with thunder

[1] Ten years later, in the winter of 1590–1, Henry Wotton stayed in the house of this same Dr. Hugo Blotz, or Blotius, 'a learned Dutchman, and librarian of the Imperial Library'. L. Pearsall Smith, *Life and Letters of Sir Henry Wotton*, I. 14.

and lightning. 'We removed into the garden there to dwell.' Later he went to visit the Emperor's garden, presumably at the Hofburg, and gave a dollar for the privilege. He bought himself Cicero's *Offices* with a commentary, and, in preparation for his journey, a horse from Archduke Ernest's chancellor, which cost 44 dollars. He got Glode, a goldsmith from Besançon, to make him 'a garland of silver and gilt wherein was engraven *Fleurs, fleurissez toujours*, my name and the year 1581'. He went to supper with Glode, where were Mathurin from Anjou, Jacques, Dr. Auberin, a bookseller. A Hungarian was thrust in the body by these Frenchmen, and Glode was put in prison by the provost. The peaceable Arthur put himself on a diet of milk from the apothecary, 8 crychers a time for 6 ounces — can it have been Hungarian *yogurt*? Delivering his trunk to be carried to Venice, paying Dr. Hugo Blotin 10 pistols for five weeks' board and giving 3 dollars in the house, he left Vienna on 20 April for his strenuous journey over the Alps.

With Throckmorton's descent into Italy in the Maytime of 1581 we reach the high point of his continental tour, the goal of his education and desire, as with so many young barbarians from the North from earliest Renaissance to latest Enlightenment, with Goethe and beyond. He made good speed, being often on horseback by five in the morning: no time for comments on Alpine scenery, nor would that have appealed to an Elizabethan anyway. He went via Freisach, where he notes 'lightning', and Villach, 'snow', where he rested on Sunday 28 May. By then he had 'outrid the Flemings', with whom he had started in company. On he pressed to Vinzon, where he lodged '*a la Fontana*'; next day he baited at St. Daniel and passing over the ferry at Pinzano — where the river Tagliamento broadens into a lake — 'I came and lay at Spilenberg *a la campagna*'. Here he rested his horse, but set out again in the afternoon. 2 June there was thunder and he lay the night at Conegliano. Next day 'I came to Treviso in coach to the inn *de la Torre*, for which coach I spent 46 soldi. Given for horse-hire £7 : 8s. from Treviso to Padua', which he reached on 4 June, hiring himself 'a chamber with a stable and a garderobe in Borgo socco in John Bassano's house'.

After his strenuous journey he rested a few days; but though the Diary has no entries we know that he at once went book-buying, for a fat little double volume of Alessandro Piccolomini's *Natural Philosophy* at Magdalen has the note, '40s a Padova 7 die de Juin 1581'. Then 'I writ to Thomas Leigh for my luting

book 6s. Bergamasco came to teach me on the lute, to whom
I gave 8 li by the month. A reader came to teach me Italian,
to whom I gave 7 li by the month.'[1] Letters caught up with
him, from his mother, Arthur Agard and Ashby. Monday the
19th: 'I was drawn upon by Bellecourt and six others as I was
taking boat to go to Venice'. To make a proper figure in Venice,
the luxury capital of Europe, he bought quantities of black silk
grogram and white taffeta, with black taffeta for lining hose and
doublet, and rich velvet. He goes to and fro between Padua,
where he boards with Antonio Milanese, and Venice where he
stops at the 'George'. He notes the English Jesuits, Fathers
Fant and Brooks, passing through on their way to Poland. He
associates with Giacomo Guicciardini, of the famous Florentine
family, who shortly leaves for home. He buys Livy's *Decades* and
Josephus in Italian (still among his books at Magdalen) for 12
li and 3 li binding, and a looking-glass for 8 li.

Quite a number of young Englishmen were in and around
Venice that summer. Early on Arthur dined with Thomas
Leigh and others — Leigh was living at the cross-roads near St.
Apostolo. Mr. Ratcliffe brought Throckmorton two pairs of
silk stockings, at 5 crowns a pair, from Milan. In August two
Scots dined with them, Mr. Sentry and James Crichton. Shortly
Neville, George Carew and Savile came on to Padua, and Mr.
Spencer brought Throckmorton 10 crowns. In September he
received bills of exchange from his mother and Mr. Agard for
120 ducats upon Argelisao Marco, and these he collected a fortnight after for his journey to Florence. His trunk caught up
with him safely at Venice. Meanwhile he was learning the lute
from Romano and to write an Italian hand, in which he wrote
his Diary while in Italy. Nor did he neglect his celestial observations: '26 July, Draco volans flied in the nether region of the
air from the north to the south between 7 and 8 at night'. In a
fray among four French gentlemen one of them was slain. Relations between these English were more peaceable: Neville and
Savile went towards Vicenza, Throckmorton sent Dr. Blotin a
letter in French by Spencer; he himself made an excursion to
Monselice and homewards to the baths of Sant' Elena by Battaglia.

It is interesting to follow Throckmorton's route to Florence
in his own words. 'Saturday, 16 September : I went from Venice
with the post Baldo of Florence to whom I give 6 crowns for
myself and 4 crowns for the carriage of my trunk and other things,

---

[1] These must be not pounds sterling but Italian libri.

which weighed 158 lb. and for every lb. I must pay 4 soldi. I set out from the "George" at Venice and came into the boat at twelve of the night and sailed all the rest of the night. We came by Porto di Malamocco and by Porto di Chioggia, 45 miles. Sunday the 17th : I came and dined at Loreo and there we changed our boat and took a *barchello* and were drawn up a drain of the river of Po and passed by Papose of the Duke of Ferrara's and forwards we were drawn all that night and before it was day we came to Francolin, which was 40 miles from Loreo. Monday the 18th : I took a coach at Francolin and before day set towards Ferrara, whither I came by 6 in the morning, 5 miles between Francolin and Ferrara. I dined at Ferrara and, after dinner, in coach went to La Scala and there lay, 16 miles. Tuesday the 19th : I came to Bologna whereat I dined and took horse leaving our coach. . . . After dinner with post horses I went and lay at Loiano, 15 miles.' As usual he says nothing of the sensational scenery, the gorges and passes of the Appennines, but merely that coming down by Firenzuola he arrived at Florence on the 20th, St. Matthew's day, to supper at the sign of the 'King'.

Next day he dined with Lorenzo Guicciardini at his house in the country. He rented a chamber at the sign of the 'Three Kings', paying 30 julios for 30 days, a gabelle of 12½ julios for his trunk at the customs, and took on a manservant. He reports on the revenues and wealth of the Medici Duke, Francesco, who has 'yearly 1,200,000 crowns, whereof he spendeth 400,000 crowns by the year and the rest retaineth. Of all marriages the Duke hath 10 in the 100 of the marriage money, yearly a portion of every man's goods according as he is rated, nothing bought nor sold but he hath a portion out of it, nothing carried out nor brought in but he hath gabelle of it, and this is by an ancient law whilst Florence was a commune wholly established and called it *la leggie dotta*.'

The moment Throckmorton was settled in he began book-buying : genealogies of the house of Medici, then of Este and of Austria. Some of these books remain : the *Historia dei Principi di Este* at Magdalen has the inscription, 'Arthuro Throckmorton, fiorenza, Septem : 23 : 1581'; Bernardini Scardeoni's *De Antiquitate Urbis Patavii* is similarly inscribed the next day. These inscriptions bring back touchingly the ingenuous young man, conscientious if not very clever, bent on educating himself, the bookshops along the Arno, those bright autumnal days in Florence so long ago, the paper books he wrote in under my hand as I write today.

He took up learning the lute once more and engaged Vincenzo Galileo to teach him to sing, at 10½ julios a month, 3 julios for a singing book. He was in regular correspondence with his friends at home and his companions abroad — Ashby, Neville and the rest; indeed one is surprised by the amount of letter-writing it was possible to carry on, communications seem to have been sufficiently reliable. He made contact with the Englishmen in Florence, some of them of rather questionable character. Anthony Standen, for example, was a Catholic exile of good family who kept in with the home-government by reporting on his co-religionists abroad; one hardly likes to call him a spy, but he was certainly an intelligence-man.[1] Throckmorton notes that Standen was in receipt of 18 crowns a month from the Duke — so he must have found him useful too. Early in October, when the weather was already turning cold, Standen came to Florence from Poggio, and on 7 October Arthur had him to dinner and supper. After this they wrote to each other quite a bit. A piece of ominous news came from Rome : John Pickering and another Englishman had been put in prison as spies. And Pickering was a Northamptonshire neighbour.[2]

On 19 October Throckmorton left the 'Three Kings' and went to live at the corner of the little street above San Pietro Maggiore in the house of a priest, Monsignor Stephano, to whom he paid 9 crowns a month. In November the Grand-duke came in to Florence from Poggio and shortly there were celebrations for the reception of the Archduke Maximilian, a masquerade on horseback. When the Archduke left for Ferrara on his way back to Vienna, he carried a bill of exchange for 20,000 crowns from the Medici and had a train of 67 mules and 21 Barbary horses. Arthur himself was enjoying the delights of high society : we find the names not only of Guicciardinis but Salviatis, Santa Fioris, Bentivoglios, Piccolominis among his acquaintance. And not only high society : on 13 November comes a suspicious note, 'Madonna Alexandrina mandata a la donna di Prison : date la 3 julie'. And shortly after there are letters to and assignations with *la camilla capraia*, who is always referred to as such and who,

---

[1] Cf. L. Hicks, 'The Embassy of Sir Anthony Standen in 1603', *Recusant History*, V. no. 3, 95 : Standen stated that he had been recommended to the Duke, who gave him 16 crowns a month, by Mary Queen of Scots. 'Despite his alleged devotion to the Queen of Scots and her son, he was for several years, as Birch rightly states, a secret intelligencer of Walsingham, one of her bitterest and most determined enemies.'

[2] John Pickering had matriculated from St. John's College, Cambridge, in 1572, and was the son of Sir William Pickering of Tichmarsh; cf. J. and J. A. Venn, *Alumni Cantabrigienses*, Pt. 1, III. 359, J. Bridges, *History and Antiquities of Northamptonshire*, II. 382.

one can only suppose, was no better than she should be. On 3 December he wrote to her 'in choler'; a week later he spent the day with her.

On 17 December, when frost lay on the ground, 'Mr. John Pickering came hither to board with the priest our host'. Two days later came sudden 'warning to depart out of Florence'. Next day at noon Throckmorton and Pickering set out with one horse between them and reached Empoli at night. The day after they got to Pisa shortly before midnight, where they put up at the 'Star'. Here Throckmorton was forced to remain until he received money for his homeward journey, which he did on the 29th — 50 crowns of gold. He at once took horse for Lerici, spending the night at San Lorenzo on the way. He made his way post up the valley to Borghetto then down to the coast at Recco, where he lay all night 'in an arrant knave's house'. Thus he spent New Year's night 1582; 'I paid to the knave my host of Recco for my horse 10 canalotti'. Next day he reached Genoa and stayed at the hostelry of 'Santa Marta'. Thence he sped by post along the main road through Alessandria to Turin, which he reached on 7 January 'by the shutting of the gates and lodged *a la Rosa Rossa*'.

Here he hired a horse, for 5 crowns, to take him to Lyons and passed over Mont Cenis in snow and mist on 9 January. Next day at St. Michel he met the Turkish ambassador coming from Paris back towards Venice and thence to Constantinople. 11 January he lay at Chambéry: 'spent at the sign of the "Golden Apple", whereat I was very badly handled, 18 carolus'. On Sunday the 13th he arrived at Lyons for the night at the 'Three Kings', but next day took a chamber at the sign of the 'Black Angel'. There he passed three days resting and enjoying the society of Anthony Bacon, Francis's clever brother, who spent many years abroad, making himself a mine of foreign information, which he came home to place at Essex's service in the 1590's. Thence Throckmorton took horse to Rouanne, and from there went by boat down the river to Orléans. From Orléans he came on foot to Angerville, and thence to Paris, where he arrived on 26 January to lodge at the 'Swan' in the Place Maubert. Here he stayed three days until the English ambassador, Sir Henry Cobham, provided him with money for his return journey, 20 crowns and 6 angels.[1]

[1] Sir Henry Cobham, 1538–1605, a diplomat by career and ambassador at Paris 1579–83, was uncle to Lord Cobham, who was condemned along with Ralegh for their part in the plots of 1603.

On 30 January he set out by post-horse by the usual route through Amiens and Abbeville to Boulogne, where he embarked at 5 a.m. and reached Dover by 10, paying 5 crowns for his passage. At Rochester he found the Queen 'conducting Monsieur le Duc d'Anjou towards his journey into Flanders and there delivered my letters'. There is a certain propriety in the fact that Throckmorton's continental experiences ended at the same moment as the strange and prolonged episode of the Queen's affair with Anjou.

Next day the young man reached Throckmorton house by Leadenhall. There follow several pages made out for entries, but none written up for several months, save for a few notes concerning the stars.

CHAPTER VI

COUNTRY AND COURT OCCUPATIONS

ELIZABETHAN diaries are hardly at all introvert, with the exception of Puritan accounts of the states of their souls; and even here the attitude is curiously that of describing an external object. It is this that gives the self-ruminatings of Montaigne their originality and idiosyncrasy. Nearly all contemporary diaries are of the nature of memoranda, a line a day mentioning its event personal or public. Throckmorton's is essentially of this character and began in this way; but from the beginning he used it to jot down miscellaneous information and, as time went on, the habit grew upon him and the very detail gives one a more intimate picture of a man's total activities than of anyone else of the age. The intimacy is both indirect and direct: a picture of the person is built up from his activities, at the same time — and this is even more exceptional — he lets us into his griefs and troubles, his most private concerns of family and heart. Yet always briefly, discreetly — often in French, sometimes in cipher and with initials in place of names. With the knowledge one has acquired of his background, one can often make these out. In the Elizabethan manner he does not indulge himself with his reflections — one has to infer. Often one longs to know more, for the rigidly confined stream — a line or two a day — to break its banks, spilling the waters over the land, that the hidden vegetation, murky as well as coloured, might spring into life.

But that would be contrary to nature, and we have reason to be grateful for what we have got: we learn a lot from Throckmorton. The tantalising gaps and silences, the feeling of for ever halting on the brink of what he might have told us — about his sister and Ralegh, for instance (for he knew everything) — are part of the perennial problem of historical evidence. And there remains always the artistic problem of rendering a life, of portraying people's lives in the round, from a succession of minute, disparate strokes in one dimension.

The young man did not resume entries of his daily doings again until September of that year 1582, by which time his trunk caught up with him from Italy, and a pretty penny it cost him — £16 : 19s.[1] Even so, it is something of a tribute to the reliability of such arrangements in a remote, and disturbed, age. He had to borrow to make ends meet — but that was usual with everyone; his mother and stepfather, with whom he had made up his quarrel, gave him presents. Before going into the country for the autumn he bought himself a grey horse of a hacker in Ratcliffe, £6 : 13 : 8, and a white horse, £7 : 5s., with saddles, bridles and other furniture, £5 : 8s. 'All reckonings paid and left in my man's hands 4s. and in my own purse £14.'

He set out via Enfield, where he stopped with cousin Middlemore, and Beddington, where he stayed a week with his uncle, Sir Francis Carew. Thence he went into Northamptonshire to look to his property, pay visits to friends and relations, hunt and enjoy country sports. He held his manor court at Silverstone, stopping with his cousin George Fermor at neighbouring Easton Neston. 'I looked over all my woods as well in the forest [*i.e.* Whittlewood] as in Paulerspury park, and lay at Gayton at Mrs. Tanfield's.' (From this family came the mother of the famous Lord Falkland.) John Tanfield went along with him to Stamford where they dined with Mr. Cave; he met his mother at Ingersby, uncle Cave's house. On Saturday, 6 October, 'I waited on my mother towards Beaumanor and lay myself at Leicester, whereat came to me my brother Robert and John Tanfield in my company'. At Leicester they met with Sir George Carew on his way south from Scotland.

They then went off to hunt the fox at Chastleton — still so unchanged on its green slopes — with uncle Anthony Throckmorton; they hunted Easton woods, stopped at Chipping Campden with uncle Smyth, at Ettington with cousin Underhill, viewed Alderminster and received his rent of £19. On to Coughton for a night at Thomas Throckmorton's, the devout Catholic,[2] thence to Haseley, Job Throckmorton's, the devout

---

[1] Throckmorton resumed correspondence with friends abroad, particularly with Lorenzo Guicciardini, one of whose letters has survived among the State Papers. He gave Throckmorton news of the English merchants and other prisoners at Rome, promising to work for that nation so much beloved by him — but the Roman Inquisition was *troppo apassionata et interessata*. *Cal. S.P. For. 1583 and Add.*, 612, 12 July 1582.

[2] In August 1580 Thomas Throckmorton was summoned before the bishop of London to answer for his recusancy. This was the beginning of his troubles, and as the dangers of 1588 approached he was consigned to the bishop's not too exacting custody. *A.P.C. 1580–1*, 166, 241; *A.P.C. 1587–8*, 348.

Puritan; relations were closer with the latter. Then to Leicester to stop at his stepfather's house, the New Wark, and at the end of the month to Brigstock, where he seems to have based himself most of the winter, probably at the keeper's lodge there.

From here he paid visits to Lord and Lady Mordaunt both at Drayton — where their grand house, with the Elizabethan wing they added to it, remains — and at Grafton. He went to market at Kettering, Oundle and Thrapston, and dismissed his man Thomas, giving him 10s. 'whenas I put him away from me'. On frosty Christmas day — one hears the frost tinkle in the brook below, in Rockingham forest round about — 'S. H. il mio servitore veniva per servirme', and he receives Christmas greetings from his mother and sister Bess. One finds him constantly writing them, and on New Year's eve, 'I sent my mother the book I made named *The Armour for Old Age*'. (Was this perhaps a translation?)

The year 1583 was to be important both for him and his sister; he was anxious to get her a place at Court, and he himself fell in love, not at first happily. On Ash Wednesday he received a token from an Italian flame, Zenobia Acciaiolli, with 'gagettas'. At the end of March he sent his stuff to London by the carrier, and paid a visit to Beaumanor, whither came 'Sir George and Lady Hastings with my mistress' — so the F. H. of the Diary might be Frances Hastings. On his way to London he stopped with his elder brother, rusticated at Tiffield. The moment Arthur arrives in town his account with his tailor soars: yards and yards of velvet and satin, ells of taffeta and sarcenet, purple cloth for liveries with crimson and yellow velvet for guarding. He went to visit Lord and Lady Lumley — Lord Lumley was the first of Elizabethan connoisseurs, responsible for the admirable Renaissance busts one sees at Lumley Castle and the fabricated antiquities in the church at Chester-le-Street. He got in touch again with Lady Stafford, about to go with her husband as ambassador to Paris; he supped with Lady Vernon, later to become mother-in-law to Shakespeare's Southampton. The Diary is a comprehensive *Who's Who* of Elizabethan society — except that one is not always sure who was who. He took his chamber at Greenwich, purged himself and was let blood, then went to Court.

His first duty was, with Lord Darcy, Lord Rich and George Hopton — whom we shall meet later as Lieutenant of the Tower — to escort the Palatine Count Laski into London. They went down to Colchester to meet him, and there Arthur 'first looked

and liked Æ' — a later hand has explained this for us: Anna
Lucas, who became his wife. But this was not before various
adventures or misadventures upset his course. She was the
daughter of Sir Thomas Lucas, whose father had been one of
those Reformation lawyers who did well out of the Dissolution.
He purchased St. John's abbey at Colchester and turned the
monastic buildings into a handsome seat — the place later
destroyed in the Civil War. Sir Thomas had married Mary
Fermor of Easton Neston, and so was a member of the cousinage.
On 27 April they met Laski outside the town, brought him in
and next day they all dined with Sir Thomas Lucas — a further
chance for acquaintance with Anna. On they brought the
Palatine to Chelmsford, supping with Sir Thomas Mildmay;
the day after to London, where they lodged Laski in Winchester
House.

In May Arthur received a useful £100 from 'goodman
Hughes' — his agent in the country; out of which he was able
to pay Sir Amyas Paulet £20 of his debt to him, £5 : 15s. to his
tailor, 20s. for half a year's wages to his man Thomas, evidently
back with him. (He seems to have been easy-going with his
menservants, and several times took them back after finding
them unsatisfactory.) Here was cash for more clothes: yards
of velvet and cloth for a cloak, a fashionable beaver hat with
silver band, a girdle with silver lace and hangers, a silvered rapier
in black velvet scabbard. Thus equipped he went down to
Rycote, Lord Norris's splendid house near Thame, where the
Palatine was visiting, attended by Lord Russell, Sir William
Russell and Sir Philip Sidney. On Sunday Kate Norris was
married to Anthony Paulet in that exquisite chapel of the
Quartermains, with the woodwork of Elizabeth's time still remaining. Next day 'the Palatine with the rest after dinner set
towards Oxford, whereat in his way entering in the university
liberties met him certain doctors, of the which Dr. Westphaling
made an oration'. The Palatine passed on his way to Woodstock and out of sight, leaving England in a cloud of debt.

Throckmorton returned to the delights, and the expenses, of
Court life. Useful sums came in to him from his woods, from
the sales of 'spires' (young trees) out of the coppice, but he was
reduced to various expedients to raise money for such an extravagant way of life. He sold outlying bits of land, one piece at
Lamport, a small estate at Beachhampton; he borrowed his
brother Robert's legacy, on which he paid interest for years, £10
a year. Later on he made a regular habit of pawning his plate.

And still he lent to his friends, as they lent to him. This was the regular Elizabethan way of going on, in the absence of banks and of an adequate supply of currency. At Court there were losses in gaming, one day £7 at primero, another day 40s. at ruff, the next day £10 — almost as much as he had got from his coppice-wood.[1] Then there were presents to be given: a 'shadoe' for Lady Darcy 40s.;[2] a pair of boot-hose for the Vice-Chamberlain, Sir Christopher Hatton; £10, a jewel for the Queen.

Above all, there was the immense cost of Elizabethan clothes; no wonder it was said that many a courtier wore an estate upon his back. Yet Throckmorton never lost his head, as some did — his friend, Lord Oxford, for instance, who, in spite of the advantage of being Burghley's son-in-law, ran through the whole of the De Vere estates and ended on the charity of a pension. Arthur remained methodical, carefully noting his outgoings, as well as his revenues, keeping a balance in his head as well as in his books. In the end he succeeded in improving on his father's estate; but this was only after he had retired from Court life.

This July he took his chamber at Court, sent his mare to Middlemore's at Enfield to grass, and put his horse into the Queen's stable. At the end of the month the Queen moved from Greenwich to Syon, then on to Oatlands, where Arthur 'first fell in love with F. H.'. Secretary Walsingham left on a mission to Scotland, and Arthur accompanied him on his way to Huntingdon and Apethorp, where they stopped with Sir Walter Mildmay. On his return a great privilege befel the young courtier: 'Sunday, 25 August, I talked with the Queen'. He was on his way up; but, of course, he was after something: a place for his sister. Hence the boot-hose for Hatton's celebrated long legs, for, as Vice-Chamberlain, he had the next to the last word in such matters. The Queen moved to Sunning Hill, to stop with Sir Henry Neville, father of Throckmorton's friend, and back to Oatlands where she received an envoy from Henry of Navarre. Arthur gave his mistress a pair of gloves, which cost 6s.

And with this the first volume of the Diary ends. The last leaf says: 'this Book contains 5 years' — and what years they had been for him: the years of apprenticeship, France and the war in the Netherlands; succession to his father's estates, the effective head, though quite young and untrained, of this branch of the family; the conscientious effort towards self-education, life

---

[1] Both primero and ruff were card-games.
[2] A kind of shade or veil to protect a lady's complexion.

at Court, the Continent — the Netherlands, Germany, the Empire, Italy, France again. Now he was falling in love.

Where the first volume ends with a page giving the names of the governors of towns in the Netherlands, the second begins with two folios of description of Italy in Italian. There follows a love poem, presumably of Arthur's own composition; if so it seems his only venture into verse and worth citing, for once, in his original spelling, if only as an example.

> O sacred sprynges out of Celestiall Centere
> Cleared by the sunne from basse and earthly breathynges,
> Inspyred from Jove with a peculier spirette,
> Noe common soulle, or generaulle beguettynge
> Thy forsse Infuses, vaynly by Adventure :
> But from that Care that Carryes well all thynges,
> Thy Bathyng blessedness thou doest Inherytte,
> Heallynge without respecte, lyke to thy lettynge.
> What are they streames now sycke ? thy waters worne ?
> For her whom Heavens have Honnor she was bornne ?

On 19 September he paid £12, and £3 before in hand, for a jewel, came to Court and gave it to Clore to be delivered. This was the form when one wanted something from the Queen. Two days later he spoke with her; the next day he received his jewel back again. Consoling himself at cards the next few days, he had considerable losses — he never, or hardly ever, seems to have won. Then the Queen sent him to London to Lady Heneage, and this may have been a kindness to advance his business, for Sir Thomas was Treasurer of the Chamber. Arthur must have received encouragement, for the next day he wrote to the Queen and Lady Stafford, and presented the jewel once more. This time it was accepted. Thus encouraged, Arthur bought himself a new suit of tawny velvet, with the usual accompaniment of tawny satin and taffeta, bands and ruffs, stockings of tawny silk and black silk, a beaver hat and two dozen points, which took the practical place of buttons in those days. He had his rapier silvered. When the Queen came to St. James's in October he took his chamber in the Strand; we find him writing to his mistress, receiving a token from Lady Stafford and sending it to his mistress. Secretary Walsingham returned from Scotland.

In November, under the sign of Sagittarius, disaster fell upon his cousin Francis and all that branch of the family, the sons of old Sir John. An entry in the Diary, in cipher, tells us that Lord Henry Howard and Francis Throckmorton were attached and sent under guard to the Tower. Anyone who knows anything about Lord Henry Howard knows what a reptile he was. A clever man, learned, devious, secretive, the dead Norfolk's brother, he was as false but far more talented. A crypto-everything by nature, crypto-papist he was also a crypto-homosexual; that gave him a bond with James I, with whom he was in high favour and whose mind he sedulously poisoned, in Elizabeth's last years, against Ralegh.[1] Though he was Elizabeth's cousin, he never had any favour from her: she knew him too well. In fact, he was a devotee of Mary Stuart. The best that can be said for him is that, very aristocratic, he was a conservative and hated the new deal; that made him pro-Spanish and Catholic, though he kept that dark, in his affiliations.

With the 1580's everything was moving towards the classic struggle with Spain; with Spain as the spear-head of Catholic, England of Protestant, Europe; other powers and forces ranged themselves, or kept out. When Mendoza became ambassador in London — there was no English ambassador in Madrid — he made himself the focus of opposition elements to the government to which he was accredited. He nursed, supported and doled out pensions to Catholic malcontents; they took advantage of the diplomatic immunity of the embassy to hear masses there. He took Mary Stuart's affairs under his protection, constituted himself her adviser (greatly to her disadvantage: she would have done far better to come to an understanding with Elizabeth). He entered into conspiracies against the Queen and was now planning, in conjunction with the Guises and James's favourite in Scotland — the fascinating Esmé Stuart, Duke of Lennox — an attempt at invasion of the country.

It was this project to which the light-headed Francis Throckmorton was fool enough to lend himself. In an Italian edition of the *Decameron* at Magdalen his cousin Arthur has a note: 'The manor of Woolavington in Somerset sold by F. T. to one Pym, a twelvemonth since or thereabouts for £1900 or thereabouts'. If this is the father of John Pym, it is not without a certain historic point. Francis was known to be sending letters to Mary Stuart and was arrested because he haunted the French embassy.[2] The French ambassador was unjustly suspected; it came out that Mendoza was the key to the plot. Francis Throckmorton was a mere agent, but he had supplied Mendoza with a list of all the possible harbours and landing-places for Guise's

---

[1] Cf. below, Chap. XIII.   [2] Conyers Read, II. 384 foll.

forces, with notes as to the local situation and likely Catholic helpers. At the end of November Francis wrote to Mendoza, in cipher on a playing card thrown out of his window in the Tower, that he had denied the document to be in his hand and assuring Mendoza that he would die a thousand deaths rather than accuse Catholic friends in the matter.[1] He did not know that the government had already given order that he should be racked.[2]

Then everything came out. Francis confessed his dealings with Lennox, with whose secretary he had conferred at the French embassy, and his contacts with the aristocratic Catholic malcontents, Northumberland, Lord Henry Howard, and the exile Charles Paget who had stolen across to England for the purpose and been hidden at Arundel Castle.[3] Lord Paget and Charles Arundel at once fled overseas; Northumberland was sent to the Tower, where he later committed suicide. That December John Somerville, a Warwickshire gentleman, set out on his crazy mission to kill the Queen, and, on his capture, incriminated his father-in-law, Edward Arden. Arden was executed, Somerville killed himself in prison. Of Francis Throckmorton's brothers, Thomas managed to escape overseas through the good offices of Lady Arundel: his mother arranged for the countess to obtain passage by ship for him.[4] The younger brother George was held in the Tower with Francis; on his release he absconded abroad for a lifetime of exile with his brother Thomas, living on money doled out by Philip or the Pope, engaged in the usual illusionary hopes of émigrés. Too late Francis saw the error of his ways: in June 1584 he made supplication to the Queen acknowledging his just condemnation, lamenting the rashness of his unbridled youth and imploring her mercy and forgiveness.[5] He was allowed interviews with his obstinate mother and his wife, and then was executed. This was the effective end of Catholic Sir John's branch of the family.

At the time of these plots there was an interesting exchange between Elizabeth and Mary Stuart, with a retrospective reflection upon Sir Nicholas's faithful dealing on behalf of the Scottish Queen. Elizabeth reproached Mary for ingratitude towards him, 'considering how well afterwards he deserved of her'.[6] She followed this up by reminding Mary that it was by Sir Nicholas's mediation that her life was spared — he had had no direction

---

[1] *Cal. S.P. Spanish 1580–6*, 510.   [2] *Cal. S.P. Dom. 1581–90*, 130.
[3] *Ibid.* 136, no. 22.   [4] *Ibid.* 124.   [5] *Ibid.* 179.
[6] *Cal. S.P. Scottish*, VI. 361, 364, 388.

to intervene. This was allowing the feminine desire to score to make her depart from the truth to her own disadvantage, for we have seen the efforts Elizabeth made to protect Mary at that juncture. On this Mary withdrew her reproaches against Sir Nicholas for his advice to abdicate. Devotion to her, and to the faith, had done enough damage to one branch of the family.

At the end of this volume of the Diary there are a few pages devoted to the young master's personal expenses, evidently by his steward, in a stylish secretarial hand : these corroborate our picture of him from the other side. Saturday, 30 November 1583 : 'for your dinner on Saturday, 18d; a pair of shoes for Leonard, 16d; for stringing of your lute, 6d; a torch, 12d'. When the master went out at night his way was lit by a flaring torch, which cost a shilling. Friday, 6 December : 'paid for your going in at the play, with two servants 4d the piece, 12d; for a torch to light you home from thence the same night, 12d; for the standing of your horse and his meat the same day, 6d'. On Wednesday, 11 December, he was 'at the playhouse in the Blackfriars', and this cost 2s. If only we knew what plays he saw, with a few comments as to what he thought of them !

Certainly the extravagance of a young courtier's attire is corroborated. Yards of purple cloth, carnation velvet, white and tawny velvets are bought — how rich and grand it must have looked. Then there was 'cloth of tinsel for your cypress suit, silk ribbon for your cypress cloak, eighteen gold buttons for your cape cloak' — the last costing the considerable sum of £6 : 1s, about a year's living at the time for a poor vicar. We find regular payments for boat-hire up the Thames from Ivy Bridge to Westminster Stairs, or the Queen's Garden Stairs — for it was the main highway to the Court. And this winter Throckmorton was fairly frequently at Court. Sometimes he spent the evening at home, alone in his bachelor chamber : one derives an impression of comfort from an entry for 4 January 1584 : 'for dressing the capon and butter to baste it, 4d; faggots spent in your chamber, 12d; bread and oranges, 3d; a quart of white wine, 5d'. It sounds a pleasant meal. Once he locked himself out from his chamber : it cost 3d. to have the lock forced open. The only note that refers to events in the outside world is that on 19 December : 'Somerville hanged himself in Newgate'.

With no further reference to these dangerous associations on that side of the family, Arthur continues his life at Court and in the country, pursues his courtship of F. H., presumably Frances

Hastings. In December she 'sent back again the plate'. One day
he delivered to his mistress's footman as much as 20s. In April
1584 he wrote to the Queen and Secretary Walsingham, and there
follow entries in his very personal cipher, which I am unable to
make out — some of them relate to his lady friends and, I suppose,
his affairs with them. In May, 'I missed my jewel and ring';
a week later he discharged John Throckmorton from his service.
In June his sister and he went to Fulham. Next month 'Sir
Philip Sidney set towards France'. The occasion of Sidney's
mission was to offer Elizabeth's condolences on the death of
Anjou; its real purpose was to persuade the French to help
resist Spain in the Netherlands. In August Lord Darcy and
Arthur, having bought a cross-bow and arrows, went hunting in
Essex, where they stopped with Sir Thomas Lucas at Colchester,
and in Northamptonshire, where Arthur stopped at Easton with
George Fermor, next day at Weston Underwood, with cousin
Thomas of Coughton, to whom this village belonged. He sent
a present of gloves to Lady Lucas by one of her men, and fell
out with brother Robert.

Returning to Court in the autumn, he presses his suit for a
place for his sister Bess. He sends a letter to the Vice-Chamberlain
for the Queen; he has an interview with him, reporting to his
mother and sister. When the Queen came to Nonsuch in November she sent Throckmorton to the Vice-Chamberlain, apparently with a ring. It meant the successful conclusion of his
long suit, for next day, Sunday 8 November: 'I came and dined
at Hampton Court. My sister was sworn of the Privy Chamber.'
This was a great opening for her, and also a necessity. For now
a girl of nearly twenty, she was practically dowerless; even the
miserable £500 left her by her father was in the hands of the
Earl of Huntingdon and could never be extracted. There was
therefore no prospect of marriage for her, unless the Queen did
something for her; all her hopes then rested on the Queen, all
her prospects on good service. No doubt this was a severe trial
for a high-spirited girl with the Throckmorton temperament;
she bore it for some seven years before her virtue succumbed.

This step was accomplished just in time, for shortly Arthur's
affairs took an ill turn, which must have permanently damaged
his prospects of a career. This seems to have been a consequence
of a love-affair, and he owed it to a woman's tongue. We hear
no more of F. H. after the return of the plate, and Arthur's fancy
turned to one of his cousins, Lady M. D., who must have been
Lady Mary Darcy. The Darcy family lived in the converted

priory of St. Osyth's, where they had made themselves very cosy after the Dissolution, in the fine red brick range the penultimate prior had built for himself. To this they added and made a fine house altogether, much of which remains as it was when Arthur used to stay there to hunt in the park they threw round the house. 'St. Tousses' he spells it, and this must represent how they pronounced it. Some of the friends he knew and hunted with are to be seen on their tombs still in their chapel in church. His first, and ominous, reference to his new girl friend, is in February 1585: 'my Lady M. D. and I fell out'. On 2 March, the day William Parry was hanged for plotting to kill the Queen, my lady went off in a huff to Nonsuch. Arthur pursued her with letters, to little purpose. In April Leicester told Arthur that his stepfather was dead; he at once went down to the country, where he found that this was not so, though Adrian Stokes must have been in his last illness. On his return to Court, 15 April: 'my kind Lady Darcy and I fell out at ten of the clock at night, whereout grew all the poison her nature could yield me, as followeth . . .'

What followed was two months' imprisonment in the Marshalsea for words he had spoken of Leicester, which Lady Darcy, either the mother or the daughter, had reported. These words must have been a serious matter, for Arthur was imprisoned at the order of a court containing those eminences, the Earls of Shrewsbury and Derby, Lord Chamberlain Hunsdon, and his friends Hatton and Walsingham; and two months was no brief confinement. What had he said? Leicester was sick and tired of being traduced, of being accused as a poisoner and what not, by his friends and now into the second generation by his friends' sons. Could it have been something about Adrian Stokes, advancing the hour of his mortality? For this was the very thing that had happened years before with Amy Robsart: Leicester was sure that she would die, and then she did die. It really was bad luck on him, or perhaps, rather, careless of him.

In the Marshalsea, which was the proper prison for these Court offences, Throckmorton would be fairly comfortable, paying his own expenses and with his servant Christopher to wait on him. His friends came to see him daily, beginning with Lord Darcy and his son: no doubt the menfolk were sufficiently sympathetic and Lord Darcy brought him a useful sum of money, which he had taken up on Arthur's behalf. Sir Thomas and Lady Lucas at once came to see him. But next day Arthur noted as a disgrace that he was committed close prisoner. This was ungentlemanly and he wrote round protesting to everybody — to Hunsdon, Hatton, Walsingham, to the Council and to Leicester himself. Anthony Shirley, a Fellow of All Souls who later became famous as a traveller, was at this time discharged from the Marshalsea, a receptacle for young hotheads. Arthur contributed 4s. towards the expenses of a fellow-prisoner on release. His mother sent Robert to see him, and more of his Darcy cousins turned up. On 5 May Arthur wrote to Sir Walter Ralegh, already in high favour and Captain of the Queen's Guard: the first reference to the man who was to marry his sister and whose fortunes would be so important to him.

From the Marshalsea he continued his unsatisfactory entanglement with the Darcy ladies. By one of his servants he sent verses to Lady Mary, who received them at Court and 'chid my sister'. Then Bess wrote him about the verses — no doubt he was making a nuisance of himself. Messages passed; Lady K. D., presumably Katherine Darcy, refused his token. His mother went to Court to plead for him. Thus May passed. In June, 'I sent Mr. Anthony Shirley 6 bottles of ale, 3s'. Arthur himself received the attentions of his doctor: he was let blood and now entered on a diet: 'I must drink a bowlful at 5 in the morning, and with my meat, and at 4 of the afternoon'. His brothers Robert, Thomas and Nicholas came to visit him, but not William; and Francis Darcy, to whom he lost 2s. at malcontent. Then the Darcys all set out for the country. Mr. John Jerningham joined him in the Marshalsea, but as a close prisoner, to whom Arthur lent 20s. On Sunday, 20 June, came the news: 'my Lord of Northumberland, as it is said, killed himself in the Tower with a dag', *i.e.* pistol. Two days later Arthur was freed — and there follows a list of payments, rent for his chamber, fees to the officers, for beer and bread and faggots, for his man-servant's keep, gifts to the maids, to the porter and, last, to the beggar at the gate. A day or two later, 'I bathed myself'. It was probably necessary.

Rebuffed by his (female) Darcy cousins, he embarked at once on a serious courtship of Anna Lucas: clearly he thought it was time for him to marry. At the beginning of July frequent letters pass between him and Lady Lucas and her daughter. The ladies come to Court, to which he has returned, and he is able to pass time in Anna's company. When she is away he sends his man Sankey — back with him again after dismissal — with messages to her. He buys himself a cod of musk, very expensive. When he next writes A. L., he sends her woman an ell of cambric. In the autumn he receives a bracelet from Anna, and sends her a gold ring set with diamonds. There followed a tiff between them, and Arthur — impulsive like his family — sent back her bracelet. Next day they were together again, and Arthur was taking medicine—the popular *confectio hamec* of the time.

On 2 November, All Souls' day, his stepfather at length died, and Arthur went down to Beaumanor for the funeral. The heir to Adrian Stokes's lands was his brother William, since he had no children. But he left Lady Throckmorton very handsomely provided for.[1] She had the manor of Langacre in Devon, in fee simple, to herself and her heirs outright, as part of her marriage-settlement: it came to Arthur.[2] Her husband left her, also, all his goods and furniture in his London house and at Brigstock park, the lease of his house in Leicester and his goods there, all goods and parcels of plate at Beaumanor specified in an inventory. The plate amounted to 1290 oz. — a great gilt bowl, a gilt bowl with the bear and ragged staff of the Dudleys, three gilt chalice bowls, Flanders cups, chafing dishes and so on. Among the pictures were portraits of Queen Catherine Parr, Queen Mary, Queen Elizabeth, Catherine de Medici, Sir Nicholas Throckmorton and old Sir Robert, Sir Francis Carew, the Earl of Devon. His stepdaughter Bess was left a gilt cup, and a bed in the Duchess's chamber at Beaumanor with the furniture to be given to her on her marriage. Bess had her own chamber there, for the hangings and furniture are mentioned. To stepson Thomas a gilt cup, to Robert his horse Grey Goodyear.

In December Throckmorton's innermost thought comes to the surface: 'God my beginner, the furtherer of my fortune, the only end of my good: Æ'. And, as if to prove that Shakespeare has expressed everything in the age (except its religious nonsense), immediately Arthur takes to music. He bought a pair of virginals, and strings; next, a bandora — the guitar-like instrument from which our word 'banjo' comes: its throbbing passionate notes provided an accompaniment to the cithern. And, sure enough, 'Spryn came to teach me of the cithern, to whom I gave 7s by the month'; in May Arthur bought his man Sankey's virginals off him.

If music be the food of love, play on . . .

But, indeed, this was the way an Elizabethan Court lady had to be wooed: music and poetry and love-talk were the language of

---

[1] For his will cf. *Notes & Queries*, 1 Series, XII. 452.
[2] It is in the parish of Broad Clyst.

the Court. And, as at all times, with presents: there are considerable payments to John White, the jeweller, for a ring — as well as for a tortoise Lady Drury presented the Queen from him. Then 'Æ refused the jewel'. No less necessary to his cause were the silk mockado and lace, the black velvet, the striped and russet satin he clothed himself in. Good relations were not interrupted: 'taken out of my desk to Æ, £4', paid for a birdcage, 20s., a fan, £3 : 10s. This was very expensive, but fans, feathered and jewelled, were the latest of Italian luxuries to come in.[1]

To clinch matters, Throckmorton sent his agent, Will Hughes, to Sir Thomas Lucas to expound to him the position with regard to his estate and the conveyances of his lands. In June, 'Sir Thomas Lucas with his counsel met me at Serjeant Puckering's lodging in Serjeants' Inn'. This was to draw up the terms of the marriage settlement: it was usual for a bride to have one-third of the husband's income settled upon her after his death, and in Throckmorton's case, he received an annuity of some £60 as Anna's dower. 3 July, 'we sealed the writings'; next day, 'I was married to Æ'. There is no evidence where the wedding ceremony took place, and the laconic entry says nothing about guests or who attended. From a casual reference some years later we learn that the Earl of Derby's brother was one of those who honoured the marriage.[2] Arthur took Dorothy Harcourt as maid to serve his wife, and at once additional expenses begin, yards of vermilion and changeable taffeta for one and the other. In a few days the Lucases with their daughter set out for Colchester, and, after taking leave at Court and receiving a useful £5 from his mother, Arthur followed them.

The young couple were setting up house at St. John's with their parents — there would be plenty of room in those monastic precincts before the savage destruction of the Civil War. There came a couple of entries in code and then the perhaps inevitable note of a jar between the new wife and her father. However, company came to distract them: Lord and Lady Lumley, Sir

[1] At the other end of the Diary are a few scribbles that witness the courtship: Arthur's signature and, in a beautiful Italian hand, Æ Throckmorton — trying out Anna Lucas's married name; on the next page it appears — Anna Throckmorton. Then there are scribbles, 'In you God send that we then shall be at your house', and, 'In hope to be at h' — as if someone came in while the lovers were writing messages. There is the nonsense-talk of love: Arthur has written, 'Anna Lucas is a naughte Guirlle and a naughte guirlle is she a'. Then their joint names: everything goes to show that it was a love-match and remained so.

[2] *H.M.C. Salisbury MSS.* V. 99.

John and Lady Petre, who, in spite of their Catholic convictions, made a desirable residence out of the monastic buildings of Ingatestone, Mr. Cornwallis and others. They all went on with the Lucases to that other monastic residence of St. Osyth's, except Arthur, who stayed at home sick. He consoled himself by sending oysters to his mother — one of the advantages of residence at Colchester — and by writing to his sister by Mr. Ludovic, the Queen's footman.

In August Arthur received £20 of his wife's annuity from his father-in-law, and the two couples set out on a journey into the West Country, to view the lands that had come to him through Adrian Stokes. Arthur equipped himself with a case of pistols, necessary for the roads in those days, and they set out along the old Icknield Way for Reading. Hereabouts they dallied for a few days to go to Newbury fair at Bartholomew-tide and to dine with the formidable Lady Russell, aunt of Robert Cecil and the Bacons, at Donnington Castle.[1] In September they viewed his land at Soulswick and went on to Bristol, where they stayed at Ashton with Mrs. Smyth, a cousin of Sir Ferdinando Gorges; a well-to-do widow, she became his fourth wife and this enabled him to protract his colonial enterprises.[2]

Leaving the family at Bath, Arthur went on to Devon alone. At delightful Bruton he stopped at the big house now vanished — but one sees its *emplacements* under the corrugated surface of the field west of the church — with Sir Henry Berkeley, who paid him his rent for Alderminster.[3] The next night he stopped at Merefield with Nicholas Wadham, later to become founder, with his wife, of Wadham College, Oxford. One of the fascinations of the Diary is the way it lays before one the landscape of Elizabethan society, with so many of its familiar figures, at any rate in the south of England. It is like the contemporary maps of the counties Throckmorton bought this year. '16 September: I came towards Langacre through the forest of Roche by Roche-castle and over Blackdown and through Gonnelly lane and by Dunkeswell abbey.' He went via Exeter to Langacre, where he kept his Michaelmas court; thence via Wells to keep his court at Enridge and so back through Marlborough. These western lands the expenses of family life would force him to sell before long.

The moment he was back again he sent to his sister at

---

[1] For her cf. my essay, 'Bisham and the Hobys', in *The English Past*.
[2] Cf. *The Elizabethans and America*, 91.
[3] For Berkeley cf. Leslie Hotson, *I, William Shakespeare, do appoint . . .*, Chap. IV.

Windsor; he was certainly devoted to her. Stimulated by his journey into the West Country he purchased a set of maps of England — whether Saxton's or Speed's there is nothing to indicate; these he had coloured and bound into a book, and later that year we find payments for colouring Mercator's maps. Throckmorton had a definite geographical interest, but it was part of his desire to inform himself about the contemporary world: we see in his purchases of books a picture of the mental equipment, the intellectual life, of the average Elizabethan courtier, a man of no exceptional intelligence: this is its value for us. Shortly he went down to Paulerspury to have the park there measured by the well-known surveyor, Edmund Osbeston, preparatory to letting it. He needed the money, and succeeded in letting it for £80 a year; he hoped to let the pasture too. He stopped at near-by Lillingstone Lovell with the redoubtable Peter Wentworth, Puritan leader in the Commons against the government, shortly to be imprisoned again for calling in question church affairs, which the Queen regarded as her own prerogative.

At Court the news at the end of November was of Leicester's return from his charge in the Netherlands, where he had had little success. It is true that it was a position where it was impossible to make much of a success, between the pressures of the Dutch to use him to commit England illimitably and the Queen's fixed resolve to have no more than a limited commitment. Her coming to the aid of the Dutch had precipitated open war with Spain anyway, and Leicester's acceptance of the offer of Governor-Generalship got him into grave trouble with the Queen. She insisted on his refusal, and nearly broke him in the process. He was returning in very chastened mood, but also in time to take part in bringing Mary Stuart at last to book. That autumn, after the exposure of the Babington plot, Parliament was summoned to give the government the support of the nation in dealing with her. The diplomatic preliminaries for isolating her were well advanced. Throckmorton notes the arrival at Court of Bellièvre, 'grand président des finances de France', to urge the French view in the matter. Meanwhile Edward Wotton, of the Kentish family into which Throckmorton's eldest daughter and co-heiress was to marry, was returning from France where he had expounded the English case against Mary.

On 2 December Parliament was adjourned, having found Mary worthy of death — Elizabeth would permit Parliament to go no further. On 6 December, Throckmorton notes that the Queen of Scots was 'proclaimed traitor by public proclamation, and all the bells in the city of London rung for joy'. This was what the English people thought of her. To end her story as it appears in the Diary of the son of Sir Nicholas, who had watched its unfolding with so much sympathy and foreboding: '7 February, between eleven and twelve in the day Mary Stuart, Queen of Scots, put to death in Fotheringhay Castle. Sir Amyas Paulet, Sir Drue Drury, my Lord Shrewsbury, my Lord of Kent, commissioners.' Two days later Throckmorton notes the bells rung and bonfires made in London upon the news of her death.

The intense strain that Elizabeth went through over all this is now understood as the genuine nervous crisis it was. She *could* not make up her mind, and for once Burghley took the burden of the decision upon himself and forced her hand, in the interests of the nation. He thereby risked his own dismissal. But he was too indispensable to go, and a lesser man, who had stuck his neck out too far, was sacrificed. '28 March: Mr. Davison brought to the Star Chamber and there condemned of a contempt and misprision, and fined at 10,000 marks and imprisonment during her Majesty's pleasure by three Judges, two bishops, my Lord of Worcester [he was a Catholic], my Lord of Cumberland, my Lord of Lincoln, my Lord Grey, Sir James Croft, Sir Walter Mildmay [he was a Puritan] etc.' Arthur must have been present, for he spent 5s.

The young man's contact with these high affairs was but marginal. He notes, during that winter of crisis, the Queen's restless movements, from Lambeth to Lord Burgh's, from Richmond to Greenwich. He himself was with other courtiers with whom the great matter would be discussed, one day with Edward Dyer (of 'My mind to me a kingdom is') at Winchester house; on another, at Barnard Castle with Lord Pembroke, son of his father's old friend, Shakespeare's patron and dedicatee of the First Folio. Arthur had intimate conversations with his friend Wotton: '8 January: I spake and entered deeply into E. W. 9 January: E. W. sounded in me fathoms.' But what would one not give to know what they said to one another? Two days later, 'old Mr. Wotton', kind old Thomas, died, and his son Edward reigned at Boughton Malherbe — the fine Tudor house in Kent of which but a fragment remains — in his place.[1] To complete this fragment of the story: on April 2 Throckmorton notes the birth of Wotton's son. A week later the child was christened, with the diplomat Thomas Randolph, Thomas Gay

---

[1] Cf. *Thomas Wotton's Letter-Book, 1574–1586*, ed. G. Eland.

and Arthur's mother as sponsors. He was named Thomas; he became the second Lord Wotton and was to marry Throckmorton's eldest daughter Mary, as yet unborn. Thus the future shapes itself for us, and thus her father's Diary came to Boughton Place to lie lost from the world until it came to light in the salvage campaign of the last war.

CHAPTER VII

FAMILY LIFE, 1587–1591

HITHERTO Arthur Throckmorton had had exemplary health: no sign of the febrile, consumptive condition that carried off his father in middle age. And indeed he must have had a good constitution, when we consider his medical treatment of himself, in spite of which he lived out his full span of life. His sister Bess was the toughest of the lot, for, in spite of the troubles and sorrows of her life with Ralegh, she lived to an extreme old age, dying in 1647 after the first Civil War. But from the time of his marriage Arthur displays a new interest in his health, perhaps regrettable though informative for us. It was not so much valetudinarianism, as offering something else to be interested in, for the Elizabethans had a narrow, circumscribed range of interests. They had to make their own amusements; amusements were home-made, rough and ready; life was lived very much within the family; they must have been easy preys to boredom. The pleasures of exoneration and copulation bulked more largely. Interest in their physical condition and its symptoms was therefore a regular thing, as with old-fashioned country folk up to a generation ago. Later on with increasing age, in the last volume of the Diary, we shall find it becoming an obsession with Throckmorton.

Now it was quickened by his wife's condition, for in January 1587 she was with child. 22 January: 'my wife took bettany water and syrup of roses, 1 quart 5s'. There are payments to Dr. Langton and a nurse, for physic, for lozenges, 'two plasters to her temples and a box of ointment for her wrists'.[1] Payments go on regularly for rolls and ointments, and on 7 February: 'my wife took two pills. I drank [*i.e.* physic]. Paid Mrs. Kemys for rolls for my wife, for ointments and for five cakes of *manus Christi* [the usual thing in such cases], 6s; for my bottle of drink,

[1] Thomas Langton was one of the more eminent physicians of the time. A Cambridge man, he was in 1581 admitted Fellow of the Royal College of Physicians, serving in various offices until he became President, 1604–6. W. Munk, *Roll of the Royal College of Physicians*, I. 76.

12s; given Mr. Heward the apothecary for oil of almonds and comfits, 3s'. A kind of competition sets in, pills and drink for one, pills and goat's milk for the other, rolls and lozenges for Anna, lozenges and an electuary for Arthur. Not even a nice concoction of myrrh, aloes, saffron and the spirit of wine did him any good: 'it gave me never a stool'. No wonder he has to record, 'I felt myself ill in my stomach and head'.

Perhaps it was a consolation to have a home and be settled, even if there were occasional rows — when, for example, his wife fell out with her mother and 'M. L., A. T., spit venom'. There was his study chamber to arrange, the green cloth for the board on which he did his studying, curtains to be put up, his books and maps to fix — he was having the *Lives of the Philosophers* bound now, and payments for books went on, even if those to the apothecary were larger. (£10 to Mr. Heward! Multiply, for its value today, by perhaps twenty-five.) Nor did he forget his sister and friends: a pearl girdle for her at Christmas cost 30s.; he gave his wife 40s. for Mr. Ludovic. Among his New Year gifts to servants is 5s. to Leicester's cook, so relations must have been renewed, visits continued.

On 15 February Parliament met again. 'Madame Bkr. m'a parlé de G. T.' This means that Lady Baker had news for him of George Throckmorton, by this time abroad in exile with his brother Thomas, living impoverished in Paris on pittances from Philip and the Pope. Within the next few days Arthur's connections on the left were also in trouble. 5 March: 'Pr. jeté en la tour de Londres'. This refers to Peter Wentworth's imprisonment for calling in question the Queen's prerogative in church matters, in regard to which this obstreperous Puritan was quite uncompromising. The character of the entry shows the familiar terms Arthur was upon with his neighbour in the country, and shortly it is followed by his cousin Job getting into trouble too. The day after Peter Wentworth was sent to the Tower, Job wrote to Arthur. In April Arthur 'was with my cousin Middlemore about J. Th.' and next day with the Lord Treasurer, evidently doing what he could on Job's behalf.[1]

On 8 April Arthur paid 'to Mr. Hubbard for my wife's picture £7'.[2] Three days later, 'ma femme avait quelques douleurs d'enfantement'. 12 April: 'my wife was delivered of

---

[1] Sir John Neale suggests that Job Throckmorton had been sent to the Tower for a speech containing 'lewd and blasphemous' criticism of James VI. J. E. Neale, *Elizabeth I and her Parliaments, 1584–1601*, 164.

[2] Miss E. Auerbach gives two references to this otherwise unknown painter in her *Tudor Painters*, 172.

a girl at half an hour past three o clock in the morning, con difficile labour, all Tuesday and all night'. There follow various payments in connection with the confinement and a large repayment of £100 borrowed from Lord Willoughby, probably the famous soldier, Peregrine Bertie, on winter leave from his command in the Low Countries. If so, he remained long enough for the christening: 20 April, 'my daughter Anna was christened by my Lady Walsingham, my Lady Stafford, and my Lord Willoughby. Mr. White preached.' A week later the nurse and Goody Hills took the child down to the country, to Bearchurch. 11 May, 'my wife was churched'. A few days later the child refused to suck and was sick; 18 May, 'my little Anna died by three of the clock in the morning'. The child was buried in the church of St. Giles within the precincts of the abbey, which served as the parish church of the Lucases.

Shortly after, his wife was ill. We may as well give her treatment in Arthur's own words for what historical interest it has. 24 May, 'my Æ was so sick as she sownded [fainted] five or six times'. There follows the doctor's treatment as prescribed: 'my wife had in the morning, noon and at night a double cloth laid upon her belly beneath her navel to both sides of her hips, dipped in plantain water and vinegar of roses in equal quantities, and another cloth likewise laid to the bottom of her back, both the which cloths must be removed a four or five times every *senerande* [bleeding] time when the party feeleth them warm; a pistary likewise of the leaves of plantain applied to the secret place and the same leaves spouted up by the pipe of a glister and a pissard in the place. She must refrain from all motions and strainings only during the times of the application of the cloths; both her arms must be tied very hard and sometime loosed and tied again, and her diet must be roasted meats without sauce, and fish sometimes. She must forbear all wines, salt and sharp waters, drinking as little as may be and that must be ale. To open a vein on both arms two or three days before the course and to let out but a little of blood but often, to open the veins four or five times a day, to let her sit from her buttocks up to her navel in a deep bowl of cold water — the advice of Dr. Atslow.'[1]

[1] Dr. Atslow was a Wykehamist and Fellow of New College, Oxford. A zealous Catholic, he busied himself designing means for Mary Queen of Scots' escape, and was in the confidence of the Earl of Arundel in attempting to fly the country in 1588 to lend himself to Philip's invasion purposes. For which the doctor was properly racked in the Tower. Munk, I. 62-3.

Dr. Atslow received 10s. for his advice. This will do for one specimen of Elizabethan medical treatment.

For Arthur's more agreeable masculine occupations, he was at this moment arranging his books and his father's papers. For these he bought a trunk covered with sealskins, and went on with his purchases of books, now an English Herbal for 13s. — William Turner's, the first of such. 'I put my books into a great standard, standing in the hall, and into two of the greatest leather chests standing in my father's study, of my father's negotiations in a chest, standing the farthermost of three from the door with others etc. in it. Plate and other things standing under the window in a little chest barred with iron. Maps in the study of Turkey, Spain, France, Tuscany. Seven French *sottises* in pictures with the Parliament at Poissy; four Queens' pictures, with a calendar in a frame. A cupboard wherein are all my deeds and writings covered with green cotton. Two curtains for the windows with the rods; a green cotton covering for the table; two tent stools.'

It is curious — the impulse that led him to record this in so much detail. No-one else has done so; this is its value: an Elizabethan interior.

The joys of married life continued to harass him, and he notes down his wife's condition in his inaccurate French. At the end of June, 'les courses de ma femme cessa [*sic*], mais elle plaigna du [*sic*] douleur en la place'. Next she complained of a chill throughout her body, then 'A se plaigna des petites pendentes en la place lesquelles jettèrent sang et eau'. On their way to St. Osyth's to visit the Darcys in July she was ill and they all had to come back. Nevertheless in August, 'ma femme avait sa maladie et ses courses'. Then there were the tiffs of family life, usually between the women, his wife and her mother, Lady Lucas. The latter demanded for their keep 13s. 4d. a week for Arthur and his wife, 4s. for each servant, and 5s. for his wife's maid. In August there was a flare-up: 'la signora signorissima entra en furie contre moi et H.' — probably his wife angry with him and some lady-friend.

In mitigation there were visits from friends and jaunts into the country. The musical Lady Kitson, patroness of the composer Wilbye, came over from Hengrave; Doctor Caesar, Judge of the Court of Admiralty, came to Colchester. In June Leicester had crossed over to the Netherlands to wind up his unsuccessful rule there, and in July Lady Leicester's brother, Sir William Knollys, visited them on his way to and from Norwich. We find Arthur writing to his mother and sister, and to the Queen. In September he goes with Sir Thomas Lucas to Court, then at Oatlands, and speaks with the Lord Chancellor — evidently a matter of business. October sees him at Paulerspury to receive the half year's rent of the park, £40, making Thomas Webb woodward, and finding that Lord Grey's man had made waste of twenty-four oak trees. Back at St. John's he crossed the Thames to go to Rochester, where he lay at the White Hart, and gave the Spanish prisoners in the *Bonaventure* 5s. He came back by way of Gravesend.

At the end of October he went to London, to find his mother very sick, and on 3 November she died. This involved him in a great deal of business, and, considering the funeral expenses for such a personage in those times, it was fortunate that a good sum towards her annuity out of the Exchequer arrived next day. Arthur reckoned up his cash and found that he had £159 : 5s. in several bags, besides money in his purse : he would need it. His wife and her mother came up for the funeral; brother William had to be polled, while hose and doublet, gown and shirts were made for him. Blacks alone cost the large sum of £77 : 18 : 6. There were payments for making gowns for the poor people attending, for 'lawn attires', to the chandler for hearsing the body and the coffin, to the heralds for exhibiting the deceased lady's arms, to the priest and the church. Lady Throckmorton was buried with her first husband in the church of St. Katherine Cree hard by Throckmorton house in Aldgate.

Then came the payment of wages, debts and legacies, the administration of the will, the settlement of family affairs. The upper servants received a quarter's wages, with a gown and kirtle if a woman, a gelding if a man. Arthur seems to have bought in his mother's coach for £26, had his own arms painted on it, and taken on the coachman at £3 a year. Lady Throckmorton's will, of which Arthur was sole executor, left to William four pieces of hangings with the Throckmorton arms, a bedstead with its furniture, table linen and, 'for the better remembrance of me, a tablet'.[1] To Arthur she left a bed with bedding, linen and embroidered cloths; to his wife, her coach and horses. Thomas got a hanging bed with its bedding, 'his own gilt jugs promised', and a jewel with a ruby and a diamond; Nicholas a similar bequest with a jewel. To Bess was left 'four pieces of hangings of imagery which did hang in the Duchess's chamber

---

[1] From the late Lady Throckmorton's MS. Note-Book at Coughton.

at Beaumanor, a sparver [canopy] of crimson velvet and cloth of
gold with five curtains of changeable taffetas belonging to the
same, a quilt of changeable taffeta, a feather bed etc. — all
which her father-in-law [*i.e.* stepfather] gave her'. She was also
to have all her mother's jewels and chains now in her custody,
with wearing apparel and linen. This, we may be sure, would
enable Bess to cut a good figure at Court; for the rest she
depended on the Queen. Lady Throckmorton left her brother,
Sir Francis Carew, a gilt bowl with cover, and 'a striking clock
to stand upon a cupboard'; her friend, William Hughes, a cup
with a cover; other small bequests to her sons Robert and
Thomas.

The first consequence seems to have been some ill-feeling,
for on 30 December, 'mon frère Thomas s'en alla de la mer
sans dire adieu'. However, in February he was back and in
favour, for Arthur lent him *Amyntas*, presumably the English
translation of 1587, which Abraham France made of Watson's
Latin poem. In the summer of 1589 he received three-quarters
of a buck from Thomas, and a year later, his will: that concluded
their relations. This year 1588 saw a composition between the
brothers and Arthur, who now took on sole responsibility as
head of the family. There remained on his father's butlerage a
debt of £199 : 10 : 6 to pay the Queen, and he made arrangements to pay this off at the rate of £30 p.a. There were payments
to be made to his younger brothers for their support, his elder
brother to be maintained. This summer we find him sending
money, by bill of exchange by Giuseppe Simone of Lucca, to
Nicholas in Italy.

These demands upon him forced him to resort to pawning
his plate. In February he pawned plate for £100 for three
months, with 50s. commodity. We remember from Shakespeare

> That smooth-faced gentleman, tickling Commodity,
> Commodity, the bias of the world.

In this case it meant a profit of 10 per cent, the statutory limit
upon usury at the time. In May his rents came in from Northamptonshire, and he redeemed his plate. At the end of the month
he had to pledge it again until August; in September he re-
pledged his silver to redeem it in November. In addition, this
February he needed to raise another £100 by bond; while at
the end of April he pledged a gilt basin and ewer, and a double
bell salt for £20 for three months, then got an extension for one
month for 5s. commodity.

During March and April this year he underwent a strenuous course of medicine, purging and sweating, which became regular with him, and still more punishing, as the years went on. He took medicine three times a day, and sometimes added a glister or an antidote. On 23 April, 'Je baignais les estruelles [pimples] de la lessive de Guaiac'. He took tamerind and cassia; but when one comes to guaiacum, one remembers that this was the Indian specific for syphilis. Can it be that he had picked up some venereal infection, perhaps on one of his continental visits? For this long course of spring purging he paid Dr. Langton the large sum of £10, and later we find him paying the doctor an annuity, or retaining fee.

In February his wife realised that she was pregnant again, and in March Arthur had her portrait painted by Jeronimo for £4. On Friday 11 May, 'ma femme commença à travailler d'enfant après diner, et enfanta à 10 p.m.'. Nothing is said of any christening, so that this child also died or was stillborn. A month later he gave the minister 12s. 6d. for churching his wife. At the same time we first find Arthur consoling himself with tobacco, 6 oz. for 20s.; and a month later a similar amount.

It is curious to find that the Diary gives no indication that this was the exciting summer of the Armada. When the Spaniards were making their way slowly from Lisbon towards the Channel Throckmorton was down in Northamptonshire keeping his courts. The Armada had been already defeated and was scudding before the south-westerlies up the eastern coast towards Scotland when Arthur returned to Mile End on August 1 and lay at the 'Limpet' at his brother Thomas's chamber. It was only now when all was over and his friend Sir Robert Sidney was being sent ambassador to Scotland, to thank James for his help in repelling the Spaniards, that a small opportunity for service came Throckmorton's way.

He had been anxious at the opening of the war, when Leicester headed the English intervention in the Netherlands, to serve under him. Throckmorton wrote to his good friend and patron, Walsingham, in March 1585: 'being thoroughly tired with an idle course, I desire in this action to be set on work, and the rather because I would cleanse the stains that some of my name and blood spotted my poor house with, by my own good and dutiful demeanour. I am not so ambitious as to catch at great matters, but shall be contented with what her Majesty and you

shall think me worthy of.'[1] They evidently did not consider him.
For one thing, Leicester was not a man to forget an injury;
and for another, the treason of his Throckmorton cousins just at
that moment made it undesirable to employ Arthur — his letter
shows that he was conscious of that.

However, Walsingham did not forget his old patron's son,
and towards the middle of August he got him the privilege of
accompanying the ambassador. It was a chance to meet King
James and greet the future. Arthur equipped himself with
cuirass, burgonet and a leading staff, two pairs of girdles and
hangers, two drums; five dozen of gold and pearl buttons, gold
lace and a stitched hat with pearled band; then there was the
making of the caff, a rich kind of taffeta, with the tassels for his
ensign. All this needed the loan of £100. He placed his servants
on board wages, delivered Martyn £60 for his charges towards
Scotland and advanced along the road to Newark, Doncaster,
York. There he supped with Lady Huntingdon, in the lodgings
of the Lord President of the Council of the North, and wrote
home to his wife and sister by Mr. Devereux's man. At Berwick
he dined with the Marshal, Sir Henry Widdrington. On 28
August, having received the King's safe-conduct, they crossed
the Border into Scotland, and next night lay in Edinburgh, 'at
a merchant's house hard by the Chancellor's'.

On 30 August he wrote to Leicester and to Walsingham.
His letter to the Secretary has fetched up among the State Papers
Scottish, expressing his grateful sense of Walsingham's love, 'in
impawning your high credit for mine honest and dutiful behaviour
here in Scotland to her Majesty'.[2] (One notices the consciousness expressed in the word 'pawning'.) He added, 'my lord
ambassador maketh good cheer and payeth dear' — the Sidneys
were all generous, and anyway in Scotland what were the English
for? While still in Edinburgh they heard the news of Leicester's
death. Worn out with his service in the Netherlands those last
years, and in England that harassing summer, he had died on
his way home to Kenilworth, his last thoughts with the Queen
he had loved and served. The poisonous tongues, whispering of
poison, that had followed him all his life did not cease to pursue
him into the grave. Only Elizabeth mourned him.

Throckmorton took the opportunity of his brief visit to Scotland to enquire for a cast of hawks, and these were brought south
after him in September by Isaac, the falconer, whom he took

[1] *Cal. S.P. Dom. Add., 1580–1625*, 140. [2] *Cal. S.P. Scottish*, IX. 602.

into his service: he proved unsatisfactory and was discharged. Altogether he had fourteen servants at this time in and about the house at Mile End, which he was engaged in purchasing and which lay conveniently for London, service at Court and for St. John's at Colchester where they resided when in the country. Immediately on his return he reported to Walsingham, to whom he presented a silver standish for his kindness. A large payment of £40 was made to Mr. Roscarrock, a Cornish gentleman from whom Throckmorton had presumably borrowed. Considerable sums were spent on books this winter, Luther's Works in several volumes, Plato's in Greek and Latin; while books necessitated bookshelves. A Turkey carpet cost as much as £8: a new luxury coming in, but one sees him throughout life building up comfort around himself.

On Candlemas day he was sworn a free burgess of Colchester, and four days later he supped in the Queen's privy chamber. His brother Thomas sold his stables and tenements by London wall for the large sum of £700 — younger sons were not wholly at a disadvantage, one observes: they did not have the obligations to support, or the upkeep, of the head of the family. In November Arthur purchased a christening cloth of white and black work in lawn — such as one sees in protraits of the time. Once more his hopes were dashed of starting a family: their third effort foundered in April with the birth of a child that did not live, and shortly 'ma femme commença avoir ses fleurs en abondance'. In early summer he was equipping his brother William with shirts, handkerchiefs and socks, silk moccado for hose and doublet, and himself with birding piece and case — the country was all round one in those days — three muskets and three cases of pistols, two cases of Scottish pistols, evidently to arm his household. He took into his service Anthony, a blackamoor from Guinea.

Earlier that year his friend William Ashby had been sent as envoy to Scotland, and their correspondence corroborates and fills out the Diary. In July Arthur heard of Ashby's recall, and wrote with the epistolary sententiousness upon which he clearly prided himself, 'you will come home hoist upon hope, which is never a jade but at his journey's end'.[1] But, Ashby was to remember the proverb: 'better half a loaf in hand than much bread in a common oven'. Ashby wrote back, 'I hope soon to see you that we may philosophise together. You will marvel

[1] *Cal. S.P. Scottish*, X. 121, 129. These letters are incorrectly calendared as from 'Michael (?) Throckmorton'.

why I seek my revocation, holding a place where I enjoy *otium cum dignitate*; you know my mind, you know my state; my health will not comport with this climate; other particulars I will satisfy you *bocca a bocca*.' Scotland was now quieter. *Vincere scit Rex, set uti victoriam nescit.* 'This young prince, chaste and continent as Hippolytus, spending the time in Diana's exercise, is now far in love with the princess of Denmark.' This view of things was to receive some queer qualifications from James's subsequent career. 'I have been so long in this climate as you may see I am grown a tratling [*i.e.* prating] Scot.' Ashby besought Throckmorton to get him recalled before winter: he was weary of the place and detested the climate.

By the autumn Ashby was involved in some trouble and had incurred Walsingham's displeasure. We cannot go into it here, but it was largely on account of Thomas Fowler, an English agent who was more intimate with James and sought to take Ashby's place as ambassador. Ashby replied on Throckmorton's friendship to do his best for him with Walsingham; he would appeal 'a Cesare irato ad Caesarem non iratum'.[1] In December Arthur reported that he had 'dealt as effectively for you as I durst. I do find him bending to a milder course than I did the last time.' Throckmorton assured the Secretary he would find Ashby more honest than his 'counter-current', *i.e.* Fowler; and Walsingham undertook to have their differences heard by Mr. Bowes on the Borders. From the Diary we learn that Throckmorton was with the Secretary on three several occasions on behalf of Ashby, who learned from Mr. Bowes how 'you have shown yourself faithful in the absence of your old friend'.

Arthur's finances in this year 1590 continued somewhat tight, though that was nothing remarkable in the aristocratic society of the time: a good deal of money came in, but more went out. Rents came in from his lands, and increasing sums for wood and trees from his Northamptonshire woodlands. In addition there was the annuity his wife brought with her from her parents. In October a goodly sum accrued from this quarter: £76 which Lady Lucas gave her daughter, besides £20 which the latter brought up with her to London, of which she handed over £14 to her husband. It was all needed, and more besides. Arthur was forced to borrow £300 from his younger brother

---

[1] *Cal. S.P. Scottish*, X. 205, 217, 220. The footnote on p. 205 should read 'Walsingham' not 'Thomas Fowler'. On p. 217 the address 'Mile End' is, of course, Arthur Throckmorton's.

Nicholas for which he paid him £30 a year interest. There were Nicholas and Robert's annuities to pay out, £40 a year to each. Thomas apparently departed this life this year, and that must have been some financial relief; while William made Arthur a gift of the thirds of Throckmorton house. Still he had to pledge a gilt basin and ewer, and a large gilt salt for £20 in August; and more plate was pledged to a London leatherseller for £50 in September.

For an Elizabethan gentleman could hardly be expected to go without his 'butt of muscadel of Candia [Crete] of the greatest size', bought of Constantine a Venetian for £18; or the Friesland cloth, cambric, damask, plush, silk stockings he was buying at the same time; or the setting of his wife's great ruby in gold. There was the brewer to be paid, £13 : 13s., a considerable sum, but the household was not a small one. As for the payments for paper, ink and quills, where should we be without them? — for this provided the paper-books, the entries we have under our eyes as we write.

His social life continues as before. Frequent letters pass between him and his sister at Court — would they had survived! — or he sends his footman with messages: evidently they were very close together, as they had always been. In August he goes to Court, which is then at Oatlands; in December to Richmond several times, for he has business to transact in regard to his lands. On 8 December he is 'before the Council's table for stocking up of my lawful assarts'. This means turning cattle into ground gained from the forest and cleared of timber. He naturally claimed that this was his own land and not royal forest, but it involved sessions, missives, messages to the Lord Chancellor, Lord Treasurer, Attorney-General and Solicitor-General. All this meant fees and gifts besides: 10s. to the lively Michael Hicks, Lord Burghley's secretary, 10s. in gold to Mr. Locke, the Lord Chamberlain's secretary. Such was the way of that world.

His wife was pregnant again. On 17 November, 'ma femme senta motion vie au ventre'. 22 January, 'ma femme se senta malade en l'estomac et avait comme une fissure'. Four days later, 'ma femme avait monstre du lait aux tettins'. In April the child was born, and this time all was well in spite of his fears. Sunday the 25th: 'ma femme commença à travailler d'enfant environ le un heures [*sic*] au matin, et elle fut délivrée d'une fille entre 8 et 9 heures du matin. Le signe étant en Libra 10 et le jour de St. Marke. Abundance.' Next day, 'my wife was very sick. Continuation. 27 April, Continuation et douleur du lait. 28, Le blanche commença à vider. 30, Given Goody Collingwood for washing, 2s. 6d.; grande abundance de fleurs coulait de ma femme, commença après diner. May 3, les fleurs de ma femme cessèrent.' On the 9th Mother Sparrow, the midwife, was paid as much as £3, and 'my girl was christened and named Mary by my Lady Lucas and Mrs. Abett and my father Sir Thomas Lucas'. The fourth effort was successful; the child was healthy, lived to marry the second Lord Wotton and carry on Throckmorton's stock in the female line.

The winter of 1590-1 saw the beginning of an acquaintance that would be important for both Throckmorton and his sister, one that quickly ripened into friendship and then moved over into uncertainty, hostility, danger: that with the young Earl of Essex and his sister Penelope, Lady Rich, the 'Stella' celebrated in Sidney's Sonnets and by so many poets. Lady Rich was an Essex neighbour at Leez priory near Chelmsford. This desirable monastic residence had been annexed and reconstructed by the first Lord Rich, most detestable of all the Henricians active in the Dissolution. He lent himself to the ruin of most of the leading figures of that black time, Cromwell, Somerset, Northumberland, but he was especially concerned in tricking and trapping the Catholics, Bishop Fisher and Sir Thomas More. Such convictions as Lord Rich possessed were Catholic; he amassed a very large fortune out of his activities, and made a pious death. His son was a Protestant and more respectable. So was his grandson, Penelope's husband; but it is hardly surprising that no-one loved the Riches, least of all the Lady Rich, who could not abide her spouse. Everyone sympathised.

She had been forced into the marriage: 'being in the power of her friends, she was by them married against her will unto one against whom she did protest at the very solemnity [*i.e.* solemnisation], and ever after'.[1] She had been intended for Philip Sidney, but, left an orphan by the death of her father, the first Earl of Essex, in Ireland, she was married off by her guardian, the Puritan Earl of Huntingdon, to young Lord Rich. (From being Catholics the Riches became Puritans.) All were agreed in that age that Penelope was very beautiful: she had a rare combination of black eyes and golden hair, a perfect forehead of the whitest skin, for her complexion, of white and rose, remained always her chief beauty. Too late Philip Sidney fell in love with her and wrote:

---

[1] q. Cyril Falls, *Mountjoy, Elizabethan General*, 59.

But that rich fool, who by blind Fortune's lot
The richest gem of love and life enjoys,
And can with foul abuse such beauties blot,
Let him, deprived of sweet but unfelt joys,
Exiled for aye from those high treasures which
He knows not, grow in folly only rich.

We can only suppose that this means that Lord Rich was un-appreciative of his treasure, while 'foul abuse' would refer to his subjecting her to frequent pregnancies. For she submitted herself to his lawful embraces and produced seven children by him, before she moved over into the arms of the brilliant Charles Blount, Lord Mountjoy, the lover by whom she had five more.

The Diary mentions that on 6 September 1590, Lady Rich was churched : this would be after the birth of her second son, who became Earl of Holland and ended on the scaffold. In August next year Throckmorton went over alone to spend a week-end with Lady Rich at Leez. One can still see from what remains of it what a splendid, characteristic Tudor structure it must have been. The first lord turned the nave of the monastic church into his great hall, the chapter house into his domestic chapel. The keep-like inner gate-house of red brick, with lofty turrets and fantastic chimneys, remains ; so does the outer gate-house with a lower range of buildings on either side.

This was the house where as a boy Essex spent his vacations from Cambridge, when Penelope was first married to her dis-tasteful lord. Now in 1590, a young man of twenty-two, Essex was a prime figure at Court, to which he had been introduced very young by his stepfather Leicester, it is said, to offset the favour Ralegh had gained with the Queen. Ralegh was some thirteen years older, and both Essex's years and his rank — for he was a cousin of the Queen — gave him an advantage with the ageing virgin who would never admit the onset of the years. She was as intrigued and taken with him as she had been with Ralegh, and before him with Leicester.

The truth is that Elizabeth spoiled him, and she was never able to keep this glittering leader of the younger generation under control as she had been his stepfather. There had already been several *contretemps* between them when this year Essex set himself seriously back by marrying. Shortly after Walsingham died in April, Essex married his daughter, Sir Philip Sidney's widow. One would have thought it a suitable marriage in every way : in those days it was an advantage to marry a widow, and Frances Sidney was not only Walsingham's sole heir but she enjoyed her thirds out of the Sidney estates. The Queen thought otherwise. In the first place, her permission had not been asked, and that was an offence. In the second place, she said that Essex was marrying below his degree. The marriage had been a secret one, until Lady Essex's condition betrayed it, and then Elizabeth was furious.

Essex went on living at Court, but he longed to get away from it all into some sphere of action where he could win the military glory he thirsted for. He had tried to escape before, but had been brought ignominiously back into those silken toils — and such is the perversity of human affections that Elizabeth would not have loved him if he had not been like that. This year another opportunity presented itself. Henry of Navarre had succeeded to the French throne, on the assassination of Henri III, and was desperately pressed between Parma in the Netherlands and the Catholic League in open rebellion and in possession of large areas of Normandy and Brittany. He was particularly anxious to recover Rouen, and this was an English interest, too. In the autumn he sent a special embassy headed by the Vicomte de Turenne to press for Elizabeth's help, and such was Essex's position in relation to the Queen that Henri IV recommended his emissaries to make interest with Essex also. From England they were to go on to seek assistance among the Protestant princes of Germany.

From this point the Diary takes up, for the French emissaries turned up at Colchester in December and were entertained at St. John's for a couple of days before embarking at Harwich for Germany. Later that month we find the first reference to Essex, though Throckmorton must have known him before: 21 December, 'I came from Court to Mile End on foot with my Lord of Essex'. From this time we have meetings mentioned, messages passing to and fro, for Throckmorton became involved in supporting Essex's ardent desire to go on campaign in Normandy. Essex had much difficulty in persuading the Queen; three times he was on his knees before her for a couple of hours, so he told the French, and was refused. At length she relented, though with no great belief in what he would accomplish; Rouen was what she had her eyes on: a pledge for Calais — as from the very beginning of her reign.

On 21 May Throckmorton was with Essex at Wanstead — Leicester's palatial country house in Essex now lived in by his formidable widow, Essex's mother. Three days later Arthur had an audience with the Queen; in June he was confabulating with

Essex again. The Earl was recruiting his forces on a personal, quasi-feudal basis, calling for contributions from tenants and friends. It was impossible for Arthur to resist his new-found friend, and in July he sent Essex an expensive case of pistols and equipped one of his men as a horseman for his forces. On 27 July, he notes, 'my Lord of Essex set towards France'.

It was this expedition to Normandy —

Our King went forth to Normandy —

with its memories of the Hundred Years War, of fighting Talbot, the terror of the French, that aroused the enthusiasm of London and launched Shakespeare upon his career as the most popular dramatist of the age. Nor did Essex ever lose the favour of the London mob through all his misadventures. The campaign went as the Queen had feared. Essex lost his opportunity to attack Rouen at once, and instead could not resist the adventure of careering dangerously across enemy country to meet Henry of Navarre. This was not warfare, but Dumas. When he got back he found that his only brother had been killed and, like a fool, the general trailed a pike along with the common soldiers. This was very popular, but it did not advance the capture of Rouen.

Meanwhile his little army melted away; Essex wrote for reinforcements and an extension of time to achieve something. We find Throckmorton sending letters to his sister at Court to be forwarded to Essex. The Diary mentions his return in October, when Arthur was with him : he had come back to use his personal charm with the Queen to extend his command. She gave way, and wept when he left. It was all to no purpose; the chance had been irretrievably lost, and she took up pen to tell him so herself. 'To this your earnest and vehement desire we were contented to assent, rather by the persuasion of divers that saw your judgment so transported with the humour of the journey, than that, by our own observation of all the course of this action, we had not apprehended both the untoward proceedings hitherto, and thoroughly foreseen the unlikelihood of any good to come hereafter, especially in such an action as had received his greatest wound even in his first beginning for want of timely proceeding, which all wise men do account the half gained in any action of importance.'[1]

[1] W. B. Devereux, *Lives and Letters of the Devereux Earls of Essex*, I. 267-8.

She was right as usual; in mid-winter he was recalled, having accomplished nothing but to waste a promising expeditionary force. Is it any wonder she became what she was — short-tempered, irritable, difficult, censorious? highly intelligent herself, not given to making mistakes or taking rash chances, she was ceaselessly involved in affairs with men of action who insisted on making them and taking them. Only the Cecils knew how never to offend.

On 17 November, her accession day — remembered and celebrated by her people for more than a century after her death — Throckmorton was at Court and, regal and gracious as she well knew how to be, 'the Queen spake to me and made me to kiss her hand'. Two days later he learned the secret of his sister's marriage to Sir Walter Ralegh, and this launched them all on a sea of troubles.

CHAPTER VIII

SIR WALTER RALEGH

SIR WALTER RALEGH was at this time, if we assume that he was born in 1554, as is probable, about twenty-seven. The Queen, perhaps it is impolite to recall, was twenty years older. *Mais ça n'empêche pas*, and all through the 1580's and until his secret marriage in 1592 Ralegh was in prime favour with his sovereign mistress: the twelve years' warfare in love, as he described it, with characteristic exaggeration, after his fall.

It is important to get Ralegh's social origins right, as his biographers for the most part have not done. In his own day those undoubted aristocrats, the De Vere Earl of Oxford and the Devereux Earl of Essex, would refer to Ralegh as 'the Jack, and an upstart', or 'the knave'. But, as Naunton observed — and this was unlike her father — 'the Queen in her choice never took into her favour a mere new man or a mechanic'.[1] And, in fact, Ralegh came from one of the oldest of Devon families. Their pedigree takes them back to the Conquest, but, without going so far, we may note that as early as the reign of Henry II a Ralegh was sheriff of Devon and was granted the Nettlecombe estate in Somerset, that Sir William Ralegh was a judge of King's Bench, and that another William was bishop of Winchester in the thirteenth century.[2]

In the later Middle Ages the family declined, and by 1500 it was noticeably down in the world from what it had been, though the Raleghs continued to marry among the best West Country families, Carews, Grenvilles, Champernownes. It seems that they lost in some way as the result of the Western risings in 1497. The family place at this time was Fardel in the parish of Cornwood, though there were other places like Withycombe Ralegh and Colaton Ralegh, Challacombe and Combe Ralegh, that bore witness to the more extensive holdings they once had had. Our

---

[1] Sir Robert Naunton, *Fragmenta Regalia* (*Arber's English Reprints*), 47.
[2] T. N. Brushfield, 'Notes on the Ralegh Family', *Trans. Devon. Assocn.* 1883, 163 foll., corrects the genealogy in J. L. Vivian, *Visitations of Devonshire*.

Walter's great-grandfather had married a daughter of the celebrated Sir Richard Edgcumbe; his grandfather, the daughter of
Sir Thomas Grenville, but he had had to sell the Smallridge
estate to John Gilbert.

The son and heir of this marriage was Walter Ralegh of
Fardel, our subject's father. This Walter was three times
married: first to the daughter of John Drake of Exmouth. This
was marrying beneath him, but it may have been convenient,
for Ralegh had given up living at Fardel to try his hand at
shipping, in a small way, from Exmouth. The son of this marriage did not make good: a George, who left only illegitimate
issue. Walter Ralegh next married the daughter of a London
merchant, Darrell; the daughter of these nuptials married an
Exeter merchant, Hugh Snedall. We find both Darrells and
Snedalls involved in Sir Walter's later fortunes. For his third
marriage the father returned to his own class, marrying Elizabeth,
daughter of Sir Philip Champernowne of Modbury near Plymouth, and widow of Otho Gilbert of Compton Castle near
Torquay. She would have brought with her something from
her father, and a little from her first husband.

The revival of the Ralegh stock came about with her. It is
impossible to escape one's notice that by her first husband she
produced Sir Humphrey, Sir John and Adrian Gilbert, and by
her second Sir Carew and Sir Walter Ralegh: all five men of
ability and remark, one of them a man of genius.

These circumstances are important to the understanding of
Ralegh, to the making of his temper and career. When he was
young, and into his adult years, he was always hard up for money:
poor, and as proud as the devil. This mixed family of Gilberts
and Raleghs had strong characteristics in common, evidently
coming through the mother. John Gilbert and Carew Ralegh
were mean and acquisitive, Humphrey Gilbert and Walter
Ralegh acquisitive and extravagant. They all had a marked
vein of intellectual interests, but (except for Adrian) they were
men of action — that was what was interesting about them:
with them ideas went to their heads, were liable to carry them
away. They were speculators, projectors, bent not only on
voyages across the seas, but voyages of the mind. Humphrey
Gilbert was almost a *fantaisiste*, for ever cruising beyond the
borders of the possible; and so he met his end. Adrian Gilbert
was a dabbler in astrology, alchemy, necromancy. Walter
Ralegh did not think as other men thought; with him an extremely sceptical intelligence went along with his soaring imagina-

tion. His heterodox opinions disregarded other men's; they rewarded him — and this was dangerous — by labelling him 'atheist'.

Passions stalked through this family. Sir Humphrey Gilbert was impetuous and rash to the verge of insanity. His brother John was perpetually involved in quarrels. Passion, rage, desperation were familiar companions with Ralegh. They were a dangerous lot. But they were gifted too: Adrian Gilbert at science; Carew Ralegh at music. Aubrey tells us that 'Sir Carew had a delicate clear voice and played singularly well on the olpharion (which was the instrument in fashion in those days), to which he did sing'.[1] The gift was continued in the next generations; so was the temper. Aubrey was at school with the grandchildren, 'excellent tuneable voices, and played their parts well on the viol; ingenious, but all proud and quarrelsome'. Walter Ralegh, as we know, had all the gifts of body and spirit, save happiness and peace of mind.

The two Raleghs were determined to make good and restore their family's position. The elder brother achieved it by marrying the rich widow of Sir John Thynne, to whom he had been gentleman of the horse. The younger brother, Walter, with far greater gifts, achieved nothing until he came into the presence of the Queen — then already a man of twenty-six, desperate to get on, with nothing to show but his looks, nothing to declare but his genius. He was not going to let the grand chance of his life pass. Naunton tells us, 'but true it is, he had gotten the Queens's ear at a trice, and she began to be taken with his elocution, and loved to hear his reasons to her demands. And the truth is, she took him for a kind of oracle, which nettled them all.'[2] By this time there was already the split in his personality by which the infection, the poison, entered; or perhaps, to vary the image, it was the irritation that secreted the pearl, his genius. But we can be sure that consciousness of his own talents, and of belonging to a very old family — much older, for example, than the Cecils — and yet to have been held back by its impoverishment did not make it any easier to bear the insults of De Veres and Devereux, gave a sharper edge to the temper always impatient to leap forth in scorn and contempt.

When Ralegh was born his parents were living at the small barton of Hayes, which his father had leased, in the parish of

---

[1] John Aubrey, *Brief Lives*, ed. A. Clark, II. 179. Aubrey explains this instrument for us: ''tis as big as a lute, but flat-bellied with wire strings'.
[2] Naunton, 49.

East Budleigh. It is, happily, not much changed: upstairs is the great chamber of his birth, according to tradition, under the thatch. The house lies on the slope away from the main road to Exeter — convenient for his father's avocations there, who had a house in Palace-gate — and for Exmouth. A stream runs down to village and church, where the manor-pew still remains — the father's first wife buried beside it — though the coat-of-arms has been defaced, possibly after Sir Walter's condemnation for treason in 1603. On the slope in front was Hayes Wood, and to the west the wide common extending into Withycombe Ralegh: very convenient for a boy's birding and coursing. To the south were the red cliffs and the sea, and from early years young Walter was drawn to wider horizons.

In 1569 his mother's cousin, Henry Champernowne of Modbury, got leave to take over a hundred volunteer horsemen to the aid of the Huguenots in France.[1] Among these were Philip Budockshide, Francis Berkeley and Walter Ralegh, *admodum adolescens*, is Camden's phrase: he would be fifteen or sixteen. Years afterwards, in his *History of the World*, he referred to the Huguenot defeats at Jarnac and Moncontour in March and October of that year, saying of the latter, 'of which myself was an eye-witness'.[2] Henry Champernowne died the year after: he had made his will, 2 October 1568, before going on campaign, and it was proved 10 December 1570.[3] We know nothing more of Ralegh in this war except that deeper down, in Languedoc, he saw men being smoked out of their caves in that war of religion.

In 1572 Ralegh turns up, at eighteen, as a student at Oriel College, Oxford, along with another cousin, Charles Champernowne, who later took part with Sir Humphrey Gilbert and Ralegh in the unsuccessful privateering voyage of 1578.[4] Other companions of this year at Oriel were the three Unton brothers, who are also found associated with Ralegh later — Edward was in Ireland with him. Another fellow student was Mr. Child of Worcestershire; and this corroborates a story of Aubrey, who says that Ralegh 'in his youth for several years . . . was under straits for want of money'.[5] Child, who was his chamber-fellow, 'lent him a gown, which he could never get, nor satisfaction for

[1] W. Camden, *History* (ed. 1675), 137.
[2] Sir Walter Ralegh, *History of the World* (ed. 1677), 593, 626, 655.
[3] P.C.C. Lyon 33.
[4] C. S. Emden, 'Sir Walter Ralegh and his Friends at Oriel', *Oriel Papers*, 9 foll.
[5] Aubrey, *loc. cit.*

it'. Though poor, he had his wits about him. Francis Bacon used to tell the story of a fellow student of Ralegh's who was a coward but a good archer. Grossly abused by another, he came to Ralegh to ask his advice how to remedy the wrong done him. 'Why, challenge him to a match of shooting,' said Ralegh.

In 1574–5 he passed from Lyon's Inn, one of the Inns of Chancery, to the Middle Temple, along with one of the Untons. Not that he meant to dedicate himself to the law, or that he gave much thought to it: it was just a part of the regular education of a gentleman, something to do with one's prentice years. Like other young sparks of the time he gave more thought to poetry. From 'Walter Ralegh of the Middle Temple' in 1576 came his first appearance in print, the commendatory verses prefaced to George Gascoigne's *The Steel Glass*, of which one couplet betrays a certain foreknowledge of his own fate:

> For whoso reaps renown above the rest
> With heaps of hate shall surely be oppressed.

Another poem from these early days, still somewhat stilted in measure, not yet having found his own idiom, yet enables us to see into his mind:

> Sweet are the thoughts where hope persuadeth hap,
> Great are the joys where heart obtains request,
> Dainty the life nursed still in Fortune's lap,
> Much is the ease where troubled minds find rest.
> These are the fruits that valour doth advance
> And cuts off dread by hope of happy chance.
>
> Thus hope brings hap but to the worthy wight,
> Thus pleasure comes but after hard assay;
> Thus fortune yields in manger oft for spite,
> Thus happy state is none without delay.
> Then must I needs advance myself by skill,
> And live to serve, in hope of your good will.

This has a convincing note: the reproach that good fortune never comes without having to wait too long for it — Ralegh's later work, especially *The History of the World*, is full of such reproaches, girding at fortune. This poem is evidently recommending himself to someone, perhaps to a lady, like others of his poems.

These were the roistering years of a young man about town, a hanger-on of the Court, waiting for something to turn up: they were formative years, and there remained always something of the adventurer about Ralegh. In December 1577 two of his servants, Devonshiremen by their name, Paunsford, were in trouble with the watch.[1] Ralegh was then living at Islington, but described himself as 'of the Court' — to which he had access by his status as a gentleman, and, in particular, through Sir Humphrey Gilbert, who had been a personal servant of Elizabeth before her coming to the throne.[2] Devonshire left its mark upon him. Aubrey records that 'notwithstanding his so great mastership in style and his conversation with the learnedest and politest persons, yet he spake broad Devonshire to his dying day'. That, too, is convincing: there was much greater regional variety in speech at the top of society in those days, a richer, more diverse and masculine effect.

A good deal of 1578-9 was taken up by Ralegh's part in Gilbert's abortive expedition of that winter, and this may afford a clue to Ralegh's way of life and how he maintained himself in these unknown years — under the wing of his half-brother, some sixteen years his senior. Ralegh was captain of the *Falcon*.[3] Gilbert made no progress beyond Ireland, and Ralegh went ahead as far as the Cape Verde Islands, hoping 'to do something worthy of honour' in the West Indies. Running short of victuals, he had to turn back and got involved in a fight at sea in which he lost many men and his ships got a battering. In the spring the Privy Council forbade Gilbert and Ralegh from any further attempts, 'and to remain at home and answer such as have been by their company damaged'. There was nothing but loss from this venture.

Restlessness, excitability, dissatisfaction may account for our next notices of him in these elusive years. In February 1580 he and Sir Thomas Perrot were sent to the Fleet for a week for an affray between them, and on their release had to give sureties to keep the peace and demean themselves quietly.[4] Now Sir Thomas Perrot, son of the famous Sir John who prided himself on his suspicious likeness to Henry VIII, had married Essex's sister, Dorothy Devereux. Next month Ralegh was committed to the Marshalsea for an affray with one of the Wingfields beside the Tennis Court at Whitehall. We can only infer that he was spoiling for action.

[1] T. N. Brushfield, 'Raleghana, Part V', *Trans. Devon. Assocn.* 1903, 547.

[2] We learn from a Chancery case years afterwards of the £10 advanced him by Adrian Gilbert when Ralegh first went to Court, and £60 to pay an Exeter draper for clothes and for liveries for his men. C. Monro, *Acta Cancellariae*, 177.

[3] D. B. Quinn, *The Voyages and Colonizing Enterprises of Sir Humphrey Gilbert* (Hakluyt Soc.), I. 43 foll.   [4] *A.P.C. 1578-80*, 384, 388-9, 421.

The opportunity came to him with the Desmond rebellion in Munster and the need for recruits and forces to subdue it. In July he was given command of a hundred footmen levied from the city of London.[1] It is not my purpose to go in detail into the complex situation or all his activities in Ireland, with which his career was so significantly intermingled; suffice it to say at the outset that it was Irish affairs that gave him his opening with the Queen.

There was no doubt about the energy with which he threw himself into action; he had the example of Humphrey Gilbert before him, who had made name and fame by his ferocity in suppressing rebellion in this area ten years before. Devonshiremen were much involved in Munster, and Ralegh based himself on Cork where his cousin Grenville and Sir Warham St. Leger had had their plantation overthrown in the previous rising. The prime mover in the new rebellion, James Fitzgerald of Desmond, who had pushed the unfortunate Earl into his fatal move, was early caught, and St. Leger and Ralegh had him strung up. Their fellow Devonshireman, John Hooker, commented, 'and thus the pestilent hydra hath lost another of his heads'.[2] This gives us the feeling in that terrible war of mutual murder and decimation described by Spenser.

Nor did Hooker fail to record Ralegh's exploits. The captain practised one on a group of kerne whom he surprised. One of these carried a load of withs, which they used instead of halters. When Ralegh asked what they were for, he got the reply 'to hang up English churls'. '"Is it so?" quoth the captain; "well, they shall now serve for an Irish kerne." And so commanded him to be hanged up with one of his own withs; the residue he handled according to their deserts.' That autumn there was foreign intervention in Ireland: the Pope sent a small expedition of some seven or eight hundred Italians, who fortified themselves upon the peninsula at Smerwick in the extreme south-west. 'When the captain had yielded himself and the fort appointed to be surrendered, captain Ralegh together with captain Macworth entered into the castle and made a great slaughter, many or the most part of them being put to the sword.' There was, in fact, no other way out in the conditions prevailing: they should not have come.

That winter Ralegh had a narrow escape himself. His energy and good service were recognised at Dublin by the grant of a

---

[1] *A.P.C. 1580-81*, 96, 97.　　[2] *Holinshed's Chronicles* (ed. 1808), VI. 433 foll.

band of horse in addition to his ensign of foot; and he was given
a commission to seize for himself the castle and lands of Lord
Barry, who had been aiding and comforting the rebels. Riding
back from Dublin, Ralegh had to pass through the enemy country
of the Seneschal of Imokilly, who laid an ambush for him at a
ford. Ralegh got through the water, but Henry Moyle, one of
his West Countrymen, had his horse founder under him and
Ralegh came back to the water to recover him. Later, that
summer, in a rash charge of his few horse against many more
foot, Ralegh's horse was killed under him and he himself might
have been slain but for a trusty servant. For his services Ralegh
was made one of the three commissioners of Munster that summer,
and based himself on Lismore, of which he later got the grant.

In early 1581 we find him in correspondence with both
Burghley and Walsingham on Irish affairs. The latter had expressed to him a 'disposition and opinion more favourable than
I can any way deserve'.[1] In return Ralegh expressed scornfully
his opinion of the bands sent over to serve : 'the officers had the
furniture, and the soldiers ran away. Besides, the men are such
poor and miserable creatures as their captains dare not lead them
to serve.' He went on fearlessly to express his opinion of the
Earl of Ormonde, the Queen's cousin : 'considering that this
man having now been Lord General of Munster now about two
years, there are at this instant a thousand traitors more than
there were the first day. Would God the service of Sir Humphrey
Gilbert might be rightly looked into, who, with the third part of
the garrison now in Ireland, ended a rebellion not much inferior
to this in two months ! Or would God his own behaviour were
such in peace as it did not make his good service forgotten and
hold him from the preferment he is worthy of !' We shall find
this become Ralegh's characteristic manner : the passion with
which he throws himself into the expression of his sentiments, the
asseveration, the readiness to swear and overswear himself.

Ralegh was anxious for some tangible reward for his services
and was pressing the Lord Deputy — Arthur, Lord Grey,
Spenser's Puritan hero — to confirm his possession of Barry
castle and island : 'I have, by great persuasion of the Commissioners [of whom himself was one], got leave to edify the same and
leave a ward therein. And if it shall please your honour to think
me worthy the keeping and custody thereof, I will at mine own
cost build it up again and defend it for her Majesty.'[2] That

---

[3] E. Edwards, *Life of Sir Walter Ralegh*, II. 9 foll.   [2] *Ibid.* 16 foll.

grand touch was also like him. So also is the contemptuous tone of his reference to the Lord Deputy in a well-known letter to Leicester, which implies that he entered public life as one of Leicester's followers. He felt himself now forgotten: 'I have spent some time here under the Deputy in such poor place and charge as — were it not for that I knew him to be one of yours — I would disdain it as much as to keep sheep'. It was an invitation to the old favourite to do better for his follower; he would shortly be in a position to do better for himself.

This arose directly from the stand he took on Irish affairs, and the advice he gave to Burghley and the Council, which showed that he had a mind of his own. He certainly had a strong point to put, an argument which has recurred often in the history of colonial conflicts. An English Lord Deputy at Dublin was apt to favour the complete subjugation and Anglicisation of the country; but this was so expensive as to tax the small resources of the English state. The home government, Elizabeth herself, were apt to wish that things would go on as they were, with the native princes ruling their septs — an indirect form of government at minimum expense. But this had broken down in Munster with Desmond's rebellion, and was to break down finally in Ulster with the great O'Neill's. Ralegh's point was that there was another alternative to subjugation — to win over the support of the lesser tribes and their chieftains, many of whom groaned under the exactions of the native princes and looked to the government. This suggested a way of cutting down the expense of maintaining English forces in Ireland. Such a position could not fail to recommend itself to Burghley, nor to the Queen when presented to her.

It was, however, in complete contradiction with the view held by the English government in Dublin, and its first consequence was to gain the ill-will of the Lord Deputy. Ralegh had been asked to submit a memorandum. Lord Grey protested, pointing out the contrast between 'the judgments of those which, with grounded experience and approved reason, look into the condition of things, and those which, upon no ground but seeming fancies and affecting credit with profit, frame "plots" upon impossibilities, for others to execute.'[1] It is true that Ralegh was always plausible, always full of projects and schemes; but the argument was going beyond the Lord Deputy, it was coming before the Council and the Queen.

---

[1] *Ibid.* 4-5.

The next consequence was that, in reward for his services, the government recommended that Ralegh should succeed to the command of another band as well as his own — that would mean doubling his poor captain's pay. To this Lord Grey replied that he had had no letter from the Queen 'which specifieth any such thing to me; and for mine own part, I must be plain: I neither like his carriage nor his company'.

But the argument was now before the Queen, and Ralegh would not need to go back a mere captain to Ireland.

Ralegh's appearance on the horizon of the Court was sufficiently striking. Aubrey tells us that 'he was a tall, handsome, and bold man : but his naeve was that he was damnable proud'.[1] He draws our attention to the extremely high, pale forehead, with the curious formation of the eyelid that must have added to the glitter of the eyes. Like all his family he had a light, sweet voice. But one cannot escape the impression of seriousness, even sadness, in the handsome face : nothing gay or lighthearted about him; high spirits certainly, but for the rest a temperament, when turned back upon itself, liable to the sombre and saturnine. One wonders whether he was not a Celt? — he had all the signs, even the stigmata : the acutely personal accent, the eloquence and lack of real humour, the intellectuality, the drama, and a certain vein of unreliability. He had not the fair hair and fresh complexion of his Devonshiremen, men like Drake or Grenville; he was pale and dark, an ivory complexion with shining wavy black hair. Aubrey tells us that his beard curled up naturally.

It was his intellectual gifts that completed the conquest of the Queen : the force and originality of his mind, the constant flow of ideas, his readiness or 'wit' as Elizabethans called it, allied to his natural eloquence and persuasiveness, the very ardour, that fascinated this remarkable woman, herself an intellectual, as much as his looks, his vigour and virility. After Leicester's marriage and settling down under the thumb of the forceful Lettice Knollys, the Queen needed a companion : who more suitable than this brilliant newcomer — who had, moreover, the cardinal virtue of being unmarried? It was the suddenness of the conquest that struck people and annoyed them so much, the elevation of someone completely out of the Court-circle. He had no real support, apart from the Queen's affection;

[1] Aubrey, II. 182-3.

he came to know bitterly what to expect from friends; he became the best-hated man in the country.[1]

To this he made no concessions, indeed there was that in his spirit that provoked it by his magnificence, retaliated upon it by his arrogance. He was notorious, even abroad, for the splendour of his clothes and jewels; we can see it still from his portraits, the pearl in his ear, the cloth of silver and satin, the capes of rich velvet sown with seed-pearls, the gems upon the long and slender fingers. Once, when people were expecting his fall, he emerged from Durham House to show them, clad in silver from top to toe. But, underneath all this, with a double dose of energy, he was a very hard-working man. As Aubrey wrote, 'a man so much immersed in action all along and in fabrication of his own fortunes (till his confinement in the Tower) could have but little time to study, but what he could spare in the morning. He was no slug; without doubt had a wonderful waking spirit, and great judgment to guide it.' He added that 'he studied most in his sea-voyages, where he carried always a trunk of books along with him and had nothing to divert him'.

At first Ralegh needed to go very carefully, watch his step, groom himself for the part. He took care to continue his education for companionship with the blue-stocking Queen. He had already gone back to his own old college to recruit someone to instruct him in mathematics and science — Thomas Hariot, who became a leading scientist of the age and shared Ralegh's good fortune and ill fortune alike.[2] Already he was known as a poet himself, and the story of his inner relations with the Queen would be told only in his poetry. He was careful to do good services with her on behalf of Burghley and Leicester, who would soon need to resort to him. He tried hard to restrain his temperament, to subject himself to the conditions of his new and unimagined rôle.

Here we are concerned only with the external evidences of his progress in favour and influence. But it is important to realise the underlying assumption that these rewards were in return for service to Queen and state. On her side she certainly attached a remarkably able man to the chariot of the state and got manful service out of him. It was probably Ralegh who persuaded her, against her better judgment, to permit Gilbert to go on his last voyage across the Atlantic. Ralegh contributed

---

[1] Cf. Anthony Bagot, an Essex follower, about this time: 'Sir Walter Ralegh he is the hated man of the world, in Court, city and country'. H.M.C. *App. Fourth Report*, 338.   [2] C. S. Emden, 18-19.

his own ship, the *Bark Ralegh*, to it, and it now fell to him to write: 'Brother, I have sent you a token from her Majesty, an anchor guided by a lady, as you see; and further, her Highness willed me to send you word that she wished you as great good-hap and safety to your ship as if herself were there in person. . . . Further, she commandeth that you leave your picture with me.'[1] Ralegh was writing from Richmond: 'your true brother'. When the Queen left Richmond for Greenwich in April, Ralegh riding by her side, it was he who reminded her of Dr. Dee waiting to be noticed.[2]

Such a personage needed providing for, and the lot fell first upon All Souls College to bestow upon him the beneficial leases extracted on behalf of the Queen.[3] This was mere chicken-feed. In May he was awarded the valuable patent for granting licences to sell wines throughout the country. This brought him in something like £1100 a year, an income at once larger than some peers had.[4] It involved him in a good deal of trouble and brought him much unpopularity, for it was a monopoly. For one thing it clashed with the privileges of the universities. On a second time of asking Cambridge received from him a letter beginning, 'I cannot a little marvel at your peremptory and proud manner of dealing. I was content to use all manner of courtesy towards you (in respect of my Lord Treasurer, my honourable good lord), but I perceive that my reasonable or rather too submiss dealing hath bred in you a proceeding insufferable.'[5] This was not the way to win the love of the dons. But there were ways of being more tactful with the great Lord Burghley, who was at this moment in trouble with his dreadful son in-law, the Earl of Oxford, and needed Ralegh's intercession with the Queen on his behalf. The Earl was a declared enemy of Ralegh's, but the latter did his best for him with the Queen; 'and the more to witness how desirous I am of your lordship's favour and good opinion, I am content for your sake to lay the serpent before the fire, as much as in me lieth, that, having recovered strength, myself may be most in danger of his poison and sting'.[6] The

---

[1] Edwards, II. 19.
[2] *The Private Diary of Dr. John Dee*, ed. J. O. Halliwell (Camden Soc.), 20.
[3] Edwards, II. 20.
[4] T. N. Brushfield, 'Ralegh Miscellanea', *Trans. Devon. Assocn.* 1909, 179 foll.
[5] Edwards, II. 28. Burghley was Chancellor of the university.
[6] *Ibid.* 22. An old courtier, Roger Manners, noticed that Ralegh was successful: when Oxford came into her presence all sins were forgiven and 'he may repair to the Court at his pleasure. Mr. Ralegh was a great means herein, whereat Pondus is angry that he could not do so much.' H.M.C. *Rutland MSS.* I. 150.

THE QUEEN AND RALEGH IN THE 1580'S

Lord Treasurer saw no reason to put any obstacle in the way of Ralegh's patent.

This monopoly was the foundation of his fortunes, and its term of years was twice extended — until the whole thing fell in with Ralegh's fall. To it was added next year, and in several more years, 1585, 1587, 1589, large and profitable grants of licences to export woollens.[1] Here Lord Burghley did think the profits excessive and that the rents to the Crown should be increased. All this gave Ralegh the resources he needed, both to support his exalted position and to perform the services he intended to the state. On Gilbert's death he at once took his place as leader of the attempts to plant colonies in America, and this spring of 1584 he sent out a vessel to reconnoitre a good site on the southern Virginia coast. His letters-patent came before Parliament for confirmation, to which he was elected as knight of the shire for Devon. He was at once called into the business of the House, and placed on committees; his own affair was committed to the care of Walsingham, Sir Philip Sidney, Sir Francis Drake, Sir Richard Grenville and others — what a committee![2]

In Ireland Ralegh's views were borne out, and his services at length handsomely rewarded. In 1582 the Lord Deputy was recalled, and the rebellion came to a miserable end with the death of Desmond at the hands of some Irish kerne. The princely earldom was not effectively revived; there was now room for the lesser clans and tribes to have more scope. After the rebellion vast tracts of depopulated and devastated lands were thrown open for settlement. Ralegh got a grant of 12,000 acres of the best in and around Cork and Waterford. With his usual energy he set about planting West Country tenants on his lands; his were better tilled and pastured than those of other grantees. His estates were administered from the former college at Youghal, where the tradition is that he introduced the potato — with its ultimate consequences for Irish history. A few years later he got from the see of Cashel the more defensible castle of Lismore, which he at once set about rebuilding to make his chief residence.

For his residence in London the Queen gave him the use of the principal part of Durham House — it was a large rambling house that belonged to the palatine see of Durham — on the site of the present Adelphi.[3] The ground floor was occupied by Sir Edward Darcy; the great hall rose with its high roof above

---

[1] Edwards, I. 62-3.   [2] D'Ewes, *Journal*, 339, 356.
[3] T. N. Brushfield, 'Raleghana, Part V', *Trans. Devon. Assocn.* 1903, 539 foll.

the river front where Ralegh ensconced himself. His study was in a turret high over the Thames, and 'had the prospect which is pleasant perhaps as any in the world' — so Aubrey thought — 'and which not only refreshes the eyesight but cheers the spirits and (to speak my mind) I believe enlarges an ingenious man's thoughts'.[1] Durham House was most convenient for Whitehall; just across Ivy Lane was Robert Cecil's house, in time to become Salisbury House. In addition, wherever the Court happened to be he had his lodgings; he was in clover.

In May 1584 he was robbed by a Welsh gentleman of some items that give us a true index to him: a jewel worth £80 (multiply), a hatband of pearls worth £30, five yards of white silk damask waiting to be made up.[2] In July he wrote a characteristic letter down to Devonshire. Where should he seat himself in the country, now that he had arrived at so much grandeur? Where but in his native-place of Hayes barton? He wrote to Mr. Duke, whose family had done so well out of the Dissolution, asking him to sell him the place. 'I am resolved, if I cannot entreat you, to build at Colaton [Ralegh]. But for the natural disposition I have to that place [Hayes], being born in that house, I had rather seat myself there than anywhere else.'[3] Mr. Duke thought otherwise; but for him we might have had something fine at Hayes.

All the same, the Queen had been in no hurry to make Ralegh a knight; she was chary of granting honours — they were very real in her time. On Twelfth day 1585, when the Court was at Greenwich, she at length knighted him.[4] This was but a prelude to the more important offices that followed that year, with which he achieved the position he was to occupy in the country for the rest of the reign. On the Earl of Bedford's death, Ralegh was in July made Lord Warden of the Stannaries; that office put him in control of the tin industry, the tinners and merchants of Devon and Cornwall. As such he was active in their interest in Parliament and outside; he drafted some of their regulations; they looked to him as their head. In September he was made Lord-Lieutenant of Cornwall, which put him at the apex of rule in that remote county, and Vice-Admiral for both Devon and Cornwall, which gave him coastal jurisdiction. In short he became the leading figure, so far as the West Country was concerned, close to the government. This meant busy ad-

---

[1] Aubrey, II. 183.   [2] Brushfield, 546.
[3] Edwards, II. 26.   [4] W. A. Shaw, *The Knights of England*, II. 83.

ministrative responsibilities, especially in regard to defence, supervising coastal preparations against invasion, levying and training forces as Armada-time drew near. It is fair to say that in all this work Ralegh performed his duties efficiently and without complaint. Hated in London, he became popular in the West Country; moreover, he made it a point of honour to look after the smaller folk.

This year, 1585, saw the most important of his colonial enterprises in its ultimate results, the planting of the first Roanoke colony. The Queen would not allow him to go on so dangerous a voyage himself; his cousin Grenville took his place. But the main burden of the preparations, the raising of the considerable resources necessary, fell upon Ralegh. No doubt he was kept busy in 1586 organising supplies for the colony, and getting into the saddle in his new employments. The war had opened with Leicester's assumption of command in the Netherlands; his acceptance of the governor-generalship precipitated a crisis in his relations with the Queen — she would have broken him if he had not given way.

The rumour was sped to Leicester that in this emergency, while he was upheld by Burghley and Walsingham, Ralegh did him ill offices. It was not true, and Ralegh asked to be allowed to take over the Queen's dispatches to contradict it. Instead she instructed Walsingham 'to signify unto your lordship, and to assure you upon her honour, that the gentleman hath done good offices for you, and that, in the time of her displeasure, he dealt as earnestly for you as any other in this world that professeth the most good will for your lordship. *This I write by her Majesty's command.*'[1] She was always having to defend Ralegh from back-biters. Ralegh took up pen for himself: 'your lordship doth well understand my affection towards Spain, and how I have consumed the best part of my fortune hating the tyrannous prosperity of that estate, and it were now strange and monstrous that I should become an enemy to my country and conscience'.[2] That was indeed a dominant theme in Ralegh's mind; it cost him his life at last. He asked Leicester to do him the justice of thinking of him as he found he deserved, good or bad — which was more than most people were willing to do. Having delivered himself of this, he was able to add a postscript: 'the Queen is on very good terms with you and, thanks be to God, well pacified; and you are again her "Sweet Robin"'.

---

[1] Edwards, I. 61-2. [2] *Ibid.* II. 33-4.

What a reversal it was for the ageing Leicester, companion of the Queen's youth, to have to accept assurance at the hand of his younger rival, his former follower! All the same, there was a difference between the Queen's relationship to Leicester and that to Ralegh. Ralegh occupied an inferior place; it is psychologically interesting that she had no affectionate nickname for him as she had for so many others in the circle around her. Leicester was her 'Sweet Robin', Burghley her 'Spirit', Hatton her 'Mutton' or 'Lids', Essex would be another 'Robin' — but Ralegh was always Ralegh or Sir Walter: there was something daunting about his personality, fascinating but contingently antipathetic.[1]

Nevertheless, in 1587 he was made Captain of the Queen's guard, in succession to Hatton, and as such responsible for her safety, a position of regular attendance which brought him into proximity to the maids-of-honour. Aubrey, commenting on 'the Queen's love to have all the servants of her Court proper men' (*i.e.* fine men), tells a story of Ralegh rejecting a gentleman's offer of his son for the guard. Ralegh would willingly have had the gentleman, but 'I put in no boys'. The father said, 'Boy, come in'. He was only eighteen, but was already taller than any of the guard and very handsome. So 'Sir Walter Ralegh swears him immediately, and ordered him to carry up the first dish at dinner; where the Queen beheld him with admiration, as if a beautiful young giant had stalked in with the service'.[2]

This year Ralegh got in reward the estates and goods of the idiotic Babington, who had ruined himself for love of Mary Stuart — and Mary too. It made a very handsome present. Hitherto Ralegh had no land of his own at all: he could not be called a landed gentleman. Now he became at one stroke the owner of three manors in Lincolnshire, a manor in Derbyshire, lands in Nottinghamshire, with all Babington's goods and furniture, forfeited by his treason, except for a curious clock reserved for the Queen. This property came very conveniently, and probably with intention, this year when Ralegh was burdened with the charges of setting forth the second Roanoke colony — the Lost Colony of American folklore and remembrance.

That summer there was a flare-up between young Essex,

---

[1] When Leicester came back finally from the Netherlands he resumed his old primacy in the Queen's affections; the rumour at Court was that because Ralegh had done him ill offices during his absence, he left suddenly for the West Country the day before the Earl came to Court. *Rutland MSS.* I. 234. This may not have been true; equally it may be an element in the mounting hostility of Leicester's stepson, Essex.   [2] Aubrey, II. 180.

aged nineteen, and the Queen on the subject of Ralegh. The Queen was on progress, and Essex's sister came to North Hall where the Queen was; she was not received, on account of her clandestine marriage with Perrot. Essex was enraged and complained that the reason for 'this disgrace both to me and my sister was only to please that knave Ralegh, for whose sake I saw she would both grieve me and my love. . . . From thence she came to speak of Ralegh; and it seemed she could not well endure anything to be spoken against him. And taking hold of one word, "disdain", she said there was no such cause why I should disdain him. This speech did trouble me so much that, as near as I could, I did describe unto her what he had been and what he was; and then I did let her know whether I had cause to disdain his competition of love, or whether I could have comfort to give myself over to the service of a mistress that was in awe of such a man.'[1] All this while Ralegh was standing on guard at the door, and the young man said everything he could think of against him that 'he might very well hear the worst that I spoke of himself. In the end, I saw she was resolved to defend him and to cross me.' Essex was convinced, quite unjustly, that the change in her attitude was owing to Ralegh and that she was trying hard to force him to be friends, 'which rather shall drive me to many other extremities'. In the end, it drove him to his death. But, meanwhile, it must have been hard for Ralegh to bear from this aristocratic stripling. Ralegh was worth ten of him any day; but it was the Earl who was the darling of the people.

Ralegh had more important things to think about. The foundering of the second Virginia colony meant a total loss and put a term to projects of empire for some years. And the Armada was on its way. Always interested in shipbuilding, Ralegh used his new-found wealth to build a splendid ship, the *Ark Ralegh*. In 1587 he handed her over to the Queen's navy, though she was not paid for, until May 1592 when she was offset for £5000 against his debts to the Crown. As the *Ark Royal* — first to bear that name so gallant in our own days — she was in time to take first place, as the Lord Admiral's flagship, in the front line against the Armada. Her quality won a tribute from him: 'I pray you tell her Majesty from me that her money was well given for the *Ark Ralegh*, for I think her the odd ship in the world for all conditions; and truly I think there can no great ship make me

---

[1] Devereux, *Lives and Letters*, I. 187-8.

change and go out of her'.[1] Ralegh's own smaller, but strongly-armed, *Roebuck*, seconded the *Revenge* in taking Don Pedro de Valdes's big *Rosario*, and brought her into Dartmouth. In the succeeding years she had an exciting record as a privateer. Both Sir John Gilbert and Adrian Gilbert had a small ship serving that month, the *Command* and the *Elizabeth*; while Carew Ralegh commanded the defence of Portland.

That spring Ralegh was a member of the important commission of experienced military men called in to advise the government on defence against invasion. His advice was listened to, and shortly he rode down to the West Country to put it into effect. He had the usual difficulty of reconciling conflicting interests even in face of imminent danger : the city of Exeter would not muster its levies along with the county forces.[2] Ralegh's position as Lord Warden of the Stannaries enabled him to levy the tinners, and he had no trouble from the county of Cornwall. In June he was able to report that in Cornwall there were 2000 special men in readiness under their captains — this was out of the much larger number of the general musters — with their wains and horses to convey them to any point in the area at a moment's notice.[3] He toured the coastal areas to oversee the defences, and was abreast with Portland when the Armada came up Channel. As the Armada moved into the straits of Dover, there was a rush of grand young men from Court down to the coast to take part in the final spectacle; even the unmilitary, though spirited, Robert Cecil dashed down so as not to miss St. Crispin's day.

When it was over Ralegh and Grenville were ordered to watch the western approaches with a small force in case of a return, and thence they passed into Ireland to look after their plantations. Grenville was renewing his earlier efforts there, but it was noticed that Ralegh had brought over more tenants on his lands than any other of the undertakers, most of whom did not carry out their obligations — or the Irish story would have been different.

Ralegh's preoccupations in Ireland prevented him from being a member of the Parliament which met in February 1589 to provide for the heavy expenses of the war. Arthur Throckmorton

---

[1] J. K. Laughton, ed., *The Defeat of the Spanish Armada* (Navy Records Soc.), I. 9, 85-6; II. 201-2.   [2] *v.* my *Tudor Cornwall*, 395-6.
[3] *Cal. S.P. Dom. 1581–90*, 496. In August he got a grant of the moiety of all penalties for offences against the statute of 7 Edward VI concerning the sale of wines. *Ibid.* 528. This would collect further unpopularity.

was elected member for Colchester, the only occasion when he served in Parliament — and perhaps that is a reflection on him.[1] He must have taken some interest in local affairs, for on 2 February 1589 he was sworn a free burgess. From the end of that year, when Ralegh was back in England, we have a letter, revealing of the jealousies with which he was surrounded at Court and the spirit with which he met them: unfortunately for himself, bitter and taunting, though it was understandable. Evidently his patience was wearing thin; there was a rumour of his losing favour with the Queen: at once all the snakes came out into the sun. To his cousin, Sir George Carew, he wrote: 'for my retreat from the Court, it was upon good cause to take order for my prize. If in Ireland they think I am not worth the respecting they shall much deceive themselves. I am in place to be believed not inferior to any man to pleasure or displeasure the greatest; and my opinion is so received and believed as I can anger the best of them. And therefore, if the Deputy be not as ready to stead me as I have been to defend him — be it as it may. When Sir William Fitzwilliam shall be in England, I take myself far his better by the honourable offices I hold, as also by that nearness to her Majesty which still I enjoy, and never more.'[2]

So far his favour held good; but what would happen to him were it withdrawn, still more if by his own offence?

The year 1590 was occupied with his duties at Court, in the West Country, his plantations in Ireland, and increasingly with the privateering activities of his ships at sea. The *Roebuck* was a strongly built and armed merchantman, constructed in accordance with his ideas.[3] He worked often in partnership with Alderman Watts, the city merchant most successfully invested in privateering. Ralegh was never so successful financially. Of the prizes he took in 1591, he commented, if he is to be believed, 'all which amounteth not to the increase of one for one, which is a small return'.[4] This was for the benefit of the Lord Treasurer, and then, with a recognisable turn of temper in the expressive phrase, 'we might have gotten more to have sent them a-fishing'.

The men of action were pushing for a more aggressive conduct of the war; and in 1591 a squadron was fitted out to lie in wait for the Spanish treasure-fleet off the Azores. Lord Thomas

---

[1] *Return of Members of Parliament*, I. 423.
[2] Edwards, II. 41-2. In that year 1589 he had received a licence to export 800 cloths in four years, a very profitable grant. *Cal. S.P. Dom. 1581-90*, 641.
[3] *English Privateering Voyages, 1588-95* (Hakluyt Soc.), ed. K. R. Andrews, 18-19, 97.　　　　　　　　　　　　　　　　　　[4] Edwards, II. 43.

Howard and Ralegh were to have joint command. For some reason, at the last moment he could not be spared — duties at Court and in the West Country, but more powerfully the solicitude of his sovereign mistress. So Grenville once more took his place and sailed on to win immortal renown in the Azores. Ralegh had a ship of his own with the expedition, the *Black Dog* — so we learn from a young Catholic serving on board her, who spent his time reading Dr. Sanders's book on the English Schism, and was fortified in his faith thereby, 'at the time Sir Richard Grenville was lost'.[1] That autumn Ralegh came before the public for the first time, though anonymously, as a writer of prose with his own immortal account of the last fight of the *Revenge*.

He went on pressing for an active prosecution of the war, with stronger squadrons in the Atlantic. For himself he wished for command of one with which to take revenge for the *Revenge*. It was his plans for such an expedition that bore fruit in the capture of the *Madre de Dios*, the richest capture of the war. Once more the Queen would not allow him to go so far way or on such a dangerous enterprise. He managed to wrest permission to go at all to accompany the fleet only so far as the coast of Spain, on condition that from there he returned. He was at this moment, the beginning of 1592, at the height of favour and influence — but he was still without a family home, or for that matter a family, in the country. Evidently he was thinking of it, if ever he were to found a family — and most Elizabethans had such dynastic ambitions.

This January the Queen provided him at last with a country seat: Sherborne Castle in the limestone-country of Dorset with that exquisite shallow valley with its pastures running south and east from it. What more convenient for his journeys and avocations between the Court and the West Country? Sir John Harington tells the contemporary story that as Ralegh was riding post between Plymouth and the Court, 'this Castle being right in the way, he cast such an eye upon it as Ahab did upon Naboth's vineyard, and once above the rest being talking of it, of the commodiousness of the place, and how easily it might be got from the bishopric, suddenly over and over came his horse, that his very face, which was then thought a very good face, ploughed up the earth where he fell'.[2] This was taken for an ill-omen, until Adrian Gilbert, who had the advantage of being an astro-

[1] *Salisbury MSS.* XII. 85.

[2] Sir John Harington, *Nugae Antiquae* (ed. 1779), I. 105-6.

RALEGH IN THE YEAR OF THE ARMADA

loger, construed it in terms not of a courtier but of a conqueror. Alas for Ralegh, the converse was true. However, it was too good for a bishop, and the Queen squeezed it out of the see of Salisbury for him; she made the bishop grant a 99-year lease to the Crown of his manors in and around Sherborne, and immediately sublet them to Ralegh.[1] Altogether it made a wonderful place for him to occupy, build on and improve, fit residence for the magnificent favourite.

But already the favourite's active mistress among the maids-of-honour at Court was far gone with child, and he had had to marry her secretly. No doubt he had planned to be away at sea, possibly to make some striking *coup*, when the news broke at Court. He had to return without accomplishing anything to offset his offence : the storm was just about to break over him.

[1] W. B. Wildman, *A Short History of Sherborne*, 170-1.

CHAPTER IX

THE QUEEN, RALEGH AND BESS

W E must now turn from the external story of Ralegh's career to the inner story of his relationship with the Queen, which is told only in his poetry. After all, Ralegh was the only man of genius among the men whom she delighted to favour; he was alone in being able to recommend himself in verse that had the principle of life in it, and indeed is still alive to us. In his own day his poetry was recognised for its force and power. After paying tribute to the Court poets, the critic Puttenham goes on to add, 'for ditty [*i.e.* song] and amorous ode I find Sir Walter Ralegh's vein most lofty, insolent and passionate'.[1] He belonged with the Court poets, 'who have written excellently well, as it would appear if their doings could be found out and made public with the rest'. It was, of course, beneath the dignity of courtiers to publish their verse like the professionals; all the same, Ralegh's poems were so much appreciated in their own day, circulated and repeated in so many manuscripts, that I do not credit the view that much of his poetry has been lost. I believe we have most of what he wrote, and the bulk of it is concerned with the Queen, or Cynthia.

It is curious that we should have had to wait till our own late day for the proper co-ordination of texts and their interpretation, with the careful techniques of modern scholarship; but at last we can put together much of the story.[2]

The first phase begins, as we should expect, rather externally with the poet moon-struck — remember that Cynthia was a name for the cold, chaste moon — with the glory of the sovereign lady who has deigned to take notice of him

> Those eyes which set my fancy on a fire,
> Those crispèd hairs which hold my heart in chains,

[1] George Puttenham, *The Arte of English Poesie* (Arber's English Reprints), 75, 77. The word 'insolent' here carries the double suggestion of 'unaccustomed' and 'powerful'.

[2] This is mainly owing to the work of Miss Agnes Latham in editing the Poems, and to Mr. Walter Oakeshott in giving them some chronological order. But in quoting them I modernise the spelling and punctuation.

> Those dainty hands which conquered my desire,
> That wit which of my thought doth hold the reins;
>
> Those eyes for clearness do the stars surpass,
> Those hairs obscure the brightness of the sun,
> Those hands more white than ever ivory was,
> That wit even to the skies hath glory won;
>
> O eyes that pierce our hearts without remorse,
> O hairs of right that wears a royal crown,
> O hands that conquer more than Caesar's force,
> O wit that turns huge kingdoms upside down.
>
> Then, love, be judge what heart may thee withstand:
> Such eyes, such hair, such wit, and such a hand.

That, with some poetic exaggeration, describes the situation, and the position that Elizabeth had fairly won for herself.

Now for her adoring subject and his relation to the deity; the poetry takes a more intimate, a more feeling tone, as always when it relates to himself:

> Wrong not, dear Empress of my heart,
>   The merit of true passion
> With thinking that he feels no smart
>   That sues for no compassion;
> Since, if my plaints serve not to prove
>   The conquest of your beauty,
> It comes not from defect of love
>   But from excess of duty.

The point could not be better put; but the poet chooses not to reveal his passion—

> For knowing that I sue to serve
>   A saint of such perfection
> As all desire but none deserve
>   A place in her affection . . .

Naturally that was what they were all after, for the streams of holy grace pouring from her meant manors, estates, power. The poet never mentions anything so coarse and terrestrial; it was, however, well understood by the deity, who once exclaimed against the 'insatiable cupidity of men'. (The word 'cupidity' has its connection with the god Cupid.) As for her grace, even kings have not won it:

> Sought by the world and hath the world disdained
> Is she, my heart, for whom thou dost endure,
> Unto whose grace, since kings have not obtained . . .

We may imagine what torments the ordinary mortal undergoes in aspiring to the mortal moon; yet, in all her changes and turns in her favour, she remains ever the same in her firmament.

> My thoughts are winged with hopes, my hopes with love,
> Mount, love, unto the Moon in clearest night,
> And say, as she doth in the heavens move,
> On earth so wanes and waxeth my delight.
>> And whisper this but softly in her ears,
>> Hope oft doth hang the head and trust shed tears.

The concluding couplet gives a pretty good hint.

> And you, my thoughts, that some mistrust do carry,
> If you mistrust my Mistress do you blame,
> Say, though you alter, yet you do not vary,
> As she doth change and yet remain the same.
>> Distrust doth enter hearts but not infect,
>> And love is sweetest seasoned with suspect.

That is to say, the insecurity of the situation, the precariousness of favour, gives an edge to it.

The next move is that the poet pretends to have been slain by his goddess.

> A secret murder hath been done of late:
> Unkindness found to be the bloody knife,
> And she that did the deed a dame of state,
> Fair, gracious, wise as any beareth life.

I find the sentiment of this poem exaggerated — though exaggeration was always true enough to Ralegh — artificial, unmoving. He is more moving to us when he exaggerates less:

> Wounded I am but dare not seek relief
> For this new stroke, unseen but not unfelt;
> No blood nor bruise is witness of my grief,
> But sighs and tears with which I mourn and melt.

This sounds convincing, as if he had been given some discountenance, some feline *coup de patte* to make him smart. We are coming to closer grips with the reality of the situation: there were ups and downs of favour; it was not all honey being a favourite. And that there were wounds in this strained and unnatural relationship we can read in such lines as these:

> These be the tyrants that in fetters tie
> Their wounded vassals, yet nor kill nor cure
> But glory in their lasting misery.

'Tyrants' refers not to Cynthia herself, of course, but to her perfections. When Ralegh came to review their relationship after the catastrophe to it, in the *Book of the Ocean* [*i.e.* Wa'ter] *to Cynthia*, he diagnosed,

> Such art to grieve, and after to make glad,
> Such fear in love, such love in majesty.

That, in fact, was the psychological situation. If we think there was an element of cruelty — we will not use the word 'sadism' — in Elizabeth's attitude, what wonder? The men could not bear it, but she was inured to it; she had had to bear it all along: she had been defrauded by life, by the circumstances of her position, of the natural fulfilment of her woman's nature. She had sacrificed that for the sake of her vocation of ruling; there had been no-one for her, and now she was conditioned to just this relationship. It was a way of keeping the men tethered, in order, with now and then a twitch on the rein to pull them up. On their side, it was not the normal love of man for woman, but of a worshipper for the deity — possession of whom meant 'the world, the power and the glory'. She knew that well enough, and that neither Ralegh nor Essex was in love with her for all they pretended. Her palace of illusion was, at heart, without any.

But time was getting on for Ralegh, even though for her it seemed to stand still; and in the increasing accents of disillusionment, we come closer to him.

> Feed still thyself, thou fondling, with belief,
> Go hunt thy hope that never took effect,
> Accuse the wrongs that oft have wrought thy grief,
> And reckon sure where reason would suspect.
>
> Dwell in the dreams of wish and vain desire,
> Pursue the faith that flies and seeks to new,
> Run after hopes that mock thee with retire,
> And look for love where liking never grew.

The closer his diagnosis comes to reality the more powerfully his poems speak to us, for he is turned back upon himself, and this is what ultimately moves him: not others, but himself.

> Restless desire, from my love that proceeded,
> Leave to be and seek your heaven by dying,
> Since you, O you!, your own hope have exceeded
> By too high flying.

And there is no insincerity or compliment in this reproach :

> And you careless of me that, without feeling,
> With dry eyes behold my tragedy smiling,
> Deck your proud triumphs with your poor slave's yielding.

Perhaps the relationship, worn by familiar contact with each other over the years, yet never satisfied, had begun to pall and they got on each other's nerves — as happened more openly and flagrantly with Elizabeth and Essex later. So far as Ralegh is concerned we have nothing to go on but the evidence of verse, and the rumours that came from Court. Both these indicate that there were ebbs and flows in his favour. In 1587, when the little Arabella Stuart was first brought to Court, her uncle reported that Ralegh 'is in wonderful declination, yet labours to underprop himself by my Lord Treasurer and his friends'.[1] He inferred from Ralegh's change from his former insolency to humility towards everyone — a pointer to his inner insecurity — that he would never rise again. Certainly there were plenty of people to hope so. In 1588 the intolerable young Essex challenged Ralegh to a duel, and the Council had to step in to prevent it. Next summer the delighted rumour was that Essex 'hath chased Master Ralegh from the Court and hath confined him into Ireland'.[2]

That summer in Ireland Ralegh visited Spenser at Kilcolman, who read him the first part of *The Faerie Queene*, while Ralegh returned with his Cynthia poems.[3] The results of this visit were important for literature. Ralegh was so much impressed with the poem that he took the poet back to Court with him and presented him to the Queen. Spenser's recognition as the laureate of the age was assured; the Queen gave him a pension to continue with his great poem, and Spenser wrote *Colin Clout's Come Home Again* describing his journey and the personages of the Court. From this we learn that there had been some trouble between Ralegh and the Queen, and Spenser presents us with his friend and patron's view of it.

> His song was all a lamentable lay
> Of great unkindness and of usage hard

[1] H.M.C. *App. Third Report*, 42.

[2] T. Birch, *Memoirs of the Reign of Queen Elizabeth*, I. 56.

[3] I should point out that Spenser's phrase, 'His song was all a lamentable lay', does not necessarily refer to one poem; it is a generalised reference to Ralegh's Cynthia poems as a whole. This amends A. C. Judson, *The Life of Edmund Spenser*, 146, and the discussion there.

> Of Cynthia, the Lady of the sea,
> Which from her presence faultless him debarred.

That is plain enough, and when we come to Book IV of *The Faerie Queene* we see, under the cloak of allegory, that the trouble was due to the attentions Ralegh was paying to some young woman.

Before we come to that, however, in Book III we are given a survey of Ralegh's relations with the Queen up to this point, as seen through his eyes; and this is revealing.[1] The form in which he represented the situation to Spenser is that which we have extracted from the Cynthia poems, but with the accent — in his disgrace — on the humility of his social station, from which the Queen had raised him up. There is the same story of his long struggle against his love for someone so far above him, and his inability to hold out against it. This was the way he put it to himself, his fantasy construction: it does not need a Freud to assure us that the struggle in reality was to make himself feel true love for the lady.

> Long while he strove in his courageous breast
> With reason due the passion to subdue . . .
> But when his mean estate he did review,
> He from such hardy boldness was restrained.

He reasoned with himself:

> But, foolish boy, what boots thy service base
> To her to whom the heavens do serve and sue?
> Thou, a mean squire of meek and lowly place;
> She, heavenly born and of celestial hue.

Long time he warred against the malady of his hopeless love, until he was quite overborne by it; conquered, rendered ill by unrequited desire. At this,

> She, gracious Lady, yet no pains did spare
> To do him ease, or do him remedy.
> Many restoratives of virtue rare,
> And costly cordials she did apply,
> To mitigate his stubborn malady.
> But that sweet cordial which can restore
> A love-sick heart she did to him envy:
> To him and to all th' unworthy world forlore
> She did envy that sovereign salve in secret store.

[1] Book III, Canto V, xli foll.

All this is plain enough too: the restoratives and costly cordials were the grants of woollen licences, the wine-licence monopoly, the offices and estates that made him rich; the sovereign salve for his pain — and this was the commonplace with all Elizabethan poets — was the last embrace denied him and all the world.

So at length he looked elsewhere, and this is referred to in the next Book, though here the Queen is Belphoebe.[1] She unfortunately came upon him consoling a young female who had been man-handled by a carl.

> There she him found by that new lovely mate,
> Who lay the whiles in swoon, full sadly set,
> From her fair eyes wiping the dewy wet
> Which softly stilled, and kissing them atween,
> And handling soft the hurts which she did get.

That was an awkward posture in which to be caught by the Queen:

> Which when she saw with sudden glancing eye,
> Her noble heart with sight thereof was filled
> With deep disdain and great indignity,
> That in her wrath she thought them both have thrilled
> With that self arrow which the Carl had killed;
> Yet held her wrathful hand from vengeance sore,
> But, drawing nigh, ere he her well beheld,
> 'Is this the faith?' she said — and said no more,
> But turned her face and fled away for evermore.

This was alarming enough, and though he followed after to make his explanations,

> He durst not nigh approach, but kept aloof,
> For dread of her displeasure's utmost proof;
> And evermore, when he did grace entreat,
> And framèd speeches fit for his behoof,
> Her mortal arrows she at him did threat,
> And forced him back with foul dishonour to retreat.

Thus the squire learnt, what many others had learned at the hands of the Tudors:

> That the displeasure of the mighty is
> Than death itself more dread and desperate.

Up to this point the interpretation is clear; but in the poem Spenser recovers Ralegh's favour with a charming episode which is much disputed.

[1] Book IV, Canto VII, xxxv to Canto VIII, xviii.

Of all the bounty which Belphoebe threw
On him whilst goodly grace she did him show,
Amongst the rest a jewel rich he found
That was a ruby of right perfect hue,
Shaped like a heart yet bleeding of the wound,
And with a little golden chain about it bound.

A dove — some think that this means Spenser himself — took the jewel back to Belphoebe and so effectually pleaded the squire's cause that he was restored to favour:

Which sorry words her mighty heart did mate
With mild regard to see his rueful plight,
That her inburning wrath she gan abate
And him received again to former favour's state.

As we know, Ralegh returned to Court from Ireland, bringing Spenser with him, who was well received and rewarded. But there must have been something seriously amiss between Ralegh and the Queen, some suspicion of misconduct, to account for all this in 1589.

We may now turn to two famous poems of Ralegh's, which seem to belong to just this time and tell us what he felt. The phrasing of the first — 'clean from sight of land', 'as in a country strange without companion' — makes me think that it was written on the way to, or in, Ireland.

Like truthless dreams so are my joys expired,
And past return are all my dandled days;
My love misled, and fancy quite retired,
Of all which past the sorrow only stays.

My lost delights now clean from sight of land
Have left me all alone in unknown ways;
My mind to woe, my life in fortune's hand:
Of all which past the sorrow only stays.

As in a country strange without companion
I only wail the wrong of death's delays,
Whose sweet spring spent, whose summer well nigh done:
Of all which past the sorrow only stays.

Whom care forewarns, ere age and winter cold
To haste me hence, to find my fortune's fold.

One notes the theme of increasing years, and this is still more explicit in Ralegh's re-working of the Walsingham ballad to apply to himself.

Such an one I did meet, good sir,
  Such an angelic face
Who like a queen, like a nymph did appear
  By her gait, by her grace.

She hath left me here all alone,
  All alone as unknown,
Who sometimes did me lead with herself
  And me loved as her own.

What's the cause that she leaves you alone
  And a new way doth take,
Who loved you once as her own,
  And her joy did you make?

I have loved her all my youth,
  But now, old as you see,
Love likes not the falling fruit
  From the withered tree.

The meaning of this is not far to seek. In 1590 Ralegh was thirty-six or seven — for an Elizabethan, on the threshold of middle age; he had given all his best years to his devotion to the Queen. Essex was only twenty-three. For the mortal moon time stood still.

But if Elizabeth was looking to someone younger, so was he. Bess Throckmorton was in this year twenty-five. This year saw the set-back Essex brought upon himself by secretly marrying Lady Sidney. So all appeared well enough between the Queen and Ralegh for the next year; though in fact it was not, for towards the end of June 1591 he gave her maid-of-honour a baby. Scandal began to circulate about them, which has also left its mark in *The Faerie Queene*: the episode of Serena and the Blatant Beast.[1] Serena was Ralegh's name for Bess, and Spenser took it from him. For Ralegh's thoughts about her, we may judge from a poem:

Nature that washed her hands in milk
  And had forgot to dry them,
Instead of earth took snow and silk
  At Love's request to try them,
If she a mistress could compose
To please Love's fancy out of those.

Her eyes he would should be of light,
  A violet breath and lips of jelly,

---

[1] Book VI, Canto VI, XII foll.

> Her hair not black nor overbright,
>   And of the softest down her belly;
> As for her inside he'd have it
> Only of wantonness and wit.

This betrays a very different spirit from the grave, tormented verses to his Sovereign mistress.

When scandal began to spot Serena's name, she took advice; and this, according to Spenser, is what she got:

> The best, said he, that I can you advise
> Is to avoid the occasion of the ill;
> For when the cause, whence evil doth arise,
> Removèd is, the effect surceaseth still.
> Abstain from pleasure and restrain your will,
> Subdue desire and bridle loose delight,
> Use scanted diet and forbear your fill,
> Shun secrecy and talk in open sight:
> So shall you soon repair your present evil plight.

But it was soon too late for this excellent advice, and from the other side Sir Walter was urging quite different measures:

> Now, Serena, be not coy,
> Since we freely may enjoy
> Sweet embraces, such delights
> As will shorten tedious nights . . .
> Nature her bounties did bestow
> On us that we might use them. And
> 'Tis coldness not to understand
> What she and youth and form persuade
> With opportunity that's made
> As we could wish it . . .

So they took their opportunity, though we need not suppose that the event fell out precisely as Aubrey tells us in a well-known story, which it is a pity to omit from his biography of Ralegh. 'He loved a wench well, and one time getting up one of the maids-of-honour up against a tree in a wood ('twas his first lady), who seemed at first boarding to be something fearful of her honour and modest, she cried, "Sweet Sir Walter, what do you me ask? Will you undo me? Nay, sweet Sir Walter! Sweet Sir Walter! Sir Walter!" At last, as the danger and the pleasure at the same time grew higher, she cried in the ecstasy, "Swisser Swatter, Swisser Swatter." She proved with child . . .' [1]

---

[1] Omitted from A. Clark's edn., it is printed in O. L. Dick's edn., 255-6.

We have seen that Sir Walter expected to be at sea on the *Madre de Dios* voyage when the lambs fell in the spring. But there were many months to get through before then, and here Arthur Throckmorton's Diary comes to our aid with exciting new information. Two days after he kissed the Queen's hand at Court on her Accession day, 17 November, he heard of his sister's marriage, and noted it down in French. It is hardly likely that Bess withheld the news for long from a brother with whom she was on the closest terms of affection. There are hardly any entries after this stunning piece of information, until the last day of the month, when Arthur had an interview with Sir Walter.[1]

In December Arthur quarrelled with Edward Darcy — a cousin who occupied the ground floor beneath Ralegh's apartments at Durham House — and was before the Lord Chamberlain about the matter. On Christmas eve he bought an expensive waistcoat, costing £9, for the Queen, and on New Year's eve two ruffs for her for £5. The family would need all the consideration that could be built up in that quarter. In January Throckmorton was watching the portents carefully: on the 13th, 'the white hen laid an egg at night in P.' [Pisces?]; 14th, 'the dun hen laid an egg in S. [Scorpio?] at night'; 16th, 'the blue hen in :/: laid an egg at night'. On the 15th the Earl of Essex returned from France to Court. Perhaps all these might have some relevance to the forthcoming event?

Meanwhile Ralegh was at Chatham toiling hard to get to sea in time. On 24 February Throckmorton sent an urgent letter to Ralegh at Chatham, and four days later 'my sister came hither to lie here', *i.e.* at Mile End. From Chatham, 10 March, Ralegh wrote Sir Robert Cecil a letter in which we now know he was lying desperately: 'I mean not to come away, as they say I will, for fear of a marriage, and I know not what. If any such thing were, I would have imparted it unto yourself before any man living; and, therefore, I pray believe it not, and I beseech you to suppress, what you can, any such malicious report. For, I protest before God, there is none on the face of the earth that I would be fastened unto.'[2]

For the next month Arthur made scarcely an entry in his Diary — he must have had plenty to think about and attend to — until 29 March: 'my sister was delivered of a boy between 2 and 3 in the afternoon. I writ to Sir Walter Ralegh, and sent Dick the footman to whom I gave him 10s.' Again, only one

---

[1] Throckmorton had difficulty in settling upon a spelling of Ralegh's name: he usually spells it Raelly.　　　　　　　　　　　　　　[2] Edwards, II. 46.

Fryday: 19: Le souer que le sauoy tomonyoge sema tour

Thursday: 25: I sent my letter to Syr walter Rawly to Chattam by Robert /

Munday: 28: my syster came hither to lye here: /

Tusday: 29: my sister was delyuered of a boye betwene 2: and 3: in the afternowne / J wryte to Syr walter Raylsy, and sent Dycke the footeman to whom J gate hym — 10 li: /

Wensday 10: Damerei Raely was baptyzed by Robert Searle & SEEEXES and Sr Throkemorton and frma throckemorton /

Thursday 27: my syster returned to the courte and the Nursse went to Enfilde

Satterday 6 Syr walter Rasly set hym selfe under sayle at faulmouth towardes the Indias

Brownne and Syr George Cathours came to bryng me seale the wrytynges betwene Syr W: Rasly and vs /

Satterday 20:

~~Munday 21:~~

Sunday: 21: the Nursse and the Chylde came hether /

Syndar 28: the hijd & and the Nurse vent to Durcashen howsse

Munday 29:

Twesday 30: Syr W: Rasly cams to Dytton:

Wensday 31: Syr w: Rasly was committed to Syr R: systridet

Iuns 30: 1592:

Thursday 1

Fryday: 2 J was at Durcan howsse with Syr W: Rasly

Saterday 3 my syster was conueyd to me wissuelfon Satyn

Thursday 14 J sent a letter to Syr R: Cicell:

Fryday: 15: Syr: water Rasly was delyuered out of the Tower

Fryday 22: my syster was delyuered out of the tower

entry before the child's christening, and by what an unexpected, dangerous godfather! Monday, 10 April: 'Damerei Ralegh was baptized by Robert, Earl of Essex and Arthur Throckmorton and Anna Throckmorton'. On 25 April, 'I writ to Sir R. Cecil'. Two days later, 'my sister returned to the Court, and the child went to Enfield'. That is to say, the child was put out to nurse, probably with the Middlemore relations, since they lived at Enfield; Lady Ralegh went back to wait on the Queen as maid-of-honour. This was equivalent to an act of perjury, putting an affront on the Queen, whom she was sworn by oath to serve faithfully, at the least a piece of brazen effrontery: it was for this that she was never forgiven.[1]

On 6 May, 'Sir Walter Ralegh set himself under sail at Falmouth towards the Indies'. 11 May, 'I was with Hunsdon, Lord Chamberlain'. Ralegh had been permitted to see his voyage off, for which he had made all the preparations and in which he was the chief investor with the Queen, only so far as the coast of Spain; and 16 May, 'Browne came from Sir Walter Ralegh hither', Arthur added that Ralegh had arrived back at Plymouth. Now there were the expenses of the childbirth: no doctor is mentioned, only the nurse. 19 May, 'paid the nurse 14 weeks' wages come Monday next, 28s. Browne and Sir George Carew came to have me seal the writings between Sir W. Ralegh and Eliz.' This would be, *ex posto facto*, the marriage settlement. But with all these people in the know it was impossible but that the news should come to the Queen's ear, though, living in her state of splendid isolation, she would not be the first to hear. 21 May, 'the nurse and the child came hither'. Three days later, 'my Lord Chamberlain's warrant came for me and my wife. My wife's answer was sent back.' 28 May, 'the child and the nurse went to Durham House' — no doubt Ralegh was anxious to see his offspring, but here was more publicity. Two days later he came to Ditton, and next day was committed to Sir Robert Cecil's custody.

This was a hardly hostile measure as yet, and on 2 June he was back at Durham House, where Throckmorton visited him. Next day, 'my sister was committed to Mr. Vice-Chamberlain' (*i.e.* Sir Thomas Heneage). The day after, the Lord Chamberlain

---

[1] This story receives external corroboration from a Chancery case years afterwards when Adrian Gilbert claimed that he had 'spent at Mile End and about London when the Lady Ralegh was first delivered of a child, and when most of Sir Walter's friends forsook him, being requested by the said Sir Walter Ralegh to visit her'. C. Monro, *Acta Cancellariae*, 180.

sent a pursuivant for Arthur, who thereupon set off for Paulerspury. He came back at the end of the week bringing brother
William with him, and reported to the Vice-Chamberlain. Still
the blow did not fall — perhaps the Queen was awaiting news
of the voyage, or sifting the evidences of the offence, making
up her mind what to do. Ralegh was sufficiently unaware of
the severity of the impending blow to be writing the Cecils,
complaining of the Deputy's treatment of his interests in Ireland :
'I wrote unto your father how I am dealt withal by the Deputy,
to whom my disgraces have been highly commended.'[1] When
his warning of further rebellion there was read by the Queen,
'she made a scorn at my conceit'. She had no further use for
his advice now; she had found him out. 'It is a sign how my
disgraces have passed the seas, and have been highly commended
to that wise governor, who hath used me accordingly. So I
leave to trouble you at this time, being become like a fish cast
on dry land, gasping for breath, with lame legs and lamer lungs.
Yours, for the little while I shall desire to do you service.' This
to the friend to whom he had lied desperately so shortly before.

It is clear that Ralegh was trying to brazen it out, and that
he had no idea how severely he would be made to pay for his
offence. The rumours of his disgrace were spreading among his
delighted enemies. At the end of July, Sir Edward Stafford
wrote Anthony Bacon from Court : 'if you have anything to do
with Sir Walter Ralegh, or any love to make to Mistress Throckmorton, at the Tower tomorrow you may speak with them; if
the countermand come not tonight, as some think will not be,
and particularly he that hath charge to send them thither'.[2] The
Queen had held her hand for a long spell before striking; what
settled the fate of the guilty couple was the utter absence of any
expression of contrition, apology or regret. If they had thrown
themselves on her mercy, confessing their fault and begging
forgiveness, they would have been treated more generously,
might even have hoped for some measure of reinstatement.[3] But
Ralegh's conduct had shown him in a bad light; they were a
couple with a front of brass, and she would teach them. They
would go to the Tower, and there they were dispatched : Monday, 7 August : 'ma sœur s'en alla à la tour, et Sir W. Ralegh'.

Finding himself within those walls, he had leisure to reflect
on what he had lost. The Queen was leaving on her summer

[1] Edwards, II. 48, 50-1.   [2] T. Birch, *op. cit.* I. 79.
[3] Cf. Sir John Neale, 'Submission and apology were the essential way to pardon
in those days'. *Elizabeth I and her Parliaments, 1584–1601*, 255.

progress; Ralegh took the opportunity of dispatching some fragment of her business that still floated around him to write to Cecil, with an eye on the offended deity. 'My heart was never broken till this day that I hear the Queen goes away so far off — whom I have followed so many years with so great love and desire, in so many journeys, and am now left behind her in a dark prison all alone.' One hears the reverberation of the phrase and sentiment from his poems. 'While she was yet near at hand, that I might hear of her once in two or three days, my sorrows were the less; but even now my heart is cast into the depth of all misery. I that was wont to behold her riding like Alexander, hunting like Diana, walking like Venus, the gentle wind blowing her fair hair about her pure cheeks like a nymph; sometime sitting in the shade like a goddess, sometime singing like an angel, sometime playing like Orpheus.' (Though accomplished on the virginals, Elizabeth's voice was shrill and harsh.) He launches into the rhetoric of self-pity, a subject that always inspired him. 'Behold the sorrow of this world! Once amiss hath bereaved me of all.' And a great deal to the same effect. 'She is gone in whom I trusted, and of me hath not one thought of mercy, nor any respect of that that was. . . . Yours, not worthy any name or title.' [1]

Clever little Cecil must have laughed when he received this missive; for, of course, Ralegh was playing a part, for the benefit of the Queen, before the mirror of himself. This was what his enemies meant when they called him a 'hypocrite'; for he was one in the literal sense, an actor playing a part. There is no evidence that Cecil showed the letter to the Queen, and it is unlikely. He now had Ralegh where he wanted him, dependent on his protection. With Essex an irreconcilable enemy, Cecil would now exert himself to do what he could for Ralegh, within limits, keeping him in a subordinate capacity to himself. That became the future pattern in his mind, and it would have been well for Ralegh if he had accommodated himself to it. Straining to fling free, to carve out a line for himself, giving way to resentment and ill-conceived ambition, at a far worse juncture in the future — the accession of a personal enemy to the throne in James I — Ralegh was to endanger, and ultimately lose, his life.

Having lost so much and put more in jeopardy, what had he gained? — Bess Throckmorton.

We can hear her voice from the Tower, in much better spirits, for we have a letter from her in her inimitable phonetic spelling.

[1] Edwards, II. 51-2.

'I am dayly put in hope of my delivery I assur you treuly I never desiared nor never wolde desiar my lebbarti with out the good likeking ne advising of Sur W. R.: hit tis not this in prisonment if I bought hit with my life that shulde make me thinkehit long if hit shuld doo him harme to speke of my deliverey: but Sir R. S. [Cecil] was somwhat deseved in his Jugment in that and hit may be hee findeth his eror: I pray you tell your ladi I reseeved heer kind lettar from Cubham [Cobham]: when wee mit wee will talke of hit: the towar standeth just in the way to Kent from Copt Hall: and who knooeth what will be com of me when I am out: the plage is gretly sesid and ever hath bin cliar heer a bout: and wee ar trew with in ourselfes I can asur you. Towar, ever asureedly yours in frinshep. E.R.'[1]

It was something to be able to write E. R., and not E. T. Not a word of regret or apology for the way she had treated her mistress, the breach of faith in her sworn service, the scandal to decorum around the Queen. Of the two women, this one may be said to have won. By risking everything she had got what she wanted — what was not on the horizon for her: marriage, her man tied to her for good, and what a man! — the man the Queen had chosen for herself, her creation. 'We are true within ourselves': it is to be hoped so, for they would have a great deal to go through together before all was done.

Ralegh was in the Tower for only five weeks when he had to be let out on the urgent business of saving the spoils of the *Madre de Dios* for the Crown. Bess was not let out until the end of the year, her offence being the greater, her utility the less. During those weeks Ralegh embarked on the long poem in which he intended to tell the story of his relations with the Queen: the *Book of the Ocean to Cynthia* about which there has been so much confusion. It would seem that he had the grandiose idea in mind of a poem in twelve books, one perhaps for each year of the association — a kind of parallel to Spenser's *Faerie Queene*, only, Ralegh being Ralegh, the poem would be intensely auto-biographical.

> Twelve years entire I wasted in this war,
> Twelve years of my most happy younger days;
> But I in them, and they now wasted are,
> Of all which past the sorrow only stays.

One notices that, working fast, with his usual impatience, Ralegh takes up this and other phrases from earlier poems in his mind:

[1] H.M.C. *Finch MSS.* I. 33-4.

QUEEN ELIZABETH, *c.* 1592

it became rather a habit with him when in prison, and it is understandable. It is natural, too, that he should begin with the most recent phase, so burned in upon his mind :

> To seek new worlds for gold, for praise, for glory,
> To try desire, to try love severed far,
> When I was gone, she sent her memory
> More strong than were ten thousand ships of war,
>
> To call me back, to leave great honour's thought,
> To leave my friends, my fortune, my attempt,
> To leave the purpose I so long had sought
> And hold both cares and comforts in contempt.

With this plan in view he wrote down rapidly and in unfinished form what would make the contents of the eleventh book, with a fragmentary beginning of a concluding twelfth, and a sonnet introductory to the whole.

And he wrote no more — for the best possible reasons : after little more than a month he was sent down to the West Country to 'toil terribly' over the indescribable confusion of the great carrack's cargo, when he came back to London it occupied him up to the end of the year settling the affairs of the voyage. Then Bess was let out of the Tower to join him and he had to set up a home for her. No further time for poetry, and in fact he wrote little in the years to come : married life occupied him and his affairs, long imprisonment ; he had lost the main inspiration of his verse, the complex, tortured relationship with the Queen.

> Out of that mass of miracles my Muse
> Gathered those flowers to her pure senses pleasing,
> Out of her eyes (the store of joys) did choose
> Equal delights, my sorrow's counterpoising.
>
> Her regal looks my rigorous sighs suppressed,
> Small drops of joy sweetened great worlds of woes;
> One gladsome day a thousand cares redressed —
> Whom Love defends what fortune overthrows?
>
> When she did well, what did there else amiss ?
> When she did ill, what empires could have pleased ?
> No other power effecting woe or bliss,
> She gave, she took, she wounded, she appeased.

The poem returns again and again to the image of the woman who had so long occupied his mind, if not truly his heart ; and nowhere, naturally, do we get a more penetrating view of what there was at the centre of her nature:

> A vestal fire that burns but never wasteth,
> That loseth naught by giving life to all,
> That endless shines eachwhere, and endless lasteth,
> Blossoms of pride that can nor fade nor fall.

Yet Ralegh, too, had no illusion when it came to the point:

> So hath perfection, which begat her mind,
> Added thereto a change of fantasy
> And left her the affections of her kind,
> Yet free from every evil but cruelty.

He did not appreciate the fact that, if she was cruel, it was a necessity of her condition, both private and public. However, his not hers was the responsibility for the overthrow.

> One hour diverts, one instant overthrows,
> For which our lives, for which our fortunes thrall.

> So many years those joys have dearly bought,
> Of which when our fond hopes do most assure,
> All is dissolved, our labours come to naught,
> Nor any more thereof then doth endure.

And so he came to where he found himself: the Tower.

> Despair bolts up my doors, and I alone
> Speak to dead walls, but those hear not my moan.

Meanwhile, the voyage he had planned made a most lucrative capture. Off the Azores his ships, with the Earl of Cumberland's that joined in for the kill, had taken the big East Indian carrack, *Madre de Dios*, with the richest booty: an immense cargo of pepper, spices, drugs; silks, calicoes, damasks; porcelain, pearl, musk, amber; besides gems and specie on board. Some spoil was made of her at her taking, and more when she was brought into Dartmouth on 7 September.[1] Only Ralegh had the information as to the respective shares of the adventurers, the proper claims of the mariners, of individuals, the dues to the Crown. It was indispensable that he should be called in, and Sir George Carew was sent to him 'to know in particular how her Majesty might be profited'. He replied, in perhaps unwelcome

---

[1] I hope to deal in greater detail with this affair in an article on 'The Spoils of the *Madre de Dios*'.

detail, showing that her Majesty's share amounted to only one-tenth, some £20,000. Then, with some distrust, 'and I know her Majesty will not take the right of her subjects from them, contrary to her hand and seal'. He added, 'and if her Majesty cannot beat me from my affection, I hope her sweet nature will think it no conquest to afflict me. Whatever her will shall be, I shall willingly obey. . . . From this unsavoury dungeon.'[1] The accents are alive with doubt.

For the Queen's service he was released 15 September: 'I hope it shall be profitable to her Majesty, and a quietness and satisfaction to the rest'. On his way down he wrote to the Lord Treasurer and Lord Admiral, with familiar exaggeration, 'if I meet any of them coming up, if it be upon the wildest heath in all the way, I mean to strip them as naked as ever they were born, for it is infinite that her Majesty hath been robbed and that of the most rare things'. Such was the disorder and flouting of authority in the West Country ports that Cecil himself was sent down to exercise the full authority of the government on the spot. He reported to Burghley that on the roads between Exeter, Dartmouth and Plymouth, 'I could well smell them almost, such hath been the spoils of amber and musk among them'.[2] Ralegh rode down swiftly after Cecil, still in charge of his keeper. Cecil reported the welcome he received from his crews, the shouts of joy from all the mariners. But 'his heart is broken, for he is very extremely pensive, longer than he is busied, in which he can toil terribly; but if you did hear his rage at the spoils . . . you would laugh as I do, which I cannot choose'. This gives one some insight into the attitude of the subtler Cecil towards the more obvious Ralegh, with his manic-depressive temperament. Sir John Gilbert wept to see his brother; but when friends congratulated him on his liberty, he kept saying, 'No, I am still the Queen of England's poor captive'. This was the part he was playing now; Cecil was anxious lest it diminish his prestige with the sailors, 'which, I do voice to you, before God, is greater than I thought for. I do grace him as much as I may, for I find him marvellous greedy to do anything to recover the conceit of his brutish offence.' These phrases discover no real liking for Ralegh in that cool Cecilian heart; nor is this surprising.

Together they worked hard to get things in order, to lay their hands on as much of the spoil as possible, for the benefit

---

[1] Edwards, II. 67-8, 69, 70-1.   [2] S.P. 12/243, 16, 17.

of the investors and of the Crown. They backed each other up on the spot; they reported well of each other — Cecil with ironical discretion, Ralegh with implausible exaggeration — to government. Ralegh wrote flatteringly to Lord Burghley, 'I dare give the Queen £10,000 sterling for that which is gained by Sir Robert Cecil's coming down : which, I protest before the living God, I speak of truth, without all affection or partiality, for (God is my judge) he hath more rifled my ship than all the rest'.[1]

When the accounts were made out and the terms of the share-out fixed at the end of the year, Ralegh found bitter reason to complain. The Earl of Cumberland, whose ships had taken part only at the last moment, was awarded a profit of £17,000 upon an adventure of £19,000. The City merchants, who had been made to subscribe £6000 by the Queen, received from her £12,000. Ralegh and his associates, who had invested £34,000 in all, were awarded a profit of only £2000, and that was not a real profit, for it made no allowance for the ships employed. Apart from the loss to him financially, it was a blow to his credit with his supporters. He was not the one to refrain from repining : 'the Earl of Cumberland is allowed £36,000, and his account came but to £19,000 ; so as he hath £17,000 who adventured for himself; and we that served the Queen, and assisted her service, have not our own again. Besides, I gave my ship's sails and cables to furnish the carrack and bring her home, or else she had perished. My ship first boarded her and only [*i.e.* alone] stayed with her ; and brought her into harbour, or else she had also perished upon Scilly. . . . I was the cause that all this came to the Queen, and that the King of Spain spent £300,000 the last year; and I lost in the last year in the voyage of my Lord Thomas Howard £1600. . . . And whereas the City only disbursed £6000 and have £12,000 again, I that adventured all my estate, lose of my principal and they have double. I took all the care and pains, carried the ships from hence to Falmouth, and from thence to the north cape of Spain ; and they only sat still and did but disburse £6000 out of the common store, for which double is given to them and less than mine own to me ; and to the Earl of Cumberland £17,000 profit, who adventured for himself, and I for the Queen.'[2]

There was an easy answer : 'all my estate', everything he had, came from the Queen. But no reply ever came ; the silence

---

[1] Edwards, II. 72.   [2] *Ibid.* 76-8.

was unbroken, no notice taken. It was more oppressive than any reply. He was being made to pay for his preferences. On Friday, 22 December, we learn from Throckmorton, 'my sister was delivered out of the Tower'. There was a new life to make.

CHAPTER X

THE DISTRACTIONS OF DISGRACE

I T can hardly be said that Elizabeth's treatment of Ralegh was vindictive; he was debarred from her presence, and that meant not exercising his office as Captain of the Guard. But he was left in possession of his important public offices in the West Country: too useful a servant of the state to forgo his services.

Hitherto, personal attendance on the Queen or other preoccupations had prevented him from taking much part in Parliament; but with the Parliament that met in February 1593 he was free to take a more active rôle, and show the House of Commons of what calibre he was. It was a mark of his disgrace that he was not returned as a knight of the shire for Devon, as before, but as member for the inconspicuous little borough of Mitchell — no more than a village with few electors.[1] He made up for this by making himself one of the most conspicuous speakers to the fore in this Parliament.

Parliament had been called because there was an urgent need for more money, with the extension of the war — the need to subsidise Henri IV, armies in the Netherlands and now in France, besides the war at sea. A new generation was coming up, personified by the militant Essex, always in favour of the aggressive carrying on of the war against Spain. Ralegh was with him over this — indeed, a hatred of Spain and all her works was a constant theme.

It is not my purpose to go in any detail into Ralegh's public career, except as a framework to his private and family life, and in so far as it throws light on the nature of the man I am pursuing. But his speeches in the House reveal the man. We may notice in passing that he was placed on a large number of committees, and so was very active in the varied business that came before the House. When it came to increasing taxation for the conduct of the war, Ralegh spoke up for the government case, 'not only, as he protested, to please the Queen, to whom he was infinitely

---

[1] *Return of M.P.s*, I. 427.

bound above his deserts, but for the necessity he both saw and knew. He very well discovered the great strength of the King of Spain, and to show his mightiness he told how he possessed all the world.'[1] It was true that the war was coming closer to our shores, with the Spanish occupation of ports in Brittany at the western approaches to the Channel; and Ralegh was responsible for the exposed front-line of our defences. On this issue he always showed himself too hot-headed a protagonist; his hatred of Spain went to his head; he had not the cool assessment of probabilities and dangers of those political heads, the Queen and Cecil. Nor had Essex. Ralegh gave an alarmist account of the strategic situation with Spanish encroachments all round. He considered 'the time is now more dangerous than it was in '88; for then the Spaniard which came from Spain was to pass dangerous seas, and had no place of retreat or relief. . . . But now he hath in Brittany great store of shipping, a landing place in Scotland', etc. This would not be grateful to King James's ear. Though there was some truth in Ralegh's view of the situation, it took no account of the growing weakness on the other side. He was never one for seeing what went on the other side of the hill.

When it came to the apportionment of the burden of taxation Ralegh showed himself, as he consistently was later, sympathetic to the poorest taxpayer. He was in favour of the three subsidies asked for by the government, but 'in them the three pound men to be spared, and the sum which came from them to be levied upon those of ten pound and upwards'.[2] In regard to procedure, there was an unexpected reversal of rôles with Cecil, usually so prudent and persuasive, and Ralegh had a marked success. The House was touchy about a conference with the Lords involving the subject of finance, thereby trenching on their own prerogative; and Robert Cecil provoked the House by an ill-tempered speech. Now it was Ralegh who played the part of the moderate, suggesting that the confusion was due to a misunderstanding, and that the proposal was for a general conference with the Lords and not naming a subsidy. This was greeted by the House with acclaim, and assented to 'by them all without any negative voice'. Evidently Ralegh was an effective House of Commons man, regarded with respect; and this was important for the tradition that came down with regard to him, helped to bring about the change in public opinion in his

---

[1] Sir Simonds D'Ewes, *Journal* (ed. 1693), 484, 493.   [2] *Ibid.* 488, 492.

favour during his long imprisonment and handed him on to posterity as a commonwealth man.

In regard to the conduct of the war Ralegh favoured an open declaration; this would put privateering on an avowed basis, when the West Country — so he averred from his own knowledge — had had £44,000 taken from them at sea, since the Parliament began.[1] As it was, 'he knew many that held it not lawful in conscience to take from the Spaniards. . . . If it might be lawful and open war, there would be more voluntary hands to fight against the Spaniard than the Queen should stand in need of to send to sea.'[2]

On the subject of relief for alien retailers of foreign goods in this country, Ralegh was just as aggressive, a thorough-going advocate of economic nationalism. The merchants in view were Dutch. 'Whereas it is pretended that for strangers it is against charity, against honour, against profit to expel them, in my opinion it is no matter of charity to relieve them. . . . The nature of the Dutchman is to fly to no man but for his profit, and they will obey no man long. . . . The Dutchman by his policy hath gotten trading with all the world into his hands. . . . They are the people that maintain the King of Spain in his greatness. Were it not for them, he were never able to make out such armies and navies by sea; it cost her Majesty £160,000 a year the maintaining of these countries, and yet for all this they arm her enemies against her.'[3] How this looks forward to the Dutch trade-wars of the next century!

Over religion Ralegh was more tolerant, as he had need to be considering the heterodoxy of his own opinions. With Archbishop Whitgift in control, strongly backed by the Queen, the Church was at last reducing the Puritans (temporarily) to order, and there was a question of strengthening the laws against sectaries. Ralegh was opposed: for 'what danger may grow to ourselves if this law pass, it were fit to be considered. For it is to be feared that men not guilty will be included in it. And the law is hard that taketh life and sendeth into banishment, where men's intentions shall be judged by a jury and they shall be judges what another means.'[4] He would shortly have experience of the dangers of popular misinterpretation of an intellectual position himself.

[1] I have adopted this figure from Sir John Neale, *Elizabeth I and her Parliaments, 1584–1601*, 308, since D'Ewes's figure, £440,000, is impossible and must be a misprint. [2] D'Ewes, 478.
[3] *Ibid.* 508-9. £16,000 is an impossibly low figure and must be another misprint: £160,000 would be nearer. [4] *Ibid.* 517.

Enough of his speechifying: we see that it coheres with our picture of him.

Parliament was dissolved 10 April 1593, and Ralegh went west to the home that he was making at Sherborne, to country occupations, his meditations and bitter girding at his lot. The moment he had got possession of Sherborne he set to work to repair the old castle and make it livable. Before his tumble from his pinnacle he appointed John Mere keeper of it, overseer of the woods, receiver of his rents.[1] On going down Ralegh first went to Bath for a cure, which did him no good, and then went on to Sherborne to pour out his complaints to Cecil, now the chief repository of his grievances and hope of his return.

Of his advice with regard to the situation in Ireland, 'her Majesty shall find it remembered to herself not long since, but the Trojan soothsayer cast his spear against the wooden horse, but not believed'.[2] He pressed his unsolicited advice — it was good advice, too — to win over the Earl of Argyle in Scotland to help control Ulster, 'but for me to speak of the one or the other, I know that my labours are prejudicate, and I cannot hereafter deserve either thanks or acceptance'. He had been driven to recall his settlers for want of being allowed to raise two or three bands of English: 'the loss shall not be alone to me' — there too he was borne out by subsequent history — 'however I am tumbled down the hill by every practice'. 'Sir, these poor countries yield no news. I hear of a frigate that taketh up fishermen for pilots in the West. I am myself here at Sherborne, in my fortune's fold. Wherever I be, and while I am, you shall command me.' He did not hold to this promise, nor many such assurances. However — 'I think I shall need your further favour for the little park, for law and conscience is not sufficient in these days to uphold me. Every fool knoweth that hatreds are the cinders of affection, and therefore to make me a sacrifice shall be thanksworthy.' There was his proud unyielding spirit, nakedly expressed; it was not in this mood that he would win his way back to Court.

He ended his letter casually enough, 'I pray remember my duty to my Lord Admiral and to your father, if it please you'. The next thing was that he was in need of Burghley's aid. In June Ralegh was back in London, pressing for a reversal of the embargo placed on the export of pipestaves from Munster to Madeira and the Canaries for wine-casks. A large number of

---

[1] *Cal. S.P. Dom. 1591–4*, 263. Mere had previously been the bishop's reeve there.
[2] Edwards, II. 78-80.

boards had already been cut and would rot on the ground;
'besides we must be forced to draw home a great number of able
men from thence . . . which will prove to be a great weakening
of the province of Munster'.[1] We perceive the discouragements
Ralegh met with in his efforts to colonise; in the end he gave
up. This theme, too, the hindrances placed in the way of Irish
exports, was borne out by a long record of frustration over the
next two centuries.

In August Ralegh was back at Sherborne, bombarding Cecil
with letters about small items of business and personal recommendations from people in the West Country. There were
country sports, so far as they could console, and he took up
falconry. From Gillingham Forest, on the borders of Dorset and
Somerset, he wrote to Cecil, 'Sir, the Indian falcon is sick of
the buckworm; and therefore, if you will be so bountiful to give
another falcon, I will provide you a running gelding'.[2]

Since he now had leisure on his hands, there was time for
reading and for poetry. Though we have no clue to the date of
two famous poems, 'The Nymph's Reply to the Shepherd', and
'The Lie', they very much express the mood of these years, the
cynicism and disillusionment of the one, the *saeva indignatio* of the
other. Ralegh had a common friend with Marlowe in Hariot,
and their circles of acquaintance intersected as well as the un-
commonness, the heterodoxy, of their opinions. To Marlowe's
celebrated poem,

> Come live with me, and be my love,
> And we will all the pleasures prove . . .

Ralegh wrote, not surprisingly, a hardly less celebrated reply:

> If all the world and love were young,
> And truth in every shepherd's tongue,
> These pretty pleasures might me move,
> To live with thee, and be thy love.
>
> The flowers do fade, and wanton fields
> To wayward winter reckoning yields,
> A honey tongue — a heart of gall —
> Is fancy's spring, but sorrow's fall.
>
> But could youth last and love still breed,
> Had joys no date, nor age no need,
> Then these delights my mind might move
> To live with thee, and be thy love.

---

[1] Edwards, II. 81-2.   [2] *Ibid.* 83.

To get the full flavour of such Elizabethan songs, we must call up the plucked strings, the dark and plangent tones of the lute. But there is no need for music to accompany 'The Lie': its savagery is sufficient to itself.

> Say to the Court it glows
> and shines like rotten wood,
> Say to the Church it shows
> what's good and doth no good.
> If Church and Court reply,
> then give them both the lie.
>
> Tell Potentates they live
> acting by others' action,
> Not loved unless they give,
> not strong but by affection.
> If Potentates reply,
> give Potentates the lie.

'Potentates' — what a word for Elizabeth, Diana, Cynthia, dear Empress! A shrewd blow is given by the reminder that they act only by others' action: it is a constant theme with Ralegh that he as a servant had to bear the toil, the hardships and dangers. Such services requited reward: what more barbed reminder than

> Not loved unless they give,
> not strong but by affection?

As for the managers of their affairs —

> Tell men of high condition
> that manage the estate,
> Their purpose is ambition,
> their practice only hate:
> And if they once reply,
> then give them all the lie.

Then, with a return to his own condition, a reminder to himself:

> Tell age it daily wasteth,
> tell honour how it alters,
> Tell beauty how she blasteth,
> tell favour how it falters.
> And as they shall reply
> give every one the lie.

Already rumours were circulating as to Ralegh's opinions, and the intellectual company he kept, not only on these matters but, more dangerous, on questions of religious belief. In 1592 the famous Jesuit Robert Parsons had published an attack on Ralegh which, being in Latin, drew attention to his heterodoxy all over Europe.[1] It said that his was an atheistic circle dominated by a certain astronomer and necromancer — a reference to Hariot — who taught young gentlemen to scoff at the old law of Moses as well as the new law of Christ. If Ralegh were made a member of the Council, as was expected, what would be the nefarious influence of Ralegh's wizard (*magus*) and sceptic (*epicurus*) in denying the deity, the immortality of the soul, life beyond death, with all the consequences of *lèse-majesté* and disturbance to the state? It was not that Father Parsons cared very much about *lèse-majesté* as far as Elizabeth was concerned — no-one had vilified her more — and he was himself a prime disturber of the state. With him any stick would do to beat a Protestant, and he was as big a liar as Ralegh; he did not care what he said, he was out to make mischief.[2]

And this made mischief for Ralegh for the rest of his life; for the truth was that he did not believe the nonsense that ordinary people fancied themselves to believe. Nor did his circle. Ralegh's was a questing mind, naturally sceptical, but anxiously seeking all his life what he could really believe to be true. Where the conduct of his life involved him in all sorts of insincerities, intellectually — at the core of his mind — he was sincere. Obviously he thought the truth was more worthy of respect than people; the latter he never much respected, and perhaps that was something of a mistake, too.

We have a vivid close-up of him at a discussion of these things at Sir George Trenchard's supper-table at Wolfeton in the summer of 1593.[3] Carew Ralegh, talking somewhat too freely, was reproved for corrupting good manners. When he asked what danger he incurred by saying what he thought, a clergyman present — an Oriel man like Sir Walter — replied 'the wages of sin is death', and not only death of the body but of the soul. 'Soul,' said Carew Ralegh, 'what is that?' He evidently thought it a term having no meaning. When the parson tried to shuffle the matter off, Sir Walter weighed in: 'I have been a scholar some time in Oxford, I have answered under a Bachelor of Art, and had talk with divers; yet hitherto in this point have I not

[1] Cf. E. A. Strathmann, *Sir Walter Ralegh. A Study in Elizabethan Skepticism*, 26.
[2] Parsons attacked Burghley and Leicester as atheists too, whereas Leicester canted with the Puritans and Burghley was almost painfully pious.
[3] Cf. *Willoughbie His Avisa*, ed. G. B. Harrison, App. III.

by any been resolved. They tell us it is *primus motor*, the first mover in a man, etc.' The parson quoted Aristotle's definition, which Ralegh rejected as too obscure and intricate. The divine then said he 'had rather say with divines plainly that the reasonable soul is a spiritual and immortal substance breathed into man by God'. 'Yea, but what is that spiritual and immortal substance?', said Sir Walter. 'The soul,' said the parson.

Ralegh thought this circular argument nonsense, and contrasted it with a mathematical demonstration on a table in the window as to the relation between the whole and its parts. The minister said that the soul was different and could only be discerned by the spirit. Nothing was more certain in the world than the existence of God, yet, being a spirit, it was impossible to subject him to the senses. For Ralegh this was another term having no meaning. 'Marry, these two be alike, for neither could I learn hitherto what God is.' Mr. FitzJames — who was on better terms with the church at Salisbury — interjected with Aristotle's *ens entium*. After a lot of further palaver Ralegh demanded of the clergyman, 'Yea, but what is this *ens entium*?' The parson answered, 'It is God.' Sir Walter gave up at this, and asked that grace might be said, '"for that", quoth he, "is better than this disputation"'; and we can but sympathise with him.

The report of this circulated all over Dorset, and in March 1594 the Court of High Commission directed an enquiry into the matter. The minister of Gillingham had heard that 'one Hariot of Sir Walter Ralegh's house hath brought the godhead in question, and the whole course of the scriptures'. Carew Ralegh was considered to argue like a pagan, while his lieutenant at Portland, one Allen, was thought a rank atheist. The churchwarden of Gillingham had heard that Sir Walter was suspected of atheism. The curate of Motcombe had heard the like report of Mr. Thynne of Longleat. The parson of Wyke Regis added that Lieutenant Allen was a blasphemer, who 'cometh not to divine service or sermons'. The vicar of Blandford had heard Mr. Carew Ralegh concede there was a god in nature. There was a good deal of talk about Allen at both Weymouth and Sherborne: 'it is generally reported by almost everybody in Sherborne that the said Allen and his man are atheists'.

Henceforth it was always open to tack this tag on to Ralegh's tail, and it marshalled further unpopularity against him from all the conventional and orthodox. Atheist, Machiavellian, Liar: such were the changes rung in the many denunciations of him set going from this time onward — and there was something in each one of them. The poem ,'The Lie', provoked many challenges :

> The Court hath settled sureness
> In banishing such boldness ;
> The Church retains her pureness
>   Though Atheists show their coldness ;
> The Court and Church, though base,
> Turn lies into thy face.

Ralegh's very name was a provocation :

> *Water* thy plants with grace divine,
>   And hope to live for aye ;
> Then to thy Saviour Christ incline,
>   In Him make steadfast stay ;
> *Raw* is the reason that doth *lie*
>   Within an atheist's head,
> Which saith the soul of man doth die
>   When that the body's dead.

When Ralegh came to trial for his life in 1603, his judges, the orthodox Coke and the puritanical Popham, did not hesitate to appeal to popular prejudice and whip up hatred against him as an atheist.

Actually it would be truer to describe Ralegh's position as that of a deist. With his later troubles and increasing age, he tried hard to bring what he thought to be true more in line with orthodox belief, and this is what is represented in the *History of the World*. With his activity of mind and the interests he shared with Hariot, the most original and ranging scientific brain in the country, he could not but reflect on these things. Apart from metaphysical difficulties teasing to an original intelligence, candid and not content to rest upon illusions, there was the special problem created for Protestants by resting so much on the 'inspired' word of the Bible. In the *Treatise of the Soul* that Ralegh wrote we find him bothered by the contradictions. 'If God (say they) create souls now, then he ceased not the seventh day ; and yet the Scripture saith he ceased.'[1] Or again, 'the Sadducees were of opinion that souls did die ; the Nazarites, that they did sleep till the day of judgment'. These doubts do not seem to have affected the idea of God, though somewhat of an abstract conception — it was hardly conceivable then that it was a superfluous one, even though not much more than the

---

[1] *The Works of Sir Walter Ralegh*, ed. Oldys and Birch, VIII. 580, 582, 589.

necessary end of the argument: 'the mind in searching causes is never quiet till it come to God, and the will is never satisfied with any good till it come to the immortal goodness'.

Amid all this, family life had its consolations, if inadequate. Ralegh and his Bess seem to have loved each other; there is the touching phrase he wrote to her at the time of his condemnation in 1603, 'remember your poor child for his father's sake, that comforted you and loved you in his happiest times'. There is no reference outside Throckmorton's Diary to the child that enforced their marriage: it must have died. Ralegh's reference here is to the elder of his two sons that lived, Walter, who was born in this year 1593, probably towards the end of October; for he was baptised on All Saints' day in the church of Lillington, a few miles south of Sherborne.[1]

In the spring of the next year Ralegh's mother died, chief link with all that Devon past. Her will, made 18 April 1594, is affecting in its directness. 'Dear sons, by my last will and testament I most earnestly entreat you that after my death you will see such debts to be satisfied as shall be demanded after my departure, and to have their due in such things as I have bestowed upon them to the uttermost farthing, to the end I may end my days towards God with a pure heart and faithful conscience. And so I bid you all farewell.' It is clear that she was not well off, though she had liveried servants. She left a large butcher's bill unpaid, smaller bills to the apothecary and 'Mr. Bodley the merchant'. She left her waiting woman, Mary Wheare, 20s., 'all the apparel that I wear, besides a writing that she hath to show' (probably for wages due to her); to Mistress Katherine Hooker 'the bed wherein I lie, my saddle and saddle-cloth, the little salt and two spoons, one pair of holland sheets, the little board with the green carpet'. Emlyn Baker was left the great salt in part payment for 40s., and there were various small sums to servants: little enough to be disposed of. She was buried with her husband in St. Mary Major in the cathedral close, the parish church of Palace-gate where they had lived in Exeter. Ralegh's father had died in February 1581, when his son was in Ireland on the threshold of his dazzling fortune. The old couple had been Protestant in their views and sympathies from right back in the latter days of King Henry VIII.

Of the other members of the family, the eldest son, George,

---

[1] For the material in the following paragraphs I am indebted to T. N. Brushfield. 'Raleghana', *Trans. Devon. Assoc.* 1896, 272 foll.

was churchwarden of Littleham, nigh Exmouth, in 1580. A ship of his was set forth on behalf of Exeter in 1588. He died and was buried at Withycombe Ralegh in 1597, leaving an illegitimate son — George Ralegh alias Blake, which gives us the mother's name — who was brought up at Exeter College, Oxford, and the Inner Temple. In these circumstances brother John succeeded to the family properties, and after him Carew Ralegh, who sold Withycombe back to George Ralegh's base son, and Fardel, old seat of the family, to Walter Hele. So, by the end of the century, were things rounded up and the Raleghs ceasing to have much of a stake in Devon.

Sir Walter was determined on building up a large estate at Sherborne, himself a new cuckoo in that nest, and it was not achieved without a good deal of local fluttering on the part of the bishop and others. The new bishop complained loudly against him, who 'of all men living least deserved' satisfying, 'in regard to his unkindness and wrong done to me, which I cannot redress by any good means'.[1] He claimed that Ralegh had lowered the rent due to be paid for his lease from the see of three of its manors, while leaving the payment of fees to the bishop; meanwhile he detained the profits and refused to pay a penny of the acknowledgment-money due to each bishop on consecration. 'It is much that he hath already, and the addition of those three manors will very near countervail the rest.' The bishop had sent and sent for the moneys due to him, but nothing had he got. 'The evil reports that I bear for him, and his evil usage of me, do make me in good faith weary of all.'

The letter bears upon its face the accents of sincerity; but we are enlightened as to the 'evil reports' the bishop bore for Ralegh, when the latter returned that he had given the Queen 'a jewel worth £250 to make the bishop', so no doubt Ralegh considered that the good prelate should be accommodating.[2] Underneath the complicated charges and coun charges, we perceive that the ecclesiastical authorities at Salisbury preferred an established Dorset landowner, FitzJames of Lillington, to the disgraced newcomer. Ralegh said that FitzJames had given 'the priests of Salisbury' a good fine to favour him, and 'he offers me £200 for my good will'. Ralegh resorted to Cecil as usual: 'I hope you may favour me so much — upon these advantages — as either to compel them to grant mine [*i.e.* lease] alone; or else that FitzJames may ease me in my charges in a more liberal

---

[1] *Salisbury MSS.* IV. 507-8.   [2] Edwards, II. 96-8.

BESS THROCKMORTON, LADY RALEGH

kind, which, of the two, I desire rather. . . . But I desire that this grant may be enrolled to the Queen . . . and then, when it is in her, perchance Master Attorney will find a way to frustrate that condition, as sure as they think they have made it.'

This was a pretty unscrupulous suggestion to make; but by the irony of fate that dogged Ralegh all his life, it was precisely upon such a legal flaw in his title that he was ultimately made to forfeit Sherborne to King James.

In the spring of 1594 there came an opportunity to strike a blow for conformity, if not precisely for orthodoxy, and stop some people's mouths by the rounding up of the flock of Recusants at the Arundell house, Chideock, and the capture of their priest, John Cornelius. 'There hath been kept in this house, as I have formerly informed you, above thirty recusants. . . . He calls himself John Mooney, but he is an Irishman and a notable stout villain, and I think can say much.'[1] Cornelius was half Cornish, half Irish, but though a foolish fanatic, much given to seeing visions, he was no villain and not at all political; he had served the Arundells quietly for some ten or eleven years without being disturbed, wrapped up in his inner mystical life and bent on the idea of martyrdom. Sir George Trenchard and Sir Ralph Horsey had tracked him down and brought him back to Trenchard's house, Wolfeton — still unchanged, with the elaborate Tudor panelling on the walls that looked on the scene — where the priest was kept for a fortnight and well treated in the hope of his renunciation. Not a hope: he would not even say grace at a Protestant table. The Catholics said that one night Ralegh sat up alone with the priest discussing matters of faith, and that he was sufficiently impressed to offer to do what he could for him. Quite unyielding, Cornelius went on his way to the martyrdom he so much desired.

No sign whatever came from the Queen, and Ralegh was reduced to planning the Guiana voyage in the hope of wresting back favour, or at least arresting her attention, with a signal *coup*. We have an early pointer in a letter written to Cecil by the hand of Lady Ralegh, which betrays by its whole phraseology that it was dictated by Ralegh and really represented his view. 'I fear that my mistress, if all hearts were open and all desires known [a quotation from the Prayer Book], might, without so great curiosity of deciphering, read her own destiny in a plain alphabet; but we are both great believers and therein we

<hr/>

[1] *Ibid.* II. 91.

flatter ourselves, and nourish our minds with what we would.'[1] Bess was incapable, on her own, of expressing such lofty and cryptic sentiments, nor even what follows. 'Now, sir, for the rest I hope you will rather draw Sir Walter towards the East than help him forward toward the sunset, if any respect to me or love to him be not forgotten. But every month has his flower, and every season his contentment, and you great counsellors are so full of new counsels as you are steady in nothing; but we poor souls that hath brought sorrow at a high price desire and can be pleased with the same misfortune we hold, fearing alterations will but multiply misery, of which we have already felt sufficient.' So we find Ralegh putting his wife up to beseech Cecil to stop his intended voyage: 'I know only your persuasions are of effect with him and held as oracles, tied to them by love; therefore I humbly beseech you, stay him rather than further him, by the which you shall bind me for ever, as yet you have ever given me cause.'

This is the kind of thing Ralegh's enemies meant by 'liar' and 'hypocrite'; and it is true that he was given to playing a part, seeing himself in the part, often exaggerating, and sometimes sitting very loosely to the truth. A worse trouble was that his antics were so obvious; subtle people like Cecil and the Queen could always see through him.

Since no sign came from on high, it behoved him to go forward with his plans for a voyage in the hope of something coming out of it. Where was he to look for quick returns? Certainly not Virginia, where there was no gold and where the colony of 1587 had been irretrievably lost. In the early 1590's a new land of promise had come on the horizon with the conquistador Berrio's discovery of a way to the upper Orinoco, with the fabled rumours of an *el dorado*, an Indian king who bathed in a remotely accessible lake, clad all in gold. This was enough to stir the exploring mind of Ralegh, who kept in touch with news from the New World. Spain had not yet taken possession of Guiana — perhaps here was a sphere for a rival (and auriferous) English Empire in South America?

Early in 1594 he sold his reversion to two of the episcopal manors near Sherborne to FitzJames 'for a good sum of money',[2] and dispatched Captain Jacob Whiddon to Trinidad to spy out the land, where Berrio killed eight of his men. For his projected voyage Ralegh managed to get the backing of both Cecil and

---

[1] *Salisbury MSS.* IV. 485.
[2] W. B. Wildman, *A Short History of Sherborne*, 171.

Lord Admiral Howard. The latter, whom he now addressed as
'kinsman', presumably through his wife, invested a ship, the
Lion's Whelp, and Cecil also invested in it. He acknowledged his
indebtedness to Cecil: 'what good shall happen in England, or
in India [*i.e.* the Indies or South America] or elsewhere, so God
favour me as I take it and confess it to be of your most honourable
friendship's towards me. . . . So, with my humble duty to my
Mistress, I leave, and am ever your servant.'[1] He added: 'I
had a post this morning from Sherborne. The plague is in the
town very hot. My Bess is on one way sent, her son another
way, and I am in great trouble therewith.'

He was always in trouble and complaining nowadays. Delay
in getting to sea ate up money. 'This unfortunate year is such
as those that were ready and at sea two months before us are
beaten back again and distressed. This long stay hath made me
a poor man, the year far spent and what shall become of us God
knows. The body is wasted with toil, the purse with charge,
and all things worn.'[2] In December, before he could get away,
he still had to resort to Cecil: 'you must esteem me for your evil
spirit that haunts you thus with so many tedious businesses'. He
had, to make more sure, as he thought, made over the conveyance
of Sherborne to his son, unknown to his wife. He was afraid of
some execution being made upon him during his absence abroad,
which would necessitate the showing of the conveyance to his
son; 'by that means my wife will know that she can have no
interest in my living, and so exclaim'. That throws an odd light
on Ralegh's relations with Bess, and, from one or two later
indications, it would appear that he stood in some awe of her.
Throckmortons were a match for Raleghs any day: she had not
only brought him to the water, but made him drink. 'On this
all my estate dependeth, and the Queen, having refused all other
graces, I hope will save me yet from the ruin of others. . . .
From Alresford, this Saturday after I left you, with a heart
half-broken.'

Early in 1595 he got away to Guiana, where we do not propose to follow him. He had a fatal stroke of luck in capturing
Berrio himself in Trinidad, for, with the usual irony of his fortune,
it was Berrio who intellectually captured him. For the last of
the conquistadors communicated to Ralegh his own fixation on
Guiana, belief in El Dorado and all. Ralegh himself explored
little of the country; he simply made a preliminary canter of

[1] Edwards, II. 100.   [2] *Ibid.* 101, 104-5.

some two hundred and fifty miles, following in Berrio's footsteps, convinced himself of the existence of gold up the Caroni river, without substantiating it, and made a hopeful impression on the Indian chiefs who would rather anything than have their country taken over by the Spaniards.[1] Then, ransoming some of the mainland towns to pay the expenses of the expedition — for this was war-time — he came home to write about it and try to persuade the Queen to take over the empire that was awaiting her in South America. She was not so persuadable. When Ralegh was gone Berrio resumed his own plans for Guiana, and proceeded to build a fort near the confluence of the Caroni with the Orinoco, which effectively blocked the passage further up where gold was thought to be. It was this that frustrated the hopes of Ralegh's last voyage to Guiana, and brought him to his end.

While Ralegh was away Throckmorton paid a visit to his sister, who was left on guard at Sherborne to bombard Cecil with her requests in place of her spouse. One of Sir Walter's kinsmen wants to go to sea: 'he being to Sir Walter as he is . . .' she knows is a sufficient reason for Cecil's favour and care of him.[2] Then her kinsman Mr. Brett has fallen out with Sir Ralph Horsey, both of them good friends of hers; but Sir Ralph is so very well friended that perhaps Cecil would 'stand indifferent for my sake in this matter . . . if it do come before you'. Now the rumour at Court is that Ralegh has come home rich; the Vice-Chamberlain congratulates Cecil 'because the world says he shall have no hurt by it'. Hugh Beeston has heard the comfortable news and sits on thorns until he shall see Ralegh's face. Bess was shortly able to correct the news: 'Sur hit tes trew I thonke the leveng God Sur Walter is safly londed at Plumworthe with as gret honnor as ever man can, but with littell riches. Kepe thies I besech you to your selfe yet; only to me lord ammerall. . . . Many of his mene slane; himself will now. Pardon my rewed wryteng with the goodnes of the newes.'

Sir Walter had not come back rich; he was a dejected man. From delectable Sherborne he wrote ungratefully, 'from this desolate place I have little matter; from myself, less hope; and therefore I think the shorter the discourse, the better welcome'.[3] Discouraged, he wrote of Philip's preparations for another Armada, 'we that have much ado to get bread to eat have the less to care for, unless much lost labour and love awake us that

[1] Cf. *The Discoverie of Guiana*, ed. V. T. Harlow, lxxxviii, 16.
[2] *Salisbury MSS.* V. 165, 289, 396.   [3] Edwards, II. 107-11.

are also thankless busied in things either beyond our capacities or cares'. Always eloquent, always exaggerating — how to take him? 'What becomes of Guiana I much desire to hear — whether it pass for a history or a fable.' He had heard that Sir Robert Dudley — Leicester's illegitimate son — and others were making for Guiana; 'if it be so, farewell all good from thence. For although myself, like a coxcomb, did rather prefer the future in respect of others, and rather sought to win the kings to her Majesty's service than to sack them, I know what others will do when those kings shall come simply into their hands.' Within a few days his mood had changed and he was all excitement to be sent out again: 'I hope I shall be thought worthy to direct those actions that I have at mine own charges laboured in, and to govern that country which I have discovered and hope to conquer for the Queen without her cost'.

Hariot was making a map of Guiana for her, and Ralegh urged that since men might fear to adventure with him on account of his disgrace someone of more sufficiency and grace might undertake it, that 'the Queen lose not that which she shall never find again'. This was rhetoric. Excitedly he reported that in addition to gold there were diamonds and pearls, but 'we must cast so many doubts, and this dolt and that gull must be satisfied, or else all is nothing'. A further letter followed at the end of the month, with a long and elaborate account of the strategic situation of the western counties and the preparations to meet the renewed threat of invasion. 'I beseech you let us know whether we shall be travellers or tinkers; conquerors or novices. For, if the winter pass without making provision, there can be no victualling in the summer; and if it be now foreslowed, farewell Guiana for ever. Then must I determine to beg or run away. Honour, and gold, and all good, for ever hopeless.'[1]

Guiana had gone to his head, as is the way with such a man, upon his return; for he was now writing about it. To convince others (and perhaps himself), to persuade opinion and retrieve fortune he wrote the first of his books to come out under his own name, in some haste: *The Discovery of the Large, Rich and Beautiful Empire of Guiana*. The dedication to his kinsman, Lord Admiral Howard, and Sir Robert Cecil reeks with his complexes but makes clear what the motive of the voyage was — simply to recover favour. 'Whatsoever shall be done or written by me

---

[1] *Ibid.* 117.

shall need a double protection and defence. The trial that I had of both your loves, when I was left of all but of malice and revenge, makes me still presume that you will be pleased to answer that out of knowledge which others shall but object out of malice. In my more happy times, as I did especially honour you both, so I found that your loves sought me out in the darkest shadow of adversity, and the same affection which accompanied by better fortune soared not away from me in my many miseries. . . . It is true that as my errors were great, so they have yielded very grievous effects, and if aught might have been deserved in former times to have counterpoised any part of offences, the fruit thereof was long before fallen from the tree and the dead stock only remained. I did therefore even in the winter of my life undertake these travels, fitter for boys less blasted with misfortunes, for men of greater ability and for minds of better encouragement, that therby, if it were possible, I might recover but the moderation of excess, and the least taste of the greatest plenty formerly possessed. If I had known other way to win, if I had imagined how greater adventures might have regained, if I could conceive what farther means I might yet use, but even to appease so powerful displeasure, I would not doubt but for one year more to hold fast my soul in my teeth till it were performed.'[1]

There, made trebly clear, was his motive. But there was also self-defence. 'Of that little remain I had, I have wasted in effect all herein; I have undergone many constructions, I have been accompanied with many sorrows, with labour, hunger, heat, sickness and peril. It appeareth, notwithstanding, that I made no other bravado of going to sea than was meant, and that I was neither hidden in Cornwall or elsewhere, as was supposed.' There we have, in his own words, exactly what Ralegh was like. We do not have to blame him for his touchiness as to what fools reported of him, for so many Elizabethans in their prefaces are like that. But I fear it is true — what seems not to be realised by his biographers — that, underneath the glitter and the excitement, he was a bore about himself, and this is an important clue to the way others felt about him in his lifetime. Shut up in the Tower he was more tolerable.

The qualities of the book are such as we should expect — eloquent, poetic in places, packed with informative facts not always reliable, not essentially different from many a narrative in Hakluyt. The one marked difference was the urgency of the

[1] V. T. Harlow, *ed. cit.* 3-4.

tone; for, never disinterested, Ralegh was pressing an argument. He had been anxious to win the sympathy of the natives. 'I made them understand that I was the servant of a Queen, who was the great Cacique of the North, and a virgin, and had more caciques under her than there were trees in their island; that she was an enemy to the Castellani [Spaniards] in respect of their tyranny and oppression, and that she delivered all such nations about her as were by them oppressed, and, having freed all the coast of the northern world from their servitude, had sent me to free them also and withal to defend the country of Guiana from their invasion and conquest. I showed them her Majesty's picture, which they so admired and honoured, as it had been easy to have brought them idolatrous thereof.'[1] All this was rather stretching the bow.

The whole argument led up to the conclusion to take Guiana and hold it, and 'after the first or second year I doubt not but to see in London a Contratation house of more receipt for Guiana than there is now in Seville for the West Indies'.[2] This was so sanguine as to be absurd. It is to be supposed that the Queen read the book, but, if so, no notice was taken and her government had more sense than to be persuaded by Ralegh's interested urgency. It would have meant an inextricable involvement with Spain in the area; the government simply had not the resources, nor would Guiana have been worth it.

The book, however, had a far greater success than the voyage. Three editions seem to have been called for in the year of its publication, 1596.[3] On the Continent it aroused even more marked attention — tribute to the fascination of the New World for Europeans. Translated into Latin twice in 1599, it had three German editions by 1602.[4] Most marked was the interest it awoke among the Dutch; translated in 1598, it was reprinted at least twice in Ralegh's lifetime. We may impute something of Dutch Guiana to its influence — as in part too, after a chequered story, British Guiana.

In literature Guiana received a tribute from the professional poet of the circle, Hariot's friend, Chapman in his *De Guiana : Carmen Epicum* :

> What work of honour and eternal name,
> For all the world to envy and us to achieve . . .
> Riches and conquest and renown I sing,

[1] *Ibid.* 15. [2] *Ibid.* 75.
[3] *Short-Title Catalogue*, ed. A. W. Pollard and G. R. Redgrave, 475.
[4] V. T. Harlow, xcix, 56.

Riches with honour, conquest without blood,
Enough to seat the monarchy of earth,
Like to Jove's eagle, on Eliza's hand.
Guiana, whose rich feet are mines of gold,
Whose forehead knocks against the roof of stars,
Stands on her tip-toes at fair England looking,
Kissing her hand, bowing her mighty breast,
And every sign of all submission making,
To be her sister, and the daughter both
Of our most sacred Maid . . .

Such was the literary propaganda coming from the circle; as a matter of practical politics the Maid thought otherwise. That Ralegh's book made its impression upon a very impressionable mind we know from the way a passage from it became transmuted on the stage. Ralegh wrote of a people there who 'are reported to have their eyes in their shoulders, and their mouths in the middle of their breasts, and that a long train of hair groweth backward between their shoulders'. Some thought this a fable; for his part Ralegh believed it to be true. In the mind of a working dramatist of the time, this became

> The anthropophagi, and men whose heads
> Do grow beneath their shoulders.

But if Ralegh was to return to favour he would need to achieve something better than this.

CHAPTER XI

BROTHERS-IN-LAW

WITH some relief we return to the less demanding avocations, and the Diary, of Ralegh's brother-in-law. After the aspirations and dejections, the insincerities and sincerities alike, the strains within and upon Ralegh, it is pleasant to come back to the simpler soul, the less ambitious occupations, of Arthur Throckmorton. Over some matters their interests converged and we shall find them co-operating, or rather, the lesser man lending himself to the purposes of the more dynamic. Throckmorton followed in Ralegh's wake on the expedition to Cadiz; he broke his friendship with Essex for his brother-in-law's sake and went over to his side. They were both engaged in the characteristic Elizabethan activity of establishing an estate and building a house, the one at Sherborne, the other at Paulerspury.

Four months after Bess's release from the Tower there came, in April 1593, a breach between her brother and her. It was the first in their lives and we know nothing of the cause; but it was serious, for Arthur was very fond of his sister, and they did not resume relations for many months. Arthur continued to be in touch with Essex and the quarrel may have been over him, for it is hardly conceivable that he did not tell the Queen what he knew about Ralegh's relations with Bess, the child-birth and christening in Arthur's house at Mile End. In July he wrote Essex several times, and on 25 July he entertained Lady Essex, Lord Willoughby, Sir Robert Sidney and Sir Matthew Morgan — those martial men — on their way from Lady Rich's.

On his journey into the West this summer to collect his rents from Langacre, increasingly interested in his health, he meant to try the waters at Bath. His brother William cannot have been wholly defective mentally for Arthur left him in charge of the housekeeping at Mile End. Arthur set out first for Colchester, where he lay at the Friars with Cousin Barker, to whom he gave a new gilt cup of pear fashion. He then proceeded across country to Bagshot, Basingstoke, Andover, Salisbury, and thence via Shaftesbury to Sherborne. It does not seem that the Raleghs were there; for though he stayed at Sherborne, he gave Huckwell of the guard 5s., while Ralegh's servants, Mere and Hancock, 'sent to see me'. He spent four days on his manor at Langacre, and then went into Somerset to stay with Sir Henry Berkeley at Bruton as before. At Bath he put up with Dr. Sherwood, who was the leading physician there for many years, and 'went into the Bath by five in the morning'. So for three days.

Leaving Bath on Monday, 17 September, he rode along the ridge-way to descend upon Tortworth, Sir Thomas Throckmorton's house: then a pleasant small gabled house within its forecourt, with moat on one side and church on the other, where now may be seen upon their tombs Arthur's host and his father, Sir Thomas, already there.[1] Thence he went up the steep escarpment of the Cotswolds to stop a couple of days with John Throckmorton at pretty Lypiatt, then a small Tudor house looking across a forecourt to tiny church and gatehouse. The Throckmortons forfeited this engaging place by being incriminated in Gunpowder Plot. Indeed in these years, the 90's, Thomas Throckmorton of Coughton was in and out of Banbury Castle for recusancy, Lady Throckmorton in and out of confinement at Gloucester for 'perverting' members of her household to the old faith and maintaining priests, while abroad members of the family continued the objectionable political activities of exile.[2]

From Lypiatt Arthur came by Chastleton to Rollright, thence to stop with cousin Underhill at Ettington. This was Thomas Underhill, eldest son of the 'hot-gospeller', who lived there many years in the small gabled manor-house with the wife who gave him twenty children; their brasses may still be seen within the tower of the ruined church.[3] He went on to stay three nights with cousin Job Throckmorton, whom a spell in the Tower had not deterred from his questionable Martin Marprelate activities. Arthur passed peaceably from one hot quarter to another on the opposite flank, all within the ambit of this variegated family.

This October he set workmen on building his house at Paulerspury, equipping himself at last with a family seat. The

---

[1] Cf. Sir Robert Atkyns, *Gloucestershire* (ed. 1768), 368, 412.

[2] *A.P.C. 1592-3*, 221, 279, 399; *Cal. S.P. Dom. 1591-4*, 258, 262, 533; *Cal. S.P. Dom. 1595-7*, 54, 178; *Salisbury MSS.* IV. 456, 571.

[3] Morrison, *The Underhills of Warwickshire*. It was from one of the Underhills that Shakespeare bought New Place in 1597.

site was below the church on the slope facing south by west, where one still sees ridges under the grass of the pastures, running down to a stream that comes out at the mill on the Watling Street. Around the shoulder of the hill to south and east lay his park, and further south in an arc around the horizon lay the forest. Throckmorton contracted to pay Green 'for setting up my building', £120; this was the builder to whom he had already given 50s. in earnest. He was down at Pury again for a week at the end of November, when he discharged the workmen for the winter, all but Bradfield the carpenter and Henchman the free mason to whom he was to give 40s. for the windows, and Adrian the paviour with his boy. In London he ordered a big brewing copper to be ready in ten days 'at the sign of the Helmet in Cornhill at one Dykes's house' — it cost £22 : 8 : 4. He was buying andirons, tongs tipped with brass, hinges, hundreds of nails and four double casements, a new supply of pewter against which he handed in a lot of old pewter at 6d. a lb. On 12 June he forwarded his stuff to Pury, a few days later he sent down his cook and prepared to follow.

In November he made it up with his sister: 17 November, 'Farrar, a Yorkshireman dwelling in Buckinghamshire, came to me with a letter from my sister Ralegh'. Next day he sent him back with an answer, giving him a rose-noble — 15s. Not until 24 June did he write to Ralegh, and went down to look to affairs at Pury. On his return Arthur gave 8s. for '*un diamant de* Cornwall',[1] which probably came through Ralegh; for next we find him visited by Sir Walter's men, Hariot, John Shelbury of Sherborne, Wood and Knyvett. To Hariot he made a present of three yards of black satin, at 12s. a yard; and bought 3½ oz. of tobacco for 11s. 6d. with six pipes for 2s. Here we watch the spread of Ralegh's influence in the noxious habit of smoking, so strongly disapproved by King James. Hariot died of cancer of the mouth: the righteous said because of his atheistical opinions, more likely from his horrid addiction.

It is pleasant to note the purchases Throckmorton made for his growing establishment: he paid the large sum of £5 for an Indian white quilt, which may have come in from some privateering capture, or from the cargo of the *Madre de Dios*. He was

[1] Cf. Richard Carew, *Survey of Cornwall* (ed. 1811), 24, on Cornish diamonds: 'diamonds are in many places found cleaving to those rocks out of which the tin is digged: they are polished, squared and pointed by nature; their quantity from a pea to a walnut: in blackness and hardness they come behind the right ones, and yet I have known some of them set on so good a foil as at first sight they might appose a not unskilful lapidary'.

buying woollen blankets, four dozen pots, a great jug, an oil pot and a glass — and 'sallet [*i.e.* salad] Candy oil excellent good at 16d. the quart'. He bought a walnut-tree table with a frame, and a little wainscot table; the closet chamber was covered with matting of fine bulrush — 40 yards at 9d. the yard; the long cushion, which would have gone the length of bench or window-seat, was embroidered with furs for 30s. The emptying of two privies cost the considerable sum of 33s. — they must have stood in need of it.

In August Hariot was with him again, to show him a letter of Lady Ralegh's. This was at the time of the birth of another child to Arthur and his wife. In the interval there had been another dead child, but this one lived: a girl named Anne, second of the co-heiresses who divided up their father's estate. Out of six children so far, only two survived. In the midst of these delights, 'J'escrivoye une lettre à madame Maria Darcy' — with an obscure impulse, for was she not an old flame? For the christening he sent to Lady Lucas and cousin Middlemore's wife; and they, with his neighbour and fellow J.P., Sir Owen Hopton, Lieutenant of the Tower, duly christened the child on Sunday, 18 August 1594.[1]

The expenses of life necessitated his pledging more silver with Mistress Haynes, his pawnbroker: six silver candlesticks, a dozen silver plates, a gilt basin and ewer, while prolonging the rest for a further period, two gilt tankards, a gilt tun, a standing cup with chased cover, sixteen silver dishes, four covered bowls. This enabled him to pay off the last of his father's debt to the Crown for his Butlerage — after thirty-five years! — for £199 : 10 : 6; this was good business and the son was to receive his *quietus est*. Building a house at Paulerspury would require more drastic measures, and in February he sold his manor of Langacre to an Exeter merchant, one Davis, for £2800. He paid off his debts: his brother Nicholas received £315, Arthur Agard £66 : 13 : 4, Mrs. Haynes her £150. At once Arthur bought £101 worth of new plate, and a feather of diamonds for £100 from Peter Vanlore, a leading jeweller in the City with whom Ralegh had many dealings.

At New Year we have a rather absurd letter from Arthur to Cecil with a proposal designed to allay the Queen's disfavour — perhaps for his part in the affair of Bess's childbirth at Mile End.

[1] The Diary tells us that Throckmorton had been sworn J.P. and took the oath of Supremacy along with Sir Owen Hopton and Lord Wentworth, 5 December 1592, and that Hopton died 25 September 1595.

'I am bold to write my determination, grounded upon grief and true duty to the Queen, thankfulness to my Lord of Derby, and to assure you I bear no spleen to yourself. If I may mind to come in a masque brought in by the Nine Muses, whose music, I hope, shall so mollify the easy softened mind of her Majesty as both I and mine may find mercy. The song, the substance I have herewith sent to you — myself, whilst the singing, to lie prostrate at her Majesty's feet till she says she will save me. Upon my resurrection the song shall be delivered by one of the Muses, with a ring made for a wedding ring set round with diamonds and with a ruby like a heart placed in a coronet, with this inscription, *Elizabetha potest*. I durst not do this before I had acquainted you herewith, understanding her Majesty had appointed the masquers, which resolution hath made me the unreadier : yet, if this night I may know her Majesty's leave and your liking, I hope not to come too late, though the time be short for such a show and my preparations posted for such a presence I desire to come in before the other masque, for I am sorrowful and solemn, and my story shall not be long.'[1]

I think we can relate this only to the disgrace that lay upon the group, and best interpret it as another attempt to allay it. For it is noticeable that after Throckmorton's visit to Court in December 1592, to thank the Lord Chamberlain and Sir Thomas Heneage for his sister's release, he had not appeared there since. Nothing seems to have come of the proposal.

This summer building at Paulerspury was in full swing, and on his way down in May Throckmorton stopped with Mr. Temple at Stowe. Arthur was interested in his cistern, which contained six hogsheads, and every yard of lead pipe weighed 12 lb. at 16d. the yard. The wainscot for Paulerspury came from Kenilworth, to be carried and set up at 20d. the yard. For those interested in Elizabethan building operations I append the details of his bargains, or contracts, with Durrant the carpenter and old Green for bricklayers' work.[2] There were other bargains with glaziers for the windows and with William Green and Story, free masons, 'for all kind of work of free masonry,

---

[1] *Salisbury MSS.* V. 99.

[2] He was to pay Durrant 12d. a day until 1 October, then 11d. a day till All Hallowtide (1 Nov.), then 10d. a day to Lady day (25 March) ; his man 10d. a day, then 9d., then 8d. during these periods; his boy 7d., 6d. and 5d. a day comparably. One notices how these wages follow the working day governed by the light. Old Green, the bricklayer, was paid 12d. a day till 1 October, then 10d. a day till Lady day ; his boy 6d. and 4d. accordingly.

but colours and pilasters, for 3d. the foot'. On 5 May Throckmorton paid a visit to Holdenby, the immense house built by Sir Christopher Hatton, perhaps to gather ideas, as Bess of Hardwick did before building the new Hardwick Hall. From there he went to Moulton Park 'to speak with James Furness the surveyor'. Next day he gave him 10 French crowns 'for directing my building' — there I think we have the architect. He had Mr. Temple of Stowe, Mr. Shirley of Aynho and Mr. Danvers of Culworth with him to give him advice. Before departing he left £100 with Temple to pay the workmen according to the detailed schedules agreed and then revised. All sorts of details were settled, the oaks to be felled, making boards, planks, setting up sawpits, making wains and wheelbarrows; stone was to come from his own quarry at Cosgrove. Before leaving, he wrote to Essex, and on 14 May set out on his summer jaunt to Bath and to pay a visit to his sister at Sherborne while Ralegh was away in Guiana.

Making for Warwick, he lay at the 'Swan'. Next day, 'I went from Warwick by Wellesbourne, leaving Sir Thomas Lucy's house, Charlecote, on the right hand and so to Over Hatherton and to Hanford bridge, to Moreton-in-Marsh and so to Stow-on-the-Wold, where I lay at the "Crown".' If only he had stopped at Stratford-on-Avon and given us some information about its contemporary inhabitants! Thence he went by Lord Chandos's house at Cubberley to Lypiatt, where he stayed three days with his cousin. While staying there, with time on his hands, he noted down in considerable detail the freehold land in Whittlebury field, and his own copyholds with the rents due to him. He worked out the costs of a cistern, evidently for Pury, and lost 10s. at cards.

On May 19 he arrived at Bath, stopping again with Dr. Sherwood. 'I found lodged at Doctor Baker's my Lady of Pembroke, my Lord being departed a little before my coming.' Next day he took a medicine previously prescribed for him by the eminent, the punishing, Dr. Paddy: it gave him twelve stools. Next day he went into the King's Bath between two and three in the morning. He made a note that his brother — he does not say which — discharged Condell from his service and gave him 10s., having paid him only 50s. for five years of service. Next day, into the Bath between one and two in the morning, and again between ten and eleven at night. 'I had the pain of the emerods!' — and, perhaps, no wonder, after Dr. Paddy. He sent off his footman to Sherborne to let his sister know of his coming.

Rewarding Dr. Sherwood with 40s. — Throckmorton was a perfect milch-cow for doctors — on Saturday, 28 May, he set out across country to Combe Hay, Wellow and by Mells, 'Mr. Horner's house, to Leighton and so to Bruton, 16 miles, where I dined at the sign of the "Hart", market day. Kyrton, Fitzjames, Biese, Hopton, Berkeley' — these would be the names of the good fellows he met there. 'I came to Sherborne to my sister Ralegh's, 10 miles, and alighted at the "New Inn".' 'Sunday, 25 May: I stayed at Sherborne, where I found Mr. Christopher Harris, Mrs. Hull, servants to my sister; Bell, Hills, Myers, Fulford, Smith the cook, John Layton, William the butler, Jockey, Peter Venn, Bromback, and Smith the cook's brother.' Such was the household, or the male household, in the absence of the master. Arthur stayed until Tuesday, when he made for Shaftesbury, where he dined at the 'Queen's Arms', over the Wiltshire hills to Salisbury and lay that night at the 'Greyhound and the Hare'. 28 May he rode to Andover, dining at the 'White Hart' and passing by Clarendon park; in the afternoon he came through Basingstoke and lay the night at Hartley Row at the 'George'. Next day he pushed on over Harford bridge to Bagshot, Egham and Staines, where he dined at the sign of the 'Bush'; at Brentford he took boat down the Thames to Ratcliffe Cross for 4s. and so home.

In June he paid brother Robert £5 of the remaining £30 of his legacy, and Robert and Nicholas went down to Sherborne to visit their sister. Later, Arthur wrote her by her messenger, Wood. He paid Mr. Mathias for excellent rhubarb at 6d. the oz., and for a lenative laxative — after Dr. Paddy! — 4s. Next day, 'I took a shilling's weight in rhubarb infused in whey, tied in a fine lawn and laid at night in the whey standing upon hot embers'. 17 June, he was at the assessing of all the J.P.s of Middlesex to raise three horsemen at £30 a horseman, every J.P. being rated for 20s. Patriotically Throckmorton provided a horseman of his own, giving Emly £25 to buy a horse; when he was sent as a light-horseman into Ireland, Throckmorton took the opportunity to write by him to the Lord Deputy, Sir William Russell, a follower of Essex.[1]

The house at Paulerspury was advancing towards completion, for Arthur was now buying a dozen locks with keys. He was contracting with a joiner in Southwark for plain wainscot at 3s. the yard and for 'French panel with mitre, cipher and pilasters, 5s. the yard'. He bought large sheets of lead in Bishopsgate

[1] There are traces of Throckmorton's work as J.P. at this time in *A.P.C. 1595–6*, 230, 292, 349.

Street, which he sent down to Pury, and 'I must pay Garret the marble-carver of Southwark £60 for making me a chimney piece of Sussex marble, alabaster, touch and rance[1] according to a pattern left with him. Whereof I must give him £30 in hand and £30 when he hath finished it and set it up at Midsummer next. He to be at all the charges and gilding whatsoever but only the carriage.' For the chief feature of his hall, a fine marble chimney-piece, coloured and gilt, Arthur was going to the leading workshop, that of Garret Johnson, the immigrant sculptor who did a prosperous trade in such things, whose tombs are still to be seen all over England and whose son sculpted Shakespeare's portrait-bust at Stratford.[2]

Out of the purchase money coming in for Langacre, he was now able to lend £200 out at interest, to buy a new Turkey carpet for £16, six college pots of silver, a silver posnet and a sugar box. Nor did he neglect books. His new interests coming from Ralegh and Hariot are represented by Blundeville's *Exercises*, his old interests by the theological controversy of Harding and Jewel, and Stow's *Chronicles*. In October he went down to Paulerspury, stopping at the 'George' at Towcester. He bargained for the repair and new setting of posts and paling about his park. The Michaelmas rent for Cosgrove was £60 : 13 : 9, of which he set aside £56 for his men to buy cattle and sheep at Banbury Fair. For the fair he went over to stop at Norton with Sir Richard Knightley, a fellow-Puritan and co-partner with Job Throckmorton in Martin Marprelate and anti-Church activities. At the fair thirty ewes were bought for £15. Ewes put to the ram this St. Luke's tide, 145 ; altogether, of all kinds of sheep, he had 344. He would much increase this number in the years of his residence at Pury. He had eight yoke of drawing oxen, two yoke of fat oxen, two fat steers, a fat heifer, a cow. A bull cost him 50s., a boar 8s. — I think this must be in addition to the regular complement of cattle pasturing on the place. We shall see the advantage of residence and direct farming in the improvement of his estate that he effects over the years.

He returned to Mile End to enjoy the company of his brother-in-law back from Guiana. On Ralegh's return to London it was observed that he 'goes daily to hear sermons, because he hath seen the wonders of the Lord in the deep : 'tis much commended

---

[1] 'Touch' was the black stone, 'rance' the reddish marble we still recognise on Elizabethan tombs and chimney-pieces.

[2] K. A. Esdaile, *English Monumental Sculpture since the Renaissance*, 117-9.

and spoken of'.[1] Perhaps more useful for the book he had in mind was to consult with Dr. Dee, the cosmographer, who dined with him at Durham House in October.[2] On Sunday, 26 October, 'Sir Walter Ralegh dined here. Ma femme se senta vive enceinte.' On All Hallows day, 1 November, Arthur accompanied Ralegh on his way home as far as Staines. He sent Lord Chief Justice Popham 4 partridges, 6 quails, 6 snipe, 2 woodcocks, 4 dozen larks — evidently for a feast. 5 December, 'I felt myself ill *in testiculis*' — the first reference to a rupture; he took a poultice, then a glister with 1 oz. of diacatholicon in it. He went on dosing himself with physic, paying Dr. Turner 10s. for his advice, and then took, more sensibly, to a half-crown truss.

Throckmorton's closer association with Ralegh this winter of 1595–6 in London is reflected in his taking up the study of mathematics and the sphere. Thomas Hood was the best practical teacher of the subject, the author of a number of text-books, and Throckmorton engaged him.[3] 13 December, 'Sir Walter Ralegh dined with me'. The next entry reads, 'I bargained with Mr. Thomas Hood to read geometry to me and do give him 20s. from this day weekly. Paid him for 3 pair of compasses 18d. the piece, and for a ruling compass 8d., and for one spring brass compass 14d.' On New Year's day he paid Mr. Hood 20s., and gave 5s. in earnest for a sphere that would cost £10.

The pleasure that it was to him to be together again with his sister may be read from the tone of his references. 10 January, 'sis et moi ensemble'. 9 February, 'la mia sorella Eliz. Ralegh venia a casa mia'. There are no further entries for a whole month, until we come to Monday, 8 March, 'received of my sister Ralegh towards our diet charges and hers — £20'. They must have been sharing housekeeping, for Ralegh was now immersed in the preparations for the Cadiz expedition on which Throckmorton was to accompany him. There may be some reflection of this in the last entries in this volume of the Diary. From mid-March on Throckmorton was laying in stocks of shirts and stuff: 116 ells of holland to make shirts, stitched russet satin, fine white cannett and yellow canvas, and stuff for six hanging beds — surely hammocks for himself and his company? The last entry is a note of Shelbury coming from Colchester, to whom Throckmorton gave 40s.

[1] H.M.C. *De L'Isle and Dudley MSS.* II. 173.
[2] *Diary of Dr. John Dee*, ed. J. O. Halliwell (Camden Soc.), 54.
[3] For Hood cf. F. R. Johnson, *Astronomical Thought in Renaissance England*, 198-203.

There the Diary stops provokingly short, for that spring the diarist would be with Ralegh on the way to Cadiz.

The expedition to Cadiz was a major measure agreed upon by the whole government to demonstrate the new offensive alliance arrived at with France in May 1596. A powerful fleet, with a small army — something like an English armada — was to be sent, which in the event delivered a shattering blow in the capture of the city and the destruction of all the shipping in the harbour, with merchandise worth millions. This brilliant *coup* sent a wave of war-weariness throughout Spain, and within two years Philip came to terms with Henri IV. Lord Admiral Howard took the project under his wing, and the expedition became essentially his. Essex as Lord Marshal was joined in equal command; but Howard was a friend to Ralegh, who was thus assured of a part in it and was given command of the fourth squadron of the fleet. His advice, enforcing a change of plan prior to the attack, was a decisive factor in its success.

In the laborious sea-preparations for so large an expedition Ralegh took a leading part with his Howard kinsmen from the start. The Lord Admiral reported, 'My Lord Thomas [Howard], Sir Walter Ralegh and myself were yesterday from eight in the morning till three in the afternoon very busy at Mr. Quarles's office, and after till it was night Sir Walter and myself were up and down on the river continually busied'.[1] The weather was bad all that spring and much delayed their preparations; there was the greatest difficulty in pressing men to serve. 'As fast as we press men one day', Ralegh reported, 'they come away another and say they will not serve. . . . I am not able to live, to row up and down every tide from Gravesend to London. . . . The pursuivant found me in a country village, a mile from Gravesend, hunting after runaway mariners, and dragging in the mire from ale-house to ale-house.'[2] Such were his complaints, vivid, passionate, as usual. This did not prevent him from finding time to pester Cecil with other requests — one day he wrote him four letters! : pressing Irish suits upon him, recommending a Puritan friend for an Irish bishopric, begging favour for a kinsman who was in the Queen's displeasure, for an Exeter man who wanted a prebend in the cathedral — 'Sir, I beseech you for my sake, because it standeth much on my credit, to favour the suit'.[3]

---

[1] *Salisbury MSS.* VI. 85.　　　　　　　[2] Edwards, II. 122, 129-30.

[3] *Ibid.* 125-32. The prebend was to be for William Hilliard, presumably a relation of Nicholas Hilliard, the painter.

Nor was Bess behindhand. With Ralegh so busy away Cecil had taken the trouble to write comfortingly to her at Sherborne. 'Sir Walter's remembrance of me to you at his last departure shall add and increase, if it were possible, more love and dear respect to him. I am in hope ere it be long to hear of him; though not in long time to see him; in which time I shall fly to you in all my cumbers as to the surest staff I trust to in Sir Walter's absence.'¹ Cecil's wife had had the goodness to wish for Bess's company; Bess replied, 'I oft wish it with her, else is an hermit's cell most fit for me and my mind at this time, being for a time dissevered from him that I am'. Here was the language of true love. Considerately, too, she chose Sir Walter's absence to sue the Earl of Huntingdon for her dower, so that the ill-feeling should not rest upon her husband. She never recovered the money.

In April the Lord Admiral wrote from Dover Roads to hasten Ralegh to the fleet. But in May he was still in the Thames chasing after reluctant mariners — he addresses a letter from Mile End, so that he found Throckmorton's house convenient for him.

Ralegh's delay rendered Essex suspicious — he was down at Plymouth with the land-forces champing to be gone.² His friends suggested that Ralegh's 'slackness and stay by the way is not thought to be upon sloth or negligence, but upon pregnant design, which will be brought forth very shortly, and found to be according to the French proverb, *fils ou fille*'.³ This was from clever Anthony Bacon — and indeed there may have been something in it. For the Queen hated the expense of such an armada and doubted whether it would accomplish any more than the Lisbon expedition had done in 1589. Her mind was turning to the idea of a less ambitious project, under commanders of lesser rank. This would have suited Ralegh, if he were in command, instead of bringing up the rear in a bigger affair — and perhaps provide a chance to satisfy his aching desire for a return to favour.

These jealousies and distrusts were endemic in Elizabethan conditions. When Ralegh ultimately got down to Plymouth, he tried to make all well with a carriage towards Essex of 'the cunningest respect and deepest humility' — according to Sir

¹ *Salisbury MSS.* VI. 104.
² Cf. Essex to Cecil, 12 May 1596: 'Sir Walter Ralegh, with the rest of our fleet, is not come; and yet he hath had (if the winds be the same there that they are here) all the wished winds he could desire, both to bring him out of the river, and after he was in the Channel along to this place'. *Ibid.* VI. 174.
³ W. B. Devereux, *op. cit.* I. 342.

Anthony Standen, an Essex follower and no friend of Ralegh's.[1]
But there came up the question of precedence between Ralegh
and Sir Francis Vere as fourth in command : between sailors
and soldiers, for Vere was Marshal of the army, and was not
backing down to Ralegh. Throckmorton stood up for his brother-
in-law and thereby got himself into trouble. Standen, his former
acquaintance abroad, gives us an unfavourable report of him.
'Yesternight, at table in drink, in the presence of my Lords-
Generals and the Flemings of the Low Country fleet, there
passed some words, the matter being taken against the Marshal
by Arthur Throckmorton, a hot-headed youth, who desborded
in such words as my Lords commanded him from the table ;
so that for all this voyage I see already the fire kindled that must
consume us inwardly, this scandal-stone being the subject of the
quarrel.'[2] He added that though the dispute was between Throckmorton and Vere, Ralegh was the cause.

Howard and Essex accommodated the matter by apportion-
ing Ralegh precedence at sea, Vere on land. Throckmorton was
reported as dismissed the army and put under guard. Before
leaving port, however, he was reinstated — after all he was not
in any command, but just a gentleman-volunteer — and went
on that famous voyage with the rest.

Arrived off Cadiz, Howard was in favour of capturing the
town, by a two-pronged landing, before entering the bay filled
with shipping and defended by forts ; and it was decided to land
troops on the Caleta, a sandy spit west of the town. By the time
set there was a south-westerly blowing and a heavy swell, which
would make the landings very dangerous. Ralegh made representations to Essex, who thereupon persuaded the Lord Admiral
to change the plan to a direct attack by the fleet upon the harbour.
In return for his advice, which was backed by the seamen, Ralegh
was given the honour of leading the fleet into the bay and being
first to attack in the *Warspite*. Lord Thomas Howard had been
desirous of the honour, but in the attack Essex thrust his flagship
the *Ark Royal* as close up to Ralegh as he could get. Ralegh
engaged both the *St. Philip* and the *St. Andrew*, 'being resolved
to be revenged for the *Revenge*, or to second her with mine own
life, I came to anchor by the galleons, of which the *Philip* and
Andrew were two that boarded the *Revenge*'.[3] The *St. Philip* and
the *St. Thomas* burnt themselves ; the *St. Matthew* and the *St.
Andrew* were taken.

---

[1] T. Birch, *Memoirs of the Reign of Queen Elizabeth*, II. 15.
[2] *Ibid.* 10-11, 17, 21.　　　　　　　　　[3] Edwards, II. 151.

It is not my purpose to relate the events at Cadiz. After the crumpling of the harbour-defences, there followed the capture and sack of the city. In all this Essex took the lead. But there was general agreement that Ralegh's insistence on changing the plan of attack was the clue to its complete success; and for once he, who 'desired to be able to sway all men's fancies, all men's courses' got the credit he deserved. Here Throckmorton was able to render him a useful service, for he got Sir Anthony Ashley away from the fleet to carry his story first to the Council and the Queen.

While their men-folk were away Lady Ralegh went up to stay with her sister-in-law, for we have a letter from her from Mile End about Captain Keymis's return from Guiana, whither Ralegh had dispatched him.[1] He brought news that the Spaniards had now moved in. Meanwhile Hariot was employed in constructing a map, based on Ralegh's notes and the information he had obtained from the Indians. Hariot was adding to it Keymis's information, who had accomplished the main purpose he was sent out for, the discovery of the coast between Amazon and Orinoco and the exploration of the mouths of the latter. Because these matters were of importance to the state, Hariot asked that his map should be kept secret between Cecil and himself, as Ralegh wished. He was willing to wait upon Cecil, but 'I dare not presume of myself for some former respects'.[2] Supposedly this refers to his delation for his opinions. The map, however, materialised — it must be the equally decorative and informative chart that has come down to us and now reposes in the British Museum.[3]

Meanwhile, in London there were rumours of disaster to the fleet at Cadiz. Young Nicholas Throckmorton carried the rumour down to his uncle, Sir Francis Carew, at Bedington that Ralegh was drowned: 'it was a general speech throughout London'.[4] This is one indication among many that Ralegh had always news-value. The truth came from 'her Majesty's city of Cadiz', that it was in English hands and that Ralegh's part in the action was so 'praiseworthy as those which formerly were his enemies do now hold him in great estimation; for that which he did in the sea-service could not be bettered'.[5]

The city lay at their feet to be ransacked, and there were liberal rewards all round. In the fleet-action Ralegh had been

---

[1] *Salisbury MSS.* VI. 308. [2] *Ibid.* 256.
[3] Reproduced in Ralegh, *Discoverie of Guiana*, ed. V. T. Harlow.
[4] *Salisbury MSS.* VI. 245. [5] *Ibid.* 229.

slightly wounded in the leg, so that he had to be carried ashore; but he got his share of the plunder. There was an absurdly liberal distribution of knighthoods by Howard and Essex — over sixty, of whom Throckmorton was one. At Court Ralegh's friends resounded his praises, and they were corroborated by the Lord Admiral's relation of the action.[1] On coming away from Cadiz, there was a question of sending the fleet, or some part of it, westward to intercept the treasure *flota* now due. Ralegh advised against it and with good reasons: the state of the ships, sickness of the men, danger from the weather. Thus the *flota* was missed, and people did not fail to impute this to him: anxious to get his plunder home, they said.

On arrival back at Plymouth he hoped he might be pardoned 'for coming about by sea, for, besides the great and dangerous infection, I am not well in health myself. Sir, I hope her divine Majesty is well, the report whereof hath encountered us all with infinite joy.'[2] Ralegh wrote his own Relation of the action, and very good it is: restrained and truthful, yet visually alive as we should expect. He concluded, 'what the Generals have gotten, I know least; they protest it is little. For my own part, I have gotten a lame leg, and a deformed. For the rest, either I spake too late, or it was otherwise resolved. I have not wanted good words, and exceeding kind and regardful usance. But I have possession of naught but poverty and pain. If God had spared me that blow, I had possessed myself of some House.'

Actually he came off better than he said: only two of the soldiers beat him markedly, his rivals, Sir Francis Vere and Sir Coniers Clifford. Of the naval commanders Ralegh came off best, so far as we know, with £1769 worth — which we must multiply many times.[3] The spoils declared by him and some other officers consisted of plate, pearl, gold ornaments, Turkey carpets, tapestries, wines, hides, with a chest of printed books.[4]

Upon the shelves of the Bodleian, it is well known, repose a number of volumes from the library of bishop Jerome Osorio taken by Essex at Faro that summer. It is not known that some of Throckmorton's takings, flotsam and jetsam from Cadiz, have fetched up on the shelves of English libraries, too. In the British Museum is a folio published at Seville in 1588, *Nobleza del Andaluzia*, with a note on the title-page, 'Taken from Cadiz the 27th of June 1596. A. Throckmorton.'[5] And on the shelves of his

[1] H.M.C. *Bath MSS.* 44-7. [2] Edwards, II. 138, 156.
[3] W. B. Devereux, I. 377. [4] *Cal. S.P. Dom. 1595-7*, 266.
[5] Information from Lady Throckmorton's Note-Book.

old college-library at Oxford are others. There is a *Tractado del Conseio y de los Conseieros de los Principes,* of 1589, in which Throckmorton has noted the words: 'Io quedo: quedaran: shall remayne. alcançar to obtayne or to reache: hallar to fynde. embiar: to sende.' They would be useful words in the circumstances of Cadiz in June 1596.

Another volume has an even more intimate interest: Çamorano's *Compendio del Arte de Navegar,* Seville, 1588. For this evidently belonged to a sea-captain or pilot, who has written on the blank pages at beginning and end directions as to the course to follow out of the bay of San Lucar to the Canaries, to Teneriffe, with descriptions of the islands, capes and headlands to note for the course to the West Indies. There are the features of Marigalante, Guadalupe and Antigua, with distances, heights of mountains to recognise from the sea; the navigation to Puerto Rico and Santo Domingo; to the harbours of the Spanish Main. The book belonged to one Joannes de Salcate or Alçaste, as he varies it; and at the beginning he has written a prayer to his guardian angel to protect him and keep him from worldly vices. 'Tuque siempre meayudaste y guardaste áyudame, guardame siempre denoche y de dia amen.'

All which did not prevent the day coming when Essex and Ralegh hove over the horizon with their splendid fleet, pillaging the city and taking Don Alçaste's goods. His guardian angel can just not have been looking that day.

CHAPTER XII

RETURN AND DISENCHANTMENT

T HE circumstances of Ralegh's return to Court show who had been responsible for keeping him away. During the years of his absence Essex reigned as sole favourite in his sovereign's heart, and he was not going to share that position with anyone. Not until he was squared could Ralegh come back, and when he did it was not on the old footing.

On his return from Cadiz the Raleghs and Throckmortons went down to Knole, where they were made much of and feasted.[1] In January 1597 Cecil's wife died, and Ralegh wrote him a lofty, much-admired letter of consolation. 'I would but mind you of this — that you should not overshadow your wisdom with passion, but look aright into things as they are.'[2] Ralegh always had this wisdom for others, but applied it less frequently to himself. And again, 'I believe it that sorrows are dangerous companions, converting bad into evil and evil into worse, and do no other service than multiply harms. They are the treasures of weak hearts and of the foolish.' There, too, he always gave way to them himself. 'It is true that you have lost a good and virtuous wife, and myself an honourable friend and kinswoman.' Lady Cecil was one of the Brookes of Cobham, the family that felt itself demeaned by Shakespeare's portrait of their ancestor, Sir John Oldcastle, in *Henry IV*, and forced him to change the name to Falstaff. In this generation she was much the best of a bad bunch; her brothers, Lord Cobham and George Brooke became the means of Ralegh's ruin, and her early death spared her the spectacle of her husband bringing them all to book and destroying her family.

The last years of the Queen's reign were a time of disenchant-ment, of war-weariness in the country and feverish feuding at Court leading to the enaction of a sombre tragedy. As yet these things were not in view, and in February Cecil went to call on his brother-in-law, Lord Cobham, at his house within Black-

---

[1] H.M.C. *De L'Isle and Dudley MSS.* II. 222.   [2] Edwards, II. 161-3.

friars where he had for neighbours the players and their private
theatre. 'It was long ere that they spake one to another', we
learn; 'there appeared the fulness of grief and passion in them'.[1]
Meanwhile, with Burghley's declining strength and health, Cecil
was in greatest credit with the Queen, who passed most of the
day in private conference with him on affairs of state, and Ralegh
hoped to be restored through his influence. He was on edge to
get back now; he was once more attending at Court, but had
not yet got permission to execute his office. Reports were constant of his standing for this or that office, at this time the vacant
Vice-Chamberlainship; but he had to be reinstated first. The
way to this was by gaining Essex's compliance.

Essex was on the worst terms with Cecil, suspicious of him
and jealous of the political confidence the Queen reposed in him.
After the fearful scattering that befell them later, it was noted
that, of himself, Essex much appreciated Ralegh's company.
They were of a type, both men of action, bent on the war with
Spain. To set against Ralegh's far greater experience and superiority of parts, Essex had much higher rank, his closeness to the
Queen — he was her cousin and Leicester's stepson — and a
deep hold on her affection. He could have afforded to be
magnanimous. That spring Ralegh laboured hard to bring Essex
and Cecil together. It was in the country's interest, he argued:
much good might grow by it, 'the Queen's continual unquietness
will turn to contentments': dispatches for all matters of war
and peace would go forward more easily. At this juncture his
own interest would be best served by such an alliance, too.

In April he achieved it. Cecil went in his coach to Essex
House, where Ralegh met him; they dined together and spent
two hours 'very private all three . . . where the treaty of a
peace was confirmed'.[2] What had the Cecils got to offer the
dissatisfied, disgruntled Essex? — Support for yet another offensive campaign at sea, such as he and Ralegh ardently desired
and the Queen as much disliked. Faced with unanimity among
her councillors, she gave way and plans were set on foot to follow
up Cadiz with what was hoped would be a knock-out blow against
Spain. The opportunity that offered was much like that in the
year after the Armada, when she had hoped for a decisive blow
against Lisbon and had been presented, by Drake and Norris,
with a fiasco. Now, again, to wipe out the shame of Cadiz,
Philip had madly driven yet another Armada to sea that stormy

---

[1] A. Collins, *Letters and Memorials (Sydney Papers)*, II. 18.
[2] *Ibid.* 42.

autumn, and had it dispersed with heavy losses of ships and men off Finistère. The remains of his fleet had taken refuge in Ferrol; both Elizabeth and Burghley hoped to end the war with an attack upon it in force. A subsidiary objective was what had been just missed after Cadiz, the interception of the treasure fleet from the West Indies at the Azores. Such was the inception of the Islands Voyage, which turned out as abortive as the Lisbon fiasco.[1]

They were only just in time in reaching agreement, for in May the Queen turned against the idea altogether — such exhaustion of her resources, the cost to the country, the chances of failure. But preparations were too far advanced to go back on it. The Lord Admiral pleaded ill-health, and Essex took command — a prime factor in its failure. Ralegh reaped his reward: a high place in the command, and restoration to his office of personal attendance on the Queen. Essex did not wish to witness the scene, and rode down to Chatham. 'In his absence Sir Walter Ralegh was brought to the Queen by Sir Robert Cecil — who used him very graciously and gave him full authority to execute his place as Captain of the Guard, which immediately he undertook and swore many men into the places void. In the evening he rid abroad with the Queen and had private conference with her; and now he comes boldly to the Privy Chamber as he was wont.'[2] What would one not give to know what passed at that private conference! Five years had passed; though time stood still with her, relations could not be on their old footing: he was now in middle age, a married, a family, man. There were no more poems.

In the enterprise on foot there was hope of private profit for those participating — prize, loot, treasure. Ralegh had the victualling of the land forces, and was given credit for doing it well; he let Essex have a generous provision, and they 'are grown exceeding great', all three often together at Cecil House prior to Essex and Ralegh's departure. Ralegh was Rear-Admiral in command of the third squadron, out of four, as for Cadiz. On their way down Channel in early July, in excellent humour they continued 'the good spirits they had enjoyed at Cecil House. Ralegh reported back, 'I acquainted the Lord General with your letter to me, and your kind acceptance of your entertainment; he was also wonderful merry at your conceit of Richard II.'[3] What was Cecil's joke on the subject of

---

[1] Cf. Sir Julian Corbett, *The Successors of Drake*, chaps. VII, VIII.
[2] Collins, II. 54.   [3] Edwards, II. 169.

Richard II? Had the entertainment, perhaps, included a visit
to a performance of the play at the Globe? No-one knows;
but the joke was to have a sinister reverberation in four years'
time, when the Essex conspirators procured a revival of the
play to put London in mind of the deposition of kings. 'I am
Richard II: know ye not that?' cried the Queen angrily.

Their plans were put out by the storms of that summer. It
has been observed by naval historians that Ralegh was the first
commander to give up and confess defeat at the hand of the
weather. On the other hand, the sea-worthiness of the Queen's
ships was not what it had been in 1588. Ralegh put back into
Plymouth, excusing himself with the vehemence of his letters:
'the storm on Wednesday grew more forcible, and the seas grew
very exceeding lofty. . . . That which most grieveth me, and
which, I protest before the majesty of God, I do constantly believe,
is that either my Lord-General himself will wrestle with the seas
to his peril or (constrained to come back) be found utterly heart-
broken, although it be not in the power of man to fight against
elements.'[1] Then Essex did give up and put into Falmouth.
Thence he went by land 'over the mountains of Cornwall' to
join Ralegh at Plymouth, who put him up in the *Warspite*. 'And
now her Majesty may be sure his lordship shall sleep somewhat
the sounder, though he fare the worse, by being with me; for
I am an excellent watchman at sea.' Time was when her solicitude had been for him.

Together they hurried up to Court to urge a change of plan,
though we know from a letter of Cecil that little was hoped of
the expedition now. They were given their head, however, and
cut down the land-forces eating up provisions at Falmouth.
Meanwhile, Lord Thomas Howard, a better sailor, had kept his
station off Ferrol awaiting them in vain. When they were together again, they had not the forces to assail Ferrol and went
on to the Azores to lie in wait for the treasure-fleet. That they
missed it was entirely due to the contradictory dispositions of
Essex. While waiting for him, Ralegh performed the only notable
action of the voyage, the capture of Fayal. This led to a dangerous breach between him and Essex, egged on by his faction, in
particular Sir Christopher Blount, who bore Ralegh an inveterate
hatred. He wanted to have Ralegh court-martialled for dis-
obedience to orders, and his life made forfeit. The breach was
patched up by sensible Lord Thomas. At Court the only person

[1] *Ibid.* 172-3, 176.

to get any credit was Ralegh: 'his friends in Court are great, and do mightily grace his doings and experience at sea'.[1]

While they were away Philip's last armada — its objective was to take Falmouth — got as far as the Lizard before being blown back. While still in the dark, the urgent thing was the defence of the West Country, to which the fleet returned in October, discouraged and denuded: Ralegh wrote from Plymouth, 'we are here made mad with intricate affairs and want of means'.[2] He was at once thrown into the work of looking to the defences of his lieutenancy. At Court Essex's proceedings, in calling Ralegh's action at Fayal before a council of war, where he might have been sentenced to death, were 'greatly misliked. Sir Walter Ralegh is happy to have so good and constant friends, that are able by their wisdom and authority to protect him and comfort him.'[3]

All these strains upon his energy did not prevent him from pursuing a quarrel with his nephew, the younger Sir John Gilbert, from which we get a glimpse of the characteristics of this stormy family. Sir John was a nasty young man, mean and grabbing. The quarrel was evidently over cash, possibly the division of prize-money. Here is his angry uncle: 'where you say you followed the worst of my fortunes in despite of envy, I pray forget not yourself; nor do not so much mistake my fortunes but that, when they were at worst, they were better than the best of your own, and were able enough to stead my friends and despise the rest'.[4] How like Ralegh this is, utterly true to character! As for the relations within this not very nice family, the uncle reminds the nephew that he had saved his parsonage[5] for him when young from the clutches of acquisitive uncle Carew, and later from cousin Thynne. 'And but in respect of me, I know how your aunt had dealt with you well enough.' And so on for pages. 'Notwithstanding, I remain your good friend. You shall not measure me by your own "good nature", for I do not labour any man against you. I may be rather ashamed to have any man know your ingratitude. I will not defile the nest, nor yet seek [*i.e.* omit] to feed those that cannot fly so well without me. Hurt not yourself. I shall leave you to your own courses, and hold this of yours no stranger than the usages of others. It being more natural to all men rather to pay [*i.e.* repay] wrongs than good turns.'

[1] Collins, II. 68.　　　　　　　　　　　　　[2] Edwards, II. 183.
[3] Collins, II. 74-5.　　　　　　　　　　　　 [4] Edwards, II. 194-7.
[5] This means some rectory, *i.e.* the rectorial tithes of a parish, in his possession.

What a lot they were! This tells us, as no romanticised biographies do, what they were really like. Sir Walter, though the most gifted of them, was not the worst.

The strain of that summer and autumn told on Ralegh, so that he remained absent from his place in Parliament till December. Parliament had met in October 1597, to raise money for the renewed activity of the war. A sign of his restoration, Ralegh had been returned knight of the shire for Dorset.[1] In October he was too busy elsewhere to attend; in November he was sick, and Adrian Gilbert, member for Bridport, obtained licence to go down to Sherborne to attend on him.[2] His vitality reasserted itself, and in December he was back to take a leading part in this Parliament of which we have but inadequate reports. These years from 1594 to 1599 were years of dearth, failures of harvest and economic distress in the country.[3] In consequence the legislation was mainly economic and social, and the bills brought forward were framed in committees of the Commons. From the moment of Ralegh's reappearance, we find him more active than ever in the committee-work of the House: on numerous committees, including all the important ones. As a Parliament man, he was indeed in a strategic position: a quasi-official member, he also represented responsibilities in, and the interests of, the West Country. No less noticeable is the confidence the House reposes in him. In the important conference with the Lords concerning amendments to some of this legislation, Ralegh was chosen to head the delegation from the Commons.[4] Again, it was characteristic that he and his fellows should have received with some distaste the fact that the Lords did not rise to them. We are more amused by his serving on a committee to restrain the wearing of excessive apparel.

In spite of the strains and cracks resulting from the Islands Voyage, in January 1598 the world wondered to see 'the too too great familiarity that is grown between the Earl of Essex, Sir Robert Cecil and Sir Walter Ralegh; none but they enjoy him, they carry him away as they list'.[5] We have a close-up of Ralegh at this moment, playing primero late in the Presence Chamber after the Queen had gone to bed, and her squire for the body that night desiring them all to give over. 'Anon after he spake to them again that if they would not leave, he would call in the

[1] *Return of M.P.s*, I. 433.
[2] D'Ewes, *Journal*, 559.
[3] Cf. Sir John Neale, *Elizabeth I and her Parliaments, 1584–1601*, 335, 337.
[4] D'Ewes, *Journal*, 580, 583, 585.
[5] Collins, II. 79, 83.

209

guard to pull down the board: which Sir Walter Ralegh seeing,
put up his money and went his ways.' The young Southampton
refused, however, and got some of his golden locks well pulled
for his impertinence.

The motives for the alliance are not far to seek. 'Sir Walter
Ralegh labours mightily to have something done for him before
Mr. Secretary's going away, and he doth importune my Lord
of Essex to be a furtherer of it.'[1] If Essex would support Ralegh
for Vice-Chamberlain, Cecil and Ralegh would contribute one
third of the prizes falling to them in their privateering partnership towards the payment of his debts. And what would Master
Secretary get out of this? He was having to go abroad to try
and persuade Henri IV not to make a separate peace with Spain.
Leaving the Court was as dangerous as entering it: he wanted
an assurance that nothing deleterious to his interests would be
procured during his absence. Having secured his rear, he was
given a fine send-off by his friends. Ralegh, Lord Cobham and
Southampton each feasted the Secretary and regaled him with
plays and banquets. How much we should like to know the
plays performed, for we know Southampton's particular relation
with Shakespeare. At this moment the young Earl was in disgrace for getting Elizabeth Vernon with child. For him the
indispensable Secretary procured licence to travel: 'his fair
mistress doth wash her fairest face with too many tears', wrote
a sharp-eyed courtier. 'I pray God his going away bring her
to no such infirmity which is, as it were, hereditary to her name.'[2]
To make doubly sure in his absence, the Secretary got the Queen
to make Essex a free gift of £7000 'out of the cochineal'.[3] Having
done these good deeds, Cecil reluctantly set out, accompanied as
far as Dover by Ralegh and his friends.

Essex was advised, however, by Cecil's jealous cousin, Francis
Bacon, to take advantage of the Secretary's absence to push
himself forward in Irish affairs.[4] Tyrone, the last native prince
of Ulster, was seeking by every means to extend his resistance to
English encroachment to the dimensions of a national rebellion,
and was constantly intriguing for Spanish intervention in
Munster. Irish affairs, the growing menace of Tyrone, were the
Council's chief anxiety, and in March they were calling Ralegh,
Sir William Russell, Bingham and other experts into session with

[1] Collins, II. 82, 86, 90.
[2] This refers to the celebrated elopement of Dorothy Vernon with John Manners,
by which the Manners family came by Haddon Hall in Derbyshire.
[3] *I.e.* from prize taken in the Islands Voyage.   [4] Devereux, II. 3-5.

them for advice. Ralegh's Irish advice seems to have been usually to the point and borne out by events; and he had the merit of having tried harder than any of the other Undertakers to plant his land with English settlers. The rumour at Court was that he would be made Lord Deputy; and then that 'Sir William Russell hath absolutely refused to go; the other doth little like it'.[1] I do not think that the Queen would have appointed him: she had not sufficient confidence in his political judgment ever to make him a member of her Council. Nor do I think that if he had been offered to be Lord Deputy he would have refused. (He would have made a kind of Elizabethan Strafford in Ireland.)

He seems to have spent this summer at Sherborne, keeping in touch with the news from Guiana, where he had left a man to spy out what gold-mines were there. With his usual compulsive energy, Ralegh was both building at Sherborne and building up the estate. When he first got the castle, which was in utter disrepair, he started repairing it. But in 1594 he changed his mind and began building a new house in a more open position, a square decoratively gabled and turreted house, which one can still see encisted in the middle of the later-extended wings and turrets of the Digbys.[2] Within, some traces of him remain, his arms from a chimney-piece, the date on the windows. He was also engaged in making orchards, gardens and groves all round it, improving the property in every way. Sir John Harington tells us that with all the money he spent on it, presents to the Queen, gratuities to the ecclesiastics, law-suits, buying up leases and 'in drawing the river through rocks into his garden, he might very justly and without offence of the Church or State have compassed a much better purchase'.[3] But Ralegh came to have a passion for Sherborne, as it took shape under his hands — it was his creation. We learn from a law-suit years later that Adrian Gilbert spent a great deal of time and money helping to make the walks and gardens, and stocking the place with cattle.[4] Ralegh was very anxious to make sure the possession of the estate and the descent to his heirs, and on this changed his mind several times. At length in 1598 he thought it safest to make conveyance to his son Walter, 'without power of revocation reserved',

---

[1] Collins, II. 94, 96.

[2] Cf. J. Hutchins, *History and Antiquities of the County of Dorset* (ed. 1870), IV. 275 foll.

[3] Sir John Harington, *Nugae Antiquae* (ed. 1779), I. 104-5.

[4] C. Monro, *Acta Cancellariae*, 177, 179. Gilbert claimed that he had spent £700 over seven years.

provided that the son paid his mother £200 a year after Ralegh's decease.[1] This was apparently kept secret, even from his wife; one sees Ralegh's dynastic intention in making it, the ardent desire to make his family and name sure of Sherborne.

In August the long-gathering storm in Ireland burst with the disaster at the Yellow Ford, where an English army was badly cut up and Marshal Bagenal killed. At once the fires of dis-affection were rekindled throughout Munster, where the settlers were too few in number to resist. Panic seized upon them as the news of killings and murders spread. Spenser and his wife fled from Kilcolman, which was fired behind him and all his belong-ings destroyed. Ralegh had settled a township at Tallow, with over a hundred able men: they all fled, the settlement was destroyed by the natives and his work overthrown.[2] This is the perspective in which to see his questionable advice to Cecil as to some 'practice' proposed for doing away with a rebel, pre-sumably Tyrone. 'It can be no disgrace if it were known that the killing of a rebel were practised; for you see that the lives of anointed princes are daily sought, and we have always in Ireland given head-money for the killing of rebels. . . . But, for yourself, you are not to be touched in the matter. And for me, I am more sorry for being deceived than for being declared in the practise.'[3] This was written to Cecil; a tell-tale postscript says, 'he hath nothing under my hand but a passport'. The more moral, or less Machiavellian, Secretary did not hold with such 'practices': he held them to be un-Christian. But then he was a Christian.

Some traces of the emergency, and of the difficulty in getting men to serve in Ireland, may be seen in Northamptonshire, where Throckmorton had settled into the life of the county and was busy as J.P. and Commissioner of Musters. In October he wrote to Essex, as Earl Marshal, of the mutiny of a contingent of London troops who were being marched along Watling Street for embarkation at Chester.[4] Out of three hundred, some two hundred refused to march farther than Towcester, challenging and wounding some of their officers. Throckmorton desired Essex to order the J.P.s of Chester to apprehend the recalcitrant and send them back for imprisonment. The mutineers were duly sent back, and Throckmorton and Sir George Fermor

[1] W. B. Wildman, *Short History of Sherborne*, 171.
[2] Cf. R. Bagwell, *Ireland under the Tudors*, III. 304. Adrian Gilbert had helped to tock Ralegh's Irish lands also. Monro, 178.
[3] Edwards, II. 198-9. [4] *A.P.C. 1598-9*, 215.

'punished them by the shame of standing upon the pillory with papers over their heads declaring the nature and naughtiness of their faults, upon St. Luke's day last' — Towcester fair-day.[1] (They must have looked still more like Falstaff's recruits.) Then they were sent back penitent to Chester, while diligent watch was set for runaways.

Of Ralegh we hear nothing more this year but that he was so discontented at thriving no better that he had a mind to follow others and go to Guiana.[2] He continued to be entangled with the priests of Salisbury over Sherborne. A new bishop expressed himself satisfied with Ralegh's friendly carriage towards him, in requital for which he had met Sir Walter's wishes; in return for this Sir Walter was soliciting Cecil to get the Queen to allow the bishop to keep his benefice in Hampshire *in commendam*. One good turn deserves another. Now the Dean, though a cousin of Sir Walter's, was troublesome, perhaps disappointed at the bestowal of the bishopric. Over the Sherborne lease, 'had I stayed [obstructed] him never so little, I might have prejudiced the lease; but of 200 angels put in my hand I took not one. . . . I must confess Sir Walter Ralegh being grateful to me, and pretending — or be it intending — afterwards my advancement to the bishopric, and I in turn, minded to show him true and uncorrupted re-gratuity . . .' yet the Dean had needed a reminder from Cecil 'not to interpose myself to draw on me the Queen's dislike'.[3] All this was very grievous to him, being now the ancientest of the Queen's chaplains, and having finished, what was though impossible, a literal translation of the Greek New Testament into Latin heroical verse. One would have thought that was a sufficient occupation in itself in the pleasantest of cathedral closes. These venerable, but loquacious, old gentlemen sleep quietly enough on their tombs there now.

In June it was rumoured that Ralegh would be made Vice-Chancellor of the Duchy of Lancaster; in July that he was the 'earnestest suitor' for the Chancellorship.[4] In August Throckmorton was agitating for the command of the fifty light-horsemen raised in his county, 'so that the pains he has taken to see them well-armed may not be bestowed upon a stranger. As he has been one of those who have angered these Spaniards in their own homes, so he would not be one of the last who should displease and displace them here.' There was need for special care

---

[1] *Salisbury MSS.* VIII. 397.
[2] *The Letters of John Chamberlain*, ed. N. E. McClure, I. 49.
[3] *Salisbury MSS.* IX. 143.   [4] *Ibid.* 198, 246, 291.

in disarming professed Recusants, as well as those whose wives refused to go to church, while themselves attended to save 'their livings and their liberties by their feigned faiths. Such here have a common saying that the unbelieving husband shall be saved by the believing wife : of which sort there are many here and of no mean estate, especially on the east side of the shire.'[1] From that quarter of Northamptonshire would come a number of the Gunpowder Plot conspirators.

Essex had made it impossible for anyone else to go as Lord Deputy and quell the rebellion in Ireland, though the Queen's better judgment wanted Mountjoy, who ultimately accomplished the task. Essex was given the largest army ever to be employed in Ireland for the job, and he was granted very wide powers with the grander title of Lord Lieutenant. To command his army he selected his own personal following — so there was a latent danger to the state in his power, for the Queen was growing old. At the end of March he set out, being given a send-off by the London mob, who accompanied him some way out of the city — as he received an undeserved tribute from their favourite dramatist while away in Ireland. There he made an even worse mess of the operations than he had done of the Islands Voyage, wasting his opportunity, allowing his superiority in the field to dribble away and Tyrone to build up prestige and power with an ill-advised truce. Worse, Essex engaged in conversation with him as to what should happen upon the Queen's death. No-one knew about this at the time, but it was clear enough that he aimed at controlling the conditions of the approaching accession and possibly restraining the Queen's freedom of action — the purpose of his insurrection in February 1601. And this was treason.

In Ireland, instead of tackling Tyrone, he was writing to the Queen, 'why do I talk of victory or success ? Is it not known that from England I receive nothing but discomforts and soul's wounds ? Is it not lamented of your Majesty's faithfullest subjects, both there and here, that a Cobham and Ralegh — I will forbear others, for their places' sakes — should have such credit and favour with your Majesty when they wish the ill-success of your Majesty's most important action ?'[2] There was not the slightest evidence but that they all longed for the end of the

---

[1] In conformity with these ideas we find Throckmorton pursuing Mr. Pinchpowle Lovett and confiscating his papistical books. *Salisbury MSS*. X. 186.

[2] Devereux, II. 40-41.

rebellion in Ireland, and they had provided Essex with the means. But persecution-mania had set in with faltering will-power, and he was egged on as usual by the swordsmen, his followers. The odious Sir Gelly Meyrick was writing against Ralegh and Sir George Carew as 'infamous here for their service'.[1] Actually, Cecil was exhausted with his labours all through August, and wanted a few days' rest at Theobalds; but it was doubtful whether he would get permission, for 'he cannot be spared'.[2] Ralegh may have been ordered to sea, to keep watch in the Channel, for he 'took his leave at Court of all the ladies and his friends'.

In September we learn that Cecil and Ralegh 'do infinitely desire to be barons, and they have a purpose to be called unto it, though there be no Parliament'.[3] The Queen thought otherwise: no notice was taken of their desire. That month Essex threw up his post, deserted his army and rushed back to Court to fling himself at the Queen's feet; his nerve had given way: he must have been crazy. No-one knew what to think, except the Queen and Cecil, and their suspicions of his intentions grew with their knowledge. Essex was placed under restraint. Ralegh had nothing to do with all this: it was beyond his sphere. The Queen took her own decisions, and at last — after all that she had put up with from Essex — became his ultimate enemy. Ralegh afterwards gave it as his opinion, and he should know, that it was Essex's terrible words that 'she was cankered, and her mind as crooked as her carcass' that rendered it impossible for him to be forgiven. In December Ralegh was sick, but all the same was suspected of the libels circulating against Essex.

In the New Year 1600 Ralegh was called into council over Irish affairs, and apparently advised in favour of a defensive war. If so, his advice was not taken: it was decided to go forward with the war and end the independence of Ulster once and for all. The whole burden of affairs fell increasingly upon Cecil, who had taken his father's place in enjoying the Queen's entire confidence. Cecil was not so inveterate against Essex as was supposed, and it must be to this time that we should date Ralegh's implacable letter to him as to his attitude towards Essex. 'I am not wise enough to give you advice; but if you take it for a good counsel to relent towards this tyrant, you will repent it when it shall be too late.'[4] After some unpleasant, though realist, arguments he recites some comparable instances which throw a grim

---

[1] *Salisbury MSS.* IX. 343.   [2] Collins, II. 117, 119.
[3] *Ibid.* 126.   [4] Edwards, II. 222-3.

light into the hard core of Tudor politics. 'For after-revenges, fear them not; for your own father that was esteemed to be the contriver of Norfolk's ruin, yet his son followeth your father's son, and loveth him. Humours of men succeed not,[1] but grow by occasions and accidents of time and power. Somerset made no revenge on the Duke of Northumberland's heirs.[2] Northumberland, that now is, thinks not of Hatton's issue. Kelloway lives that murdered the brother of Horsey, and Horsey let him go by all his life-time.'

We have to remind ourselves that this was the sixteenth century. Sir Walter went on, 'let the Queen hold Bothwell while she hath him.[3] Princes are lost by security, and preserved by prevention. I have seen the last of her good days, and all ours, after his liberty.' Such was the world they lived in. He concluded with a look into the future: Essex's son 'shall be the youngest earl of England but one, and, if his father be now kept down, Will Cecil shall be able to keep as many men at his heels, and more too. . . . Lose not your advantage; if you do, I read your destiny.'

This letter has given much concern to Ralegh's more sentimental biographers. But he was not a man of sentiment, and here we have what his mind was like. Without embarking upon morality, we may at least remark the unwisdom of committing such thoughts to paper. As if they would be necessary, either! For all his experience of the Queen, he could not read her political mind: she would always do her duty.

Moreover, she had taken his measure and knew that his political judgment was unreliable, that it was flawed and faulty. He was desperately anxious to be made a member of the Privy Council, and this March he was pressing to be made a commissioner for the treaty-negotiations taking place in the Netherlands. 'But her Majesty, as it is thought, begins to perceive that if he were one, he would stand to be made a Councillor ere he went, which she hath no fancy unto.'[4]

Very discontented — and everybody knew it — Ralegh left the Court in March and went into the country. On his way his new friend, the Earl of Northumberland — not a very wise choice, for the Percies had been touched with treason in the last two generations — made him a dinner at Syon House. Ralegh

---

[1] This means that they are not inherited.

[2] Ralegh means Somerset's heirs — in fact, they were in no position to do so.

[3] In Scotland Bothwell had recently got away after several outbreaks against James VI.   [4] Collins, II. 178.

took with him Cecil's young hopeful, the boy William, who had been sickly, for the good air of Sherborne to amend him. Here we see a pleasanter side to Ralegh's nature, that which appealed to boys, as it did with Prince Henry later. In spite of everything, Ralegh was a good family-man. 'Because I know that you can receive no pleasinger news from hence than to hear of your beloved creature', he wrote to Cecil, 'I thought good to let you know of his good health. . . . His stomach, that was heretofore weak, is altogether amended, and he doth now eat well and digest rightly. I hope this air will agree exceedingly with him. He is also better kept to his book than anywhere else. This is all I can say from this poor place, and that I am ever your poorest and truest friend and servant.'[1]

In this we already hear the accents of discontent that would take such a dangerous turn in the next two years, particularly with the company he kept. Cobham was becoming his closest friend, but, though the Queen's favour for a moment beamed upon him, he was not a good friend for any one : he was unstable, light-headed and full of schemes, unable to keep anything to himself, ambitious to play an important part in affairs yet totally incompetent to do so. Ralegh and Cobham had this in common that they were both discontented, yet knew that a change of monarch would not favour them. In April Ralegh wrote to Cobham, 'I can write your lordship nothing from hence, but that we live . . . if there be neither honour nor profit, I must begin to keep sheep betime'.[2] The next thing is that the Raleghs went to Bath specially to meet Cobham and waited a week there for him. 'My wife will despair ever to see you in these parts if your lordship come not now. We can but long for you and wish you as our own lives whatsoever.' Cobham was a poor exchange for Cecil, but the latter was immersed in affairs of state, at this moment the complex negotiations in the Netherlands that might lead to a general peace.

For this purpose Cecil desired to see what might be material, especially in regard to the question of diplomatic precedence between England and Spain, in Sir Nicholas Throckmorton's negotiations. His son sent what he could find among 'those my father's painful and unprofitable papers (I mean unprofitable only to himself).'[3] He accompanied them with a compliment to the Secretary's father, 'the chief guide of our so long good . . . nothing being more happy amongst the heaps of happiness which

[1] Edwards, II. 202-3.   [2] *Ibid.* 203, 206.
[3] *Salisbury MSS.* X. 125.

came from your father's faithful hands to this state than was the league and amity broken between France and Scotland, made by him at Leith sincere and entire between us and them'. Throckmorton gave it as his simple judgment that a Dukedom of Burgundy, severed from both France and Spain, would suit English interests and the cause of peace best — as indeed the Secretary needed no telling. 'Thus humbly desiring you to take a clown's contemplation in as good part as it is meant.' In Elizabethan English, a 'clown' meant a country cousin, and Throckmorton was referring politely to his rustication from the delights of the Court. He was best off, to quote a court-follower: 'it is a world to be here, to see the humours of the time. Blessed are they that can be away, and live contented.'[1]

But Ralegh could not live thus contented — *sua si bona norint*. In June he was back once more agitating for the Vice-Chamberlainship.[2] In July he advised in favour of sending over the titular Earl of Desmond, to help keep Munster in allegiance — though, being a Protestant, he had no sway with the tribesmen whatever. In July Ralegh and Cobham 'stole over' to Dunkirk, in Cecil's phrase: they went to see the operations from the States' camp, but it gave an opportunity for more dangerous cogitations and contacts in regard to peace. Back in August Ralegh at last got the Queen's promise of the government of the Isle of Jersey, for which Cecil had backed him. Later that summer Cecil and Cobham were expected at Sherborne, 'where young Mr. Cecil, his son, is brought up'.

From this summer we have a charming letter from William Cecil that shows Ralegh in the most attractive light as playmate with the boys. The boy had been at Bath for three weeks in Dr. Sherwood's care, and was now able to report to his father — or his tutor for him — 'nunc autem reversus sum Sherborniam optima valitudine'. To his grand playmate he wrote, 'Sir Walter, we must all exclaim and cry out because you will not come down. You being absent, we are like soldiers that when their Captain are [*sic*] absent they know not what to do: you are so busy about idle matters. Sir Walter, I will be plain with you. I pray you leave all idle matters and come down to us.'[3]

When he did come down, he went across from Weymouth to take over the government of the island of Jersey. Bess and 'little Wat' brought him aboard the ship, which left in fair weather and then ran into contrary winds that kept him two days and

[1] Collins, II. 129.   [2] *Ibid.* 196, 206, 209, 214.
[3] *Salisbury MSS.* X. 459.

nights at sea. He took the oath of office on 20 September, and was royally entertained.¹ He found Jersey the pleasantest island he had seen, but was disappointed at its value — not the third part that was reported or that he had expected. However, energetic as ever, he gave orders for the completion of the fort, *Isabella Bellissima*, and reprieved Mont Orgueil Castle from demolition, placing men in it at his own charge until further instructions.

While he was away there was a fire at Durham House, which Lady Ralegh was glad went 'noo fardar other wies, hit had rid ous of all our pooar substans of plat and other thinges. Unly now the loos is of your cumpani [Cecil's] wich I thinke by this menes wee cannot injoy this wintar. Hit will now be a fit time for you to get sum intres in that rotten houes for yourself and your frind: other wies I knoo none so un wies that will besto so mani hundred pounes as Sur Wattar hath dun, without fardar interest or asurans of hit.'² Lady Ralegh's idiosyncratic spelling has a phonetic interest for us: we can hear her voice with its broad a's and liberal aspirates. We see too that, like her own family, she was a schemer. It would have been well for the Raleghs if they could have got a lien on the bishop of Durham's house, for one of the first things James did was to hand it back to the bishop. (He much preferred bishops to fighting men.) Bess was glad too that 'this mischans of feeiar cam not by ani neckelegans of ani sarvant of mine, but by me cossin Darci's sarvant — a woman that delleth just under our logging, and anoyeth ous infenitly. I hope hee will now remoueve heer.'³

In the final stages of Essex's self-destruction Ralegh had much less part than is usually supposed. His was a duel not with Ralegh, or even with Cecil, as he thought, but with the Queen: he never seems to have realised that in the end she had become his mortal enemy, in the interests of the state. He was in touch with James, hoping to use his leverage on his own behalf — and James was sympathetic; he was in touch with Mountjoy, his follower in command of the army in Ireland, hoping to use him. In January 1601 he summoned his supporters from all parts of the country to London, mostly discontented army officers. When he made his ill-conceived outbreak into the City on 8 February,

¹ T. N. Brushfield, 'Raleghana, Part V', *Trans. Devon. Assocn.* 1903, 555.
² Edwards, II. 404-5.
³ A robbery occurred at Durham House in 1602 when two men stole two linen pillow-beres (*i.e.* -cases) fitted with silk and gold, worth £10, a cushion cloth adorned with silk and gold £5, and a diaper table cloth. Brushfield, 'Raleghana, Part V', *Trans. Devon. Assocn.* 1903, 558.

he used Ralegh and Cobham's names as an excuse: they would have him murdered in his bed, they had sold England to the Infanta of Spain. (She was now ruling in the Netherlands — and some of these aspersions stuck.)

That morning Ralegh had an interview with his kinsman, Sir Ferdinando Gorges, who had deserted his command at Plymouth at Essex's summons. Gorges would not come to Durham House, so each put out in a boat on the Thames. Ralegh advised him to go back to his command. Gorges refused, but at least he made no attempt to capture or kill Ralegh, as Sir Christopher Blount wished him to do. (Blount was now Essex's stepfather, third husband of the much-married Lettice Knollys.) From the bank of the Thames Blount fired several shots at Ralegh. When the insurrection sputtered out that day, it was Gorges who released the Lords of the Council whom Essex was holding as hostages in Essex house. At his trial it was the evidence of Gorges that told most heavily against him. Gorges was imprisoned, but not for long; no doubt he had a powerful advocate in his kinsman.

At his trial Blount made amends to Ralegh, confessing that his and Cobham's names had been used only 'to colour other matters'. But Blount had more on his conscience: he had been one of those in whom Ralegh inspired a perfect hatred, and after the action at Fayal he had sought to have Ralegh's life. On the scaffold he expressed an 'infinite desire' for Sir Walter's forgiveness. At Essex's trial, when Ralegh was called in witness, the Earl said, 'what booteth it to swear the fox?' But on the scaffold he, too, acquitted Ralegh and Cobham of his imputations of supporting the Infanta's claim to the English throne, and said that they were true servants of the State. As Captain of the Guard Ralegh had to be present at Essex's execution, and approached the scaffold to be within hearing of the Earl's desired reconciliation. His presence was so much resented, however, that he had to retire within the Armoury, from a window of which he watched the scene. This was misrepresented by his enemies, who put it about that he had gloated over the sad spectacle. Actually it was observed by those near him that Ralegh was sunk in gloom that day — as well he might be, considering the uncertainty of his own future, the insecurity of tenure, depending on the life of an old woman exhausted by the struggle.

For, what these people could not realise was that it was neither Ralegh, nor even Cecil, who had brought Essex to the block, but the Queen: it was her last effort for the independence of the throne.

These last years of a great reign were sad and depressing, bitter with cynicism, people's nerves on edge with expectation of change, hope, anxiety, revenge. The heroic spirit of the earlier phase of the war had gone out of public affairs; people were in them for what they could get out of them for themselves. The Jacobean age of opulence and vulgar ostentation, and with its moral velleities, was already on the way.

For the time, things went on as they were, with everyone waiting the Queen's death. Cecil was almost as unpopular as Ralegh, and over the country they were abused together, now in Suffolk, now in Warwickshire.[1] They appeared together in the libels that circulated:

> Little Cecil tripping up and down:
> He rules both Court and Crown . . .

> Ralegh doth time bestride:
> He sits twixt wind and tide,
> Yet uphill he cannot ride,
> For all his bloody pride.
> He seeks taxes in the tin,
> He polls the poor to the skin,
> Yet he swears 'tis no sin —
> Lord, for thy pity![2]

In fact, he had always done his best to look after the interests of the tinners, and in Parliament pleaded for the poorest class of taxpayer. It is true that there were pickings from the wreckage of the Essex conspiracy, and Ralegh appears to have been paid a sum to procure pardon for Sir Edward Baynham.[3] Such things, though resented by those who did not share in them, were legitimate then.

A small trace of the disturbance in London is reflected in Throckmorton's affairs in Northamptonshire. He was at once given command of the county's horse-bands, with a testimonial from the Council that he was 'known to be of good skill and experience and hath already taken pains to see the numbers made complete and other defects amended'.[4] The Commissioners of

---

[1] Ralegh was so unpopular at this time that even his sexual prowess was depreciated. A naughty prisoner in Newgate said that the Queen 'gave most liberally to those who were best weaponed; thus the Earl of Leicester and Lord Chancellor [Hatton] might spend £50,000 a year, Sir Walter Ralegh £10,000'. *Cal. S.P. Dom. 1598–1601*, 373.   [2] S.P. 12/278, 23.   [3] Birch, *Memoirs*, II. 496.
[4] *A.P.C. 1600–01*, 382; *Salisbury MSS.* X. 224, 257, 465.

Musters replied that Sir William Lane had been appointed captain in 1588 and they thought him a very fit man for the place. They thought the like of Sir Arthur: would the Council appoint which of them was fitter? Throckmorton applied to Cecil at length: Sir William had had charge of the horse at Tilbury, and since that time never took care of them: 'whose place so near about the prince deserves all his attendance, and might be sufficient to content, without any country ambition, *un abil homme*'. The Privy Council suggested a compromise: the band of 100 horse to be divided 50–50 between Sir Arthur and Sir William. This did not suit a Throckmorton, who used his sister to carry his remonstrances to Cecil: 'for these thirteen years (until my Lord of Nottingham appointed myself, wherein I stand to their judgments that will not forbear me of my care and behaviour) Sir William Lane never did so much as to look on a horse or ever took order for them'. No doubt, no doubt.

At Sherborne we see Ralegh opening a letter of Cobham's by mistake: brought at midnight, 'I opened it in a bad light and half asleep, thinking it had been to myself. I hope your lordship will be here tomorrow or a Saturday, or else my wife says her oysters will be all spoilt and her partridge stale.'[1] Cobham stayed but a night and then went on to Cornwall. For Cecil's building operations, Ralegh was bargaining for timber. 'Rushmore will not be fit for you to come to this year. It is so ruined as I cannot lodge you or myself therein. I pray believe that when all hearts are open and all desires tried, that I am your faithfullest friend to do you service.' With such personages, these are the accents of some mistrust. 'Bess returns you her best wishes, notwithstanding all quarrels.'

Back in London in September Ralegh found that no provision had been made for the reception of the French Marshal Biron. The Duke, companion at arms of Henri IV, was a very eminent guest, but Ralegh 'never saw so great a person so neglected': not one nobleman or gentleman to guide the company.[2] So Ralegh took them to see the monuments in Westminster Abbey, and to the Bear Garden which they enjoyed. He had sent to and fro, and laboured like a mule to see that they were properly entertained. 'The French wear all black and no kind of bravery at all, so as I have only made me a black taffeta suit to be in, and leave all my other suits.' Ralegh was in attendance on the Queen on her summer progress; she was anxious to see Cobham, and

---

[1] Edwards, II. 226-7.   [2] *Ibid.* 233-6, 245.

'will take it exceeding kindly and take herself more beholding unto you than you think'. Lord Cobham was resolved not to come; Sir Walter excused him on the score of sickness. Ralegh himself was sick on his return to Sherborne and so unable to take the waters at Bath this year. He was plagued with suits with his former agent Mere, who was upheld in Dorset by Lord Howard of Bindon — and this made another enemy for him in the powerful Howard clan. Bess had made Cecil a pair of gloves, and 'says that she must envy any fingers whosoever that shall wear her gloves, but your own'. While Ralegh was away, Cecil paid Sherborne a visit — Bess said 'in an unseasonable time, and had no leisure to look abroad; and that every day this place amends, and London to her grows worse and worse'.

They were all together again in London for the Parliament that met on 27 October. Money was more badly needed than ever: the war in Ireland meant an immense drain; the Queen was having to sell Crown lands to support her government, and even, according to Ralegh, jewels. The memory of the ever-popular Essex was an unspoken reproach. At the opening of Parliament, as the Queen 'went through the Commons very few said "God save your Majesty" as they were wont in all great assemblies'.[1] Ralegh had been returned knight of the shire for Cornwall,[2] and since this Parliament is more fully reported than any of the reign it would be possible to follow his part in it in some detail. Here we wish only to indicate what throws specific light on his personality and opinions.

It is obvious that he was a foremost member, and regarded so. He appears more frequently than any other member except Cecil, who operated as government leader of the House, and Francis Bacon, who had wormed his way over from Essex's side before his fall and was now obsequiously following the cousin he always envied. We can also observe Ralegh's independence of mind; supporting the government's essential demand for three and even four subsidies, he took an independent line on other issues. With him, it was probably a case of *Ich kann nichts anders*. There was a bill for the compulsory sowing of a proportion of hemp. Ralegh did not like 'this constraining of men to manure or use their grounds at our wills; but rather let every man use his ground to that which it is most fit for, and therein use his own discretion'.[3] Again, his sympathy was for the poor cultivator, who could not afford to buy the seed.

[1] D'Ewes, 602. [2] *Return of M.P.s*, I. 437.
[3] H. Townshend, *Collections*, 188.

His mind was consistently bent towards freedom. When the statute of tillage came up, he argued that poor men could not provide the seed for as much corn as they were bound to plough. I think this represents, too, a West Country view, where pasture was more in keeping with natural conditions. But most countries had surpluses of corn and he favoured more freedom of trade. In this he came up against both Bacon and Cecil, who was at least candid as to his own experience: 'I do not dwell in the country nor am I acquainted with the plough. But I think that whosoever doth not maintain the plough destroys the kingdom.'[1] On the burden, and the incidence, of taxation, Ralegh effectively exposed Bacon's humbug. Bacon argued for not exempting the poor any more than the rich, with a Latin tag: *Dulcis tractus pari iugo* (easy is the pull with an even yoke). 'Call you this *par iugum* an even yoke,' said Sir Walter, 'when a poor man pays as much as a rich? And peradventure his estate is no better than it is set at, or but little better. When our estates that are £3 or £4 in the Queen's Book, it is not the hundredth part of our wealth. Therefore it is neither *dulcis* nor *par*.'[2]

It is to be feared the Ralegh was without that element essential to a politician, and the successful running of politics: humbug.

The uncanting, free-ranging nature of his mind is to be seen again in his opposition to still further measures to compel attendance at church. He showed how ridiculous it was for two churchwardens from every parish in a shire to bring offenders to sessions — what multitudes there would be, besides the absurdity 'of giving authority to a mean churchwarden'.[3] Here one is very close to Ralegh's spirit: the contempt for ordinary standards and judgments, with the consequence of more freedom. No less characteristically, he got into trouble by expressing his contempt too freely. The House divided 105 to 106, but someone had been pulled back by the sleeve from giving his vote. There was some fuss made, and Ralegh said 'Why? It is a small matter to pull one by the sleeve, for so have I done myself oftentimes.' There was an uproar at this —a mistake so openly to challenge people's cant. He had to submit to be reprehended by the Comptroller of the Household — a heinous offence, a very loose conscience, he should be ashamed of himself. There we have the man to the life, spoiling a good case by indiscretion; this was what contemporaries meant by his 'bold face', a certain brazenness.

---

[1] H. Townshend, *Collections*, 299. [2] *Ibid*. 204. [3] *Ibid*. 320-1.

Yet, that he had no ordinary sensibility we know from both his poetry and his prose; and this Parliament witnessed it on one occasion when monopolies were being discussed and that of playing-cards was mentioned, which he held; for it is recorded that 'Sir Walter blushed'.[1] I do not know of any other instance among these hard-faced men. It is the combination in him, the contradictory qualities, that make him so complex, difficult to understand and teasing to study. In the very same debate he defended himself, with a good sense of tactics, not in regard to the playing-cards, but on his tin-patent as Lord Warden of the Stannaries. For this went with his office: 'I am urged to speak in two respects; the one, because I find myself touched in particular; the other, in that I take some imputation and slander to be offered unto her Majesty'. There, again, he was going too far, being too aggressive. He had no difficulty in showing that before he was granted the patent, with the price of tin fluctuating extremely, the poor tinners never had but 2s. a week; 'but since my patent, whosoever will work, be tin at what price soever, they have 4s. a week truly paid'.

He spoke sharply, and nobody could deny him; but it was reported that, after his speech, there was 'a great silence'.

Some lack of sympathy, some disaccord, is observable between Ralegh and Cecil, sitting beside each other, in this Parliament. In the summer Ralegh had again been expecting to be made a member of the Council, and he blamed Cecil for obstructing it. Some years later he described his fortunes in the last phase of the Queen's reign as 'at a stand'. How far the breach had gone one can only learn from Cecil's secret correspondence. On the surface there was insincerity in both, though Cecil, as an accomplished politician, was far better master of himself. Here is an outburst of Ralegh's against Lord Howard of Bindon, who was thought in Dorset to have poisoned his wife (his daughter was certainly a poisoner, Frances Howard, Countess of Somerset, who poisoned Sir Thomas Overbury). 'I will not endure wrong at so peevish a fool's hands any longer. I will rather lose my life. And I think that my Lord Puritan [*i.e.* Lord Justice] Periam doth think that the Queen shall have more use of rogues and villains than of men, or else he would not, at Bindon's instances, have yielded to try actions against me, being out of the land.'[2]

Bess was also contributing her quota to antagonising the numerous Howard clan. She was now on bad terms with a

---

[1] *Ibid.* 232, 235.   [2] Edwards, II. 250.

former friend in Lady Kildare, who was Lord Admiral Howard's daughter — a former patron of Ralegh, now an enemy. Bess was pulling every string she could to get back the Queen's good will, and she learned that Lady Kildare had dealt unfavourably in regard to her with the Queen. 'I unly say this, that for the honnar I beear heer name and the auncient aquaintans of heer, I wish shee wold be as ambitious to doo good, as she is apte to the contrari.'[1]

In these quarrels around the Queen the reign was sputtering out. At the end Ralegh was wanting some further assurance of his patent for wine-licences. 'It grieves me to find with what difficulty and torment to myself I obtain the smallest favour. Her Majesty knows that I am ready to spend all I have, and my life, for her in a day; and that I have but the keeping of that I have. . . . Let the Queen, then, break their hearts that are none of hers. There is little gain in losing her own. These things should not torment me if I were as others are.'[2]

And to the Queen, to whom he had had the tactlessness to offer a paper on the Succession: 'your Majesty may, perchance, speak hereof to those seeming my great friends, but I find poor effects of that or any other supposed amity. For, your Majesty having left me, I am left all alone in the world, and am sorry that ever I was at all.'

That was but as she had found him; and this would be his last letter to her.

[1] Edwards, II. 405-6.   [2] *Ibid.* 257, 259.

CHAPTER XIII

RALEGH AND KING JAMES

T WO issues dominated everybody's mind in the governing circle at the end of Elizabeth's reign: the question of the succession and that of the peace with Spain. The resolution of the second came to depend on the first, and both, in the circumstances of those days, were extremely dangerous to touch. This did not stop Ralegh from meddling with both of them — and in the worst possible conditions, having incurred the mistrust of the man who had proved himself his strongest friend, Robert Cecil. The unwisdom of it all is made the more pointed by the circumstance that Cecil was in the key-position to control the solution to both these great questions. Ralegh's conduct at this critical juncture, however, was not controlled by reason, but by pique; and Cecil's reaction was not only one of mistrust, but of resentment at ingratitude. By August 1601 he was writing that he was 'left to seek new friends'.[1]

Ralegh was piqued because Cecil would not help to make him a member of the Privy Council. It is doubtful if Cecil could have done anything in the matter, even if he had wished, for it is clear that the Queen did not have that confidence in Ralegh's judgment. But why should Cecil wish it? He expressed his view to Ralegh's cousin, Sir George Carew: 'he shall never have my consent to be a Councillor without he surrender to you the Captainship of the Guard, to which we will easily add some matter of profit'.[2] We perceive the suggested bid to Sir George to come over to Cecil's side; on the other hand, it would give Ralegh an intolerable advantage over the Secretary if he were both a Councillor and retained his position in constant personal attendance on the Queen. Cecil did not think he was being ungrateful to Ralegh and Cobham, but he resented 'the mutinies of those whom I do love and will (howsoever they do me)'. As if things were not difficult enough, with the Essex crisis only

---

[1] *Letters from Sir Robert Cecil to Sir George Carew*, ed. J. Maclean (Camden Soc.), 89.
[2] *Ibid.* 85-6.

just past and the great change looming ahead! Cecil added, 'for the better man, the second wholly sways him, and to which passions he is subject who is subject to his lady, I leave to your judgment and experience'. This gives us Cecil's opinion of Ralegh's relation to his wife, and what Cecil thought of her.

Both Ralegh and Cobham were very indiscreet, given to railing openly in the presence-chamber; and Cecil warned Carew to be careful what he wrote, 'for they show all men's letters to every man'.[1] He himself, like the politician he was, concealed his feeling that his 'two old friends use me unkindly; but I have covenanted with my heart not to know it, for in show we are great, and all my revenge shall be to heap coals on their heads'. This was being too Christian for a politician; but Cecil was a dab at concealment. He was still in partnership with Ralegh in privateering as late as early 1603 : he left the manning of one dubious ship to Ralegh's discretion, though he was ready to undertake half the victualling of her himself. 'But now, sir, that you know all these particulars, I pray you as much as may be to conceal our adventure, at least my name above any other. For though, I thank God, I have no other meaning than becometh an honest man in any of my actions, yet that which were another man's *pater-noster* would be accounted in me a charm.'[2]

By now Cecil had something far more important to conceal : his secret understanding with James in Scotland. No-one can deny that this was in the interest of the country and of a quiet transition at the Queen's death, but if it had come to her knowledge it might have been a serious matter for Cecil. James, a sympathiser with Essex, had hitherto been no friend to the Secretary; but here Lord Henry Howard came in very useful and laboured to bring about an alliance between the two. As an old supporter of Mary Queen of Scots, Lord Henry was *persona grata* to King James; but they shared other interests. They were much interested in religion, or at least theology, in which they were both learned; they were both pacifically inclined and this made them lean towards Spain, and they had other tastes in common. To James this Howard was 'dear Lord Harry', 'my long-approved and trusty Lord Harry'.

Lord Henry effected the junction, and Cecil wrote his first letter to his future king. It is a masterpiece of circumspection and political tact how to deal at such a moment. It is perfectly direct and sincere — and none the less clever for that. 'If I

[1] *Letters from Sir Robert Cecil to Sir George Carew*, ed. J. Maclean (Camden Soc.), 108, 116.   [2] *Salisbury MSS.* XII. 599.

SERO, SED SERIO.

ROBERT CECIL, EARL OF SALISBURY

could accuse myself to have once imagined a thought which could amount to a grain of error towards my dear and precious sovereign, or could have discerned that you had entertained an opinion or desire to draw me one point from my individual centre . . .'¹ James was no fool: he understood this kind of loyalty when he saw it: here was a prize to win. Having established his ground, Cecil went on to give him straight advice: 'your best approach to your greatest end is, by your Majesty's clear and temperate courses, to secure the heart of the Highest, to whose sex and quality nothing is so improper as either needless expostulations, or overmuch curiosity in her own actions. The first showing unquietness in yourself, the second challenging some untimely interest in hers.'

What could be more direct, or more salutary? James had been of opinion — he never was very good at gauging the position in England — that following the breach between Queen and country over Essex, Cecil was 'king there in effect'. So far from that, the old woman was never more autocratic than in her last days. Cecil confided to Carew that 'but myself, I know not one man in this kingdom that will bestow six words of argument to reply, if she deny it'.² There is a tradition in the Cecil family that when a letter from James once arrived in her presence, immediately suspicious, she wanted to know what it was. Quick-witted as always, and relying on her hatred of anything ill-smelling, he said 'Faugh, it smells vilely', and took it out of view. Of any mention of the succession Cecil warned James that 'the subject itself is so perilous to touch amongst us, as it setteth a mark upon his head for ever that hatcheth such a bird'.³ Then, too, 'what was possible for art and industry to effect against the person of a successor, in the mind of a possessor, hath been in the highest proportion laboured by many against you'.

Cecil followed this up later with a damaging attack on Ralegh and Cobham's discourses, 'how contrary it is to their nature to resolve to be under your sovereignty; though they confess (Ralegh specially) that natural policy forceth them to keep on foot such a trade against the great day of mart. In all which light and sudden humours of his, though I do no way check him, because he shall not think I reject his freedom or affection, but always use contestation with him . . . yet, under pretext of extraordinary care of his well doing, I have seemed to dissuade him from engaging himself too far.'⁴ Cecil went on to disengage

¹ *Correspondence of King James VI with Sir Robert Cecil*, ed. J. Bruce (Camden Soc.), 4 foll.   ² Maclean, 139.   ³ Bruce, 13.   ⁴ *Ibid.* 18-9.

himself completely from his unwise friend in James's estimation, praying that 'whatsoever he shall take upon him to say for me, upon any new humour of kindness, whereof sometimes he will be replete (upon the receipt of private benefit), you will no more believe it, be it never so much in my commendation'. This may be taken to have effectually blocked any way to James's mind that Ralegh might try. Cecil — like James, an orthodox religious man — made doubly sure by invoking religious prejudice: 'would God I were as free from offence towards God in seeking, for private affection, to support a person whom most religious men do hold anathema'. One hardly knows which to admire more in that sentence — the smug self-approbation or the treachery. 'But why do I thus far presume to trouble your ears so much with my poor private griefs at this ingratitude to me?'

How often in this age one has reason to remember the sad saying of Cecil's cousin, Francis Bacon: 'there is little friendship in the world, and least of all between equals'. Having thus corroborated James's distrust of Ralegh, he could safely 'leave the best and worst of him' to Lord Henry, since it was unsafe for the King and the Secretary to write too often 'upon needless grounds'. With Lord Henry Howard in control of the correspondence, the King's mind was safely poisoned with 'the worst' of Ralegh; for Howard was inspired by an inextinguishable personal hatred of him. Not that Ralegh had done anything against him, but that he stood for all that Howard hated: Protestant stock, inclining to free thought and unbelief; war with Spain; the favour with his cousin the Queen which himself could never command; the masculine good looks, the virility, that were offensive to his own ambivalent type.

Howard took up his pen; the first and most constant charge that ran off it was the 'atheism' of Ralegh's circle, their 'diabolical' principles. The 'diabolical triplicity', Ralegh, Cobham, Northumberland, were meeting every day at Durham House for consultation.[1] Howard was equally vicious against Northumberland, who was unhappily married to Essex's sister, Dorothy, Perrot's widow. Having been 'reconciled *usque ad conjugalem copulam* [it was characteristic of the curial mind of Howard to flavour his letters with Latin tags], which was not *in more* two years before, they departed in passion, not according to the rule of the philosopher, that *omne animal post coitum triste*, but by the

---

[1] *Secret Correspondence* (ed. Edinburgh, 1766), 29, 32.

distemper of an atheist that, besides Ralegh's Alcoran, admits no principles.' Howard himself was, of course, a guardian of ortho- dox morality, like King James.

A second line of attack with Howard was that Ralegh's group were insinuating to the Queen that Cecil was sold to James 'by the sorcery of the Howards'. There may have been something in that, while it was an obvious self-recommendation of the Howards to James; at the same time, Howard throws an un- pleasant light on Cecil: 'I dare undertake, out of my knowledge of the sense he hath of wrong, according to his former custom in these cases, he would make their hearts to ache for it.'[1] When James's personal emissary had been in London, Ralegh lost his opportunity of making interest with James by giving him a gallant answer that 'he had been over-deeply engaged and obliged to his own mistress to seek favour anywhere', he refused to 'diminish his sole respect to his own sovereign'. He then wanted Cecil to let the Queen know the line he had taken. Cecil cleverly put him off by suggesting that 'it would be thought a motive only to pick a thank, and in the present by dishonour, and in the future by danger, do more hurt than it could ever do him good anyway'. Clearly Ralegh was no match for such a politician; he should never have set himself up against him, but kept in step with him — after all, he had been his best friend.

At the end of 1601 Howard was able to report, 'Cecil swore to me this day that *duo erinacii*, that is he and they, would never live under one apple-tree'.[2] Cecil now regarded their position as a miserable one, 'fain to put their heads under the girdle of him whom they envy most . . . they cannot escape his walk with all their agility'. The next move was an attempt to bring Lady Ralegh back into personal attendance on the Queen. 'The league is very strong between Sir Walter Ralegh and my Lady Shrewsbury and Sir Walter Ralegh's wife. Much hath been offered on all sides to bring her into the Privy Chamber to her old place, because she is a most dangerous woman, and full of her father's inventions. *Sed canunt surdae.*' An envenomed letter of Howard to Cecil, bristling with hate, tells us that Lady Ralegh 'as furious as Proserpina with failing of that restitution in Court which flattery had moved her to expect, bends her whole wits and industry to the disturbance of all motions, that may disturb the possibility of others' hopes, since her own cannot be secured'.[3] With his ear at every key-hole, very well-informed, Howard

---

[1] *Ibid.* 39, 47-8.   [2] *Ibid.* 52, 68.   [3] Edwards, II. 439.

was able to report that the next move would be to get North-umberland — whose family had suffered along with Mary Stuart — to make interest for Ralegh with James. And, surely enough, Northumberland produced a testimonial of good behaviour, all the more convincing for not being biased in Ralegh's favour, and based on sixteen years' acquaintance. 'I must needs affirm Ralegh's ever allowance of your right. And although I know him insolent, extremely heated, a man that desires to seem to be able to sway all men's fancies, all men's courses, and a man that out of himself, when your time shall come, will never be able to do you much good nor harm, yet must I needs confess what I know, that there is excellent good parts of nature in him . . . and whom I wish your Majesty not to lose, because I would not that one hair of a man's head should be against you that might be for you.'[1]

This strikes one as a balanced summing up of Ralegh's case. No attempt at any justice of mind with Howard : 'Hell did never spew up such a couple, when it cast up Cerberus and Phlege-thon'.[2] Lord Admiral Howard had turned against Ralegh since Cadiz days, wishing 'from his soul that he had but the same commission to carry the cannon to Durham House that he had this time twelvemonth to carry it to Essex House, to prove what sport he could make in that fellowship'. Lord Henry had a disquieting image for discontented persons watching the worthy arrive at their port of honour : 'either they grow familiar, or a piece of bread with a pin will quiet them'. Evidently this way of dispatching curs was a familiar thought with this Howard. Lord Henry had no desire to be found wanting in his duty, as if 'our Blessed Saviour should come again and say to us, as he did to the deaf and blind man in the gospel, Ephphatha' — Be opened. Lord Henry needed no such adjuration : he was all ears. And he had Holy Writ constantly in mind : if things continued another year on their present footing, Sir Walter Ralegh could expect against the Prophet David, 'that affirms the age of man, but not as he will think the age of woman, to be seventy years'.

But the woman whose life was so bandied about among these creatures did not reach her seventieth year ; on 24 March 1603 she died.

As James rode south that delightful April, equipped with all this friendly information, the English nobility and gentry streamed

---

[1] Bruce, 67.   [2] *Secret Correspondence*, 131, 132-3, 154.

up the Great North Road to greet the rising sun. All kinds of rumours circulated in London about Ralegh, that he had been dismissed, that he was ordering up his horses from the West Country;[1] at last he could bear the suspense no longer and set out to meet the King, in spite of a proclamation intended to stop him and Cobham. Ralegh met James at Burghley House, the palace that Lord Burghley had built out of the pickings of office and excused himself so humbly for building. Lord Henry was already in attendance, and Ralegh had a very chilly reception. The tradition is that James received him with, 'I have heard *rawly* of thee' — if so it was true enough, and very true to James, who was more like a punning don than a king. Ralegh requested his instructions from the new sovereign regarding the Duchy of Cornwall. The King said he should have a letter for continuance of process until he had determined what to do with it. An ominous note was sounded, the King ordered the letters to be made out at once so 'that Ralegh may be gone again'.

A fortnight later Ralegh was dismissed from his office as Captain of the Guard, and his place given to a Scot, Sir Thomas Erskine. This was reasonable enough: the King could not trust his personal safety in the hands of a malcontent. And Ralegh was given a fair exchange: he was excused his considerable debt to the Crown, and the payment of his £300 a year rent for Jersey. Ralegh had another audience of the King at Beddington, where his wife's uncle Carew lived. Ralegh presented James with his *Discourse concerning a War with Spain*, and offered to raise two thousand men at his own expense to invade the country. Nothing could have been more contrary to the King's intentions, for he was determined on peace and to reign as *Rex pacificus*; nothing could have been more tactless, for it roused all James's fears of the marauding Scots swordsmen who had filled his life with alarms, so that he could not bear the sight of naked steel. All that he wished to leave behind him.

In May Ralegh was ordered to give up possession of Durham House to the bishop, and within a fortnight. He expostulated that he had had possession almost twenty years and had spent £2000 of his own upon it — if so, another unwisdom as Bess had pointed out. The meanest gentleman in the kingdom would have been given six months, the poorest artificer in London a quarter's notice by his landlord. He had made provision for forty persons in the household and for almost twenty horse — one

---

[1] *Salisbury MSS.* XV. 11. This was reported by Sir John Popham, shortly to be one of the judges at Ralegh's trial.

sees the lordly scale upon which he lived. 'Now to cast out my hay and oats into the street at an hour's warning, and to remove my family and stuff in fourteen days after, is such a severe expulsion as hath not been offered to any man before this day.'[1]

In July there broke the news of a conspiracy of crazy Catholics to capture the King, which came to be known as the Bye Plot and centred upon a vain and conceited priest, Father Watson, who felt himself personally let down by James's failure to relax the Recusancy fines and tolerate Catholicism.[2] (James was in advance of public opinion in his day and would have gladly done so, had it been politically possible.)[3] Watson recruited a couple of dissolute swordsmen, Sir Griffin Markham and one Copley who went forward in the idiotic atmosphere of Catholic ecstasy, 'mush less doubting but to find amongst the Host of Heaven that blessed Queen, his Majesty's mother, at my elbow in that hour'.[4] (She had in her life-time been quite used to such doings.) These fools got in touch with George Brooke, the still baser brother of Lord Cobham. Brooke's confession implicated his brother; and one day towards mid-July, while waiting on the terrace at Windsor to ride in attendance on the King, Ralegh was called in before the Council to say what he knew about Cobham's activities.[5] After examination Ralegh wrote a disingenuous letter about Cobham's dealings with Arenberg, with regard to peace and pensions from Spain, which clearly told less than he knew. That fatal flaw in his nature, the fact that he was a liar, gave a bad impression from the start, and from this time henceforth he was inextricably involved.

We must remember the nature of sixteenth-century treason-trials, difficult as it is for English-speaking people to envisage them — yet we have had the Russian purges, the concept of the 'people's justice', before our eyes to enlighten us. When the government's investigations were completed and a fabric of evidence built up, a state-prisoner was not held to be innocent: it was for him to prove his innocence. And this Ralegh could never do: he relied upon flat denials of the charges that were brought against him. Cobham made no bones about confessing

[1] Edwards, II. 270.

[2] Information was relayed to the government through the Bishop of London by the Archpriest Blackwell, who was a partisan of the Jesuits and an enemy of the seculars.

[3] We must remember that there was no question of toleration in Catholic countries like Spain and Italy.

[4] S. R. Gardiner, *History of England, 1603–42* (ed. 1900), I. 113.

[5] Among his examiners was Lord Henry Howard, now promoted to the Council.

his guilt, that he was to receive an enormous sum of half a million crowns to disburse in pensions for putting through a Spanish peace, and Ralegh would receive his quota. The island of Jersey would be convenient for these operations.

Ralegh knew too well the impossibility of proving his innocence: he was incriminated, he had discussed these plans with Cobham, had never attempted to dissuade him from them, and was involved in a way no-one fathomed. He well knew the atmosphere of prejudice in which the matter would be brought to trial; losing his nerve, he made every mistake — until he came to the stage of the trial itself. Everybody believed Ralegh to be guilty — with the probable exception of Cecil, who understood better than anyone how the case lay, and exerted himself to see that Ralegh got a chance at the trial.

No wonder, when Ralegh found himself once more incarcerated in the Tower, that he behaved badly as he did. The split in his personality expressed itself along with the neurotic, hysterical symptoms with which his genius was probably allied: on the one side, intellectually he would never budge, he always stood on his entire innocence; on the other side, he behaved as if he were guilty. His keeper, Sir John Peyton, 'never saw so strange a dejected mind. I am exceedingly cumbered with him. Five or six times in a day he sendeth for me in such passions as I see his fortitude is not competent to support his grief.'[1] (Might Sir John have Sir Walter's delectable government of Jersey for his pains? He might, and did.)

There was a rumour in London that Throckmorton had been arrested with the other conspirators;[2] but this was a mistake, and we find our faithful friend begging Cecil to allow him to go up and console his sorrowful sister, now in the Tower too.[3] He would be contented to yield her in this grief all lawful brotherly comforts. Bess's presence may have been more disquieting than consoling; for next her husband made an attempt at suicide, and the motive was clear — to save Sherborne to his family for fear it should be forfeit by his condemnation. But Ralegh's will to live was too strong, as always: he stabbed himself under the right pap, and, for greater effect, while the Commissioners were in the Tower examining the prisoners. In a few days, he was 'very well cured, both in body and mind'. The theologian on the throne was more concerned for Ralegh's soul, and instructed the Lords to take a good preacher with them, 'that he may make

---

[1] *Salisbury MSS.* XV. 204, 205.   [2] *Cal. S.P. Venetian*, 1603–7, 71.
[3] *Salisbury MSS.* XV. 207, where Arthur is miscalled Thomas.

him know that it is his soul that he must wound and not his body'.[1] Perhaps this was still harder to bear — for a distinguished intellect from a Scotch Calvinist.

Meanwhile the case was being built up against him. Ralegh's letter to the Council about Cobham's practises with Arenberg had been shown to Cobham, who immediately retaliated by accusing Ralegh of having led him into these mischiefs, and been the instigator all along. Now Ralegh got a message through to Cobham that he had cleared him of all, and that one could not be condemned for treason on the evidence of one witness. In return Cobham retracted his charges and exculpated Ralegh. But when it came out that there had been collusion between them it made an even worse impression — as Cecil wrote, 'the retractation so blemished by the discovery of that intelligence which they had, as few men can conceive that it comes from a clear heart'.[2] Gardiner sums up, 'it is almost impossible to avoid the conclusion that he knew more of Cobham's plans than he chose to avow'.[3] Both Cobham and Ralegh were liars, and now Ralegh added to the impression of falseness by denying boldly that he had sent Cobham any such message.

It has always been an unsolved mystery why an intelligent man like Ralegh should have put his head in the noose with a totally unstable, psychotic type like Cobham. Historians have been unable to explain it — perhaps because they are too respectably minded, perhaps because they lack imagination to penetrate the mind and atmosphere of the time. We have seen that, at the top, almost anyone would betray almost anyone else. We have seen that Ralegh was already in desperate case so far as James was concerned : he would need to do something desperate, perform a striking service, if he were ever to recover himself. It is curious that historians have not followed up the hint that Aubrey gives us — after all, Aubrey knew various members of the Ralegh family, was at school with his great-nephews and knew people who had known Sir Walter. Aubrey gives us a clue, which came from the governing circle of the time, that 'as to the plot and business about the Lord Cobham, etc., he [Ralegh] being then governor of Jersey would not fully do things unless they would go to his island and there advise and resolve about it; and that really and indeed Sir Walter's purpose was, when he had them there, to have betrayed the plot and to have then

[1] *Salisbury MSS.* XV. 212.
[2] *Memorials of Sir Ralph Winwood*, ed. E. Sawyer (1725), II. 8.
[3] Gardiner, I. 136.

[them ?] delivered up to the King and made his peace'.[1]

I find this the only convincing explanation by which all the otherwise inexplicable features of this transaction fall into place. Of course it is surmise as to Ralegh's motives — but the motive was strong enough. Of course he could not plead this in exculpation — at the expense of his character for ever. At the same time he never wavered, now or at any other time, in asserting his innocence of any treasonable intent against the king, nor is he likely to have had any. It is simply incredible that he was *such* a fool as to have engaged himself in genuine treason against a king whose inevitable succession was accepted by the whole nation. On the other hand, since this was the only chance of putting himself right with James, and the means could never be confessed to, he could never establish his innocence. No wonder Cobham was mad with him. All historians have thought that Ralegh was holding something in reserve : I have little doubt that this was what.

In this atmosphere the trial was held at Winchester in November — everybody believing that Ralegh was guilty, provoked by his standing so brazenly on his innocence, all the more so because of the difficulty of bringing it home to him. There had been so much lying by Cobham, accusation, retractation, and then withdrawal of the retractation, that the truth was as difficult to come by as in the Alger Hiss case in our own time. In fact, nobody ever has extracted the whole truth in the case of Ralegh — we can only guess and infer from what we know of his character. When he was taken through the City on the way to Winchester, the London mob did not fail to express their detestation of him : it was 'hob or nob' whether he 'should have been brought alive through such multitudes of unruly people as did exclaim against him. If one hare-brain fellow amongst so great multitudes had begun to set upon him, no entreaty or means could have prevailed, the fury and tumult of the people was so great.'[2] This had always been the attitude of the people towards Ralegh ; but the trial was to set in motion a spreading process of reversal.

Ralegh, like the actor he was, needed an audience. When he came face to face, alone and undefended, with the concentrated political and legal ability of his day, his performance was a very able one and roused much admiration. It must have been gall and wormwood to James at neighbouring Wilton to read the reports : one spectator affirmed that 'never man spake so

---

[1] *Aubrey's Brief Lives*, ed. A. Clark, II. 187. [2] Edwards, I. 386.

well in times past, nor would do in the time to come'; another
that 'when he saw Sir Walter Ralegh first, he was so led with
the common hatred that he would have gone a hundred miles
to have seen him hanged, he would, ere they parted, have gone
a thousand to save his life'; a third, 'never was a man so hated,
and so popular, in so short a time'.[1] This was partly due to the
bullying he was subjected to by the Crown lawyers, particularly
by the harsh and offensive Coke, rising hope of the stern unbending Puritans. Some part of Coke's fury, we may surmise, arose
from his consciousness of the difficulty of proving Ralegh's guilt
— if we may judge from an argument of this quality: 'the
Peace pretended by Sir Walter Ralegh is merely a jargon, for it
is clear the money was for discontented persons. Now Ralegh
was to have part of the money; therefore, he was a discontented
person; and therefore, a traitor.'

The Crown lawyers could not proceed except by using the
evidence that came from the confessed 'treason of the priests' to
smear Ralegh. When Ralegh protested that he had nothing to
do with that, was not even charged with it, and asked that the
evidence against him should be taken point by point, this was
refused: the Crown's built-up case, inference, innuendo and all,
had to be taken as a whole. When Ralegh went back to the
famous argument of Sir Nicholas Throckmorton at his trial, the
legislation regarding constructive treason, and the necessity of
two witnesses, this also was disallowed. He asked that he
might be brought face to face with his accuser, Lord Cobham;
though the request was supported by Cecil, it was refused. The
question became whether Ralegh was to be believed, 'of as
much wit as the wit of man can devise, he useth his bare denial'
— or Cobham, who had confessed his treason and inculpated
Ralegh. And here the fact that there had been intelligence
between them in the Tower made the worst impression. That
excellent, religious man, Attorney-General Coke, did not fail to
appeal to people's prejudices on the score of Ralegh's atheism
in his final address: 'O damnable Atheist! He hath learned
some text of Scripture to serve his own purpose, but falsely alleged.
He counsels Cobham not to be led by the counsels of preachers as
Essex was — *he* died the child of God. God honoured him at his
death', etc.[2] (Actually, he had been bullied by Coke at his trial
much as Ralegh was now.)

After this, there could be no doubt of his condemnation, any

---

[1] Edwards, I. 410, 415.   [2] Edwards, I. 432-3.

more than of the judgment, in after years, of one of the very judges who sat on the bench in the hall of Wolvesey castle: 'that trial injured and degraded the justice of England'.[1]

We are taken into the recesses of Ralegh's heart with the letter he wrote to his wife on the night before his execution was to take place. This letter became well known in his own day, to judge from the number of copies that have survived: evidence of the *réclame* his personality elicited, and a pointer to the way in which the popular opinion of him would be reversed. Before the trial made the verdict against him inevitable, every effort was made by Ralegh and his wife to appeal for mercy.[2] The Victorians considered his appeals rather base and abject — all very well for them who were so secure in their lives; but we, in the insecurity of our time, have a worse reason for apprehending the sweetness of life and cannot blame him.

It is true that he blamed himself, and asked Bess to get back his letters to the Lords — Lord Henry Howard among them, who had had the pleasure of being one of the Commissioners to try Ralegh — begging for his life. 'God knows that it was for you and yours that I desired it.'[3] He at last apprised her of the conveyance of Sherborne to their son, for safety's sake; he had meant to leave her his wine-patent, or what he could purchase by selling it, with one half of all his goods. 'When I am gone, no doubt you shall be sought unto by many, for the world thinks that I was very rich. And no greater misery can befall you in this life than to become a prey, and after to be despised.' Still, it would be best for her to marry again, for her protection and their child's. 'Remember your poor child for his father's sake, that comforted and loved you in his happiest times.'

The letter confirms that Ralegh really loved Bess: 'I send you all the thanks my heart can conceive, or my pen express, for your many troubles and cares taken for me, which — though they have not taken effect as you wished — yet my debt is to you never the less; but pay it I never shall in this world. . . . My love I send you, that you may keep it when I am dead, and my counsel, that you may remember it when I am no more. I would not, with my last will, present you with sorrows, dear

---

[1] *Ibid.* 388.

[2] Among those who made suit to James was an unexpected figure from the past, Thomas Morgan, Mary Stuart's old agent in Paris, who wrote that Lady Ralegh's father 'was a Protestant, but yet in his time did very grateful service in England to you and your mother; which should lead you to have compassion upon her in case he suffers death'. *Cal. S.P. Dom. Add. 1580–1625,* 430.

[3] Edwards, II. 284-7.

Bess. Let them go to the grave with me, and be buried in the dust. And, seeing it is not the will of God that ever I shall see you in this life, bear my destruction gently and with a heart like yourself.' The eloquent and pathetic phrases roll off his pen, as they had always done — 'when you have travailed and wearied your thoughts on all sorts of worldly cogitations, you shall sit down by Sorrow in the end'. These noble thoughts, grandly expressed, were what pierced the hearts of his readers in his own day and, it must be confessed, have never ceased to exert an appeal. (King James, however, was allergic to Ralegh's eloquence.) The condemend man came at length to an end : 'God knows how hardly I stole this time, when all sleep; and it is time to separate my thoughts from the world. Beg my dead body, which living was denied you; and either lay it at Sherborne, if the land continue, or in Exeter church by my father and mother. I can write no more. Time and death call me away.'

In fact, up to the last — according to the Bishop of Winchester, who was sent to offer spiritual consolation and also to worm out what had been the truth between them — both Ralegh and Cobham entertained 'a lingering expectation of life and busy inquisition what certainty I had of their deaths'. So Ralegh had not repelled the bishop's presence, 'but pretendeth or findeth a dulness or coldness to receive that comfort which I offer him'. His beliefs, whatever they were, were his own and not to be accepted at anyone else's hand. The poor bishop found himself not able to cope with Ralegh as he would, so he called in another 'to ripen those needful points of Christian repentance that I propose to Sir Walter'. Nor did this ineffective emissary get any further on the political front. Cobham stood to his story that foreign forces were to have been landed at Milford and the money conveniently brought to Jersey. Ralegh persisted in his 'denial of all, save giving patient ear to the Lord Cobham's unwise and lavish projects'.[1]

The alien king, with whom a pawky humour was an unendearing characteristic, and whose lack of taste was equalled by his lack of tact, was planning a grim surprise : he would turn tragedy into farce. While the Court waited at Wilton for news of the executions at Winchester, James, unknown to anyone, sent a Scottish lad of his Bedchamber, one Gibb, to stay the executions at the scaffold itself. One after the other, Sir Griffin Markham, Lord Grey and Lord Cobham, were led to the scaffold, left there

[1] *Salisbury MSS.* XV. 305, 306.

in the rain to pray at length, make their edifying peace with God and the King, and then, totally mystified, were led off again with their heads on. James had a natural lack of dignity in his person, and everything he touched bore this stamp. It was said by an observer of the distasteful scene that Sir Walter 'beheld the comedy played out by his companions with a smiling face'.[1]

The new king naturally wanted to begin his reign with a popular act of clemency, but what a way to do it! Cecil gave a sycophantic account of the circumstances in a letter for foreign consumption. 'I doubt not but you would equally with us admire the excellent mixture of the King's mercy with justice; for even after he had first absolutely taught us all our duties, to leave all mediation in this case (Mercy being only his)', he signed the death-warrants for Cobham, Grey and Markham, 'pretending to forbear Sir Walter Ralegh for the present, until the Lord Cobham's death had given some light how far he would make good his accusation.'[2] James made no soul privy to his intention — naturally not wishing to share the credit for mercy, or give people to suppose that he was acting on advice; but the effect at Winchester, with each on the scaffold expecting the stroke when reprieved, was received by everyone with 'such joy and admiration as so rare and unheard-of a clemency most worthily deserved'.

We may conclude that it was, anyway, better than being executed.

[1] Edwards, I. 450.   [2] *Winwood's Memorials*, II. 11.

CHAPTER XIV

IN THE TOWER

THE duel with King James now continued, in one form or another, all the rest of Ralegh's life and beyond it. Never was there a more active prisoner within the walls of the Tower, one who was more alive and kicking. Once he had recovered from the shock of the catastrophe and, after a time, given up his sanguine hopes of a speedy release, he kicked back the whole time. He never gave up the struggle; he never would admit guilt. If only he had been willing to, if he had been ready to bow the head and submit, he might have made some sort of peace with the Stuart Court. But that would not have been like Ralegh.

So far as the law went, he was a man 'civilly dead'. We must do James the justice of recognising that he believed him guilty: why then could he not be grateful for his life, keep quiet and let the world forget him? So far from this Ralegh asserted his innocence of treason, and took every possible step to appeal to public opinion and assert his existence. In all his years behind those walls, people could not forget him; indeed, they were constantly reminded of him. At one time the Lieutenant of the Tower had to complain that, given liberty to walk on the walls, he was showing himself to the people, who flocked thither to gaze on one of the sights of London. Lady Ralegh, with all the spirit of a Throckmorton and the pride of a Ralegh, drove grandly in and out of the Tower in her coach. Any number of people clamoured to visit him, on one excuse or another, and many came to be admitted. After Gunpowder Plot that sombre character, the 'Wizard' Earl of Northumberland, came to join him; and a famous circle they made in the Tower, recruited by the mathematicians, Hariot, Hughes and Warner. The 'school of atheism' continued under more distinguished patronage than ever. Ralegh gave up a good deal of time to chemical experiments, which he engaged in in a shed in the Lieutenant's garden, turned into a still-house. Here he produced his celebrated

Cordial, the ingredients of which have been lost, but which won a rather fabulous character in the succeeding century. James's own wife, Queen Anne, fancied herself to have benefited by it; it was administered to the dying Prince Henry, in the vain hope of saving him; one of the first entertainments of the restored Charles II was to watch its compounding, by Pierre Lefèvre, who wrote an account of it.[1]

One begins to see what an aura came to surround James's prisoner, what a myth-making personality his was.

Of more immediate effect, too: since Ralegh would recognise neither guilt nor that he was civilly dead, from his eyrie in the Bloody Tower, where his apartments were, he came to take more of a hand in politics. Since he could not speak in Parliament or Council, he wrote tracts offering his advice on matters of state. Once and again, either with plain lack of tact or an unconscious, unspoken taunt, he dedicated them to the King. His advice was extremely unwelcome, his existence not recognised, no notice taken. So, as the King's son grew up, the extrovert, active Prince Henry — given to martial exercises and keenly interested in the Navy and shipbuilding — Ralegh captured the son's sympathy away from his father. 'Who but my father would keep such a bird in a cage!' said the Prince. Ralegh already had the support of Queen Anne, for what it was worth — the poor lady neglected in these years for the long-legged Carr.

It was important to the King's government to keep Ralegh under lock and key: at first in the interest of making peace with Spain, and later in that of maintaining good relations. When relations deteriorated and James's foreign policy, under the prudent direction of Cecil, took a turn less favourable to Spain — as it did in 1610–1 — Ralegh came nearer to being let out. After Cecil's death, with the temporary ascendancy of the far less intelligent, the simply pro-Protestant Winwood, Ralegh was let out, to embark on the final disaster of Guiana. Willy-nilly, and of course he willed it, he became a figure of some importance in international politics: a knight, or a pawn, on a chess-board.

So long as Cecil was in power, things did not go seriously wrong — though James superfluously offended Parliament with his lack of tact, of *rapport* with the nation, his pedantic habit of lecturing them on the the divine attributes of monarchy, when he did not possess even the dignity. So Ralegh came forward

[1] *The Diary of John Evelyn*, ed. E. S. de Beer, III. 336.

with his tractate, 'The Prerogative of Parliaments', with its doctrine that there could be no loss to the King in winning the affections of Parliament, with its unwelcome reminders of the ways of Queen Elizabeth in government, her success as a ruler, and its uncomfortable questions: 'is it a loss to the king to be beloved of the commons?'[1] One might think the question was ironical, except that Ralegh was not much given to irony; he was more directly sardonic, but the question was not without its sting. When things went ill with James's rule, everything that Ralegh was — the last survivor of the heroic age — rose up as a reproach. There, incarnate in a famous figure in the Tower, was the alternative, the perpetual opposition, the reminder.

And Ralegh did everything he could to remind the nation — since he could not speak or appear — now by his writings. In addition to everything else, he became a professional, full-time writer: no longer the amateur, the poet of his romantic phase at Elizabeth's Court, but one of the grandest and most voluminous of prose-writers, an immense influence on his century. His energies were indeed prodigious, as always; with their exertion upon the active duties of office cut off, he had all the more to devote to the more significant occupations of study, of reading and writing, apart from the scientific experiments and concoction of medicines, the conduct of his affairs, the family and social life within the Tower. He wrote a number of tracts and discourses, some of a technical character, like those on Ship-building, on the Navy and Sea-Service. Most of his writings were on politics — some on immediate issues like those on the marriages proposed for Prince Henry and the Princess Elizabeth, upon which the Prince had asked his advice, and it went clean contrary to his father's wishes. Some shorter essays were philosophical, like 'The Sceptic' and 'A Treatise of the Soul'. At length Ralegh devoted himself to a master work, his *History of the World*, with which he won another sort of immortality.

The sympathetic Bishop Hall pointed out that to his imprisonment 'we are beholden, besides many philosophical experiments, for that noble *History of the World*, which is now in our hands. The Court had his youthful and freer times, the Tower his later age: the Tower reformed the Court in him, and produced those worthy monuments of art and industry, which we should have in vain expected from his freedom and jollity.'[2] We owe his longest poem, *The Book of the Ocean*, to his first experience

---

[1] *The Works of Sir Walter Ralegh*, ed. Oldys and Birch, VIII. 213.
[2] *q*. T. N. Brushfield, 'Raleghana, Part VI', *Trans. Devon. Assocn.* 1904, 181.

RALEGH IN LATER LIFE

of that gloomy place. For posterity's sake, no less than for his own — if only he had known it — he was best off there.

Now that Cecil, on his way to become Earl of Salisbury, had got Ralegh where he wanted him, he once more became his best friend — or at any rate his most powerful friend to extend a measure of protection to him and his. Politics at the summit is apt to be a cut-throat occupation, and Cecil had gone over to the Howards, who were able to offer him so much more powerful support and to reinforce him with James. (Ben Jonson, who knew Ralegh well and what he thought of Cecil, told Drummond, 'Salisbury never cared for any man longer nor he could make use of him'.)[1] With Ralegh out of the way the peace with Spain could be negotiated without opposition, and Cecil achieved a personal triumph by bringing the proud Spaniards to London and ending the long war on terms that recognised the newly united Britain's place in the world. Such services deserved signal recognition, and it was Cecil and the Howards who got the Spanish pensions that Cobham and Ralegh had so foolishly gaped for. The hungry Howards got a great deal more out of the wreckage: Lord Henry, on his way to become Earl of Northampton, got Cobham's office as Warden of the Cinque Ports, where he was in a favourable position for surreptitiously undermining the country's laws by letting Catholic priests in and out. (No wonder the number of open Catholics began to increase markedly.) The Lord Admiral, Earl of Nottingham, got Ralegh's valuable patent for wine-licences; but, not content with that, began to press for the arrears Ralegh had not been able to collect in the last few agitated years. Already Ralegh had had to sell to him the rich hangings of Durham House for £500 cash. Such were the consequences of making a disastrous move in high politics — and these were only the beginnings of his losses.

Cecil now stepped in, with his splay foot, to take him under his (qualified) protection. He advised Ralegh to write his thanks to the King, to whom he would deliver any letter of his, and assured him that he would be glad of his future good — not the less irritating, we may feel, for being just. Ralegh duly wrote to offended majesty, smugly self-satisfied with his clemency: 'seeing it hath pleased your Majesty to breathe into dead earth a new life . . . whereas your Majesty hath reason to reckon me among those who have wickedly intended the greatest ill towards the greatest goodness', etc.[2] To Cecil Ralegh made no such

[1] C. H. Herford and P. Simpson, *Ben Jonson, the Man and his Work*, I. 142.
[2] Edwards, II. 288-9.

admission; he went no further than to say that he had failed 'in friendship and in judgment', and that in future the pursuit of fortune, or rather vanity, should not again turn his eyes from Cecil. Once more we see that in adversity Ralegh was capable of self-knowledge, and his own diagnosis was true enough: vanity had been at the root of his fault, vanity and bad judgment, egged on by jealousy of Cecil and pique at not getting higher office. All Ralegh's biographers place the blame on Cecil and exonerate Ralegh: this is very innocent of them, largely owing to their incapacity to grasp the essentially political mind.[1] In fact it was Cecil who in all this displayed much more intelligence, a better sense of justice as well as judgment — in a word, more sense.

The rewards of submission at once began to appear. Cecil saved Ralegh from the depredations of the Lord Admiral, prevailed on him to stop pursuing Ralegh for uncollectable arrears. The now all-powerful Secretary weighed in to stop any further dispersion of Ralegh's goods and chattels; whereas under his attainder they were all forfeit to the Crown, they were now made over in trust for the maintenance of his wife and child. Ralegh's affairs were very complicated — far more so than we can explain here; indeed, Ralegh could not get to the bottom of them himself. He had always been extravagant, and he did not possess a cool, business head. Furthermore, in the absence of banking in that age, a grandee's affairs were complicated by bonds and assignments, and reassignments, of them; debts owed in both directions, both to as well as from; leases and assignments of them; plate in and out of pawn; trusts to deal with landed estate: the whole thing involving law-suits to sort it out, and as often leading to further law-suits just to complicate it further.[2]

We are in pursuit of the personal, and it so happens that a Chancery case some years after Ralegh's death throws a light into the crevices of his affairs in his first year in the Tower.[3] We learn of a magnificent jewel that Queen Elizabeth had given him, of diamonds worth £1000, a very large sum in those days. Lord Treasurer Buckhurst would have given him as much for it, but Ralegh was forced to part with it to Peter Vanlore, the Jewish jeweller and money-lender. Ralegh had difficulty in persuading

---

[1] We must except Edwards from this stricture.

[2] We have an example in the Chancery suit brought by Adrian Gilbert against Ralegh in November 1612. Gilbert claimed £3303 debts from Ralegh, as against Ralegh's payments to and for him of £1150: 17s. C. Monro, *Acta Cancellariae*, 176 foll.   [3] C24/497/107.

Bess to let him have it, partly because of their unsatisfactory
dealings with Vanlore before. And again Vanlore seems to have
dealt sharply with them, keeping £600 upon the sale for a debt
already paid and letting Ralegh have only £400. We see how
preoccupied and unbusinesslike Ralegh was, saying to his steward
John Shelbury, 'It is marvel how you and I should forget this
bond. It was as quite out of my mind as if it had never been
made. But for your discharge and quietness, I was enforced to
accept the £400 and to persuade my wife as well as I could to
patience.' Lady Ralegh was not of the most patient disposition.
Her doctor, who had known her from childhood, one day asked
Sir Walter why she did not come to dinner with him at the
Tower; he replied that she was angry with him and Vanlore
for making her part with the jewel.

Vanlore told Shelbury that Sir Walter had 'dealt with him
the most nobly of any gentleman that ever he had to do withal
. . . and was the best payer of his debts that ever he knew'.
But to help pay his debts even before the Queen's death — one
sees the familiar element of cash-necessity in these conspiracies —
Ralegh had pawned most of his plate to Thomas Offley, the City
merchant, for £800; his troubles made it impossible for him
ever to redeem it.[1] All this is borne out by the letters with which
the Raleghs bombarded Cecil. We learn that his debts at £3000
were treble the value of his goods; that he had lost £3000 a year
with his offices, and there remained to him only Sherborne. Its
yearly value was some £660, of which he paid £260 rent to the
bishops of Salisbury and £50 in fees, leaving not £400 a year.
That was all the family had left now to live upon, and at Sherborne 'my tenants refuse to pay my wife her rent. Alas, all
goes to ruin of that little which remaineth. My woods are cut
down; my grounds waste; my stock, which made up my rent,
sold. And except some end be had, by your good favour to the
King, I perish every way.'[2] Cecil's favour held good: his word
went down to Sherborne to stop the depredations. Ralegh wrote
gratefully, 'as God liveth, I shall never forget your true honour
and remorse of me'.

With regard to Sherborne the situation was hardly less complicated, and more insecure than Ralegh realised. In January
1603 he thought he would make all safe by a deed of trust between himself on one side, and Throckmorton, Alexander Brett

---

[1] In 1603 Ralegh sold the manor of Leigh Durrant in Cornwall, by which he
hoped to raise £1000 at the time of his trial. *Salisbury MSS.* XV. 265.

[2] Edwards, II. 293, 295.

(a cousin of Lady Ralegh) and Hariot on the other, conveying the land to his eldest son and heirs male, reserving only a life interest to himself.[1] (Unfortunately, unknown to him, the engrossing clerk in copying out the deed omitted the phrase making the deed legally operative, by pure mischance.) This did not as yet come to notice, and Ralegh thought that Sherborne was safe. In reward to Hariot, for Ralegh was not ungenerous, he had given him a long lease of Pinford, and an outright gift of an abbey in Waterford, which he had had from the Queen, and of which Hariot had made £200.[2]

The only way to make assurance sure was that of a pardon, and already in 1604 Ralegh was in hope of obtaining one. Lady Ralegh gained an interview of Cecil, who told her — what gave some ground of hope — that it could not yet be done, but that he would help in the matter of conveying Ralegh's lands to feoffees in trust. Too sanguine, as ever, Ralegh was willing, if he might have a pardon, 'to be confined within the hundred of Sherborne; or, if I cannot be allowed so much, I shall be contented to live in Holland, where I shall perchance get some employment upon the Indies'.[3]

Our friend Throckmorton comes up this summer with a curious letter to Cecil, since he was involved in Ralegh's affairs and was in some trouble of his own. 'I have chosen rather to trouble you with my writings than with my words, place nor your leisure serving at my last waiting upon you to give you satisfaction of those suspicions wherewith, you seemed, I should be touched. . . . My fortune is not so favourable as to make me wanton, nor my folly so great as to forget your force; my wishes are that in so unequal a rank we might right one another. . . . I am glad you but take hold of untruths, yet sorry to see you so forward to finger them. For Brigstock, it never entered my thoughts to mislike therewith, much less to complot any complaint. And for Sir John Gilbert, whatsoever I had I received from Sir William Strode, and delivered without naming any man.'[4] This is a very lofty tone to take with the most powerful man in the kingdom. Evidently Throckmorton identified himself with his sister and her husband in their troubles, and did not hesitate to press for access to Ralegh. Later in the year Cecil agreed and wrote to the Lieutenant of the Tower on his behalf. The Lieutenant feared that the Secretary must be

---

[1] W. B. Wildman, *A Short History of Sherborne*, 172-4.
[2] *Salisbury MSS.* XVI. 260-1, 433.   [3] Edwards, II. 304.
[4] *Salisbury MSS.* XVI. 265-6, 362.

much troubled with such requests, but the times were less dangerous now than before the trials, and Throckmorton gained admission.

In the Tower Ralegh had warrant for two servants, one to attend on him, the other to go about on his business. With the relaxation of close imprisonment in 1604 he had 'drawn unto him a preacher and three boys in ordinary'.[1] When the Lieutenant asked him to get warrant for them, Ralegh railed and complained, as he did about everything. Actually he was allowed to walk in the Lieutenant's garden, and several times various courtiers finding the gates open walked in and 'complimentarily' talked with him. Among those permitted access were Lady Ralegh, their doctor, Sir Alexander Brett, Peter Vanlore, Mr. Shelbury and Talbot, a schoolmaster — evidently for Ralegh's son Walter. In the relaxed circumstances of this unglad summer Bess became pregnant again.

This gave Ralegh no joy: it merely added to his worries, and their troubles imposed a strain upon his relations with his wife. 'Since the time that my wife was last with your lordship I have withered in body and mind.'[2] She reported a sad change in Cecil's favour towards him. 'For the times past, whatsoever your lordship hath conceived, I cannot think myself to have been either an enemy or such a viper but that this great downfall of mine, this shame, loss and sorrow, may seem to your lordship's heart and soul a sufficient punishment and revenge.' He complained of loss of health, of palsy and want of breath. And now the plague had come into the Tower: 'my poor child having lain this fourteen days next to a woman with a running plague sore, and but a paper-wall between, and whose child is also this Thursday dead of the plague.' So that Lady Ralegh had been driven to take herself and her boy away from his company. In November Philip Gawdy, who had been on board the *Revenge* at Flores, wrote from Court to his brother, 'I stood this last Sunday hard by an old mistress of yours, my Lady Ralegh, who with her son were petitioners to his Majesty; but he would no way respect them nor so much as look towards them.[3]

In February 1605 their second son was born, either within the Tower or in lodgings just outisde, for he was baptised in the chapel of St. Peter ad Vincula inside the walls on 15 February by the name of Carew. His godfather was Richard Carew of

---

[1] *Ibid.* 192-3. [2] Edwards, II. 314-5.
[3] *Letters of Philip Gawdy*, ed. I. H. Jeayes (Roxburghe Club), 152-3. Bassingbourne Gawdy had done much better for himself by marrying a rich, comfortable heiress.

Antony,[1] who had dedicated his *Survey of Cornwall* to Ralegh in such warm terms three years before. Ralegh then bore authority over their bodies and estates in Cornwall, 'but in whose hearts and loves you possess a far greater interest by your kindness. Your ears and mouth have ever been open to hear and deliver our grievances, and your feet and hands ready to go and work their redress.' Here is the better side to Ralegh, spoken from his own West Country, where he seems always to have been popular; it is pleasant to record this loyalty in an eminent Cornishman to the dejected prisoner in the Tower.

No word came from Cecil concerning Ralegh's long suit for the assurance of his estate, and now he was leaving London for the country. When Lady Ralegh heard this, 'I shall be made more than weary of my life by her crying and bewailing who will return in post when she hears of your lordship's departure and nothing done. She hath already brought her eldest son in one hand and her sucking child in another, crying out of her and their destruction, charging me with unnatural negligence, and that having provided for mine own life I am without sense and compassion of theirs.'[2] Nor was this the end of his troubles at Bess's hands, of whom he seemed to stand in some awe — still less of her troubles at his. If he had known what griefs it would all bring with it, would he have given her such pledges in 1591–2?

The immediate result of his *cri de cœur* was that Cecil moved James on Ralegh's behalf for Sherborne, and the King declared himself disposed towards the relief of Lady Ralegh and her children, but not the father. Once more Ralegh had to express himself deeply grateful for Cecil's intervention, and added politely, if insincerely, that he wanted to free Sherborne to bargain with Cecil, now Earl of Salisbury and Viscount Cranborne, for it; 'for there is no seat within the compass of your titles so fit for your lordship as that . . . your lordship may save £10,000, in respect of building, imparking and settling elsewhere'.[3] A draft warrant was made out saying that, though by rigour of law Ralegh's lands might come to the Crown, 'seeing his conveyance [*i.e.* to his son and heirs] was made in the Queen our sister's time . . . all our title and interest may be passed over to his wife and children that we be no more troubled with their pitiful cries and complaints for that business'.

Ralegh would have done far better to let sleeping dogs lie and not have stirred up the matter. For when Lord Chief

---

[1] Cf. *D.N.B. sub* Ralegh.   [2] Edwards, II. 318.
[3] *Salisbury MSS.* XVII. 624.

Justice Popham went into the conveyance, he found it defective, 'upon a plain omission of that which should have made the assurance perfect; which nevertheless, I think, grew by the omission of the clerk in the engrossing of the book'.[1] If that was not an evil stroke of luck — surely the devil was in it! For this meant that the estate remained in Ralegh and so was forfeit by his attainder to the Crown. It lay wide open for the asking to whoever was close enough to the King to make interest for it and to whom James felt under such obligation as to have to grant it.

The last months of 1605 were filled with the agitation of the Gunpowder Plot, which gave James the fright of his life, made an indelible impression on the country and finally strengthened Cecil's hand in dealing with the Catholics. The new Earl of Northampton had to show himself conspicuously zealous in dealing with the conspirators to avert suspicion from his inner sympathies. In this atmosphere of general alarm Ralegh was once more brought before the Lords of the Council and questioned. One Whitlock, who had spent the summer suspiciously in the Spanish Netherlands, had afterwards had access to Ralegh: that was enough. He protested to the Council, in the accent of anguished sincerity, 'I beseech your lordships to call to mind my many sorrows and the causes, and to remember my services and love to my country, and I beseech you in charity and for the love of God not to make me more odious than ever the earth brought forth any, by suspecting me to be knowing this unexampled and more than devilish invention'.[2]

Down at Sherborne the yokels were making merry and saying that though Ralegh stood in danger of his life, yet he would escape and come to greater matters.[3] One of the Thynnes, who were supporters of his, quarrelling with Mere, who had been upheld against Ralegh by Lord Howard of Bindon, pointed to Prince Henry's favour and said that he himself would bear Ralegh out of the Tower on his back rather than that he should tarry there. On the road between Shaftesbury and Salisbury the rumour was that Ralegh's muskets and pistols were being made ready. It seems that the unfortunate Bess had chosen this autumn to have the armour at Sherborne cleaned. Again one sees what an aura Ralegh had, becoming a legend in his own lifetime; people had always taken sides hotly about his intransigent, outsize personality, and now in adversity they were coming round to him.

[1] *Ibid.* 242.   [2] *Ibid.* 480.   [3] *Ibid.* 502.

Like the actor he was, Ralegh exploited every chance. The new Lieutenant at the Tower, Sir William Waad, complained to Cecil that everybody knew Ralegh had been before the Lords, and now he was showing himself 'upon the wall in his garden to the view of the people, who gaze upon him and he stares at them, which he does in his cunning humour that it might be thought that his being before the Lords was rather to clear than to charge him'.[1] Ralegh claimed that the Lords had allowed his son, Walter, more liberty to go out and about and for his doctor to come in. Waad was no friend, and proceeded to put Ralegh under closer restraint again; the little garden where he had his still-house and spent all day at this time in his distillations had only a slender paling, so that Ralegh could see everybody who came in and out the Lieutenant's lodgings: Waad had a brick wall built so that Ralegh should neither see nor be seen. He got Cecil to reprove Ralegh: 'how your message has wrought you may in part perceive from his handwriting. It is not possible for any man to protest more ignorance in the matter than he does, laying all these rash errors and frantic parts on the folly of her whose imperfections he should conceal; wherein what he says is fitter to be related than written.'

It is sad that their troubles were wearing out love, the strain of the circumstances of their marriage bringing out the faults of her temperament no less than his.

Down in Northamptonshire Gunpowder Plot brought Bess's brother momentarily to the fore; for some of the leading plotters were Northamptonshire men — notably the handsome Catesby and the febrile Tresham, who betrayed the plot — and Throckmorton was this year sheriff of the county. Instructed to search suspect Catholic houses and seize the goods of the traitors, Throckmorton needed to show all the more devotion to duty in that so many of the conspirators were his kinsmen, descended from old Sir George of Coughton. And indeed Coughton came once again into the picture, for tall Sir Everard Digby borrowed the house for the occasion, heard mass there and had his horses ready for action, if things had gone well in London and James and his Parliament been blown sky-high.[2] Instead, the tradition of the house is that the women of the family waited for news of their men-folk in the room above the gate — to hear all was lost.

The sheriff's detailed bill of expenses incurred in the emergency reads like a missing page from his Diary: how he rode

---

[1] *Salisbury MSS.* XVII. 378, 548, 551.   [2] *Cal. S.P. Dom. 1603–10*, 248, 261.

down post from London to Paulerspury, with six horses and a guide, sending out letters to the other Deputy-Lieutenants — Sir Anthony Mildmay, Sir William Fitzwilliam and others — to meet at Rushton to search Tresham's house and send up his servants.[1] Thence they went on to Drayton — Lord Mordaunt was sent to the Tower: 'his house a receptacle of most dangerous persons and there is a continual concourse between it and foreign seminaries.'[2] Other houses searched were Tresham's Lyveden, Pipewell, Silsworth, and the Catesby house at Ashby St. Ledger's. Altogether there were some thirty Recusant houses in the eastern division of the county, fifteen in the western.

Such zeal aroused the opprobrium of his kin, and Throckmorton was glad to win Cecil's approbation to offset it. 'It is no small comfort to understand how gracious a construction, in the midst of the outcries of my unkind kindred, you pronounced of my carriage, wherein I have been many ways wronged . . . as appears by the inventories of the goods by me seized and now delivered up to Lady Tresham . . . all things being delivered up to the least trifle; only one new book, written from Aristotle to Alexander, I have reserved for my Sovereign, if you think it meet for so great a Majesty, wherewith, when I am out of my physic, I will attend you.'[3] Being in a course of physic is a familiar note from the Diary, and the next we hear does not surprise us. 'My being so near at the gate of the grave and the weakness the unexpected recovery has left me in have kept me from giving testimony of the comforts I received of your vouchsafing to present from me the books to his Majesty and the favourable words for me at the Council table, persuading the payment of my poor bill, which yet rests unanswered. And last by the exceeding joy you put me in, dying, and my woeful wife, touching the obtaining of the wardship of my children after me. . . . I have now sent you the picture you desired (too plain a piece to possess any place in your house), as also the old manuscripts. My sickness and absence from London make them come thus in their old coats. There are eleven of them in number, all I assure you I have; some of them are rare, witty and pithy.'

One consequence of Gunpowder Plot was to bring a former friend of Ralegh's, Northumberland, into the Tower for company. The Earl was a known malcontent and no friend to Cecil;

---

[1] *Salisbury MSS.* XVIII. 38-40. Actually Tresham had time to wall up his papers; they were not discovered at Rushton till 1828. *v. D.N.B. sub* Francis Tresham.

[2] *The Montagu Musters Book, 1602-13,* ed. Joan Wake, xliii, 224.

[3] *Salisbury MSS.* XVII. 644; XVIII. 448.

he is said to have protested against the treatment of Ralegh. He had had the negligence to admit his kinsman, Thomas Percy, one of the conspirators, as a gentleman pensioner in attendance on the King without administering the oath of supremacy. Percy was a Catholic and, as the Earl's steward, proposed to devote his Michaelmas rents, some £4000, to the purposes of the rising. The government chose to regard the Earl's negligence as criminal, deprived him of all offices, sentenced him to imprisonment for life and imposed the enormous fine of £30,000 on him. Northumberland always held that he owed these amenities to Cecil's enmity; his residuary claim to the throne exposed him to danger. A difficult, saturnine, deaf man, of distinguished intellectual interests, mathematics and astrology, medicine and alchemy, a student of Machiavelli and Italian literature, he was an eminent accession to the group of unorthodox spirits collected in the Tower. For with his wealth the Wizard Earl was able to take Hariot into his regular employ, and Warner and Hughes followed: the Earl's 'three Magi'.

What the orthodox thought of these unquiet spirits may be gathered from the effective verses circulated as supposed to have been written by 'that Atheist and traitor Ralegh':

> When first this circle round, this building fair,
> Some god took out of this confusèd mass —
> What god I do not know nor greatly care —
> Then everyone his own director was,
> Then war was not, nor riches was not known,
> And no man said then this or that's my own . . .
> Then some sage man among the vulgar wise,
> Knowing that laws could not in quiet dwell
> Unless they were observed, did first devise
> The name of god, religion, heaven and hell,
> And gain of pains and fair rewards to tell —
> Pains for these that did neglect the law,
> Rewards for him that lived in quiet awe.
> Whereas indeed they were mere fictions,
> And if they were not, yet I think they were,
> And those religious observations
> Only bugbears to keep the world in fear
> And make them quietly the yoke to bear . . .
> Indeed I must confess they were not bad
> Because they keep the baser sort in fear.
> But we whose minds with noble thoughts are clad,
> Whose body doth a richer spirit bear,
> Which is not known but flieth everywhere,

KING JAMES I

> Why should we seek to make that soul a slave
> To which dame nature such large freedom gave ? . . .[1]

(On which we may comment, why indeed ?)

A more important consequence of Gunpowder Plot for Ralegh was that it was improbable now that he would ever gain his freedom; gone was the relaxed atmosphere of security prevailing in 1604, and with it his sanguine hope of pardon. He recognised that it was unlikely now, for it was from this time that he settled down to work on what would take him years, his *History of the World*. We find him writing to the antiquary Sir Robert Cotton to lend him a whole series of early chronicles in Latin, French and English; and no doubt he made other requests, drawing upon scholars to aid him and setting himself to his studies with all the force of concentration, and more, that he had previously given to voyages, war, privateering, politics, the vain pursuit of power.

Gunpowder Plot ended James's honeymoon with his new kingdom, and shortly there were other evidences of *malaise* in high places. James had noticed a sadness in Cecil's face and, apprehensive as always, took it for a sign of distrust. Cecil expressed the hope, 'if you have noted any sadness in my face (being the true seat of love and cares) that you will judge thereby how deep an impression the least shadow of distrust will work in those spirits whose affections no art hath power to dissemble. . . . The changes which I observed (as became me) in former times (when the age and sex were full of change and passion) did not so much trouble me as the least cloud that I should see gathering in your countenance.'[2] And so on. It seems that the reptilian Northampton had been up to his tricks again; for James wrote at length assuring Cecil of his trust, but closing with a warning against Northampton: 'what large and eternal proof of 3 [Northampton] his fidelity ye best know, and yet I would no more trust him than one of the corruptest lawyers in the trial of a mean error upon one of his dearest friends'. He added, 'set another leg beside mine, I warrant 3 will swear the King's sweet leg is the far finest'. Donnishly conceited as he was of his learning, his wisdom and his theology, the spindle-shanked King had no illusions about his legs.

Far finer were the legs of Robert Carr, which had first attracted the attention of the royal eye. James had been pathetically starved of affection from his earliest years, and now he demanded it in those around him. An affectionate nature and

[1] H.M.C. *Bath MSS*. II. 52-3 ; actually from the anonymous play, *Selimus*, 1594.
[2] *Salisbury MSS*. XIX. 20, 50.

not unkindly disposition — except where Ralegh was concerned, who was not his type — needed someone to love, and during these years he was in love with Carr. Now Carr's eyes fell upon Sherborne, and it was not possible for James to resist the desires of the man he loved. Early in 1609 the long suit to determine the legality of Ralegh's conveyance to his son terminated against him, and at once Carr pressed for Sherborne. Ralegh wrote him a remonstrance of grave dignity: 'it is come to my knowledge that yourself (whom I know not, but by an honourable fame) have been persuaded to give me and mine our last fatal blow, by obtaining from his Majesty the inheritance of my children, lost in law for want of words. . . . Sir, seeing your day is but now in the dawn, and mine come to the evening — your own virtues and the King's grace assuring you of many good fortunes and much honour — I beseech you not to begin your first buildings upon the ruins of the innocent, and that their griefs and sorrows do not attend your first plantation.'[1] All to no avail; nor did it bring Carr, in the end, any good.

Lady Ralegh, by now a practised and inveterate suitor, had knelt to the King at Hampton Court that autumn for her husband's liberty and received no sign of recognition. Now this Christmas she knelt to him again for Sherborne, the apple of their eye, all that remained to them of their hopes. But James, too, was under pressure; all he would say, in his broad Scots, was 'I maun hae the land; I maun hae it for Carr'. He was a generous man — always excepting Ralegh — and that he had a bad conscience about it may be gathered from the terms accorded to Lady Ralegh and her sons. She was to be given £8000 as purchase-money for the life-interest in the estate and a pension of £400 a year during her life and the elder son's. These were not unfair terms of exchange; but of course they disregarded the declining value of money, the irregularity of its payment and the increasing value of land. It was always land that counted.

Comments in London were what we might expect: now that the land had gone beyond recall, Ralegh might 'say with Job, Naked came I into the world and naked shall I go out. But above all, one thing is to be noted that the error or oversight is said to be so gross that men do merely ascribe it to God's own hand that blinded him and his counsel.'[2]

Certainly the indomitable man was much buffeted by fortune; wherever he turned he was checkmated, all his hopes turned to

---

[1] Edwards, II. 327.   [2] *Letters of John Chamberlain, ed. cit.* I. 280.

dust, yet strangely he never gave up hope. (It must have been a function of his excessive vitality.) He never gave up scheming, for example, about Guiana; various English enterprises were on foot to explore and settle on that coast: he kept in touch with them and out of his much diminished resources subscribed to one or two. In 1607 he tried to interest Cecil in some promising minerals brought home from thence; later he was writing to the King to consider the advantages of the riches of Guiana before it was too late. Cecil kept a close eye on behalf of English interests in relation to the whole diplomatic situation; in 1610 he moved over to a more anti-Spanish line, in support of Sir Thomas Roe's expedition to explore the possibilities of English settlement and of finding gold in Guiana. This raised Ralegh's hopes; but Roe's negative report convinced the wise Cecil that it was not worth risking war with Spain for a doubtful quantity. It was not true that Cecil was playing with Ralegh, but that he 'consistently refused to commit himself until a concrete demonstration had been provided'.[1] It was not forthcoming.

Whatever the issues between them, Cecil can hardly have relished the task of addressing a rebuke to Ralegh on behalf of the Council, upon unspecified charges in 1610. Once more he was put under close restraint for three months and Bess ordered to remove herself, her children and womenfolk from the Tower to her own house on Tower Hill. This brought a request from Ralegh that 'my wife might again be made a prisoner with me, as she hath been for six years last past'.[2] Otherwise it meant his keeping two establishments, to his impoverishment. Next year, further suspicions fell upon him — perhaps in regard to his writings and discourses — and it clearly gave Northampton pleasure to take him down a peg once more. Northampton wrote to Carr, with whom he was very familiar, in spite of his being the King's favourite: 'we had a bout with Sir Walter Ralegh, in whom we find no change, but the same boldness, pride and passion, that heretofore hath wrought more violently, but never expended itself in a stronger passion. Hereof his Majesty shall hear when the Lords come to him. The lawless liberty of the Tower, so long cockered and fostered with hopes exorbitant, hath bred suitable desires and affections. And yet you may assure his Majesty that by this publication he won little ground.'[3] It is all in the old Lord Henry's inimitable style.

At this low ebb in his fortunes Ralegh derived strength —

[1] V. T. Harlow, *Ralegh's Last Voyage*, 21.   [2] Edwards, II. 328.
[3] *q*. Stebbing, 253; *Cal. S.P. Dom. 1611-8*, 58-9.

and no doubt the jealousy of others — from the support and sympathy of Prince Henry, the heir to the throne. What would happen if James were to die? There can be no doubt: the famous prisoner in the Tower would command the confidence of the new king. That gave Ralegh a renewed contingent importance, and reinforced the hostility of those in possession. It can have given James no pleasure that both his wife and his son were keen supporters of his prisoner. Ralegh now in 1611 wrote to Queen Anne to protest against his stricter treatment, 'who, after eight years' imprisonment, am so straitly locked up as I was the first day'.[1] He complained that his 'extreme shortness of breath doth grow so fast on me, with the despair of obtaining so much grace to walk with my keeper up the hill within the Tower'. Long before, when he had more hope, he had petitioned the Queen to undertake a Virginia voyage — what possibilities it opens to the imagination if he had been allowed to plant the colony at Jamestown in 1607! A petition to the Queen in verse survives from this time, and it is noticeable how his mind echoes his former phrases when he turns, as rarely now, to verse:

> My days' delight, my springtime joys foredone,
> Which in the dawn and rising sun of youth
> Had their creation and were first begun,
>
> Do, in the evening and the winter sad,
> Present my mind (which takes my time's account)
> The grief remaining of the joy it had . . .
>
> Moss to unburied bones, ivy to walls,
> Whom life and people have abandoned,
> Till th'one be rotten stays, till th'other falls.[2]

The Queen begged again for his release, but nobody took any notice of that poor lady.

Renewed hope came this summer of 1612 with Cecil's death, at Marlborough on 24 May, hurrying back from a vain attempt to recuperate his health at Bath and to counter the machinations of enemies, and friends, flocking round upon the failure of his powers. Cecil's prisoner had survived him to write a bitter epitaph on the dead Lord Treasurer:

> Here lies Hobinol, our pastor while ere,
> That once in a quarter our fleeces did shear . . .[3]

[1] Edwards, II. 335.   [2] *Poems of Sir Walter Ralegh*, ed. Agnes Latham, 68-9.
[3] This refers to Cecil's office as Lord Treasurer.

For oblation to Pan his custom was thus,
He first gave a trifle, then offered up us;
And through his false worship such power he did gain
As kept him o' the mountain and us on the plain.
Where many a hornpipe he tuned to his Phyllis
And sweetly sung Walsingham to's Amaryllis.
Till Atropos clapped him, a pox on the drab,
For (spite of his tarbox) he died of the scab.[1]

This summer, too, there died Sir Philip Sidney's daughter, the Countess of Rutland; and Ralegh, whose personality people could not let alone, was 'slandered to have given her certain pills that despatched her'.[2] Actually it is true that the Rutland family, like others, resorted to him for medicines. As early as 1606, we find among the Rutland accounts a payment 'to Sir Walter Ralegh's man that brought a water for my Lord for the colic, 20s.'[3] There were also payments for tobacco and pipes sent to Belvoir. Ralegh was, of course, the conspicuous patron of smoking — another discommendation in the eyes of King James, who in 1604 had published his *Counterblast to Tobacco* in a vain attempt to dissuade from a filthy habit 'neither brought in by king, great conqueror, nor learned doctor of physic . . . but by a father so generally hated'.[4] For once our sympathies are with King James, who pointed out that the popularity of tobacco was as 'an antidote to the pox, a filthy disease whereunto these barbarous people [the American Indians] are very much subject . . . a stinking and unsavoury antidote for so corrupted and execrable a malady, the stinking suffumigation whereof they yet use against that disease, making so one canker or venom to eat out another'. King James's habits exposed him the less to the contemporary disease that so ravaged society.

Ralegh's hopes rose once more to their height with the strengthening of his ties with James's heir: the Prince now asked his advice not only with regard to maritime matters but affairs of state. The question of his marriage and that of Princess Elizabeth was coming to the fore. James would have preferred a Spanish or a French marriage. Not so the Protestant Prince, who asked Ralegh to propound his views and argue the case for him. Ralegh responded with two effective tracts, impressive for their knowledge of European and English history. He was opposed to the idea of marrying the Princess to the Catholic

---

[1] *Poems*, ed. Latham, 53.   [2] *Letters of John Chamberlain*, I. 374.
[3] H.M.C. *Rutland MSS*. IV. 507.   In 1612 we find extract of amber for plasters and chemical oil of amber directed by Ralegh to be sent down to Cambridge for one of the family. *Ibid*. II. 353.   [4] *A Royal Rhetorician*, ed. R. S. Rait, 36, 55.

Prince of Piedmont; he preferred the Protestant Prince Palatine of the Rhine. (That was the marriage that came about — by which the popular Elizabeth, adored by the poets, became the 'Winter Queen' of Bohemia, mother of Prince Rupert of Civil War fame.) For similar reasons Ralegh was opposed to marrying Prince Henry to a daughter of Savoy; so was the Prince.

No wonder Ralegh's mind, as we see from other writings of his, was filled with historical knowledge and reflection, for his great *History* was getting on apace. It was announced for publication in 1611, and then something happened to delay it. 'It was for the service of that inestimable Prince Henry . . . that I undertook this work. It pleased him to peruse some part thereof, and to pardon what was amiss.'[1] It seems that Prince Henry induced Ralegh to change the plan of his book and make it larger; he wanted to read in greater detail the more interesting history of the Persian Empire, the Greeks and Romans, than the history of the chosen people with which the book began. This meant more work — but to that Ralegh never objected. And it was a vast compliment and encouragement that the heir to the throne should take this personal interest in it. The rewards might be expected to be correspondingly rich.

The Prince got his father to promise Ralegh's liberation that Christmas; he certainly purchased Sherborne from his father's favourite, it was said with the object of restoring it to Ralegh. It would have been a very appropriate reward for the *History of the World*. Then, in November, the Prince was struck down with typhoid, and was obviously dying. The Queen insisted on sending to the Tower for Ralegh's Great Cordial. There followed a vehement debate among the Lords of the Council and the doctors, and only as a last resort was it administered. Here, too, every act of Ralegh's was ground for controversy: he wrote that the medicine would take effect against fever, but not against poison. The result was that when the Prince died, after a temporary rally, Queen and people were convinced he had been poisoned. For Ralegh it was the overthrow of his last hope; in laying down his pen at the end of the first folio volume, of his projected three, he wrote, 'it hath pleased God to take that glorious Prince out of the world, to whom they were directed; whose unspeakable and never enough lamented loss hath taught me to say with Job, Versa est in luctum cithara mea, et organum meum in vocem flentium'.

[1] *q.* Sir Charles Firth, 'Sir Walter Ralegh's *History of the World*', in *Essays Historical and Literary*, 39-40.

THE DEAD QUEEN

CHAPTER XV

RALEGH IN HIS WRITINGS

RALEGH'S writings in the Tower come back again and again to the theme of Fortune, the accidental turns and twists of man's life, particularly a public man's life, throwing him up unexpectedly on the heights and the next casting him into the depths.[1] He had experienced it over and over in his own career. It is not my purpose to analyse his writings in detail, but to scan them for the light they throw on a personality hitherto so enigmatic, controversial and contradictory, now becoming clearer to us. 'The success of all human actions', he tells us, 'seems rather to proceed from fortune than virtue.'[2] Again, 'it is no wisdom ever to commend or discommend the actions of men by their success; for oftentimes some enterprises attempted by good counsel end unfortunately, and others unadvisedly taken in hand have happy success'. 'Neither can I think that the virtue or sufficiency of any man, without the favour of the heavens, can advance him.' And lastly, with an inward turn, 'rarely or never can we consider truly of worldly proceedings, unless first we have felt the deceits of fortune'. These thoughts that crop up across the surface of his various works have the connection of inner meditation: they are his reflections on his experience of the buffetings of life.

From what he had felt in his own hide he was able to say: 'the course and quality of men's lives serving in Court is of all other the most uncertain and dangerous'.[3] There, among other things, 'great men do study not only to hold their own but also to command and insult upon inferiors'. Here we see Ralegh, who had been proud enough himself in prosperity — though, oddly enough, we do not hear of his persecuting inferiors — now in adversity, on the way to popularity. The element of autobiography is obvious in the reflection, 'whoso aspireth to any dignity must resolve himself to endure the envy of men'; and

---

[1] There is a similar emphasis in the writings of Churchill, for a similar reason.
[2] *Works, ed. cit.* VIII. 60, 86, 96, 120.   [3] *Ibid.* 44, 57, 101, 104, 113.

particularly in the thought, 'any exterior behaviour or garment presenting pride or greatness, chiefly in persons lately advanced, though no man be thereby injured, doth move in others a certain offence'. But there is not much point in paying attention to what others think of one, either their disapprobation or even their applause; for, though 'everyone seest what thou seemest to be, but few can understand what thou art indeed'.

In these circumstances, and with this disillusioned view of human beings and their society, 'there is no course more comely, nor any resolution so well beseeming a wise man . . . as to retire himself from Court and company'.[1] Though Ralegh could see that well enough in the silence of the Tower, outside it he would nevertheless not have practised that wisdom: his own temperament would have been too much for him, too much vitality, too many chances offered. All the same the truth remained that 'for such men as have gained unto themselves reputation and are accounted virtuous, to maintain that conceit and eschew envy there is nothing better than a life retired from daily conversation, and chiefly of the multitude'. In fact, it was only by force of his imprisonment that Ralegh found the fruitful solitude whence sprang his works.

Nevertheless, it would be more than human were Ralegh not to resent it against those who had placed him in that solitude with no such kindly motive. In his dedication of 'The Prerogative of Parliaments' to King James he wrote, 'it would be in me more doglike than manlike to bite the stone that struck me . . . seeing their arms and hands that flung it are most of them already rotten'.[2] There was a bitter satisfaction in that, and this was what he really felt about Cecil and company who had put him there. When they were dead he was there to get his own back; he would continue the feud. James — such a contrast with Elizabeth — was at loggerheads with his very first Parliaments: 'the people were as loving as ever, and so his Majesty had found them in his last two Parliaments, if he had not been betrayed by those whom he most trusted'. Whether just or not, Ralegh's writings would have their influence with posterity in the formation of the anti-Stuart Parliamentary tradition. And, another kick for Cecil, for daring to take, even by exchange, 'princely Hatfield' from the Crown, 'which the greatest subject or favourite Queen Elizabeth had never durst have named unto her by way of gift or exchange'. The further implication of that was that a

[1] *Works, ed. cit.* VIII. 106, 114.   [2] *Ibid.* 15, 153, 177, 179.

Scottish king was whittling away the possessions of the English Crown — as he was. If one connects up the divers reflections from various places in Ralegh's writings, a consistent attitude emerges, ominous in its undertones for the Stuart monarchy. A king should 'gratify his courtiers and attendants by such means as not to pleasure them with the hurt and injury of his people'.

Everything that he wrote, in spite of the formal flattery that did not take in James, rose up to accuse the alien king. There was the insistent contrast with the living memory of a great queen. 'Queen Elizabeth would set the reason of a mean man before the authority of the greatest councillor she had'; for 'she was the Queen of the small as well as of the great and would hear their complaints'.[1] 'She much desired to spare the common people', and we learn that when Ralegh rose in Parliament to plead the case of the poorest tax-payer, 'I did it by her commandment'. No wonder we hear the reproach set against the accents of affection: 'is it a loss to the King to be beloved of the commons?' . . . 'our late dear sovereign kept them up'. She had not been afraid to go about among her people — there were still the unforgotten memories of Tilbury: a king should 'show himself oftentimes graciously, with state and majesty, to his people, and receive complaints of his suppliants and suchlike'. But James had a craven fear of crowds: no popular progresses for him, nor could he ever compass dignity, let alone majesty, in his public appearances. So that Ralegh's adjuration sounds like irony: a king should 'so order and behave himself that he be loved and reverenced of the people'. No-one could love or reverence James.

An unspoken reproach is present in every article. 'There is no art or other knowledge so seemly and necessary for a prince as the art military.'[2] James was notoriously a coward, with no physical courage at all. 'A prince ignorant of martial knowledge, among other misfortunes, cannot be esteemed or trusted of his own soldiers.' Was it any wonder that the country's prestige had sunk so low? 'I myself may remember when one ship of her Majesty's would have made forty Hollanders strike sail and to come to anchor.' Not so now: the Dutch were even superior at sea. Unfair as this observation may have been, Ralegh repeated it; it was not without significance that when the Civil War came, the Navy and all the seamen were on the side of Parliament. Even Ralegh's personal tastes were antithetical to James's, not

---

[1] *Ibid.* 14, 187, 195, 213.   [2] *Ibid.* 102-3, 327, 568.

only with regard to sex : James could not bear a smoker, equally
Ralegh could not bear a drunkard. 'It were better for a man to
be subject to any vice than to it . . . a drunkard will never
shake off the delight of beastliness ; for the longer it possesseth
a man, the more he will delight in it ; and the older he groweth
the more he shall be subject to it.' So James found.

All this while, as the deeper burden to these varied notes of
his activities in the Tower, there proceeded the *History of the
World*. There was all the reading and research that went into
it — over six hundred authors are quoted — and then the magnificent writing of the book, one of the elaborate, learned, poetic
fabrics of the age, the more splendid for being built on the
frontiers between the Gothic inheritance of the English past and
modern baroque. The learning and the idiom are traditional ;
the spirit, sceptical, questing, unquiet, is modern.

Since the eighteenth century and the rise of simpler modern
prose, with its different idiom, this masterpiece — so influential
in its own century — has been neglected and even underestimated.
But this has chiefly been by the pure critic, incapable of such a
work himself or of appreciating either what goes into it or what
it achieves. The best historians, who know, have always admired
it at its true worth. Hume, for instance : 'they were struck with
the extensive genius of the man who, being educated amidst
naval and military enterprises, had surpassed in the pursuits of
literature even those of the most recluse and sedentary lives ; and
they admired his unbroken magnanimity which, at his age and
under his circumstances, could engage him to undertake and
execute so great a work as his *History of the World*'.[1] In our time
Firth has most judiciously summed up the values of the work :
its living qualities, the characters standing out clearly, the way
that great men work out the providences of their time. (We, in
ours, would state that the other way round : the ways in which
the forces of a time work through the historic figures.) There
is a constant human interest in the book, besides the immense
intellectual energy imposing rational order, so far as was possible
then, upon the chronology and making what sense could be made
out of Biblical nonsense, the assumptions of sacrosanctity imposing inhibitions upon the reasoning faculties. With Ralegh's
sceptical intelligence, all that was at a minimum. And this
makes him, though the truth is not realised, far more readable
than the prose-works of Donne or Lancelot Andrewes, now so

[1] D. Hume, *History of England* (ed. 1824), III. 38.

adventitiously fashionable, but so much of whose prose is in fact dead.

This even applies to the style, as others have noticed : it is far more modern than that of the contemporary theologians, or Milton. If the book were given modern punctuation only, its readability would become obvious. Then there is the personal accent, which, some do not sufficiently realise, is what gives a book life, difference, idiosyncrasy. Ralegh is always 'near at hand, sometimes in front'; and personality is never obsolete.[1] Hence the book's appeal to those best qualified to judge. Charles James Fox's infallible taste named Bacon, Ralegh and Hooker as the supreme writers of prose in the period between the Armada and the Civil War. Bacon and Hooker were professionals, but what an achievement for the soldier, sea-captain, privateer, Irish planter, voyager, coloniser, courtier, poet, official, politician, to rival them! Hallam, too, has pointed out how clear and racy, flexible and flowing, besides eloquent, Ralegh's writing is, blessedly 'free from the affectation and passion for conceits, the snare of contemporary historians, preachers, and essayists'.

Of course there were not wanting mean-minded persons to say, as they do with Churchill's *History*, that Ralegh's work was done for him by others; and the cases are not dissimilar. Ralegh used the advice of specialists — for example, for Hebrew, which he is the first to tell us he did not know; but the information he gathered from them, like a sensible man, is absorbed so that every paragraph emerges, as with Churchill, with his personal imprint on it. Some fillip to misinterpretation was given by Ben Jonson saying that he had written 'a piece to him of the Punic War, which Sir Walter altered and set in his book'.[2] This passage has been identified as that dealing with the revolt of the mercenaries against Carthage; but indeed if one looks into Jonson's words one sees that it offers no exception to my statement of the position.

The work was licensed for publication in 1611, but did not appear till three years more, in 1614. Since Ralegh was a man condemned of treason, 'civilly dead', the book appeared without title-page or name of author. However, the author was very much alive, with his double dose of vitality, in the long and extremely personal preface which served as his *Apologia pro Vita Sua*.

We learn from it that he intended to come at length to a

[1] Stebbing, 276-8.   [2] *q*. Firth, 37.

history of Britain. 'I confess that it had better sorted with my
disability, the better part of whose times are run out in other
travails, to have set together the unjointed and scattered frame
of our English affairs, than of the universal: in whom, had there
been no other defect (who am all defect) than the time of day,
it were enough — the day of a tempestuous life, drawn on to the
very evening ere I began.'[1] How much reason we have to regret
that he did not get on to recent history, we can see from the revealing things he lets out by the way. He had a remarkable
knowledge of the inwardness of events, their personal and private
motivations in the century and a half before — offering us an
illuminating parallel with Shakespeare's cycle of plays on English
history. *What* a history of the reign of Elizabeth Ralegh could
have given us, if he had dared! But he was well aware of the
danger — everything he said or did gave offence. 'I know that
it will be said by many that I might have been more pleasing
to the reader if I had written the story of my own times, having
been permitted to draw water as near the well-head as another.
To this I answer that whosoever, in writing a modern history,
shall follow truth too near the heels it may haply strike out his
teeth.'

Everything in the book, like everything in Ralegh's life, only
added to King James's vexation. It was no use Ralegh's writing
in a passage to flatter the king, James knew well enough what
Ralegh really thought; while references to his clemency, without
any of the foul spots upon his predecessors, sounded either like
an irony upon himself or an impertinence towards kings. Indeed
the outrageous man did not hesitate to say exactly what he
thought about kings — and by this time we know enough about
Ralegh to know that, where intellectual truth was concerned, he
was unable to restrain himself. His very genius made it impossible for him to be anything but honest, independent, uncompromising; he would never compromise over what he thought: too
proud, too contemptuous of others. (And, indeed, contempt
must have been a tower of strength to him in all those years, a
fortification of the spirit as strong as ever were the walls of the
Tower.)

The fruits were to be seen in such things as his savage indictment of Henry VIII. No-one, except exiles safely abroad, had
ever dared to write about that monarch — the nearest the English
have ever had to an Ivan the Terrible or a Stalin — as Ralegh

---

[1] Ralegh, *History of the World*, ed. 1677. All quotations are from this edition, but
the Preface has no pagination.

did. 'Now, for King Henry the eighth, if all the pictures and patterns of a merciless prince were lost in the world, they might all again be painted to the life out of the story of this king. For, how many servants did he advance in haste and with the change of his fancy ruined again, no man knowing for what offence? To how many others, of more desert, gave he abundant flowers from whence to gather honey, and in the end of harvest burnt them in the hive? How many wives did he cut off, and cast off, as his fancy and affection changed? How many princes of the blood (whereof some of them for age could hardly crawl towards the block), with a world of others of all degrees did he execute?' And so on. There had been no such plain speaking about a king, especially by a leading public figure; look how careful that prudent man William Shakespeare was in handling that dangerous theme about the same time! No wonder King James, though accustomed himself to exclaiming against Henry in private, was annoyed.

Nor can Ralegh's tribute to Elizabeth have helped much; for one thing, James was understandably jealous of her hold upon her people's memory still; for another, Ralegh asserted himself by the reminder of his special relationship to her. 'I know that I lost the love of many for my fidelity towards Her whom I must still honour in the dust, though further than the defence of Her excellent Person I never persecuted any man.' It is a curious fact — one of the many contradictions in this conflicting man — that the most outspokenly contemptuous of them all, he was also one of the more humane. We have no record of his persecuting small folk as with others of his smoother contemporaries; where he governed he seems to have been genuinely popular.[1] It was his equals, but without his gifts, who were jealous of him and disliked him. Of his own overthrow he added, 'of those that did it and by what device they did it, He that is the supreme judge of all the world, hath taken the account' — for Cecil was dead. The very last words of the Preface return to draw attention to Ralegh's fate, and what he owed to them. 'I am on the ground already, and therefore have not far to fall.

---

[1] Cf. Carew's tributes to Ralegh for his efforts on behalf of the Cornish; in regard to the pre-emption of tin 1599–1600, where Ralegh did his best for the tinners; in protecting the ancient customary tenures, favourable to the tenants, on the Duchy manors against an attempt to screw more money out of them; and in procuring the revocation of a patent granted to some speculator that 'none should salt, dry or pack any fish in Devon or Cornwall without his licence. . . . The Cornish Justices of the Peace, through the never-failing forwardness and backing of Sir Walter Ralegh, obtained a revocation.' Carew's *Survey of Cornwall*, ed. 1811, 56-7, 113, 206.

. . . All the hope I have lies in this, that I have already found more ungentle and uncourteous readers of my love towards them, and well deserving of them, than ever I shall do again. For had it been otherwise, I should hardly have had this leisure to have made myself a fool in print.' As for James, would any-one be likely to mistake the portrait of Ninias, successor of the famous Queen Semiramis, a king 'esteemed no man of war at all, but altogether feminine, and subjected to ease and delicacy?'

In adversity Ralegh had come, as is usually the case, to have God more frequently on his lips, a useful reach-me-down in default of rational explanations. But indeed his philosophical position seems always to have rested on a deistic basis — though that was the same as 'atheistic' in terms of popular abuse, for Ralegh was never an orthodox Christian. The whole turn of Ralegh's mind and temper was sceptical. 'It is not truth, but opinion', he says with disgust, 'that can travel the world without a passport.' His conviction obviously was that it should be truth; but how much truth can feeble human intelligences either take in or stand? He never lets up on his contempt for the standards of the mass of mankind; 'fool', 'idiot', 'idiotism', are words always on the tip of his tongue and very revealing of his temper. Frequently there are phrases that betray both his scepticism and his contempt together: 'neither the false beauty of our apparent actions, nor all the formality which, to pacify the opinions of men, we put on' . . . 'Everyone is touched most with that which most nearly seemeth to touch his own private, or otherwise best suiteth with his apprehension.'

He applies this to people's religious pretences in a very un-comfortable fashion. 'We are all in effect become comedians in religion; and while we act, in gesture and voice, divine virtues, in all the course of our lives we renounce our persons and the parts we play. For charity, justice and truth have but their being in terms, like the philosophers' *materia prima*.' As for *what* people believe, the 'doctrine of faith touching the Creation in time (for by *faith* we understand that the world was made by the word of God) being too weighty a work for Aristotle's rotten ground to bear up', what are we left with? 'For myself, I shall never be persuaded that God hath shut up all the light of learn-ing within the lantern of Aristotle's brains.' Ralegh shared the anti-Aristotelianism of the moderns of his day. What certainty is there in man's knowledge; what do we know of the mystery of the universe, or of our place in it? 'Man, saith Solomon, that can hardly discern the things that are upon the earth and with great labour find out the things that are before us; that hath so short a time in the world as he no sooner begins to learn than to die; that hath in his memory but borrowed knowledge; in his understanding nothing truly; that is ignorant of the essence of his own soul, and which the wisest of the Naturalists (if Aristotle be he) could never so much as define, but by the action and effect, telling us what it works (which all men know as well as he) but not what it is, which neither he nor any else doth know.'[1]

This was what Ralegh really thought, this was what he was like: it all adds up to something very different from a pious, orthodox Christian.

Both Preface and the book itself are full of personal touches and reminiscences keeping it alive. There are references to plays and players, one of them referring to Tamburlaine in a visual manner that makes one feel he had seen — as surely he had — Marlowe's play. 'God, who is the author of all our tragedies, hath written out for us and appointed us all the parts we are to play, and hath not in their distribution been partial to the most mighty princes of the world . . . that appointed Bajazet to play the Grand Signor of the Turks in the morning and in the same day the footstool of Tamburlaine.' At the same time there is Ralegh's touchiness about people calling him a play-actor: 'great pity it is that such mad dogs are oftentimes encouraged by those who, when they themselves cannot touch a man in open and generous opposition, will wound him secretly by the malicious virtue of an hypocrite.'[2] Then, too, there were those given to the chimeras of divinity, who 'condemn all such, in the pride of their zeal, as atheists and infidels that are not transported with the like intemperate ignorance'. But perhaps both sorts of mad dog had a point against Ralegh.

There is a touching reference from the man shut up in the Tower so many years to the swelling waves we observe, 'for so we do in the West of England, before a southerly storm'.[3] He recalls at one moment the fig-trees he had seen in South America, at another the very old Countess of Desmond — supposed to have been married in Edward IV's time — whom he had met in Ireland. Knowledge of recent astronomical discoveries, observations of Venus and so on, he would owe to Hariot; while he kept himself in touch with the new accretions to geographical knowledge, like the information about Sinai — important for Biblical

---

[1] Notice how consistent this is with Ralegh's conversation at Sir George Trenchard's table at Wolfeton in 1593; *v.* above p. 176-7.

[2] *History, ed. cit.* 215.   [3] *Ibid.* 26, 45, 59, 157, 593, 612, 626, 655.

history — coming from the travellers to the monasteries there in
1588. His graphic memories of his early soldiering in France
we have already remarked on — after Jarnac and Moncontour,
and what he saw in Languedoc. His personal acquaintance with
France and the Netherlands, his experience at sea, illuminate
many pages.

Most informative are his references to contemporary history
— indeed Firth says that his reflections on English history alone,
if drawn together, would make a considerable tract. Ralegh
points out, for example, the confused strategy behind the Armada:
'for to invade by sea upon a perilous coast, being neither in
possession of any port nor succoured by any party, may better
fit a prince presuming on his fortune than enriched with understanding. Such was the enterprise of Philip II upon England in
the year 1588, who had belike never heard of this counsel of
Artabanus to Xerxes, or forgotten it'.[1] His anti-Spanish reflections were no more likely to commend him to James, who had a
snobbish respect for the Spanish monarchy and was bent on a
pro-Spanish foreign policy. Ralegh reminded the country of the
18,000 Netherlanders 'cut off in those six years that Alva governed
by the hands of the hangman, besides all his other barbarous
murders and massacres'. To what purpose? At the end of it all
'he hath paid above an hundred millions and the lives of above
four hundred thousand Christians, for the loss of all those
countries, which for beauty gave place to none, and for revenue
did equal his West Indies; for the loss of a nation which most
willingly obeyed him, and who at this day, after forty years' war,
are in despite of all his forces become a free estate and far more
rich and powerful than they were when he first began to im-
poverish and oppress them.'

In June 1614 Throckmorton made suit to the Council to
repair to him in the Tower, and was granted licence as his
occasions required.[2] Throckmorton was a trustee, as we have
seen: but owing to the gap in the Privy Council Registers from
1604 to 1613 we do not know why he had to get special licence
or whether he had discontinued his visits. In the spring the large
folio, first of the ambitious three projected, appeared. Though
without title-page, it had a remarkable frontispiece drawn to
design laid down by the author to illustrate his conception.
There was History, the Mistress of Life, attended by Experience
and Truth, treading down Death and Oblivion and holding up

[1] *History, ed. cit.* 427, and Preface.   [2] *A.P.C. 1613–4*, 455-6.

the globe, upon which were marked the Orinoco as the only river, as Ralegh's own, and ships, which might be his, engaged in the Atlantic and sailing the seas. On either side of the globe were Good Fame and Ill Fame; while above, the eye of Providence (or Fate) presided over the history of the world. Ben Jonson contributed the verses opposite describing the frontispiece:

> From Death and dark Oblivion (near the same)
> The Mistress of man's life, grave History,
> Raising the world to good or evil Fame,
> Doth vindicate it to eternity.
>
> High Providence would so: that not the good
> Might be defrauded nor the great secured,
> But both might know their ways are understood,
> And the reward and punishment assured . . .

In short, History was

> Time's witness, herald of antiquity,
> The light of truth and life of memory.

The immense folio was printed by William Jaggard, who in a few years' time had a still more important undertaking on his hands, the First Folio of Shakespeare's Plays.

At the end of the year James made an attempt to suppress the great work. The Archbishop of Canterbury wrote to the Stationers' Company, 'I have received express directions from his Majesty that the book lately published by Sir Walter Ralegh, now prisoner in the Tower, should be suppressed and not suffered for hereafter to be sold'.[1] In January 1615 Chamberlain reported, 'Sir Walter Ralegh's book is called in by the King's commandment, for divers exceptions, but specially for being too saucy in censuring princes. I hear he takes it much to heart, for he thought he had won his spurs and pleased the King extraordinarily.'[2] If so, it is one more instance of Ralegh's lack of tact and failure to understand the man irrevocably hostile to him. But he need not have taken it to heart, for he was winning this round of the duel. The attempted suppression only increased the demand for the book; there were three separate issues of the first edition. In 1617 two more editions were needed, and so it went on: between its publication and the Revolution of 1688 there were no less than ten distinct editions, with numerous variant issues. It was not only the best-seller of the century,

---

[1] Brushfield, 'Raleghana, Part VI', *Trans. Devon. Assocn.* 1904, 184.
[2] Chamberlain, *Letters*, I. 568.

after King James's Bible, but it made its own contribution, with Ralegh's other prose-works, to the tradition that culminated in the Whig Revolution. From his own point of view King James was quite right : the *History* became the favourite reading of, and an inspiration to, revolutionaries like John Hampden, Milton and Oliver Cromwell.

The third edition came out in 1617 with a title-page and the name of the author at last, with, opposite, his portrait to remind his countrymen of that unforgotten appearance : the splendid long head, the tall brow and pointed beard, the magnificence and air of command, for he was holding his baton now as general in command of the Guiana expedition. For which purpose he was once more a free man.

CHAPTER XVI

THROCKMORTON IN
NORTHAMPTONSHIRE

WHILE Ralegh was building a monument to himself by his works in the Tower, Throckmorton had settled into the landscape and life of Northamptonshire, and was quietly but unmistakably prospering. No longer the pawning of plate as in his early married days, the borrowings, the sale of land — though, as we saw, that had not contracted his expenditure; now, in spite of the increased expenses of family life, of having to marry off his daughters, building and equipping his house, of entertaining largely and making presents — he was always generous — he carried every year a large surplus of cash and was in a position to lend.

His is a very interesting case to consider, factually and concretely, in the too generalised and splenetic controversies that have convulsed academic historians over the rise of the gentry.[1] For the historian, it is always better to follow the facts than to lay down the law.

For one thing, Throckmorton profited by having given up Court-life with its hazards, its extravagance and ostentation. Most of those who followed it lost by it: hence their feverish scramble for offices, perquisites, grants, licences, patents; only a favoured few — personal favourites, successful politicians, and lawyers — made by it. In consequence, Throckmorton was able to direct his attention to his own estates, make a full-time job of it, and go in for direct farming of his lands, which was the way to see that the increasing returns from improved breeding and cultivation accrued to himself. Particularly, in Northamptonshire, from raising sheep.[2] This was the way the Spencers had

---

[1] I much agree with Sir George Clark in preferring local knowledge to generalisations and thesis-history: 'it enables us to think in concrete terms . . . not of enclosures of so many hundred acres, but of Rushton and Hazlebeech, not of landowners but of identifiable Montagus and Knightleys and Treshams'. 'Jacobean Northamptonshire, 1603–25', *Northamptonshire Past and Present*, 1958, 216.

[2] Cf. M. E. Finch, *Five Northamptonshire Families, 1540–1640* (Northamptonshire Record Society).

made their large fortune in the course of the century; one of the ways by which John Isham built up his pleasant estate around him at Lamport; the chief method by which the Treshams managed to hold on to their estates in spite of too many children to provide for, too much building, prodigal housekeeping, heavy Recusancy fines and the idiotic course of their heir, Francis Tresham, in the Essex conspiracy and Gunpowder Plot, involving himself in a large fine, the necessity of a handsome bribe, death. (His death, however, was a good thing for the family.)

The convictions of the Catholic Treshams were conservative, but their conduct in running their estates was radical. They had no objection to racking their tenants, coming down heavily upon then with exactions and fines and, worst of all, depopulating villages for sheep, turning the folk out to fend as best they could or perish. In 1603 the poor tenants petitioned the King not to renew a lease of Sir Thomas Tresham's from the Crown, for they were 'utterly undone by the extremity of their fines, rents, payments and services innumerable, as by vexations with processes and enclosure'.[1] In 1604 the Puritan, Sir Edward Montagu, had had, as knight of the shire, to represent their grievances, 'the depopulation and daily excessive conversion of tillage into pasture'.[2] In May 1607 the poor peasants broke into revolt at various places, but with noticeable unanimity and animus on the Tresham estates at Rushton and Hazlebeech.[3]

Nothing of this transpired on Throckmorton's estates, but then he was not greedy or a grinder of the poor; it is obvious from the Diary that remains, covering the years 1609 to 1613, that he was easy-going with them and, though conscientious and careful in his accounts as always, treated his people well. He, too, went in for sheep, though on nothing like the Treshams' scale: where they doubled their flock in a decade, from three thousand to over six thousand, his remained around twelve hundred. He did not depopulate. His estates were smaller and more varied: plenty of tillage as well as pasture, and there was the peculiarity of proximity to the forest of Whittlewood, which added variety to the economy, with returns from timber and coppice, pasture of cattle, the fallow deer.

He was not an engrosser; but he seems to have been able to

---

[1] Finch, 88.

[2] E. F. Gay, 'The Midland Revolt of 1607', *Trans. Roy. Hist. Soc.* 2nd Series, XVIII. 212.

[3] It must be added that the extremely Puritan Knightleys were depopulators too. Clark, *loc. cit.* 214. Perhaps the sensible, middle-of-the-road Anglicans were more respectworthy than either of the extremes?

make a valuable addition to his inheritance in the manor of Burton Dassett in Warwickshire. He did not succeed with his suit for the keepership of Brigstock parks,[1] but in February 1597 he received a small recompense for his service at Cadiz, the grant of 16 acres in Paulerspury park belonging to the Crown's manor of Grafton.[2]

If only we possessed his Diary between Cadiz and 1 September 1609, when the third volume takes up — covering his adventures there, Essex's last years and the death of the Queen, as much information about Ralegh's later affairs as he recorded of his earlier disgrace! But Ralegh was a man under attainder — too dangerous: he is not mentioned. Throckmorton is now away from the centre of affairs; his Diary has another interest. I find the daily life of the Northamptonshire squire, the routine of quarter-sessions and musters, hunting in Grafton park or the forest or hawking at the brook, quarrelling with his wife or entertaining neighbours, laying in provisions for the winter, shearing his sheep and counting his cash, ordering books from London along with oranges and lemons, wax candles and tobacco pipes, his care for his girls and his household, making a garden and plashing his fruit trees — I find these country occupations more affecting, more refreshing than the rise and fall of dynasties. For, with his doings, we are more immediately in touch with life, its satisfactions and its pathos, its poetry and prose.

By the time the third volume opens — the writing larger and older, the entries fuller and more spread out, inkier, and the paper less good — his family has taken its final shape: four daughters ('dafter' Throckmorton always writes) and no son to carry on his name. The year before, 6 June 1608, the eldest daughter Mary was married to Sir Thomas Wotton, son and heir of the first Lord Wotton.[3] Lord Wotton, of the Kentish family seated at Boughton Malherbe, was a distinguished diplomat who had been Sir Philip Sidney's companion on his journey to Vienna in 1574–5, and subsequently envoy to Portugal, Scotland and France. At this time, actually from 1602 to 1616, he was comptroller of the Household, and had been one of the commissioners for the trial of Cobham and Ralegh. There was nothing distinguished about Lord Wotton's son: an addict of horse-racing and country sports, he seems to have had nothing else to him and

---

[1] It was awarded to Sir George Carey, son of Lord Hunsdon, the Queen's cousin, in 1592. H.M.C. *Montagu of Beaulieu MSS.* 23.

[2] *Cal. S.P. Dom. 1595–7*, 176.   [3] G. Baker, *Northamptonshire*, II. 202.

was certainly no company for the bookish, serious-minded Throckmorton. The marriage bound Arthur more closely to his old friend, the celebrated Sir Henry Wotton, with whom and *his* friend Donne, Throckmorton had been on the expedition to Cadiz.[1] No doubt the two cronies had made the marriage; it was a suitable one, into the peerage, and it was happy enough.

The Diary opens with a close but fair day, 1 September 1609, when 'there dined here, besides Sir Edmund Bacon and my Lady Sibs Ouseley[2] and Morgan le fay (Bess)' with a number of young men. We at once recognise the authentic Throckmorton touch, the gentle archness of the Arthurian reference; while Sir Edmund Bacon, head of the family at Redgrave in Suffolk, was a friend of both Sir Henry Wotton and Throckmorton. Next day is no less recognisable from of old : 'ma femme était insensée en colère. I was to see my Lady Clifton and my Lady D'Aubigny at Grafton, where Sir Thomas Wotton killed his fee two bucks.'[3] So young Wotton, we gather, was keeper of Grafton, and poor Throckmorton had not been allowed to go and meet the ladies. At home he received a letter from the tenant of Alderminster, Thomas Russell, friend of Shakespeare and an overseer of his will — so that we are justified in thinking of the dramatist turning in along the road to Stratford to visit him.[4] If only Throckmorton had been present! Next day 'Mr. Pey came hither to supper and brought word of Sir Francis Vere's death some ten days before'. Two days later the Bacons left for home, and 'ma femme renouvella sa colère en extrémité'. Four days later, 'j'écrivais une lettre à ma femme'. She clearly needed more than that; Throckmorton gives a mellowed, gentler impression.

He continues his old habit of violent purging, and is now in the care of Dr. Chenell of Oxford, to whom he frequently sends Timothy for physic.[5] Not content with eight stools in a day, he took a potion with some powder in it which gave him twelve stools. 'Brought from Oxford an electuary to take before I

[1] Sir Henry was half-brother to the first Lord Wotton.

[2] The Ouseley family lived at delightful Courteenhall.

[3] Lady Clifton was the daughter of Sir Henry Darcy; her daughter, Lady D'Aubigny, married James I's cousin, Esmé Stuart, 3rd Duke of Lennox. *The Complete Peerage*, G.E.C. VII. 608. As Darcys these ladies belonged to Throckmorton's old acquaintance.

[4] Cf. Leslie Hotson, *I, William Shakespeare, do appoint Thomas Russell, esquire . . .*, 24. But Alderminster was not a manor of Russell's, he was Throckmorton's tenant there.

[5] John Chenell was a Fellow of Corpus Christi College, admitted to the practice of medicine 1596, M.D. 1605. J. Foster, *Alumni Oxonienses, 1500–1714*, I. 269.

sweat, 2s.; three purging potions, 7s. 6d.; bottles of small and strong diet drink, 7s. for each lot; four purgations, 12s. . . . I drank of the strong diet drink at four and when I went to bed, and once at supper of the small.' Then there are purges for his wife, who needed them more. Next, 'I was very ill in my stomach at night', so he took another potion which gave him twelve stools. He was accustomed to sweat half an hour 'in the stove', and at the end of the month was let blood, '9 oz. better blood than the last time'. For all this he paid Dr. Chenell and the apothecary £4 : 15s. Let this be enough.

This year he had 1275 fleeces of all kinds wound, and paid the woolwinder 27s. The winter provisions came from Stourbridge fair : 200 dozen of haberdine (salted cod), two quarters of great and green ling, 20 bushels of bay salt, mustard seed, starch, a barrel of soap, pepper and hops. He had a fat buck from his park salted in and then hung up to raise. Labourers were to work about Cuttle mill, clearing the dam and ponds, and scouring the brook that runs down the little valley outside the boundary. On 24 October he signed conveyances of his lands to three daughters — the fourth, Katherine, was as yet only ten[1] — and settled annuities of £100 a year each upon them after his death. From Lord Wotton he received half a year's rent for Burton Dassett, £300, of which he paid his son-in-law £200 for his half-year's annuity — a pretty penny to pay for a son-in-law, £400 per annum.

A map of the manor of Alderminster was being made, and Throckmorton sent Timothy over with a message; Thomas Russell was away from home, 'but where his wife knew not'. From delightful Hillesden in Buckinghamshire Sir Thomas Denton sent him a couple of spaniels; while out of Wales came thirteen goats — a dozen does and a buck — purchased from Mr. John Wynne, presumably of Gwydir. 'The price of a very good goat in Wales is 4s.' His half-year's rent for Cosgrove was now £63 : 8 : 8. In mingled sunshine and rain he set out on 6 November 1609 for a visit to London, £18 in gold in his purse, £5 : 18s. in silver, with Mr. Southerton for company and five servants in attendance. At St. Albans they had musicians, supper, fire, sugar and cloves, feed for their horses. Arrived at his lodging by Whitehall he set about laying in stocks : large quantities of cloth, fustian, bays, taffeta for upholstering, feather-beds, ticks, bolsters; three dressings for the three girls, cuffs and a beaver hat for

[1] She had been baptised 24 December 1598. Paulerspury Register.

Paul; for himself a Brussels cloak, a hawking bag, a brush and a looking-glass. Then, from Sir Baptist Hicks, yards of cypress[1] for his wife and three girls, six pair of Jersey stockings for these. 'Mrs. Mercer the midwife went down to my dafter Wotton at Paulerspury.'

He continued his buying: Rouen canvas for servants' sheets; quantities of paper, wax, pens; the winter stocks of groceries, sweet Candy oil, Spanish olives; 20 gallons of muscadel, the same of canary; cut-fingered and whole-fingered gloves; a white feather for his wife's hat, and a speckled red and white fan; hawk's bells for the goshawk, and a hood and jesse; 10 lb. of potatoes at 6d. a lb. — one sees that they were rare at that price. He bought a new felt hat for himself, and a lace ruff, an inexpensive jewel for Paul — who must have been his favourite servant, perhaps a page. Then there are his purchases of books: three volumes of the indispensable, inescapable, unbearable Perkins; 'nine loose play-books and four bound together' — of far more value, for among them would be a play or two of Shakespeare. (If only his collection of plays had been preserved, as the Ishams kept theirs!)[2] In addition, he bought volumes of play-books, paying as much as 16s. Meanwhile, he went to see the tombs at Westminster, and Spring Garden, like any tourist, himself a mere visitor now to London. Altogether he had now disbursed some £246 : 2 : 5, his servant Adrian keeping the cash, and he still had a good deal left.

He now expended large sums for his wife: black Florence satin, a doublet and round kirtle, black and silver parchment lace, silver buttons, silver loop lace and silk. Still larger sums went on plate, silver candlesticks and snuffers, spoons and forks, chargers and dishes: equipment for Paulerspury. He supped with Sir Robert Banastre at his chamber in Court;[3] visited Sir William Browne at his lodging by Baynard's Castle; and when he stayed at home his cousin, Sir Clement Throck-

---

[1] Cf. Milton,

'And sable stole of cypress lawn
Over thy decent shoulders drawn.'

[2] Till the nineteenth century, alas.

[3] Sir Robert Banastre was a Court official, whose fine portrait bust, perhaps by Nicholas Stone, may be seen in the church of Passenham looking down upon the chancel he built and beautified with splendid Renaissance woodwork and the walls with fine frescoes of the Prophets, upon which the Victorians riveted their indifferent tablets. This exceedingly fine Caroline monument deserves admiration and restoration. Banastre was 'bred up in the Court where he served three Princes eminent. A man prudent, charitable and very industrious.' He died 15 December 1649, aged about eighty.

morton or Sir Robert Osborne, came to see him.[1] He went to
consult Attorney-General Hobart about his assart lands (clear-
ings made in the forest), to whom he gave £10 — one of the innumerable pickings that went into the building of Blickling.
Before setting out from London he bought his daughter Wotton
a grand waistcoat for £3 : 6 : 8. And now he received the large
sum of £318 : 10s. wool-money, of which he sent £100 into the
country.

What about the rise of the gentry? There is no doubt that
Throckmorton — a fair specimen of the class, no special case —
had received a marked accretion of prosperity.

He got back just in time for his daughter's delivery of a girl,
with its attendant circumstances. Lord Wotton asked Throckmorton to be his deputy at the christening, and sent a basin,
ewer and two standing cups, worth £40. Little Kate was then
christened by Arthur, his wife and Lady D'Aubigny, who gave
a gilt cup worth £20. The midwife received £20 from Sir
Thomas and '£5 from my daughter, borrowed from me'. More
interesting were the books received from the binder, Du Bartas
in English, Dr. Rainolds upon the inexhaustible subject of
Divorce for Adultery, and *Nova Francia*.[2] On 20 December, a
day of wind and sunshine, Throckmorton betook himself to
Luffield and 'went forth with my goshawk'. At Christmas he
distributed pieces of beef and groats to twenty-one poor persons;
and the last days of the year he dined, as his custom was, the
village people near by, two townships at a time.[3] He was able
to make an offer of £430 to cousin Clement for the tithes of
Alderminster.

In the New Year book-buying continues with Dr. Bilson's
Survey and Donne's *Pseudomartyr*, recently published — Throckmorton always bought Donne's rather sparse publications in
these years.[4] He lent Sir Thomas Denton the Book of the Union,

[1] Sir William Browne, a soldier in the Netherlands, was deputy-governor of
Flushing under Sir Robert Sidney; Sir Robert Osborne lived at Kelmarsh in Northamptonshire.

[2] Marc Lescarbot's *Nova Francia or the Description of that Part of New France which is
one Continent with Virginia*, translated at Hakluyt's suggestion and published, with a
dedication to Prince Henry, 1609. G. B. Parks, *Richard Hakluyt and the English Voyages*,
266.

[3] Tuesday, 26 December, a day of rain and snow, he dined Plumpton end and
Church end; 27th, 'frost, windy, fair, I dined Pury end and Heathencote'; Sunday,
31st, 'windy, rain, I dined Whittlebury men'.

[4] Sir George Clark suggests that 'our knowledge of Jacobean Northamptonshire
would evidently gain in depth if we knew who did buy books, and what books, and
who read them', *loc. cit.* 216. Here Throckmorton's Diary provides fuller information
than any other source I know.

presumably the Union with Scotland; and when cousin Clement gave him six lampreys, he passed on three of the horrors to Denton. Meanwhile he was still being sued by Lord Compton and Lady Mordaunt for his actions at Drayton when sheriff at the time of Gunpowder Plot in 1605. They now presented him with the bill, and a privy seal was served on him to appear before the Council. More books were sent down from London by his agent, Mr. Southerton, and more purgatives from Oxford. In February he lent his son-in-law £10, who now owed him £30, for a visit to Redgrave, from which he came back with a letter from Sir Henry Wotton in Venice. 'I will therefore present you the service of a poor scholar, for that is the highest of my own titles and, in truth, the farthest end of my ambition.'[1] Sir Henry commended himself to 'your whole house, with which we are now so particularly conjoined'. This was very flattering from one who was both an eminent figure in the world and a scholar, either of which Throckmorton would have been pleased to be.

In May he was in correspondence with the Solicitor-General about his land, with that of others, being taken in to enlarge Grafton park to serve James's mania for hunting. Throckmorton was buying cattle at Banbury fair and branding sheep in his park and at Luffield: altogether he had 1166 sheep this year and had bred 482 lambs. Loads of stone, Harleston being best for the door-frames, were brought home for his garden walls: Harleston, being of a rich dark brown colour, would punctuate well the local grey limestone of the walls.[2] In June Adrian Wright and Robert Pound, his confidential servants, were sent up to London with £200 and £32 : 17s. for charges, to establish his rights to his assart lands. In July the reliable Adrian came back with the patent for them — it had in all cost £246 : 17s. The fleeces wound this year totalled 1221.

Throckmorton paid parson Pilkington 10s. for teaching Paul Ashton. On Mayday Arthur went to christen his friend Jasper Ouseley's girl Mary, and gave six gilt spoons, with 20s. to the nurse. Later Ouseley and Baldwin Wake came to stay a night; young Sir Thomas Wotton went into the Duchy — *i.e.* Duchy of Lancaster land — to course hares. In July he went up to London to take leave of his father going ambassador to France. On the young man's return, we read 'Sir Thomas Wotton *me fit injures*'. An old friend, Sir Edward Hoby, came to stay, and various Throckmortons, young Simon frequently. Arthur was

---

[1] *Life and Letters of Sir Henry Wotton*, ed. L. Pearsall Smith, I. 483.
[2] I owe this information to Miss Joan Wake.

in correspondence with his cousin, Sir John, who had had a successful military career in the Netherlands and was for long Serjeant-major of Flushing; he forwarded his son's account of the siege of Jülich, where he was serving.[1]

In July the Queen passed by, going from Tyringham to Holdenby. Sir Christopher Hatton's magnificent mansion had been bought by James in 1608; it became a favourite summer residence of both James and Charles I, until the deplorable Civil War, in consequence of which the splendid house, along with many other good things, was destroyed. On 17 August, a fair windy day, 'the King came to Grafton and the Prince to Pury Lodge. My Lord of Montgomery killed a buck in my park and supped here. Sir John Grey lay here.[2] Saturday, 18th. The King hunted and dined at Salcey forest. Sir Thomas Wotton went thither and Sir John Grey. Monday, 20th, windy, fair. My Lords of Pembroke and Montgomery dined here and killed three bucks. The King came hard under my house and through my park.' He did not call on Ralegh's brother-in-law, and next day he went on from Grafton, restless, for ever on the move. Next day, *ma femme et moi en colère*. Eighteen sheaves of his wheat were stolen, after sun setting. His neighbour, Sir Robert Banastre, an official of the royal Household, went on his progress to provide fish for it. Throckmorton lent his rude son-in-law another £30, making £60 in all, and the Wottons set off for Boughton Malherbe 'in my carroche'. More to the point was Throckmorton's bargain with four Essex clothiers to sell his two-years' wool for 24s. the tod.[3] The Witham men weighed it at 312 tod, which amounted to £374 : 8s., the money to be delivered at Pury. His last sale of wool, at 27s. the tod, had brought in £418 : 10s. He sold 110 wethers, and bought conies at 12d. a couple and 15d. a couple of the best.

In September Throckmorton embarked on the final stage of making Paulerspury a pleasant habitation, designing a garden, laying out walks, paving and paling the paths, planting hedges, fruit-trees, wardens, vines, artichokes. We know from Bacon's essay 'Of Gardens' how contemporaries thought they should be laid out: the formal square within walls for shelter, the fair alley in the midst, covert alleys on either side the green 'upon

[1] For Sir John Throckmorton, *v.* H.M.C. *De L'Isle and Dudley MSS.* II and III *passim*. He was an able soldier, a follower of Essex who quickly skipped over to Cecil on Essex's fall; he deserved to rise.
[2] Sir John Grey, son and heir of Lord Grey of Groby, had been at Cadiz with Arthur and was knighted there. J. Nichols, *History and Antiquities of the County of Leicester*, IV. Part II. 633.　　　　[3] The tod is 28 lb.

carpenters' work about twelve foot in height, by which you may go in shade into the garden', the stately hedges and the fountain of water, 'the fruit-trees as well upon the walls as in ranges': the whole providing a setting for the trees, fruits and flowers which in the Essay read like a Jacobean nurseryman's catalogue.

Throckmorton's garden followed closely the fashion laid down there. The gardener of Mixbury[1] came to 'draw the ground walled in to a hanging level as the foundations of the walls would suffer,[2] and by taking out stones and superfluous earth to proportion all my walks and quarters to see how they may receive the good mould of the pheasant-run. To plant, spread and nail all my apricot trees in good mould against my house and other places fittest.' For this the gardener was to have £5. The paviours had already paved the causey to the stable; now a great deal of sawing boards was necessary to make rails, 'with three chequered doors for a walk from the causey before the south door alongst the wall and to turn up to the park at the churchyard, 11 foot wide with 42 posts turned, and to make a double strong door into the churchyard, 4 foot wide, with a fair head of timber garnished, and to pale up from the pond to the door, the pales to be 8 foot high from the ground'. There were to be seats, one by the garden door over against the church, the other within the rail-fence against the stables; seats also for the bowling place and pales for the orchard strong and straight.

We can see it all — though, if we go to Paulerspury today, there is nothing but a bare humpy hillside running down from the church to the brook.[3]

Soon the masons were building the walls, the railed-in walks to the church being levelled. Bilson of Mixbury broke off his bargain and left work. Daniel, Lord Stanhope's French gardener, came from Harington to give advice, and the gardener of Holdenby bargained to make the garden at 1s. a day, with meat and drink. There were eight labourers at work, and Throckmorton set 229 artichokes altogether, besides the old roots. In November he was moving apricot trees into the new garden, and in December was setting fruit trees from London, five apricots, two mellacottons,[4] two yellow peaches, two primordian plums, two cherry plums, two orange plums, two pescoo (peach) plums, bluepear,

[1] Near Brackley, just inside the Buckinghamshire border.
[2] As the ground is on a slope, this would mean sloping banks and terraces.
[3] The humps mean that the foundations of the house are there for any Elizabethan archaeologist to expose.
[4] Melocotón is the Spanish for peach, so these would be Spanish peach trees.

redpear, whitepear plums, and cherry trees red and white. The cherry plums were set one each side of the parlour door, and the rest in order which he gives in detail. In all thirty-four fruit-trees from London cost £3 : 7 : 10.

In January 1611 he bought some thousands of privet sets at 3½d. the hundred, and willow twigs at 6d. the thousand, to plant his hedges and fences. By now the battlements were being set upon the garden walls; vines were sent to him out of Kent. He bargained with Thomas Foster, plumber, from Northampton 'to make a double force of brass to bring water to my house' — all work, lead and labour to cost £103 : 10s. More thousands of privet sets and willow twigs were planted, and in February he uncovered the artichokes. Thomas Shipton came from Holdenby to be the gardener of both his gardens for £6 a year wages, a livery and 'the overplus (my house being found) of all herbs, sallets and artichokes, and to have the yard before his lodging for a nursery for fruit-trees for me and himself'. He bought an acre of timber from Grafton park for hedging and ditching his fields. The rails were all oiled and coloured by painters from Stony Stratford. It must have looked enchanting.

Now the plumbing went forward. Labourers were set on work 'about the force for water at the spring head'. One day he 'found the young plumber playing the knave with Jane'. (Plumbers will be plumbers.) A few weeks later, 'I turned away Richard Bunch the butcher and Jane the foul. I spake with Mr. Whalley about this business' — he was the parson of Cosgrove, and no doubt Jane's business might involve child-birth, for which the parish would have to pay. Our ancestors were properly anxious to avoid that. By July the long walk in the great garden was levelled, and loads of gravel in place upon all the walks. At last, on 13 July, he was able to say, 'I did eat a very ripe apricot out of my garden'.

And now, of all that labour and design, such forethought and care — nothing remains.

All that autumn and winter of 1610–11, while Ralegh's hopes of release ran high, life at Paulerspury had gone on as usual: letters passing between Throckmorton and Thomas Russell at Alderminster — if only he had gone over and caught a glimpse of Russell's friend, the busy dramatist, some of whose plays must have been among the playbooks he bought. He bought Camden's *Britain*, with the maps, on its publication in English this year, 1610. Mr. Southerton sent him down two of Lancelot

Andrewes's *Sermons* and his *Answer to Bellarmine*, a playbook for
6d.; in May Throckmorton paid Southerton 47s. 4d. for books.
When he reckoned up his cash in November, he had in a little
box £35 : 8s. in gold, in a coarse canvas bag £100 : 8s.; in several
bags in the iron chest £400, besides £10 lent Dick Lydcote and
£100 of Lord Wotton's — 'in all and lent £510 : 8, besides
money in two drawers of my desk to pay the labourers in the
garden'. He had been able to lend his neighbour Sir Austin
Nicolls £500, of which £250 had been repaid to him.[1] When
Sir Austin repaid the rest in August, Throckmorton reckoned up
his cash and found he had £680 : 14 : 9 in the house.

There is no doubt that this gentleman, without the burdens
or hazardous rewards of office, had — financially speaking —
risen.

In March his daughter was delivered of a boy; the proud
father went off to Brackley to run a horse-race with Wenman
from Oxfordshire. The christening arrangements fell to Throckmorton, who invited Sir Henry Wotton, went over to Astwell to
invite Lady Compton, sent to Gloucester to buy fish for the
party — three salmons and fourteen horrible great lampreys
from the Severn — and sent Adrian to London for provisions,
besides lending his daughter £5. On 6 April Sir Henry Wotton
— who was away from Venice from 1611 to 1616 — arrived in
time for supper with Dr. Walsall of St. Benet's, Cambridge.
Next day the child was christened Charles by the grandfather,
Lady Compton and Sir Henry, who, chronically impecunious,
seems not to have presented even a cup. Throckmorton, as
usual, paid up — 40s. to the nurse and midwife. But, then, he
was now well off. At Lady day a couple of tenants paid him
£300, of which his son-in-law had £200, and £100 went to buy
sheep and beasts at Stow-in-the-Wold fair. However, Sir Henry
sent down four pots of Venice treacle: *theriaca Andromachis
senioris fideliter confecta in officina duorum Aethiopum Venetiis*. Throckmorton was always grateful for a purgative.

In May Sir Henry wrote Arthur the news from Court: 'the
King goeth to Windsor, there to honour with his presence both
his sons and his favourites at their instalments'.[2] This meant
that, along with the young Prince Charles, the handsome leg of
Robert Carr, now Viscount Rochester, was to be decorated with
the Garter, for his services. In Germany another member of
the confraternity, the Emperor Rudolph — whom Arthur had

---

[1] Sir Austin Nicolls lived at Hardwick, where he is buried under a brass in the
church.   [2] L. Pearsall Smith, I. 506.

known in earlier years in Prague[1] — grown more and more eccentric and recluse was displaced in favour of the Archduke Matthias: 'so as having first spoiled him of obedience and reverence, next of his estates and titles, they have now reduced him to so low a case that he is no longer patron of his own voice'. This was a small return for his obligations, but Throckmorton was well content to be kept in touch with the world he had quitted by so eminent a figure on the stage. Scholarly in his tastes, he liked to be in correspondence with scholars. When Dr. Chenell came over from Oxford in May, to supervise his spring purging — which we will not go into — he brought a letter from Bodley's first librarian, Dr. James, to whom Throckmorton presented a buck in the summer. In spite of his present of £5 to Dr. Chenell, he 'went away in a chafe', and later wrote back 'an humourous [*i.e.* ill-humoured] letter'. At the end of May, Sir Henry Wotton sent Arthur a cipher for their correspondence, and later a picture of an Italian banquet, *Gustare Guastfare*. On 27 May, 'Sir Hatton Fermor brought Walter Ralegh here and supped here'. That is Ralegh's elder son, and it is the only reference to the Raleghs in this volume of the Diary.

The older generation were going out, the affairs of the younger demanding attention. In May uncle Sir Francis Carew died, and Arthur's brother Sir Nicholas, who took the name of Carew, succeeded to Beddington.[2] Brother Robert's daughter, Anne, came to stay a few days on her way thither to claim her portion. Sir Thomas Lucas died at Colchester, leaving Arthur and his wife a small legacy of £30. The question of marrying their second daughter, Anne, now came to the fore. A Northamptonshire neighbour, Thomas Elmes of Lilford, had put in a bid for her for his son; but since she was a co-heiress she could do better. In September 1611 'Sir George Throckmorton moved a match for Mr. Heneage of Lincolnshire and also of Sir Lewis Watson[3] for Anne my dafter'. Michael Throckmorton, who had succeeded to his father's position as Serjeant of the hawks,[4] engaged himself for Sir George Heneage. Next followed a negotiation

---

[1] See above p. 85-6.

[2] Before this fortunate event Nicholas had been very hard up. He wrote in 1604 to his father-in-law, Sir George More of Loseley — he was therefore brother-in-law of the poet Donne: 'my plate is all to pawn, credit I have none . . . you know whereon I do hope and to whom I am indebted, which may frustrate my hopes if I should not content and please. . . . No less than £200 at Midsummer next can make me show my face in any company, and £100 at Michaelmas next, which if I cannot have I must leave my country, and my wife and children to the parish.' *The Loseley Manuscripts*, ed. A. J. Kempe, 361.   [3] Of Rockingham Castle.

[4] In April 1597. *Cal. S.P. Dom. 1595-7*, 397.

with Sir Robert Cholmondeley, which was almost concluded and then was broken off with some ill-feeling. A still more important proposition came into view, for a match with the immensely rich Attorney-General Coke's eldest son. This broke down when it was discovered that that nasty type was simultaneously, and characteristically, negotiating underhand with someone else.

Actually Anne was not married until after the Diary ends, on 5 July 1614, when she married Sir Peter Temple of Stowe, a neighbour who visited frequently at Paulerspury.[1] Temple got, with his treasure, the manors of Luffield and Dodford; then in January 1620 his wife died in childbirth. Not getting the second daughter Mr. Elmes came back with a motion for the third, Elizabeth, for his son. He did not get her either: she went to Richard Lennard, Lord Dacre of the South, who got with her Cosgrove and Tiffield. They were married 14 July 1617, but she too died before her father, in 1625. This left Mary, with Paulerspury and Silverstone, in the hands of the Wottons.

In August young Wotton 'used some tricks to me'; this did not prevent him from calling on his father-in-law to lend him money. With the money, Arthur gave him 'the Precepts for the well bringing up of his son Charles'. Compiling such precepts was a fairly common thing with such persons in that age: Ralegh himself left a well-known set of 'Instructions for his Son'.[2] But Throckmorton's proved unnecessary, for on 21 June 1612 'little Charles Wotton died about six in the morning'.[3] His father was away in London; 'my daughter had letters from Lord Wotton and her husband consolatory'. It seems that the grandfather, with his sympathetic nature, was more touched than the father; actually, if they had known it, this meant the end of the Wotton peerage, for Sir Thomas had no more sons. For the Wotton inheritance, too, a generation later was dispersed among co-heiresses.

---

[1] Baker, II. 202, and Paulerspury Register.

[2] *v.* below, p. 326-8. Another example from Northamptonshire, in marked contrast to Ralegh's in tone, is the virtuous Montagu's. Cf. L. Stone, 'Lord Montagu's Directions for his Son', *Northamptonshire Past and Present*, 1958, 221-3.

[3] He was buried the same day. Paulerspury Register.

CHAPTER XVII

JACOBEAN COUNTRY GENTLEMAN

I N his fine new house with the garden growing up around,
along the shoulder of the hill his spacious park with the deer,
to the south, bounding his horizon, the crescent shape of the
forest, well-off with money coming in increasingly from both
arable and sheep-pasture, Throckmorton was in a position to
entertain constantly and generously. He was a natural host,
rather than a guest; one does not find him going to stay much
in other people's houses : they came to stay with him. He would
have a bowling party, to which Throckmortons and Fermors
came; or a match at bowls against the Longfields with whom
Charles Wake and Shakerley Marmion dined. Himself would
go over to Grafton of a summer afternoon to eat cherries with
the Whalleys. Among neighbours who came was Shakerley
Marmion, father of the Caroline dramatist, from Aynho, which
he was forced to sell to the Cartwrights in 1616 — they remained
there right up to the family catastrophe in our own time. In
September 1611 Shakerley Marmion went off with a goshawk
Throckmorton gave him. Francis Beaumont brought word of
Sir John Grey's death of smallpox at Lady Newdigate's.[1] One
cannot tell whether this was the dramatist, for a Francis Beau-
mont is qualified as 'old' on another visit. On 1 November,
'Lord Carew passed by this way out of Ireland and sent Sir
Geoffrey Fenton's son to see us'.

To entertain his guests over the Christmas holidays Throckmorton offered five fiddlers from Stratford, either Old or Stony
Stratford, 50s. with meat, drink and lodging. They stayed the
whole twelve days, Arthur paying 40s. and son Wotton 10s.
There are payments to other musicians at intervals, and Throckmorton took his usual care with a dancer named John Renolds
to whom he paid 6s. 8d. the week. When he left he got into
trouble, for the master sent him 20s. in prison. In July 1612
Renolds came back; he had been before King's Bench with

---

[1] The Newdigates lived, and live, at Arbury in Warwickshire.

Lord Vaux and at the Keeper of Newgate's house with Mrs. Vaux, inveterate Recusants. Evidently the dancer, like so many people connected with the arts, was a Catholic. After all, one would hardly expect a dancer to be a Puritan, or a Puritan to dance. He stayed three weeks, and on his leaving kindly Throckmorton gave him 20s. — a useful sum in those days. At New Year 1612, 'we had my Lord Chandos's men that played two plays for 30s.'. There was always the entertainment of cards, particularly gleek, at which Throckmorton fairly regularly lost.[1]

His book-buying continued as full, and of as much interest as ever. On 21 November 1611 Robert Pound came back from London with Murray's *Sophonisba*, Tourneur's *The Atheist's Tragedy*, and Donne's *Anatomy*, all published that year; as also King James's *Bible*, for which Throckmorton paid 47s. and presented it to the parish. In December Southerton, who wrote him always a newsletter with his books, sent him du Plessis Mornay's *Mysterium Iniquitatis*, 14s. 8d., and Mr. James's book, 2s. 4d. On 21 December there came 'a book of Don Quixoto', which cost 3s. 6d. — this was the volume read by Shakespeare, and which had its influence upon the lost play *Cardenio*.[2] In January 1612, when Throckmorton had £768 : 2s. in the house, the remainder of his wool-money was in Christopher Southerton's hands. On 19 January he sent Mr. Southerton a great Banbury cake, and shortly received the *Syntagma Amandi Poloni*, 2 vols. for 16s., *Britanno Romano* 4d., and wax sises or tapers, 2s. 10d. In the same month came from Southerton Pierre Matthieu's *Life of Henry IV*, translated by Edward Grimeston, 2s., Willet on the Romans (*i.e.* papists), 8s. 6d., and the King's book against Conradus, 1s., evidently the Declaration against Conrad Vorstius. The theologian on the throne, instead of occupying himself to more point with the country's finances, was at this time engaged in an absurd controversy with the Dutch professor on predestination and other exquisite points in Calvinism. James took the orthodox, illiberal view and succeeded in driving him from his professorship, if that established his point.[3] The Jacobean public lapped up this kind of thing with relish.

Meanwhile young Wotton 'jarred with us', or hurt his nose at the foils; went about the country to Brackley races, or to

---

[1] Gleek was played by three persons with forty-four cards, each hand having twelve and eight being left for the stock. A gleek was three of the same cards in one hand together; to gleek therefore meant gaining a decided advantage. J. O. Halliwell, *Dictionary of Archaic Words*, I. 403.

[2] This ante-dates the year of publication in *S.T.C.* (4915) for Shelton's translation of Part I, given as 1612. [3] Gardiner, II. 128.

Northampton 'to running for the snaffle'. A party of menfolk
went from the house to Brackley for the race on Baynard's green
for the bell; Michael Throckmorton, being a sportsman, joined
them and Lords Montgomery and Compton came to see Sir
Thomas's horse race Babington's for a wager of £50. The race
was deferred on account of the weather till the Saturday, when
Sir Thomas's horse Styllein won. Then 'my dafter Wotton
quickened of her child'. One sees where Sir Thomas's interests
lay. Only occasionally did he do something useful, like viewing
the deer in Grafton park — there were 660 in all. He was a
perfect out-of-doors fellow. In March Throckmorton sent a
horse to London to bring the more useful Southerton down, who
brought with him a dozen preserving oranges, the same of lemons
and Jordan almonds. Sir Henry Wotton's half-nephew and
secretary, Albertus Morton, came with a letter to say that Sir
Henry was to go ambassador to Savoy and evidently asking for
aid. For Morton was given £5 in gold, and William Leet sent
to wait upon Sir Henry during his mission. Southerton sent Dr.
King's Sermons upon Jonas on 27 March; from Oxford Dr.
Chenell sent bottles and bottles of strong diet drink, trusses, pills,
lozenges, coltsfoot, potions that gave sixteen stools.

Throckmorton was now able to spend £1600 a year and more.
From 1 January to 13 December 1611 'I spent £1597 : 17 : 6½
in all manner of expenses, besides Paulerspury half-year rent
which my wife received'. In the house and about the place he
had seven women servants and twenty-four men, including the
miller and cooper. For wages Rose Throckmorton got £8 a
year, far more than anyone else; perhaps she was a poor relation
or an illegitimate sprig of the family, as was often the case. Sir
Arthur had had before now to chide her for 'her carelessness
and cursedness and unthankfulness'. The indispensable Adrian
Wright and Robert Pound, at whose influence young Wotton
took exception, got no more than £3 a year each. When Throckmorton cast up his wool accounts in May, he found he had sold
1265 fleeces this year — more than ever; so was the total cash
in his chest, £836 : 15 : 6.

He could well afford to indulge his taste for books — Donne's
two *Anniversaries* for 6d.; Ben Jonson's *Alchemist*, 6d.;[1] the
Proclamation against Lord Sanquair, 'a murdering Scot. Peevish
Pilkington read the Proclamation unknown to me in the church.'[2]

---

[1] He received Donne's *Anniversaries* on 10 May, Jonson's *Alchemist*, 15 May 1612.

[2] Throckmorton presented William Pilkington to the living in 1602, who quitted
in 1625. Baker, II. 205.

Along with half a salmon and three lobsters, Southerton sent three
no less rebarbative books of Vorstius; more amusing, Throckmorton was expecting Ben Jonson's *Epigrams* for 6d. The chief
news in May was that 'Robert Cecil, Lord Treasurer, died in the
way from the Bath at a house that was the Lady Sharington's'.
A few days later Arthur 'sent my tear for Cecil' to his cousin
Clement — the reference suggests a certain hostility: the traditional Throckmorton feeling for Cecils, perhaps reinforced by
sympathy for Ralegh.

On a fair hot day at the end of July 1612 Throckmorton set
out for London with Paul, who had grown into a close companion, possibly a personal valet. They took with them £50 in
silver, £51 : 18s. in gold, and stayed at the 'Black Swan' in
Holborn. At Sir Baptist Hicks's they bought tawny velvet
wrought in grain, large quantities of taffeta, sarsenet, fustian;
two shirts and a pair of stockings for Paul. They removed to
the 'Bear' at Smithfield, but had 'our dinners at the "Pope's
Head".' A second visit to Hicks's shop procured 'a loose gown
for myself', wrought nightcaps, quantities of velvet, two pairs of
Spanish leather boots. On Sunday, 2 August, clearly for old
times' sake, 'I went to the sermon at the Italian church, given
there 6d.' Paul bought two looking-glasses, and they supped
at the 'Pope's Head'. Throckmorton paid a visit to Lady
D'Aubigny, and returned on 7 August to find Sir Clement
Throckmorton awaiting him.

Visitors were more frequent than ever; the young men —
Wotton and Charles Wake — went to Northampton fair, but
came back to supper. 'Old Francis Beaumont' with others came
to dine, and then the King and Prince came to Holdenby and
Grafton, with a grand following, to hunt. Two of the Prince's
officials dined at Paulerspury; and on 23 August 'I went to my
Lords of Pembroke and Montgomery to Sir Robert Osborne's'
— that is, to Kelmarsh. This was a Sunday, and Scott the Sub-
Almoner preached at Grafton. Next day Lord Pembroke, with
a distinguished company, came to dine; and 'after dinner the
King drank here, for the which came Sir Walter Chute, Sir
Walter Stuart, Sir Edward Zouche etc.' Some of the King's
party came to dine next day, and on the 26th James moved on
to Woodstock for more hunting and other diversions. More
important, 'all my corn harvest was inned'. On 27 August Lady
Wotton produced another daughter; her husband went off
immediately to Woodstock with his prize-winning horse as a
present for the Prince.

Throckmorton went off, more sedately, for a night at Oxford, where he stopped with Dr. Chenell, who had Dr. Abbot, Master of Balliol, the Principal of Hart Hall and other academic worthies to meet him. He paid a visit to Bodley's Library, presenting the librarian — who complained of being underpaid — with a 20s. piece, 2s. for the porter. At Chenell's house he gave liberal rewards of 10s., and at Wadham College, then newly building and which he wished to see, 12d. With three books, which cost 1s., and medicines from apothecary White for daughter and granddaughter he went back to Paulerspury for the christening, and to lend son Wotton more money, which came now £20 : 15 : 4. A large party came to hunt in his park — Lord Exeter, the Lord-Lieutenant, Sir Francis and Sir George Fane, Sir Peter Temple and others. Throckmorton had several days hunting at Grafton and Hartwell; a fat buck he killed on Wakefield Lawn he sent to the indigent, the appreciative, Sir Henry Wotton. Later in the month Arthur sent him 'my dappled grey gelding'; for this generous present Sir Henry managed 40s. for the groom that brought him.

Son Wotton borrows £30 to go to Market Harborough fair with Adrian; but it is Adrian whom Throckmorton entrusts with £50 to buy a dozen heifers in calf. He does not find his son-in-law useful for any purpose, except to hunt with occasionally, nor does he entrust him with any business. One day Wotton quarrels with Sir Thomas Denton, Arthur's friend and Arthur succeeds in making 'all friends' again. We do not think highly of young Wotton. Paul receives 30s. for fustian and linings for doublet and hose, and sometimes cash or a dozen points; clearly Paul is becoming quite a figure. The 'Swan' at Market Harborough is noted as the best inn; it still is. In London the Palsgrave of the Rhine arrives in September to marry Princess Elizabeth; Southerton sends down a newsletter with his picture. But in November the news comes of Prince Henry's mortal illness. On Saturday, 7 November, 'I writ to Pilkington to pray in the church for the Prince's recovery'. But not all the prayers in all the churches could make any difference. And it is from the Diary that we learn that Sir Thomas Chaloner was suspected — quite unjustly — of the Prince's death.[1]

Throckmorton now made the acquaintance of another doctor, a Dr. Cotta, author of a *Short Discovery of the Dangers of Ignorant*

---

[1] Sir Thomas Chaloner was governor and subsequently chamberlain to the Prince, and was given to chemical and other experiments. That was enough for the credulity of the time.

Practisers of Physic, from which theme, generally applied, Throckmorton might have profited and suffered less disturbance of his system. Dr. Cotta came to stay, received £3, and two good spoonfuls of syrup of roses gave Throckmorton fourteen stools. (His record was twenty-two.) Among books bought in December was *Purchas his Pilgrimage*, newly out, for 10s. On 17 December, a day of wind, sun and rain, 'Queen Anne's players came hither and played, for the which they had 13/4'. Sir Richard and Lady Gargrave were stopping that night; Sir William Tate[1] and Sir Thomas Temple dining next day. Sir Arthur distributed his usual largesse at Christmas: twenty-four large pieces of beef and 24s. to the poor; a doe to Sir Austin Nicolls, another for Sir Euseby Andrew, high sheriff;[2] 5s. a piece to daughters Anne and Bess, little Kate Wotton and Paul, who is treated almost as a member of the family. On Boxing day Shakerley Marmion came over, and Throckmorton entertained a lot of young fellows, a Greville, two Moolles, two Yorks, Richard Foxe, Sykes and 'young Washington'.[3]

The musicians played all through the twelve days of the holidays and received 40s. Throckmorton lost large sums of money at play (dice) and at cards. He was much bothered by county business as a Deputy-Lieutenant and Commissioner for Musters. But still more by his wife. At New Year, 'ma femme se monstra mal contente'. So next day he sent her — perhaps they were not on speaking terms — 20s. Result: 'continuation de la colère de ma femme'. Next day and the next day, 'continuation de ma femme'. Lady Gargrave was staying, with whom Arthur was on friendly terms, and his wife may have been jealous. The day after Lady Gargrave left, 'given my wife 20s.'; and, more consoling, Dr. Cotta came to stay.

On 23 January 1613 Throckmorton heard that his brother Nicholas was sworn Chamberlain of the Exchequer. This must have given pleasure, since it was the office by which the Throckmortons had risen and which their father, Sir Nicholas, had held. The eldest son, William, was still alive in this year, for we have

[1] Sir William Tate of Delapré was an active colleague of Throckmorton's as Deputy-Lieutenant; he had been sheriff the year before the latter, in 1603-4; he died in 1617. Joan Wake, 'Delapré Abbey', *Northamptonshire Past and Present*, 1958, 230.

[2] The Andrew family lived at pleasant Charwelton on the Warwickshire border, where their monuments in the church remain, and their manor-house close by.

[3] Young Washington would be the eldest son of Lawrence, who with his father had sold Sulgrave four years before and moved to Brington, where they were buried. Young Washington's brother John went to America and was the great-grandfather of the President.

SIR HENRY WOTTON

a rare entry for clothes and things for him in June. But Arthur's attentions are directed more towards Paul, who gets special treatment: doublet and hose made for him, knit stockings; when Sir Arthur and he go to Northampton for training the musters, Paul is given 40s. In October a tailor's bill for clothes for him came to £4:12:5: one can only conclude that Paul was regarded as a gentleman.

At the end of January Throckmorton received a letter from Sir Henry Wotton, with a manuscript '*Terra Sigillata*' — presumably the Christmas Day Meditation on Christ's Pilgrimage on earth — which Arthur sent on for Sir William Tate to read. Next month he received Wither's *Abuses Stripped and Whipped* for 2s. Wotton rewarded his friend for his gelding, not by precisely inviting him to London for Princess Elizabeth's marriage — that Sir Henry could not afford — but suggesting that he should come. The gelding had been much admired, 'and I have had a great deal of love made unto me for him by no small ones. I mean to persuade you, I am sorry I cannot say to invite you (for my mind would bear that word better than my fortune) to bestow yourself and your whole family upon us this Shrovetide, at the conjunction of the Thames and the Rhine, as our ravished spirits begin to call it. I will add that out of your own store at home, you may much increase the beauty of this assembly, and your daughters shall not need to provide any great splendour of clothing because they can supply that with a better contribution, as hath been well authenticated even by the King's own testimony of them. For though I am no longer an ambassador, yet I am not so bankrupt of intelligence, but that I have heard of those rural passages.'[1] So James, it seems, had been gracious to Ralegh's nieces, and such a letter from the scholarly Wotton would go a long way with one of Throckmorton's disposition.

When the judges came to Northampton assizes in March Throckmorton met Lord Chief Justice Coke, who was the first to propose the match for his son with Throckmorton's second daughter. Meanwhile, Lord Wotton wrote to him about the possibilities of young Peter Temple; Mr. Wynne had already proposed the match to Lord Spencer for his son. At the end of the month Arthur went to meet Coke on the road from Warwick and brought him to supper and stay the night. But in May Sir William Tate was able to tell him that Coke was in hand with Mr. Berkeley, on behalf of his son Sir Robert Coke. And this

---

[1] L. Pearsall Smith, II. 11-2.

marriage took place, after a further complication which we learn from Sir Henry Wotton. 'A match treated and managed to a fair probability between my Lord Coke's heir and the second daughter of Sir Arthur Throckmorton is suddenly broken; the said Lord Coke having underhand entertained discourse about the daughter of the late Sir Thomas Bartlett [Berkeley], who in defect of her brother shall be heir of that name.'[1] But we see a better chance coming up for Anne when, in September, Sir Thomas Temple brought his whole family over from Stowe to sup and spend the night: the eldest son Peter was the one who became Anne's husband.

Throckmorton was not the kind of person to go underhand or to play tricks; completely honest and generous, he yet managed his own affairs prudently and with success. This year, for instance, gives us the highest figures yet for his wool-crop and his cash in hand: 1341 fleeces worth over £200; in his iron chest he had £728 : 19 : 6 in gold and silver, besides wool-money to come, and cash for wood in Foxhole copse. When all was in, his cash reached the record figure, 'money of all sorts in the house, £967 : 18s.' This position enabled him to entertain on a magnificent scale when Lord Wotton came down in the summer for a fortnight's hunting. Impressive preparations were set on foot; an immense stock of food and good store of fish bought — lobsters, crabs, trouts, perches, pikes. A special cook was brought from Oxford, one Gosteloe, who had been Lord Cobham's; Lord Compton's musicians were engaged for the whole period. On Saturday, 24 July, Throckmorton and Sir Thomas set out to meet Lord and Lady Wotton, who had several in attendance, including a groom and a dwarf. Every day Lord Wotton hunted in the parks around, Paulerspury, Grafton or Stoke; in the second week he hunted at Cuthbert Ogle's, at Hanley near Towcester, or in Hasleborough walk. Every day some of the neighbours came to meet the eminent diplomat; every night Throckmorton lost handsomely at gleek. Quantities of delicacies were consumed: 18 teals, 14 quails, 2 bitterns, dotterels, and a heron; 20 fat wethers, 3 beeves, 40 couple of rabbits, veals, capons, chickens, pheasants; 20 hogsheads of beer, a hogshead and a half of claret, quantities of canary, sugar and spice; loads of hay, pease and oats for all the horses. The musicians cost £5, the cook 50s., rewards for venison, which otherwise cost nothing, 37s. 6d. The total cost of entertaining Lord Wotton for seventeen

---

[1] L. Pearsall Smith, II. 29.

days was £187 : 12 : 1. No-one could say that Throckmorton was not a good sort.

He was similarly generous to the university of Oxford which issued an appeal at this time for the building of the Schools : he sent 20 marks, £13 : 6 : 8, to the Master of Balliol for the purpose. Dr. Chenell had died in April; that summer Arthur sent to Oxford for his prescription. This sounds an ominous note, for this time he made himself ill with his violent purgations. 23 September : 'I was very ill of my rupture. I lay upon my bed and applied warm cloths and made a truss of two napkins. 24th : I drank the strong drink three times. My wife and Rose made me a little truss with a bag to bear up my cods.' (Hence the Elizabethan word codpiece, so relished by Lytton Strachey.) At the end of the month 'I caused to be gathered a handful of St. John's wort, so of groundsel, so of chickweed, so of hollyhocks, so of hound's tongue, so of camomile, so of wormwood, and caused them to be stamped in a mortar, boiled in milk and with bran flour made it to the consistency of a thick poultice and applied it as hot as I could endure it'. In the midst of his torment he did not forget to send the Master of Balliol a doe- and red-deer pie.

Charles Wake and one or two more went gathering herbs for his poultices, which he applied hot every night on going to bed. There follows a long prescription for his rupture : take linseed, aniseed, fennel seed bruised in mortar with malmsey and sack and oil of camomile, sponge the whole side of the rupture each side of the cods . . . keep the sponges 'so clipped with some napkins close trussed up that the cods hang not down . . . when you feel the pain gone and your cods well lessened, which will be in three or four days, then be shaven thereabouts and put on Fernel's plaster *contra Herniam* and wear a truss close with a bloster on that side and one other truss to hold up your cods that they may not hang down.'

With relief we read that he left off his physic, went out of his chamber and returned to his usual avocations on 10 October. I cite these disagreeable details only for their interest to students of Elizabethan medicine. This was the kind of thing our ancestors took to, if anything untoward happened to their physical condition.

Still rather feeble, and now with a numbness and swelling in his knee, he took up again the duties of his station : local affairs, the business of a J.P. and Deputy-Lieutenant of the shire, the family and friends. On 27 October Gregory Isham and his whole family came to stop the night; and on Preservation day, *i.e.* 5 November, they came to visit, when Lady Throckmorton gave her god-daughter, Penn Isham, 11s. For Queen Elizabeth's Coronation day, which continued to be celebrated still into the next century, Throckmorton gave the ringers of the church bells 5s. The last two pages of the Diary have various prescriptions, including Dr. Chenell's in Latin for a strong diet drink containing black guaiacum, sassafras root and sarsaparilla, prepared over a slow fire with aniseed added. One would suppose it to be for the pox. These last pages have the margins nibbled by mice — presumably among the débris of Boughton Malherbe to which Throckmorton's papers were transported, owing to the failure of male heirs to Paulerspury. It would seem that the Diary was continued, for it breaks off short at this point. What a mass of papers he must have collected altogether — like his books, which would make a rare and splendid library now, if only the English volumes, folios, maps, pamphlets, playbooks, had been kept together like his foreign books at Magdalen. For he was a collector, of facts as well as books and papers, especially facts about himself and everything that happened to him — in other words, a born diarist.

A newcomer to Northamptonshire, whose family had no long continuance there — effectively only for some thirty years from Throckmorton's settling there to his death — he was yet anxious to take his full share in local affairs, in county government, particularly in military matters, training and providing for the musters, on which he prided himself and which conferred a kind of prestige. The multifarious business of a J.P. was not only a matter of prestige but of necessity: it was the way society was knit together, law and order enforced, a rustic people with plenty of undisciplined energy ruled. At the apex of the structure sat the Council in Westminster, and there were its orders to be carried out in the localities.

The villages in the neighbourhood for which Throckmorton was immediately responsible as J.P. were Paulerspury with a population of some 300, and Silverstone with 120.[1] There were many parishes in the county, compared with its neighbours, but they were small ones. Most of the countryside was unenclosed, and both Camden and Norden wrote glowingly of its beauty and its amenities. Sir Edward Montagu of Boughton, an upright

[1] From an unpublished thesis by P. A. J. Pettit, 'The Economy of the Northamptonshire Royal Forests, 1558–1714'.

and public-spirited Puritan, writing in 1614 was anxious to write down its economic value for purposes of taxation.[1] He said that as an inland county the commodities it produced went for low prices, they had so far to go; and for the same reason what they needed to buy cost them dear. Then the county included many royal forests and parks. We may say that it was that that made the county cheap to keep house in, and gave it an agreeable diversity for a gentleman's pleasures. Altogether Northamptonshire was a delectable county to live in.

For the subsidies granted by Parliament in 1597 and 1601 we find Throckmorton a commissioner along with persons much senior in the county, of families far longer rooted there.[2] Sir Richard Knightley of Fawsley and Norton was the richest of the gentry and had a certain precedence. But he had been badly hit for his Puritan proclivities: fined heavily in Star Chamber for allowing the printing of the Marprelate Tracts on his premises under Elizabeth, now under James, for petitioning against the ejection of Puritan ministers, he was struck out of the Commission of the Peace and fined £10,000.[3] It would not be fully exacted, of course — these large fines rarely were; and he remained the richest of the gentry, rated at £40 for the subsidy. Next came Sir George Fermor of Easton, who was a part-time conforming Catholic, Sir George Shirley of Astwell, who was another, and Robert Spencer of Brington, rated at £30. Throckmorton came into the £20 class, along with Sir William Lane of Horton, John Wake of Piddington, Edward Cope and Erasmus Dryden of Canons Ashby and others. Robert Washington of Sulgrave came well down the scale at £3, but he was hard up and had to sell his place in 1608.

For the musters the leading gentry had to contribute horsemen: Knightley, Fermor, Shirley, two demi-lances each; Sir Valentine Knightley, Sir William Tate, Throckmorton and others one each. Money was levied upon the parishes in proportion to population for the supply of munition, their part in the expenses of training — Paulerspury and Heathencote together 12s. one year, 28s. 9d. another when a drive towards greater efficiency and readiness was promoted by the Lord-Lieutenant, Burghley's elder son, Lord Exeter. In this Throckmorton took an enthusiastic part. Paulerspury contributed 27

---

[1] *The Montagu Musters Book, 1602–1623*, ed. Joan Wake (Northamptonshire Record Society), xiv-xv, 235.

[2] *Musters, Beacons, Subsidies in Northamptonshire, 1586–1623*, ed. Joan Wake (Northants. Record Society), 53 foll.　　　　[3] *Ibid.* xxi.

able men to the musters; the local store of arms and munition was at Towcester, the county store in Northampton Castle. The county was divided into two divisions, each of ten hundreds; and each division, east and west, raised 300 foot and 50 horse. Paulerspury was in the western division. We have already seen Throckmorton's keenness to have command of the horse; in 1612 he became one of the Deputy-Lieutenants, tribute to his activity and public spirit.

In local affairs the question of Catholic Recusants gave more trouble than anything else, especially after Gunpowder Plot. Parliament was eager to signalise the danger from which it had narrowly escaped by imposing severer Recusancy laws, a new oath of allegiance and making 5 November a day of thanksgiving for ever.[1] All this is faithfully reflected in the Diary. 5 November is usually denoted 'Preservation day: Papists' Conspiracy'. At suitable intervals Throckmorton and his household receive Communion according to statute. On 9 April 1610, it is noted when 'Sir George Fermor was at the sermon at Towcester'. The new oath of allegiance made a sensible distinction between those Catholics who would still uphold the Pope's power to depose kings, and those who would not: between disloyal and loyal subjects.

These matters involved correspondence and consultation with other J.P.'s, and then there was imposing the oath, applying the laws. In August Throckmorton had to go to Northampton about the matter, and then the Justices met at Towcester and 'sent warrants out, but nothing to purpose performed'. Very likely: there was immense obstruction and interest made at every stage on this. And trouble varied very much from county to county. Northamptonshire had a not inconsiderable minority of Catholic gentry, especially in the east division, where were the Vauxes at Harrowden, Mordaunts at Drayton, Brudenells at Deene, Treshams at Liveden, with their tenants and dependants; in the west Sir George Shirley and a number of lesser people. When Throckmorton went to administer the oath at Towcester in September, he noted that the tiresome Mrs. Vaux, who was an ardent proselytiser, was at Sir George Fermor's. At Quarter Sessions at Northampton in October the J.P.s received the verdict about Recusants' goods liable according to the statute. Mr. Elmes kept badgering Throckmorton to know if he was going to certify those who refused the oath of allegiance; and when

---

[1] S. R. Gardiner, *History of England, 1603–1642* (ed. 1900), 286-8.

Elmes sent him the certificate with the schedule of Recusants' names, 'I refused to set my hand'. It was all so unneighbourly; nevertheless the J.P.s had next to meet at Easton Neston on the matter.

On 2 July 1612 a commission came down to enquire into the lands and goods of Lord Vaux and his mother, who had all the obstinacy of the Catholic Ropers in her veins. A few days later the commissioners met at Wellingborough and found Lord Vaux in a premunire, but put off executing it — it would involve a measure of confiscation — till September. There Throckmorton met Sir Edward Montagu, Sir William Lane, Sir Gilbert Pickering — whose son John had been Arthur's companion in their Florentine adventure years before — the feodary and escheator for the county. Lord Vaux's case was argued for him by his lawyer, the King's by Sir Austin Nicolls, with whom Arthur stayed a couple of nights. A jury was impanelled, and 'after dinner we heard arguments on both sides, but at last dismissed the tediousness and intricateness of this great business to the trial of Exchequer Chamber'. At Westminster two-thirds of Lord Vaux's lands were taken into the King's hands for nonpayment of Recusancy fines, though he and even his mother were now prepared to take the oath.[1] Nevertheless, that it was possible to avoid the last consequences of refractory obstinacy in the more tolerant atmosphere of England, by contrast with Spain or Italy, is witnessed by the fact that the Vauxes are still at Harrowden.

Trouble was caused by a robbery committed by the Sparrows at the end of 1611, for the neighbourhood neglected to pursue them with hue and cry, and thereby became liable to reimburse the victim. The sheriff sent to Throckmorton orders to rate the townships within Mr. Furtho's hundred, *i.e.* Cleley, where the robbery had taken place. But not till the summer did the assessments collected by the constables come in: £5 each from Paulerspury, Cosgrove, Ashton, Hartwell, £4 from Potterspury and so on. Slow as it was, one sees how justice was disseminated, how society worked. What came in with more alacrity was a rude letter from Mr. Furtho, who 'sent his man Joiner with a foolish letter unto me, of the which I read the first two lines and threw his letter away'. The Furthos of Furtho were a very old, autochthonous family in Northamptonshire, now extinct. When one goes to their place, nothing is left but a farm, the large

---

[1] G. Anstruther, *Vaux of Harrowden*, 401-2.

dove-cote of the old manor-house, and the pretty Jacobean church on its mound of graves, unenterable, falling into ruin.

The multifarious activities of the J.P.s were overseen by the Judges of Assize when they came to Northampton. Throckmorton regularly contributed a buck to their feast, and himself dined with them. When he was in physic and could not go, Adrian did his business for him there. One needed to be a J.P. to protect one's property from the depredations of the people, and to keep them in order. On Sunday, 23 December, 'Toby Clitheroe of Newport, tanner, and Caparns of Towcester coursed and killed a deer in my park with a brace of dogs, the fellow dog being taken and hanged'. The men may have had a good Christmas dinner of venison, and the tanner the skin, but Caparns saw the inside of prison for his escapade. It is clear, however, that Throckmorton was no tyrant: a year later, 'I forgave all the Blisworth offenders in Tiffield woods', and it is sufficient evidence in itself that, under his benevolent rule, his people gave him no trouble, unlike the Treshams'.

Early in 1613 there was a scare of another attempt by the Catholics, and more disagreeable work accrued as the result of the Council's orders to seize the arms in Papist households. Throckmorton corresponds with Knightley and Tate as to what they are to do; then 'the Sheriff and Sir Edward Montagu began the disarming of the Papists on the east side'. The west followed suit: 'we went to Astwell, Sir George Shirley's, where we sealed all the armours'. It is not surprising that at the next assizes Throckmorton and Henry Shirley had words. Orders continued to come down from the Council, however, and Throckmorton had to write round to the Puritan Knightley, the sheriff, and Erasmus Dryden, grandfather of the Catholic poet.

More important in Throckmorton's eyes were the musters, in regard to which he had from the first pressed for greater efficiency. Miss Joan Wake tells us that his poor opinion of Northamptonshire's showing, inland and secure, was probably justified. At assizes in March 1613 he was much concerned with musters business, taking a new turn with Captain Fisher sent by the Council and Lord-Lieutenant to be muster-master. On 12 March, a windy fair day, 'Sir Richard Knightley and I took the musters of four hundreds at Towcester. Spent 18s. He lay there with me, with Captain John Fisher, muster-master, Sir Seymour Knightley and Ferdinando Knightley with him.' A few days later they went to Daventry to muster the men, and lay at the sign of the 'Sheaf'.[1] Next day they mustered the hundreds of Fawsley, Guilsborough and Chipping Warden, and lay at Norton, Sir Richard Knightley's house. On to Northampton, where they stayed with Sir William Tate at Delapré and mustered the town, Wymersley, Spelhoe and Newbottle. 19 March was frosty and fair: they mustered the horse at Northampton. Altogether he spent £9 : 7s. at three musters, and so home to supper. Letters passed between him and Tate about a longer day to certify the musters, and shortly he went in to Towcester to view the defects and absents. Captain Fisher was paid in all £50 for his full satisfaction to Lady day — no small sum; 20s. to his man. Later Tate came to dine to consider Lord Exeter's letters about training the men.

The first three days of June they spent on the job. It rained, but 2 June, 'I began the training at Towcester with Sir William Tate. Paid at the ordinary for myself and Captain Fisher 5s.' They all came to stay for the night. The next two days training continued in spite of the rain. On the last day at Towcester 'paid 34s. 4d. for my dinner [he must have entertained the rest] and 22s. in gold for the best shooter at the butts. Gave out of my own purse to the muster-masters 20s.' So, on to Northampton where 'Tate and I mustered Wymersley, Spelhoe and New-bottle grove hundreds, out of which we took 90 men to be trained soldiers, armed them and delivered them over to Captain Fisher, Captain Belcher and Lieutenant Catesby.' Next day they selected 20 men from the town of Northampton to be armed and trained by the officers, inspected the horse and exercised horse and foot together.

The Diary, in fact, bears out the better view of historians now that the Jacobean government did take pains to keep the armed forces of the country in shape.

Evidences of Throckmorton's activity continue beyond the Diary. In 1616 a drive was made to substitute the musket for the old-fashioned caliver and Sir Arthur was especially eager to forward this.[2] In June 1618 he took offence at receiving no instructions from Council or Lord-Lieutenant about musters or trained bands; he felt slighted and asked Montagu, whom he much respected, to excuse his absence from Sessions, 'being now forced by some occasions of weight nearly touching me'. We do not know what these were; but Ralegh was on his way home from utter disaster in Guiana; the *Destiny* arrived at Plymouth

[1] Still there as the 'Wheatsheaf'.
[2] *Montagu Musters Book*, ed. Wake, lvii, 177, 239.

on 21 June. Throckmorton was anxious to keep Montagu's good opinion, and wrote again in August: 'let me entreat you not to be carried away with any misconceit of me, who have ever borne an excellent opinion of your worth. . . . I cannot but impart unto you what I have received from Oatlands about an untoward accident fallen out between Dr. Williams and yourself, for a Bacchanalia to be kept at Grafton Underwood: which, as it seems, is eagerly followed by him whose calling, methinks, requires rather a restraining of sin, especially upon the Sabbath day, than suffering a soiling of the same. Although he may begin his new office with his diligence to see his Majesty's declarations in so pleasant a matter performed, wherein it had been meeter for his ministry rather to have suffered than to oppose, yet I think he will have small credit or content thereby, his Majesty from his wisdom countenancing many things in the remote places of his realm which he will not do in the centre of his kingdom, for many things may become the borders and skirts, as guards of many colours which will disgrace the heart of the garment.'

This is convincingly, long-windedly, but none the less effectively expressed; it is true Throckmorton, with its image from clothes — how many references to coloured guards we have cited from the Diary! What is new is the marked vein of Puritan sentiment: he disapproved of James's *Declaration of Sports*, tactlessly issued for the clergy to read from the pulpit. Dr. Williams, rector of Grafton Underwood, had gladly fallen in with the King's wishes — he had just been made chaplain to the King and was on his way to become Lord Keeper, Bishop of Lincoln, Archbishop of York. It is still more revealing, if unexpected, to us to find Throckmorton touched at last by Puritanism.[1] He had been no Puritan in the glad days of youth and the Queen; now in the Jacobean age he was affected by the movement of opinion and feeling that bore the country onwards to the Civil War.

It is this kind of thing that gives the person, the career, the Diary of Arthur Throckmorton a symptomatic importance to a student of the time, watching its changing colours and currents.

In September he wrote his friend Sir Edward Montagu, 'you may well judge that my head was intoxicated and troubled with some discontentful businesses — mistaking, as I hear, in one letter your Christian name, and in another forgetting to set to

---

[1] In March 1612 he entertained Knightley's Puritan preacher from Norton.

my hand'.[1] He asked pardon, and would write to cousin
Knightley with the rest 'to ease me for this time in the muster
of the horse. . . . And so remembering my assured love unto
you I end, hoping in God to meet you at the Sessions.'

He had plenty to worry him: Ralegh was now once more
back in the Tower, Throckmorton's sister taken into custody and
in graver trouble than ever before.

[1] *Montagu Musters Book*, 240.

CHAPTER XVIII

RALEGH: THE LAST ACT

I N Ralegh's last years we find the main themes of his life brought together, recapitulated more starkly than ever in the brief space that remained to him. There is the obsession with Guiana, now more clamorous since it offered the only chance of liberty, of escape from the Tower. There is the self-justification, the continued assertion of his innocence, now fortified in his mind, if in no-one else's, by King James letting him out to go on the voyage. The voyage itself was an anachronistic return, in quite changed conditions, to the days of Elizabeth, haunted with memories of Drake, Grenville and Cadiz. Ralegh was twenty years older, an ageing man; but we see the same traits of character more sharply accentuated than ever in too sanguine hope and final failure. We see the worst and the best of him, in concentrated form : as gambler — though one cannot blame him for gambling his way out of the Tower — promoter, plausible schemer, actor. We see him energetic, ingenious, persuasive; unreliable, hysterical, despairing; obstinate and unyielding, in spite of everything unable to relax his hold on life; he might break, but he could not yield. It is an excellent perception of Edwards's to note his 'unconquerable love of hitting hard, whatever the recoil'; whatever else of psychological there is in that, there is also the artist. Above all, in this last act he is an actor : at times a very bad ham-actor, feigning illness, taking medicines to simulate disease upon him; at the end, when his destiny becomes clear, a superb actor, a consciously heroic figure, himself arranging his departure from the scene, stamping it imperishably upon people's minds.

The scenes are familiar, too. Once more he is out and about London, a *revenant* from Queen Elizabeth's time recognised in the streets. Then the voyage takes him home to the West Country, to places familiar in earlier years : to Plymouth and Falmouth, the region where he once bore rule, to Cork, which he had hoped would be the capital of his Irish domain, now another's. Into the Atlantic — blue water after looking out on the muddy Thames so many years — the Canary Islands, the coast of Guiana. And then the sad return to Plymouth, through the childhood lanes of Devon into Dorset, having to pass by Sherborne, also another's: 'all this was mine, and it was taken from me unjustly'. No wonder he girded against fate: 'is it possible that my fortune should thus return upon me again?' Once more the gates of the Tower closed upon him, until the last scene hard by Whitehall, of his earliest triumph when the world was young, not far from St. Margaret's where his dissevered body now lies.

In September 1613 Carr's former friend, Sir Thomas Overbury, was poisoned in the Tower. The deed was procured by Northampton's niece, the beautiful Frances Howard, jealous of Overbury's influence on her prospective husband, the favourite who married the murderess in December. The trick that had got Overbury incarcerated was thought up by Northampton, and to judge from the suspicious letters he wrote to the Lieutenant to dispose at once of Overbury's body, he knew more about the murder than was befitting a Councillor, let alone a pious Catholic.[1] For, before anything could be brought home to him, in June 1614 he fortunately died, reciting of the Faith, with St. Jerome: *in qua fide puer natus fui in eadem senex morior.* Immensely rich from the pickings of office, he left it all to the Howards, including his splendid mansion, Northumberland House, which remained at Charing Cross right up till the last century. So passed from the scene, in the odour of piety if not precisely of sanctity, Ralegh's most inveterate enemy.

Ralegh's prospects were brightening, too, with the appointment of Sir Ralph Winwood as Secretary of State; for Winwood — a Northamptonshire man, and, like Throckmorton, a student at Magdalen — was a firm Protestant, bent on an anti-Spanish policy. Moreover, King James had met a very handsome youth while hunting in Leicestershire, the courteous and affable George Villiers, who was now on his way up. In June Throckmorton got leave to repair to Ralegh in the Tower, as his occasions should require.[2] We know that Arthur had been a trustee for his brother-in-law, but it does not appear that he invested in any of his Guiana enterprises: he had a better use for his money. Early next year Ralegh made himself ill from one of his chemical experiments; people said it was apoplexy, but it sounds like a

[1] Winwood's *Memorials*, III. 481, 482.
[2] *A.P.C. 1613-14,* 455-6.

slight stroke which left him henceforth a bit lame.[1] Discouraged, too, by the King's reception of his book and attempt to suppress it, according to Aubrey, he burnt 'the apparatus for the second part . . . and said, "If I am not worthy of the world, the world is not worthy of my works".'[2] That sounds convincing.

On the other hand, with the changed political scene — the weakening of the Howards, the strengthening of the anti-Spanish faction — the chances of a voyage to Guiana were going up. They always had depended on the contrary pulls of persons and politics at Court, of foreign policy, and would continue to do so, fatally for Ralegh. Not really a political type, though people called him 'the old fox', he did not fully appreciate this in all its bearings. A soldier rather than a politician, he was over Guiana partly an imperialist, partly a gambler. The attempts to plant colonies there by the Leighs and by Robert Harcourt had been failures; Sir Thomas Roe had come back with the conclusion that the talk of the city of Manoa and an El Dorado was a fable. Shut up in the Tower so many years, Ralegh can hardly be blamed for losing touch with reality, for an element of fantasy in his wishful thinking. He was convinced that there was a gold-mine near St. Thomé; after Cecil's death he wrote to the Council wagering his liberty against Keymis's return with half a ton of the ore, if he might but send out a couple of armed ships.

At the back of his mind Ralegh never gave up the idea of an English empire in South America, and fighting the Spaniards for it. His fixed view was that *he* had taken possession of Guiana for the Crown; to that day the Spaniards were not in effective occupation. The truth was that it was not worth it — here I dissent from the views of our maritime and empire historians; I would point out that James's government did not differ from Elizabeth's in holding that it was not worth fighting Spain for Guiana. And I am bound to own, without prejudice in his favour, that James's judgment on this was better than Ralegh's. It is a political judgment.

James had got himself — not only by his personal extravagance and hand-outs to favourites, but by his congenital inability to cope with the country's finances — heavily into debt: he was now over £700,000 down. Since he was no good at managing Parliament, he too was reduced to taking a gamble. He much preferred a Spanish marriage for his son Charles, with half a

---

[1] *Cal. S.P. Dom. 1611–18*, 275.   [2] Aubrey, ed. Clark, II. 191.

million dowry. That was not immediately forthcoming; what of the alternative — a Ralegh voyage, after the pattern of Drake's, bringing back half a ton of ore to the country? The King's better judgment told him that this was quite improbable, and he was right. He was really opposed to the voyage all along; but his hand was forced — by the changed balance in his Council, and by the public clamour stirred up by Ralegh's supporters, fed by his propaganda. Between this and his ardent desire for the Spanish marriage, James was caught in a tormenting dilemma; between the one and the other Ralegh's fate was settled.

Ralegh saw it as a struggle to gain liberty, but it engaged him in another round of his long duel with the King. Nor did he repine at that; we do not have much evidence that he had any consideration for another's point of view or attempted to accomodate himself to that person's difficulties. On the contrary, he exerted himself to overpower the King's opposition. He won over the King's Secretary of State to his scheme; he did not hesitate to bribe the King's new boy-friend for his freedom, with a handsome present to Villiers's half-brother and a friend. And, 'if it succeed well, a good part of the honour shall be yours; and if I do not also make it profitable unto you, I shall show myself exceeding ungrateful'.[1]

With the egotism which formed the hard core of his nature (and his genius), Ralegh saw the issue as a personal one, as we discern from his letter to Winwood. 'What I know of the riches of that place, not by hearsay but what mine eyes have seen, I have said it often, but it was then to no end: because those that had the greatest trust were resolved not to believe it — not because they doubted the truth, but because they doubted my disposition towards themselves, where (if God had blessed me in the enterprise) I had recovered his Majesty's favour and good opinion.'[2] What Ralegh's disposition towards them was we need not doubt: 'his Majesty hath sometimes answered that his Council knew me better than he did — meaning some two or three of them — and it was indeed my infelicity. For had his Majesty known me, I had never been here where I now am; or had I known his Majesty, they had never been so long there where they now are.' The impudence of this — it was meant for the King's eye — still takes one's breath away, and also the impercipience, for he had had plenty of evidence of James's detestation of him. And with reason, for he was now engaged

[1] Edwards, II. 341.   [2] *Ibid.* 340.

in forcing the King's hand against his better judgment. Nor did he fail to assert his innocence once again: Prince Henry had been very curious to find out what the nature of his offence could possibly be; the Queen had informed herself from the beginning; her brother, the King of Denmark, was thoroughly satisfied of his innocence — or none of them would have spoken up in his favour.

To Ralegh's other characters, we must add that of a hardened, unscrupulous, effective propagandist.

In March 1616 he was released to go about his business, making preparations for the voyage that had gained him his liberty. His lodgings in the Tower were immediately occupied by Carr and his lady, whose misdeeds had at length caught up with them. Ralegh was still under the surveillance of a keeper, and 'we think good to admonish you (though we do not prejudicate your own discretion so much as to think that you would attempt it without leave) that you should not presume to resort either to his Majesty's Court, the Queen's, or the Prince's, nor go into any public assemblies whersoever, without licence'.[1] He was still a man under sentence. With undiminished zest, curiosity of mind alert as ever, he went about London 'seeing sights and places built or bettered since his imprisonment'. He was himself one of the sights, noted by one observer as the only man left of those who had beaten the Spaniards in '88. There was Northumberland House for him to view, and, beside Durham House, Salisbury House — monuments to his successful rivals; and in the Abbey lying upon her sumptuous tomb, the familiar profile of his mistress, hawk-nose, high cheekbones, the wide-awake eyes.

Meanwhile, the preparations for a powerfully armed expedition went forward. Ralegh was building a fine new ship, the *Destiny* — an ominous name. In June the rumour was that he would be pardoned, for unless he were the gentlemen-adventurers would not hazard going with him.[2] Then it became known that he would not be pardoned until his return: the threat remained suspended over him throughout the whole enterprise. In these circumstances it is no small tribute to his aura that he was able to gather as much support around him as he could put into it himself. He called in the £8000 compensation for Sherborne, which he had out on loan, and raised another £5000; while Lady Ralegh sold her property at Mitcham to invest in the

---

[1] *A.P.C. 1615–16*, 456.   [2] *Cal. S.P. Dom. 1611–18*, 374, 425.

RALEGH AS COMMANDER OF THE GUIANA VOYAGE

Destiny.[1] His co-adventurers — among them her connections, the Earls of Huntingdon and Pembroke, and the Earl of Arundel — raised another £15,000. Altogether there were some seven ships, large and small, under his command, and there were complicated negotiations for a French contingent to join him. It seemed quite like old days — though it was not. In November we find him supping at Winwood's with a number of friends, some of them familiar to us as Throckmorton's companions abroad: Sir Henry Savile and Sir Henry Neville, Sir Maurice Berkeley, Sir Robert Killigrew, a Seymour 'and I know not how many ladies and gentlewomen of that race and alliance'.[2]

At Court the arguments went to and fro: James was under strong pressure from both sides. Spanish interests were represented, as never before, by an ambassador clever, learned, insinuating, who established a personal hold over James by community of interests and his conversation: the Galician Gondomar, who had begun his career fighting against Drake. Gondomar protested from the first, and, since the King was overborne by his Council, pressed conditions which hamstrung Ralegh from the start. Thus not only was a free pardon refused but Ralegh was to bear the penalties of any aggression against Spaniards in the area. James pledged his word as a king that Ralegh would inflict no injury on them. All Ralegh's preparations were known to Gondomar and reported back to Spain; but not all his intentions, for Ralegh was in negotiation for a French contingent, which in his plans might have borne the brunt of any aggressive action necessary and so have exculpated him. That this contingent failed to materialise at the last moment meant that Ralegh would have the sole responsibility if things went wrong in Guiana. Gardiner summed up, 'for James there was to be everything to gain; for Ralegh there was to be everything to lose'.[3] We may not agree with the first term in this proposition, but there can be no doubt about the second.

Rumours flew around London to the last that the expedition would be overthrown, by the machinations of the Spanish ambassador and its opponents, of whom Prince Charles was one. At the end of March 1617 Ralegh had to make haste away for fear he should be countermanded. A good friend of his wished he

---

[1] V. T. Harlow, *Ralegh's Last Voyage*, 24.
[2] *Letters of John Chamberlain*, ed. McClure, II. 34.
[3] Gardiner, *ed. cit.* III. 43.

might be for his own sake — in verse, according to the manner of the time:

> Ralegh in this thyself thy self transcends,
> When hourly tasting of a bitter chalice,
> Scanning the sad faces of thy friends,
> Thou smil'st at Fortune's menaces and malice.
> Hold thee firm *here*, cast anchor in this port,
> *Here* art thou safe till Death enfranchise thee.
> Here neither harm nor fears of harm resort,
> Here, though enchained, thou livs't in liberty.[1]

Why could not Ralegh have heeded, and stayed at home? It would not have been Ralegh if he had; everything was now staked on this last throw, pride, ambition, loyalty to friends, to his own idea, life itself.

The voyage began with no good omens: the winds were contrary and delayed him, thus exhausting provisions, his 500 men were a lot of rag-tag-and-bobtail, 'scum of men', as he called them. But at Plymouth, where the town was putting up in the Guildhall Drake's portrait and Hawkins's arms — mementoes of the heroic age — Ralegh, another memento, was welcomed. We find traces of him in the town's accounts: the Mayor, Robert Trelawny, was allowed £9 'for entertaining Sir Walter Ralegh and his followers at his house, which was done by a general consent'.[2] And then, 'paid the drummer for calling Sir Walter Ralegh's company aboard, 12d.' He got faithful support, as ever, from the West Country: Sir Warham St. Leger, son of Grenville's old companion in Munster; William Herbert, one of his Pembroke kinsmen; George Ralegh, his eldest brother's son, and John Chudleigh. Lady Ralegh's kinsman, Edward Hastings, and a brother of Lord North were with him; Ralegh's own son, young Walter, went as a captain, while at Plymouth he was joined by his faithful henchman, Keymis. Contrary winds blew the expedition back into Falmouth harbour, and again off the Irish coast into Cork, where he was well received by his old acquaintances, Lord Barry and Lord Roche. Richard Boyle, to become the 'great Earl of Cork', came down to greet him from Lismore, where he was piling up an immense fortune on Ralegh's foundation. All the scenes of his earlier life were passing before him, as before the eyes of a drowning man. He told Boyle there was nothing now for him but 'perish or prosper'.

---

[1] q. Edwards, I. 598.

[2] *Cal. Plymouth Municipal Records*, ed. R. N. Worth, 150.

They made slow progress southwards and across the Atlantic, and that gave time for disease to ravage the fleet. By the time Ralegh arrived in Guiana he was a very sick man. In November he wrote home to Bess, 'Sweet heart, I can yet write unto you but with a weak hand, for I have suffered the most violent calenture [burning fever] for fifteen days that ever man did and lived'. Then, at the end, with a characteristic turn, a resurgence of vitality: 'to tell you that I might be here King of the Indians were a vanity, but my name hath still lived among them'.[1]

Ralegh was too weak to take command into the interior; he remained behind with the ships on the coast, while Keymis led the men upstream to St. Thomé which guarded the diggings for gold. (There was auriferous ore in the vicinity, but nothing like sufficient to justify all this: Guiana was no Mexico or Peru.) There was some hope of the town's betrayal or peaceful surrender; if so, this was ruined by young Walter's 'unadvised daringness', who leaped forward to the attack with 'Come on, my hearts! This is the mine you must expect! They that look for any other mine are fools!' and so was killed at the onset.[2] This language, this bravado, is not only completely characteristic of the Ralegh temper, but it betrays the ambivalence of purpose in the father — mine or empire, peace or war with Spain?

St. Thomé was captured, at the cost of casualties on both sides, and later the town was burnt to the ground. There was no mine, at least nothing that could be called a mine. Nothing was achieved, except a fine piece of endurance under George Ralegh's command, exploring two or three hundred miles up the Orinoco for a possible approach to the riches of New Granada on a future occasion. But what was the point of that? — there would be none. 'Such was the poignant contrast between dream and reality. The dream — Ralegh sailing home with a cargo of precious ore, and afterwards as the founder of an Anglo-Indian Empire and conquistador of the "New Kingdom": the reality — the mine undiscovered and discredited, a Spanish town in ruins, and the shadow of the scaffold.'[3]

One can imagine Ralegh's anguish and despair when he heard what had come of it all, or rather we have evidence of what he felt. Grief-stricken at the death of his son, he treated the faithful Keymis with unfeeling harshness. Keymis was no natural leader, and he had failed Ralegh; but he had followed his master's fortunes through good and ill alike. Ralegh blamed

[1] Edwards, II. 347-9.   [2] Harlow, 344.   [3] *Ibid.* 79.

his incompetence for the disaster and refused to forgive him. 'I know then, sir, what course to take', said the poor fellow, who went to his cabin and killed himself. There was no end to the tale of disaster. Ralegh wrote a report of it all to Winwood; but before the end of the year, the Secretary — his chief mainstay and support — was dead. To Bess, Ralegh poured out his troubles, while trying to console her: 'I was loth to write, because I knew not how to comfort you; and God knows I never knew what sorrow meant till now. All that I can say to you is that you must obey the will and providence of God, and remember that the Queen's Majesty bare the loss of Prince Henry with a magnanimous heart. . . . The Lord bless and comfort you that you may bear patiently the death of your valiant son.' Later, he took up his pen to add a long postcript telling her the whole story, from which we may gather the precursors he had in mind: 'I protest before the majesty of God that as Sir Francis Drake and Sir John Hawkins died heart-broken when they failed of their enterprise, I could willingly do the like'.[1]

But, with his unabated vitality, he survived to come home.

James, too, now had to face the consequences. Gondomar at once pressed him to keep his word and hand Ralegh over to judgment. Before he got back the King rushed out a proclamation disclaiming responsibility: in the licence given for the voyage 'we did by express limitation and caution refrain, and forbid them from attempting any act of hostility, wrong or violence whatsoever upon any of the territories, states or subjects of any foreign princes with whom we are in amity: and more peculiarly of those of our dear brother, the King of Spain, in respect of his dominions and interests in that Continent'.[2]

By this Ralegh stood exposed to judgment. James was understandably angry at the position the intolerable man had forced him into. The Spanish marriage for his son was in jeopardy, he himself under pressure from Spain to make reparation for the damage done, under threat that measures would be taken against English trade in recompense. James had no nerve; Elizabeth would have brazened it out: over Drake she had told the Spanish ambassador, 'the gentleman careth not if I disavow him'.

On 21 June 1618 the *Destiny* arrived at Plymouth, and Bess went down to meet her husband. She was able to report to him the situation in London, the changed atmosphere, the menace

---

for him; she tried hard to persuade him to escape the country while there was time. Strict orders came from the Council to Sir Lewis Stukeley, Vice-Admiral of Devon — another kinsman — to bring him up, and only then Ralegh did make a half-hearted attempt from Plymouth Sound. But what could a new life abroad hold for him? He refused to take refuge in France, and was brought slowly up through the West Country, while debate raged round the King as to what to do with him.

Indecision prevailed in Ralegh's mind, too, and with will-power suspended he seemed to go to pieces; certainly hysterical symptoms appeared in his conduct on the way up, partly neurotic, partly conscious acting a part. Altogether it makes the most uncongenial passage in his life, but we must remember how very much less under control contemporary people were; however sophisticated or intellectually brilliant, they appear more naïf, more childish when the controls fail. On the other hand, it adds very much to their interest.

The King was on his summer progress at Salisbury, and Ralegh wanted time to compose his 'Apology for the Voyage to Guiana' to place before him. So he asked the French physician, who was in attendance on him with Stukeley, to give him a vomit to counterfeit sickness and so gain a few days' grace. Next he procured an ointment with which he smeared himself to simulate the symptoms of some loathsome disease; he feigned madness. Thus he won a respite during which he wrote his last state-paper, recapitulating his arguments for the Guiana enterprise, defending his own conduct, blaming poor Keymis. All to no purpose so far as James was concerned — he was more than sick of him. But Ralegh was now hoping to appeal to anti-Spanish feeling in the country, and his propaganda about Guiana was not without effect.

Ralegh's slow progress in Stukeley's custody brought him at length in August to his wife's house in Broad Street, whence an attempt to escape down the Thames was arranged by Stukeley in order to betray it to the government. Once again Ralegh's own conduct gave the worst impression of him, and one cannot but think that the government intended that it should. Chamberlain thought 'it was a foul *pas de clerc* for an old cozener to be so cozened and overtaken'.[1] King James used to give it as his opinion later that Ralegh was 'a coward to be so taken and conveyed, for else he might easily have made his escape from so

---

[1] Chamberlain, II. 165.

slight a guard.'[1] The very next day he was taken back to the Tower. Lady Ralegh was placed under strict guard in her own house, no-one to have access to her, for fear of her conveying away jewels that would be needed to offset the losses people had suffered from the expedition.[2]

Still the government hesitated how to deal with him. They wanted more evidence about his contacts with France, and the negotiations for a French contingent to the Guiana expedition, so as to fix a treasonable colour upon his proceedings. Sir Thomas Wilson was therefore planted upon him in the Tower to report his conversations. Ralegh was more guarded than he usually was, and Wilson learned nothing about the French project, which, if carried out, might have implied a joint Anglo-French attack on the Spanish empire — there were no limits to Ralegh's ambition. He certainly was a danger to peace. Wilson did learn that Ralegh would have attacked the Plate Fleet, if he had had the chance: no-one was called a pirate for millions! Ralegh talked a great deal to him of his inventions, boasting of his services to the state and of what he might have done. Once again, a more conventional soul was shocked: 'the things he seems to make most reckoning of are his chemical stuffs, amongst which there is so many spirits of things, that I think there is none wanting that ever I heard of, unless it be the Spirit of God'.[3]

In September Ralegh was ill, and wrote pathetically to Bess: 'I am sick and weak. . . . My swollen side keeps me in perpetual pain and unrest.'[4] She replied with the comforting assurance of a good wife: ''tis merely sorrow and grief that with wind hath gathered into your side. . . . God in mercy look on us.' Ralegh wrote one last plea to the King: 'my mutineers told me that if I returned for England I should be undone; but I believed more in your Majesty's goodness than in their arguments'. James scorned Ralegh's 'roaring tedious letter'; he was at last coming to a decision about him. Realising this Ralegh turned to the favourite, to the Queen, with his pleas. Queen Anne, at least, had always been kind: he addressed her once more in verse, to which he always turned for consolation in trouble:

> O had Truth power, the guiltless could not fall,
> Malice win glory, or revenge triumph;
> But Truth alone can not encounter all.

---

[1] Aubrey, II. 188. We may discern that this betrays an uneasy conscience on James's part — perhaps a wish *ex post facto* that he had been rid of his embarrassment, and, a coward himself, a mean desire to have Ralegh thought so too.
[2] Chamberlain, II. 167.   [3] Harlow, 271.   [4] Edwards, II. 368-70.

Mercy is fled to God which mercy made,
Compassion dead, faith turned to policy,
Friends know not those who sit in sorrow's shade.

For what we sometime were we are no more,
Fortune hath changed our shape, and Destiny
Defaced the very form we had before . . .

Ralegh's themes and phrases are very recognisable, continuous
with his past: Fortune, Destiny, Sorrow and the desertion of
friends; his truth and guiltlessness (of course); appearance and
reality, time and circumstance defacing the very form of things,
'for what we sometime were we are no more'.

James, prompted by Spain, had now made up his mind: he
would have Ralegh brought to account in England, but first
there would have to be an investigation of his new offences, if
only to set himself right with opinion. A public trial would
make him too popular: James remembered how last time he
had 'by his wit turned the hatred of men into compassion of
him'.[1] Chamberlain's forecast was pretty accurate: 'it is generally thought that Sir Walter Ralegh shall pay this new reckoning upon the old score'.[2] Early in October Ralegh and Bess
were winding up the affairs of the voyage, so far as they could,
preparatory to the end; it seems that she must have joined him
in the too familiar Tower for the last time, for on the 5th there
was an order for her liberation.[3] At the end of the month he
was brought privately before the Council, where he answered
the new charges as well as he might. He excused himself for
feigning madness by King David's example in the Bible. Once
again he asserted his innocence in 1603, and had the hardihood
now to say that 'he verily thinketh that his Majesty doth in his
conscience clear him of all guiltiness for his fault' of that year.[4] He
even quoted Judge Gawdy's death-bed condemnation of the trial.

On 28 October Ralegh was taken to Westminster Hall and
brought before King's Bench to authorise the execution of the
sentence of 1603. On his way through the corridors of the ancient
palace, an old servant accosted him, shocked at the magnificent
master's fallen appearance: feverish, lame, unkempt, the hair
that had been so splendid needing a comb. 'Let them kem it
that are to have it', he said, and then, noticing the man's dejec-
tion, attempted to cheer him up with, 'dost thou know, Peter,

---

[1] Harlow, 296. [2] Chamberlain, II. 167.
[3] *Cal. S.P. Dom. 1611–18*, 583-5. [4] Harlow, 299-300.

of any plaster that will set a man's head on again, when it is off?'
In Westminster Hall the attitude of the Judges towards him was
in marked contrast to that of the odious Coke and Popham at
Winchester fifteen years before: now it was one of respect, a
signal indication of the change of feeling about him. The
Attorney-General went out of his way to pay him a compliment:
'Sir Walter Ralegh hath been a statesman, and a man who in
regard of his parts and quality is to be pitied. He hath been as
a star at which the world hath gazed; but stars may fall, nay,
they must fall when they trouble the sphere wherein they abide.'[1]
The Lord Chief Justice was no less respectful: 'I know you have
been valiant and wise, and I doubt not but you retain both these
virtues, for now you shall have occasion to use them. Your faith
hath heretofore been questioned, but I am resolved you are a
good Christian for your book, which is an admirable work, doth
testify as much.' The Crown's Judges were anxious, as ever, to
get an admission of Ralegh's guilt back in 1603: 'you had an
honourable trial, and so were justly convicted; and it were
wisdom in you now to submit yourself and to confess your offence
did justly draw upon you that judgment which was then pronounced against you'. But this he would never admit: he had
had no treasonable intent whatever against the King; as to his
motives in regard to Cobham, he always maintained an absolute
silence. After sentence of execution was granted, he had only
one plea: that he might not, as he had feared, be cut off suddenly
in the Tower. He had a great last scene to prepare for the world.

From Westminster Hall he was taken to the Abbey Gate-
house, whither Bess came to take her farewell of him. Distraught,
she wanted at least to have the burying of his body on the morrow.
Faced with the certainty of death, no need of any further twisting
and turning for life, Ralegh was perfectly resolved and calm. 'It
is well, dear Bess, that thou mayst dispose of that dead which
thou hadst not always the disposing of when alive.' Some time
during the night, resorting as of old, when most alone with himself, to poetry — 'the refuge of them that have not the Church'
— he recalled some earlier verses much to his purpose:

> Even such is Time which takes in trust
> Our youth, our joys, and all we have,
> And pays us but with age and dust:
> Who in the dark and silent grave,
> When we have wandered all our ways,
> Shuts up the story of our days.

[1] Harlow, 302-3.

316

Now, facing the mystery of death, he took up pen and added:

> And from which earth and grave and dust
> The Lord shall raise me up, I trust.

He was determined to make a good end, though when the Dean of Westminster came to attend him out of this world, he was surprised that Sir Walter made so light of death. The Dean feared that 'this extraordinary boldness might come from some false ground'.[1] It seems that of death in itself Ralegh was not at all afraid. He was able to reassure the Dean as to the state of his soul by communicating in the early hours. 'He was the most fearless of death that ever was known, and the most resolute and confident; yet with reverence and conscience.'

When morning came he dressed himself with care for the scaffold: black velvet gown, black waistcoat and breeches, ash-coloured silk stockings. He bore himself erect and smiling, made brave jokes which were remembered and repeated a thousand times afterwards, as he went; for his hour of triumph had come. He was only afraid that his light voice, enfeebled by illness, might not reach the friends who had come to see him die; so the lords joined him on the scaffold to hear him better. He welcomed them with familiar courtesy, shook hands with each, was glad to see Arundel there, for to him he had given his word before the voyage that he would return, when he might have got away. 'It is true', Arundel corroborated. The speech yielded not the slightest consolation to the government. His phrase that he had trusted too much to the King's good will — when he might have demanded a pardon before undertaking the voyage — fixed the responsibility squarely on James. Everyone could see that this was not an act of justice, but the political sacrifice of the last survivor that had fought the Armada to the demands of Spain. It was all bound to do damage to the Stuarts and to count against them with the English in years to come.

The more pious his end, the more effective with the people. So he forgave his enemies, naming Stukeley in particular who had betrayed him. He went back to Essex's death, about which he had been maligned: 'I take God to witness that my eyes shed tears for him when he died'.[2] Nevertheless, 'I have many, many sins for which to beseech God's pardon. Of a long time my course was a course of vanity. I have been a seafaring man, a soldier, and a courtier, and in the temptations of the least of

---

[1] Edwards, I. 695.   [2] *Ibid.* 704.

these there is enough to overthrow a good mind, and a good man.'
He was dying a Christian, as he hoped to be saved. This was
very edifying, and fastened further obloquy on the King who was
making a sacrifice of him. Among the throng of spectators between the Parliament house and the Abbey was John Eliot, who
never forgot or forgave the Stuarts that scene. It was time to
make an end: 'I have a long journey and must bid the company
farewell'.

He showed no fear whatever of the axe, but tried its edge
with his thumb. Kneeling down, he refused to be blindfolded:
'think you I fear the shadow of the axe, when I fear not the axe
itself?' The axe fell: two strokes sufficed to sever his head;
the blood that poured out made one spectator conclude that he
had years of life left in him. When the head was held up, a
shudder passed over the throng, and a voice spoke out loud in
the silence: 'we have not such another head to be cut off'.
Among the things found upon his body was 'one ring with a
diamond which he weareth on his finger'. Upon which a scribe
annotated, *Given him by the late Queen.*[1]

That day Bess wrote: 'I desire, good brother, that you will
be pleased to let me bury the worthy body of my noble husband,
Sir Walter Ralegh, in your church at Beddington, where I desire
to be buried. The Lords have given me his dead body, though
they denied me his life. This night he shall be brought you with
two or three of my men. Let me hear presently [*i.e.* immediately].
God hold me in my wits. E.R.'[2]

[1] Edwards, II. 496.   [2] *Ibid.* 413.

CHAPTER XIX

POSTERITY

I

Bess obtained the disposing of her husband's head only, not of the body, which was buried in St. Margaret's, Westminster to the south of the altar. Ralegh's head, upon its severance from the body, 'was showed on each side of the scaffold and then put into a red leather bag, and his wrought velvet gown thrown over it, which was afterwards conveyed away in a mourning coach of his lady's'.[1] It seems that Bess had it embalmed and kept it with her to her dying day, and after her it came to their son Carew, with whom it was buried. Bishop Goodman, in his account of the Court of King James, wrote that 'no man doth honour the memory of Sir Walter Ralegh and his excellent parts more than myself; and in token thereof I know where his skull is kept to this day, and I have kissed it.'[2] This is somewhat curious coming from a bishop, even from a bishop addicted to ritualistic practices and inclining to Catholicism: one hardly thinks of Ralegh's head as a holy relic.

Nevertheless, in a more encouraging clime, there might have come about something like a cult of that noble, scheming organ. At the execution, when the head was lifted up, a spectator said that it should be on the Secretary of State's shoulders. Some time later, when the King was having difficulties with the Spaniards — he never did get the Spanish marriage for which he had offered up this sacrifice — the rumour went round that he wished Ralegh's head on his shoulders again. This is improbable, though James had good reason to regret the execution; it is only another indication of what people had come to think of that head.

Nothing the government did could undo the damage the execution wrought: not all the time the royal theologian spent, between his decision and the act, in composing his 'Meditations

---

[1] q. T. N. Brushfield, 'Raleghana, Part VIII', *Trans. Devon. Assocn.* 1907, 242 foll.
[2] q. *Ibid.* 253.

on the Lord's Prayer' — certainly not the measure of content expressed by Philip III at the enactment. The government had to rush out its *Declaration* in a vain attempt to justify itself, and much taken aback by the revulsion of public opinion. The task fell to Bacon, grateful for promotion to the summit of Lord Chancellorship at last — it was all in the day's work for the euphoric lawyer, who had performed a similar task for Cecil's government upon the fall of his former friend Essex. One of the least convincing of the great lawyer's pieces of advocacy, it had no effect and got 'little credit'. People's minds were made up for them not by argument but by the fact.

Sir Lewis Stukeley, henceforth known as Sir Judas Stukeley, was regarded with general opprobrium for his part in the affair. He put forth an *Apology*, and then, finding that it removed nothing of the stain clinging to him, got a Devonshire clergyman to write a more cogent *Petition* to disperse the ill matter. This made some relevant points, drawing attention to the contrast between the charitable spirit Ralegh had expressed to the Dean of Westminster and the vindictive manner in which he had fixed public blame and shame on Stukeley; between Ralegh's real motives and the piety for public consumption on the scaffold. Stukeley — or rather the cleric behind him — said, 'this man's whole life was a mere sophistication . . . and such was his death'.[1] His last piece of play-acting had been the most effective of all, his masterpiece; his aim, 'to gain reputation upon his Sovereign . . . and to spread by those whom he had invited the contagion of his seditious humour unto others'.

There was a good deal in that; but can we blame Ralegh? So far as he was concerned, this was the last act in his prolonged duel with King James: the King could do no more hurt to him, he was taking all that he had with his life. But it would not be Ralegh not to make him pay for it, and the consequences to the Stuart monarchy would be incalculable.

Stukeley went on to declare that Ralegh had meant to break the oath he had taken on the Bible not to desert the ship's company, 'which perjury, his Lady hath said, was the cause of all his ruin'. If so, very simple of Bess: she was no intellectual, unlike her husband. Ralegh, said his kinsman, had never been true to any but himself. There was something in that, too: he was an egoist first and last; all his work, all his career, his writings, his poetry, had been inspired thus. But, if so, what

[1] *q.* T. N. Brushfield, 'Raleghana, Part VII', *Trans. Devon. Assocn.* 1905, 284 foll.

then? Would we forego the achievements of that inspiration?
His contemporary was William Shakespeare, least egoistic of men;
but the accomplishment of one was as valid as that of the other.

Ralegh, his cousin said, had been a constant equivocator —
like the Jesuits. If he had succeeded in escaping abroad, he
would have made a dangerous Antonio Perez. He was 'desperate
of any fortune here agreeable with the height of his mind'.
There Stukeley's cleric scored a bull's eye: it was indeed the
crux of the matter. No Coriolanus had a heart more vindictive,
who died like a saint too.

All this had no effect: nothing they could do could wash off
the stain Ralegh had fixed on them by his end. Stukeley sought
help from the King from the general defamation of his character.
Little sympathy was to be had in that quarter: 'were I disposed
to hang every man that speaks ill of thee', said James, 'there
would not be trees enough in all my kingdom to hang them on'.
Within a few months Stukeley had taken Ralegh's place in the
Tower, for a less dignified offence than treason — clipping coin.[1]
Released, he is said to have died mad on Lundy Island; certain
it is that he died a youngish man of about forty in 1620, less than
a couple of years after his betrayal of Ralegh.[2]

John Pory summed up the effect of the last scene in Westminster, in which it had been 'impossible to show more decorum,
courage and piety': Ralegh's death would do much harm to
the pro-Spanish party.[3] A month after, Chamberlain reported
that the town was still talking of nothing else and that almost
every day brought forth something about it, besides ballads some
of which were suppressed by the government. We have probably an instance of its intervention in the cutting of some passages
in the penetrating portrait of his fellow Devonshireman by the
dramatist, John Ford: 'a man endowed not with common
endowments, being stored with the best of Nature's furniture,
taught much by much experience. . . . Yet behold in him the
strange character of a mere man, a man subject to as many
changes of resolution, as resolute to be the instrument of change;
politic, and yet in policy so unsteady that his too much apprehension was the foil of his judgment. For what man soever leans
too credulously to his own strength, not supported by the firm
pillars of constancy and virtue, that man cannot choose but fall
under the weight of his own burden.'[4] Beneath the artificial

---

[1] *Cal. S.P. Dom. 1619–23*, 7, 8.   [2] J. L. Vivian, *Visitations of Devon*, 722.
[3] *Cal. S.P. Dom. 1611–18*, 588.
[4] T. N. Brushfield, 'John Ford . . . and his *Linea Vitae*', *Western Antiquary*, V. 49 foll.

antitheses of a fashionable style, fanciful and unpersuasive, this comes fairly close to our own sober prose estimate: the independent-mindedness, the independence, playing a lone hand against great odds; the pride, thinking that in such a world it could do without the support of others.

There remain the consequences for the family for us to trace — the threads of life to be taken up anew by Bess and her surviving son. Actually both their lives were dominated by that mighty shadow in the background, by Ralegh's fame that did not diminish but grew with the years, by the circumstances of the catastrophe. There was the family to be provided for from the shipwreck of their fortunes. Immediately, the nasty Sir Thomas Wilson suggested to the King that he should take possession of all Ralegh's sea-charts, his manuscript treatises and his library of some four hundred books, chiefly on history, science and divinity.[1] Upon this Lady Ralegh begged that a stop might be put to the depredations on the library — it was all that was left to his poor child. The unfortunate lady was by now an adept at begging — the truth was that it was by no means all that was left. A year later, November 1619, Wilson was still agitating for a final decision about Ralegh's books; but it does not seem that James was so mean as to take them, and a stream of Ralegh's papers came upon the market for publication in future years, the ultimate source appearing to be the family.[2]

The failure of the Guiana voyage left complicated financial troubles in its wake. In 1620 Lady Ralegh got a privy seal from the King that the Lords of the Treasury should agree with her for her ship, the *Destiny*, 'for which she was contented in all humility to take the lowest sum their lordships allowed unto her'. Now Mr. Herbert, one of the adventurers, claimed a fourth part of her portion in the ship, 'which she thinketh is not due unto him at all, or if it be, yet she offereth to prove that it is not payable by her'.[3] It was decided to allot three-fourths to her, and to deposit the remainder until it was settled whether Lady Ralegh was in the right or to pay Mr. Herbert out of her portion. Certainly the government handed over £2250 to Lady Ralegh for her investment in the *Destiny*.[4] £700 was detained in the Exchequer, being claimed by Herbert. In October 1621 there

---

[1] *Cal. S.P. Dom. 1611–18*, 589, 592.

[2] *Cal. S.P. Dom. 1619–23*, 100. It would be good to have a study of the dispersal of Ralegh's books and the whereabouts of those that have survived.

[3] *A.P.C. 1619–21*, 177.   [4] *Cal. S.P. Dom. 1619–23*, 428.

arrived a Spaniard claiming £700 for damage done by Ralegh in Guiana.[1] In July 1622 the Council made an order for the transfer of £750 for claims upon Lady Ralegh out of the £2250 already paid her. We learn that the Earl of Huntingdon had lent Ralegh two great pieces of brass ordnance, sacres of Queen Mary's time marked MR, which were to be restored to him.[2] Years later we find Phineas Pett, the famous shipwright who built the *Destiny*, claiming that the failure of the voyage meant a loss of £700 to him.[3] It is impossible now to estimate the losses to various people, the upshot of it all.

Meanwhile Lady Ralegh's financial transactions with the government regarding her pension and compensation for Sherborne are no less complicated. We recall that James had compounded for Sherborne for £8000 and £400 a year to Lady Ralegh and her son for their lives. To raise money for Buckingham's Rochelle expedition in 1628, the government was glad of a loan of £4000 from Lady Ralegh and the surrender of her pension of £400 a year, in return for a payment to her of £1000 arrears of her pension, and £2400 for her surrender of it and upon which she was to receive 8 per cent until the payment of the sum.[4] We do not know what to make of this: on the face of it, it looks like a bad bargain for her; all we can say is that Bess was certainly not in need — she seems to have had money not immediately needed, to lend Charles I's more indigent government. Meanwhile, too, she was following suits regarding her elusive dower, from more than fifty years back, now with the Earl of Cork, to whom the Earl of Huntingdon must have transferred his debt. She is unlikely ever to have recovered it. In November 1623 her house in the City was burnt down — the poor lady had no luck — and after that she went to reside in the parish of St. Martin-in-the-Fields, for her name appears in a list of grandees headed by the Duke of Buckingham and including many peers, who refused to contribute to the mending of the highways.[5]

In the country Lady Ralegh lived at West Horsley; thence

---

[1] *Ibid.* 297-8.   [2] *A.P.C. 1619-21*, 137.   [3] *Cal. S.P. Dom. 1631-3*, 85.
[4] *Cal. S.P. Dom. 1628-9*, 97, 179; *A.P.C. 1627-8*, 473, 494, 505. The Privy Council reserved its judgment with regard to £600, seized upon Ralegh's attainder and found not to belong to him but to Lady Ralegh. I fear the Privy Council must have found Bess a very pertinacious woman. It is nice, however, to find that she was to receive her 8 per cent out of the impositions on tobacco. *Cal. S.P. Dom. 1631-3*, 120-2.
[5] H.M.C. *App. Fourth Report*, 286. She took the opportunity of the fire to rustle the Lord Treasurer for £200 due to her; and *Cal. S.P. Dom 1625-6*, 392.

we have a few fragments of her intimate correspondence with her brother, Sir Nicholas Carew. In 1629 he writes that he has been importuned by Mr. Everman for the principal and fee of £500 due to him. 'I wonder that you will not pay the fee money at the day, which is but £20 for six months : the not paying of it will breed distrust both of yourself and of your sureties and doth make them hasten to call in the principal.' Bess replied, with feminine logic, 'Brother, I have never stirred out of this town this half year or three quarters, and ever kept my doors open to great and small, therefore I wonder why we should be mistrusted though we break an oath. Mr. Everman shall be paid the principal and interest presently [*i.e.* immediately]. . . . Your friend has seen one hundred discharged to a jettison ; the rest shall be discharged as fast as I can, for I find no pleasure nor profit to pay so much interest.' Later, she excuses herself for not coming to Beddington, 'I have such occasions this term', *i.e.* law-suits to follow. She helps her brother with housekeeping advice, however. 'Brother, I have never a still here but a tin one, which is broken since Joan went, for I have distilled no more rosewater since. But I will send for a glass body and head to London for you . . . but if it please you to send them hither we will set it up here and distil them for you. Or any other thing that Mrs. Quarles did, Kate shall do here, but I will not spare her you thither, you have too much green fruits.' Later, she does a good office by recommending a possible match for a daughter of the house of Beddington. 'Brother, this gentleman Mr. Kechar, is desirous to see and to be seen ; he is in my opinion worthy of a welcome, being a proper gentleman and his father's heir and his uncle's which is rich and was never married — God must give the success, and to God I commend you and yours.'[1] Bess lived on to the immense age, for those days, of eighty-two — long enough to see the ruin of the Stuart monarchy : dying in 1647, with Charles I's execution not much more than a year away, upon a scaffold not far from where Ralegh's had been.

Of their two sons Walter, as we have seen, was killed at St. Thomé. He is said to have been the image of his father ; he certainly was very like him in temperament.[2] Ralegh sent him to Corpus Christi at Oxford, where he remained from 1607 to 1610 under Daniel Featley as his tutor. Aubrey's cousin Whitney

---

[1] Lady Throckmorton's Note Book, from B.M. Add. MSS. 29596/6; 29598/10, 11; 29599/34.
[2] I expect that the boy appreciated the white curled feather the Earl of Northumberland gave him in 1599. H.M.C. *App. Sixth Report*, 228.

was at Oxford with young Walter, and remembered him as 'a handsome, lusty, stout fellow, very bold and apt to affront. Spake Latin very fluently, and was a notable disputant and courser, and would never be out of countenance nor baffled; fight lustily and, one time of coursing, put a turd in the box and besmeared it about his antagonist's face.'[1] Walter's ways stood out even among the crudities of the seventeenth century. In 1612 Ralegh got his acquaintance, Ben Jonson, to take charge of the youth as tutor on a tour abroad — though 'take charge' is hardly the word for so irrepressible a scapegrace who behaved as he did to Jonson. While in Paris there took place a disputation between Featley and a Catholic exile on the profitless subject of the Real Presence; both Ben Jonson and John Pory were there and, it would seem, young Ralegh, to whom it suggested the next jape to practise on Ben. Jonson himself told Drummond, 'this youth, being knavishly inclined, among other pastimes — as the setting of the favour of damsels on a codpiece — caused him to be drunken and dead drunk so that he knew not where he was; thereafter laid him on a cart which he made to be drawn by pioneers through the streets, at every corner showing his governor stretched out and telling them that was a more lively image of the crucifix than any they had'. There is the authentic Ralegh touch — dangerous sport, too, in fanatically Catholic Paris shortly after the Wars of Religion. 'At which sport young Ralegh's mother delighted much, saying his father young was so inclined, though the father abhorred it.'[2] We need hardly be surprised that on their return, tutor and pupil parted, 'I think not in cold blood'.

We have a notice of Walter's fighting proclivities from the sedate Sir Henry Wotton. In May 1615 young Ralegh went over to the Netherlands to fight with one Jay of his own shire at Utrecht: to cover their intent they ate together at Leyden. Wotton sensibly had Walter brought to the Hague: some months before he had dangerously hurt Jay in a private chamber, now Jay had challenged him and Ralegh got leave to travel only for this purpose.[3] In the days of his prosperity Sir Walter planned a marriage for his son and heir with a rich heiress, Elizabeth Basset. On his attainder the contract was broken, and this profitable piece was also picked up by the Howards: the girl was married to a son of Lord Thomas, who became Lord Treasurer Suffolk,

[1] Aubrey, ed. Clark, II. 194.
[2] Herford and Simpson, *Ben Jonson*, I. 65-6, 69, 140-1.
[3] Wotton, ed. Pearsall Smith, II. 79.

subsequently imprisoned for embezzlement on a grand scale from the Treasury of which he was in charge. It was said that the girl always held that she should have been young Ralegh's bride — he certainly had what appealed to a girl — and it was probably over this that he fought the duel with Jay, a gentleman of the Lord Treasurer's. His father recommended him to Prince Maurice, who for Sir Walter's sake, took him into his service.[1]

Next year he was pardoned to come back and serve on his father's — and his — last voyage. It must have been to this interval that Aubrey's story of him relates. 'Sir Walter being invited to dinner to some great person where his son was to go with him, he said to his son, "Thou art expected today at dinner to go along with me, but thou art such a quarrelsome, affronting [fellow] that I am ashamed to have such a bear in my company". Mr. Walter humbled himself to his father, and promised he would behave himself mighty mannerly. So away they went. He sat next to his father and was very demure at least half dinner-time. Then said he, "I, this morning, not having the fear of God before my eyes but by the instigation of the devil, went to a whore. I was very eager of her, kissed and embraced her, and went to enjoy her; but she thrust me from her and vowed I should not, 'For your father lay with me but an hour ago'". Sir Walter, being strangely surprised and put out of countenance at so great a table, gives his son a damned blow over the face. His son, as rude as he was, would not strike his father, but strikes over the face the gentleman that sat next to him, and said, "Box about: 'twill come to my father anon". 'Tis now a common-used proverb.'[2]

We may surmise that if young Walter had lived, we should have had some exploits from him during the Civil War.

Notwithstanding Walter's looks, his younger brother Carew is the more congenial character — gentler, though he too has the recognisable Ralegh temper. All his life was lived in his father's shadow, faithfully defending his memory, advancing his cause, struggling to get back Sherborne, with a perfect fixation upon it, in the end succeeding to his father's old governorship of Jersey. It was for him, to judge from Ralegh's covering letter, that he wrote his famous *Instructions to his Son* — one of the first instances of this strictly private form to be published.[3] Such was 'the lustre

[1] *Cal. S.P. Dom. 1611–18*, 344.   [2] *Aubrey's Brief Lives*, ed. O. L. Dick, 256.
[3] Agnes M. C. Latham, 'Sir Walter Ralegh's *Instructions to his Son*', *Elizabethan and Jacobean Studies Presented to F. P. Wilson*, ed. H. Davis and Helen Gardner, 199 foll.; Oldys and Birch, *Ralegh's Works*, VIII. 557 foll.

of wisdom', according to the publisher, such the fame of the author that, published in 1632, the little book ran into six editions in the next four years. From the grave we hear Ralegh's authentic voice: 'great possessions would make thee lazy, I would have thee to be the son of thine own fortunes as well as my son. I have ever aimed at a competency and God hath fitted me thereafter; nevertheless I deny not but that I have affected promotion.' His aim had been to do good in the commonwealth, and the same 'just ambition I bequeath to thee, my dear and well-beloved son. I feel no more perturbation within me to depart this world than I have done in my best health to arise from table when I have well dined and thence to retire to a pleasant walk. I have had my part in this world and now must give place to fresh gamesters. Farewell. All is vanity and weariness, yet such a weariness and vanity that we shall ever complain of it and love it for all that.'

And so we come to the singularly realistic view of life, without any illusions, that so bothered Victorian admirers of Ralegh's genius. 'Public affairs are rocks, private conversations are whirlpools and quicksands' — he had certainly found them so. 'Thy adventure lies in this troublesome bark; strive, if thou canst, to make good thy station in the upper deck; those that live under hatches are ordained to be drudges and slaves. Endeavour rather to be part of the timber of the house than lath or mud-wall.' The worst thing of all was to be poor. 'Make election rather of thy betters than thy inferiors, shunning always such as are poor and needy . . . if thou be poor withal, thou and thy qualities shall be despised. Poverty is a shame amongst men, an imprisonment of the mind, a vexation of every worthy spirit. Thou shalt neither help thyself nor others; thou shalt drown thee in all thy virtues, having no means to show them; thou shalt be a burden and an eyesore to thy friends, every man will fear thy company; thou shalt be driven basely to beg and depend on others.' There is the worst fate: to be dependent.

These maxims, so much maligned, need no defence; for, from a worldly point of view — and Ralegh's was never other-worldly — these are the principles that obtain in the world. The shocking thing was nakedly to state them, for people do not much relish hearing things called by their right names. It may indeed be that they cannot support life without illusions; and this added to the difficulty of living for Ralegh, who had none, when almost everybody in the seventeenth century had at least the illusions of religion to support them.

Nor did the Victorians relish any more Ralegh's realism

about sex. There were advantages, for a young man, in taking a mistress rather than a wife — for 'how many mistresses soever thou hast . . . when thy humour shall change, thou art yet free to choose again, if thou give thyself that vain liberty'. Nor are there any more illusions about wives. Great care should be taken in choosing one, for 'every man prefers his fantasy in that appetite before all other worldly desires, leaving the care of honour, credit and safety in respect thereof'. He himself could speak from experience as to that. All the same, 'let thy time of marriage be in thy young and strong years, for, believe it, ever the young wife betrayeth the old husband. . . . Have therefore ever more care that thou be beloved of thy wife rather than thyself besotted on her.' It would seem that it had been this way with Bess and Sir Walter. On the other hand, 'if thou have a fair wife and a poor one, if thine own estate be not great, assure thyself that love abideth not with want, for she is the companion of plenty and honour'.

Here young Carew followed his dead father's precept rather than his example : by marrying a rich widow he lived happily enough.

We first catch a glimpse of the boy begging mercy of the King for his father : 'greate Lord, conceit not too grievously the error of a despairated minde, torne with everie misfortune, whilst his lounge shiftings for life perswaded the fittest for the capacities of humors not his own. And, greate Lord, though meritt and reason cannot requier, yet let the priviledge of old age and the innocency of a fatherless child begg mercie from your Majestie.'[1] I think we may judge this to be a composition of his own, at the age of fourteen : its spelling is so much superior to Lady Ralegh's.

Next year he was entered at the new West Country foundation at Oxford, Wadham College, its buildings then going up at the hands of Somerset builders, looking like a more spacious Jacobean manor-house. There Carew remained till 1623, an intelligent youth writing sonnets and later on poems, like 'Careless of love and free from fears' contributed to Lawes's *Airs and Dialogues*. On coming down from Oxford, he was presented at Court by his kinsman, the Earl of Pembroke ; but James, with whom everything relating to Ralegh indicated a bad conscience, found him too much like his father's ghost, and the young man departed for a year's foreign travel. In 1621 a bill passed through the House of Lords restoring him in blood, but the government would not proceed with it. In 1624 a provisional settlement for

---

[1] Edwards, II. 488.

his future was arrived at: the King continued the pension of £400 a year to him, as formerly to his brother Walter, and the father's goods and chattels were granted in trust for the family.[1] This restitution was not to prejudice the Digby Earl of Bristol's grant of Sherborne, now confirmed by the House of Lords.

After Carr's condemnation as accessory to the murder of Overbury, James had granted Sherborne to Sir John Digby for his services as ambassador to Spain, where he had met his own charges, and for £10,000 besides.[2] This was in October 1617, when Ralegh was out of the Tower and very angry he had been made by it. He felt, justly enough, that he had built the house and made the place what it was. His son Carew spent most of his life trying to get it back. Not till his last years did he give up hope, in spite of the special reservations made to protect the rights of the Digbys. In 1624, for instance, an act of Parliament to restore Carew Ralegh in blood, *i.e.* recover him from the effects of his father's attainder, passed both Houses of Parliament, though it was specifically not to apply to Sherborne. Nevertheless, James refused his assent — he had his obligations to the Digbys and had committed himself — though we are not sorry that Ralegh's affairs troubled James to the last. In 1626, the first year of Charles I's reign, the act was submitted to Parliament again; not until 1628 did it receive the Royal assent, with the proviso that Carew should resign all claim to Sherborne.

It was only then that he bought Bishop's manor in the parish of East Horsley in Surrey — which had once briefly belonged to Sir Nicholas Throckmorton — where to seat himself and his family.[3] For about this time he married Philippa, the rich widow of Sir Anthony Ashley — a former follower of his father and companion of Throckmorton's at Cadiz.[4] The marriage was fruitful: two sons and three daughters. Carew was well-received at Charles I's Court, where his Carew and Herbert relations were in high favour; in 1630 we find him dancing in Ben Jonson's masque, *Love's Triumph*.[5] Five years later he was made a gentleman of the Privy Chamber. Already in 1634 he was petitioning Charles's impecunious government for £2765 arrears of pension due to his wife, Lady Philippa.[6] In 1639 an incident while in attendance upon the King revealed a couple of Ralegh characteristics, not only the familiar temper. The King was unwell

---

[1] *Cal. S.P. Dom. 1623–5*, 218, 247. [2] *Cal. S.P. Dom. 1611–18*, 426.
[3] O. Manning and W. Bray, *History and Antiquities of Surrey*, III. 31, 40.
[4] *v.* above, p. 201.
[5] Herford and Simpson, *Ben Jonson* X. 437. [6] *Cal. S.P. Dom. 1633–4*, 465.

while hunting at Oatlands, and Ralegh who was at the fall of the stag in the forest reported to the King he had but two or three horns, whereas he had four or five. A dispute followed with Sir William St. Ravée, whom Carew struck and drew on in the outer court of the palace. For this he was sent to the Fleet, discharged only on a bond in £1000 to appear before a court of honour next term.[1]

Soon the Civil War came down upon these fooleries and they all had other things to think about. In 1643 his uncle Sir Nicholas died, and Carew succeeded to the manor of West Horsley, in addition to the property he already possessed in East Horsley. He was not doing badly. His attitude in the Civil War was a sensibly equivocal one : a personal servant of the King, he could not, with his estates in close-by Surrey, go against Parliament. Moreover, his father's tradition lived on in growing proportions on the Parliamentarian side. When Charles I left Hampton Court for the last time — to make his attempt at escape from the Isle of Wight as Sir Walter had from the Thames, each to be brought back to the scaffold — the King honoured Sir Walter's son with 'a kind token'.

The victory of Parliament brought the cult of Sir Walter Ralegh as a martyr to the Stuarts, which had been growing ever since his death, to its full proportions, and at the same time seemed to open an opportunity for the recovery of Sherborne, for the Digbys were Royalists. Carew was bent on the full restoration of his family. He sat as member for Haslemere in the Rump Parliament from 1650 to 1653. Another new member in that House of Commons was the Earl of Salisbury, the House of Lords having been abolished by the Commonwealth : it is somehow touching to think of Ralegh's son and Cecil's son sitting there together after the years and all that had passed.[2] The next thing we hear is that Ralegh was committed to the Tower for a few days for 'passionate words' spoken at a Parliamentary committee. However, his membership gave him the chance to bring several petitions during the Interregnum for the return of his father's estates. In 1651 he went before the committee for the sale of delinquent estates, since the Digbys were delinquents in addition to being malignants, in good Puritan terminology, to give evidence as to the particulars of his father's deprivation. Commonwealth justice did not go so far as to reinstate the Raleghs, but it awarded Carew £500 a year out of the estate. This came to

---

[1] H.M.C. *App. Fourth Report*, 294.
[2] D. Masson, *Life of John Milton*, IV. 114.

an end with the Restoration, when the Digbys came back for good, and this, along with the death of his elder son and heir, ended Carew Ralegh's hopes.

We can trace the growth of Sir Walter's fame in the crowding publications of the time, while his son always stood up for his memory. Carew took offence, for example, at James Howell's reference in his *Epistolae* to the mine in Guiana as a 'mere chimera' and exacted an apology from the author. The tribute of that other victim of the Stuarts, Sir John Eliot, to Ralegh is well known. He, too, during his years in the Tower had time to write a number of learned works. In his *Monarchie of Man* he has a long encomium upon Ralegh at his execution, speaking rhetorically as an eye-witness: 'all the preparations that are terrible presented to his eye, guards and officers about him, fetters and chains upon him, the scaffold and executioner before him, and then the axe . . . and what did all this work on the resolution of that worthy?' etc.[1] Eliot makes the point that it turned men's minds to admiration; we observe that Ralegh had become a Parliamentarian worthy, on his way to becoming one of the heroes of the Revolution of 1688 and taking his place with Eliot and Hampden in temples of liberty at Wentworth Wood-house and Stowe. We know the cult that John Hampden vowed to him: he is said to have paid an amanuensis to copy out Ralegh's manuscripts at length. John Eliot himself transcribed Ralegh's *Prerogative of Parliaments*: the copy still exists at Port Eliot in Cornwall.[2] Ralegh's sentiments and arguments entered into the speeches of these leaders of Parliament against the Stuarts.

Even more important in their general effect in forming opinion would be the widespread circulation of Ralegh's manuscripts and the frequent publications of his works throughout the century.[3] With Parliament's victory in the Civil War it was possible to publish, in 1648, an account of the Trial of 1603 and the Proceedings of 1618. *The Prerogative of Parliaments* had been first published in Holland in 1628; now that it was open to publish Ralegh's political tracts in England, his *Remains*, which

---

[1] Sir John Eliot, *The Monarchie of Man*, ed. A. B. Grosart, II. 158-9.

[2] H. Hulme, *The Life of Sir John Eliot*, 31. I take this opportunity to assure Professor Hulme that the first generation of Eliots in Cornwall were *not* rich, as he thinks (p. 1.). If he thinks £66 p.a. rich for an Elizabethan gentleman, he little knows what riches were in the period. The first Eliots belonged to the lesser gentry in Cornwall, as opposed to greater gentry like the Arundells, Grenvilles, Edgcumbes, Godolphins, or the immensely new rich Robartes family.

[3] Cf. Brushfield's Ralegh Bibliography, *Western Antiquary*, V. *passim.*

also included poems and letters, came to rival the *History* in popularity: there were editions in 1651, 1656, 1657, 1661, 1664, 1675, 1681, 1702. Ralegh's *Judicious and Select Essays and Observations* came out with a dedication to Carew Ralegh in 1650, and was re-issued. Carew himself turned author with his *Brief Relation of Sir Walter Ralegh's Troubles*. The *Maxims of State* was published in 1642, and in 1658 Milton printed Ralegh's most considered work on politics, *The Cabinet Council*. In publishing it Milton said that he had had the manuscript by him many years, 'given me for a true copy by a learned man at his death, who had collected several such pieces. . . . I thought it a kind of injury to withhold longer the work of so eminent an author from the public.'

Numerous separate pieces dropped from the press all through these years, and shortly came the biographers. William Winstanley was the first with his in 1660, then John Shirley's biographical Preface to the *History*, very popular and frequently reprinted. Meanwhile, in the second generation on, co-eval with Ralegh's grand-children, John Aubrey was taking down his valuable notes, for in Wiltshire he was close to reliable sources of information about the Raleghs and knew people who had known Sir Walter well. Then in 1691 came Anthony Wood's Oxford account, and in 1701 John Prince's life in his *Worthies of Devon*, which was the best up to that time and brought local knowledge to bear on the subject. And this besides character sketches and portraits such as John Ford's, Naunton's and Fuller's in his *Worthies*.

We have an indication of people's interest and the way Carew Ralegh met it by a letter of his to Lord Conway in 1652, sending him 'a parcel of papers, old, rotten and dirty, such as a person less intelligent would hardly understand — all receipts, most in my father's hand'.[1] And then, with authentic Ralegh touch, 'I have many other of verses and discourses of several kinds, which, on the return of these, shall be sent you, if you desire it'. For the continued interest in Ralegh's medical receipts, we note that in 1671 the still-rooms at Belvoir and Haddon kept, along with the 'marmalett' and the conserved roses, Sir Walter Ralegh's Cordial. When William III was dying, in 1702, the doctors gave him the cordial, 'which they have some hopes in', as a last resource.[2]

In the high summer of 1658 John Evelyn dined twice with

---

[1] *Cal. S.P. Dom. 1651–2*, 303. 'Receipts' here means medical, or chemical, receipts or compounds.   [2] H.M.C. *Rutland MSS*. II. 169, 338.

Carew Ralegh at Horsley.[1] Next year Carew took his place in May in the restored Rump Parliament, and thereafter was very busy in the last stages of the drift towards the Restoration. A Commonwealth man, he was out of sympathy with, and had no part in, Cromwell's military dictatorship. This year, until the Rump was once more extruded, Ralegh was one of those members most regular in their attendance, with protagonists of the 'good old cause' like Haselrig, Henry Vane, Ludlow, Neville.[2] In June he was allotted official lodgings in Whitehall — so too Andrew Marvell.[3] In December he was reinstated with other members of the restored Rump, and throwing in his lot with the moderate, cautious General Monk, who sought to realise the general will of the nation, Ralegh became a member of the new Council of State, from January to April 1660.[4] In February he got his reward from the General, who appointed him to his father's old office of Governor of Jersey.[5] Everything was on the move, like an avalanche, towards the Restoration.

On Charles II's return Carew was offered knighthood, as one of those who had supported Monk in bringing about what the country undoubtedly wanted; but this he declined in favour of his eldest son, who became the second Sir Walter in June 1660. Carew had settled the Horsley estates upon his two sons, Walter and Philip; but Walter's early death upset this, and the father sold West Horsley to Sir Edward Nicholas, Secretary of State, and East Horsley to Henry Hildyard.[6] Carew Ralegh retreated to his London house in St. Martin's Lane, which had no doubt been Bess's before him. Here he died at the end of 1666 — though the parish register of St. Margaret's, Westminster, described him as 'killed' — a characteristically Ralegh ending.[7] We have no information, but that his end was sudden and unexpected we know from a nuncupative will having to be made, testifying that on the day he died he uttered these words, 'I do make my wife my sole executrix, And I give unto her all my estate whatsoever'.[8] This was said, or supposed to have been said, in the presence of his son-in-law Sir Peter Tyrrell and his wife Dame Philippa. Nothing whatever is said of his son Philip: he cannot have been on good terms with him. There is some

[1] *Diary of John Evelyn*, ed. E. S. de Beer, III. 219.
[2] Masson, *Milton*, V. 454, 465.   [3] *Cal. S.P. Dom. 1659–60*, 27.
[4] Masson, V. 519, 537, 545.
[5] Bulstrode Whitelock, *Memorials* (1853 ed.), IV. 401.
[6] *V.C.H. Surrey*, III. 353–5.
[7] Brushfield, 'Raleghana, Part VIII', *Trans. Devon. Assocn.* 1907, 247.
[8] P.C.C. Carr 10.

question, too, where Carew Ralegh lies buried, and with him his father's skull — for Ralegh's head still dogs us. There is no doubt that he was first buried in St. Margaret's. But the parish register of West Horsley says that he was buried in the burial place of the manor in September 1680.[1] Perhaps this was a re-burial? And what about the sacred head he had kept by him all his life? Sir Edward Nicholas's son was convinced he saw that a severed head was buried in Ralegh's son's grave.

Philip Ralegh carried on the tradition of his grandfather into a new century, by publishing in 1702 three of his discourses : on the War with Spain, on the Cause of War, and on Ecclesiastical Power. The grandson married a Buckinghamshire, not a West Country, Grenville and had four sons, all of whom pre-deceased him. Three of them were called by names so familiar to us in this story. Walter, the eldest, died young; then in 1698 died two sons : Carew, lately an officer in the King's ship *Breda*, and Brudenell, 'now intending a voyage to the West Indies', leaving his father power of attorney to collect his pay, bounty and prize money due to him 'in any of his Majesty's ships of war' : he must have died, then, on that voyage to the Caribbean, which had cast a spell on the famous great-grandfather. This left only Grenville Ralegh, formerly of the Marine Regiment, who died a captain in the army at Chester in 1717.[2]

Philip Ralegh died in 1705 and this was effectively the end of the family, though not of Sir Walter and Bess's progeny; for, without the tie of land, a family as such disappears into the soil from which it raised itself, in this case with so much effort in the centuries before.

II

The fate of the Throckmortons of Paulerspury was in some contrast. Where Ralegh's stock held good in the male line for some generations, fighting a rearguard action to maintain themselves, but sinking down at last among the people, the Throckmorton co-heiresses married into their own class, and into the peerage, their name thus absorbed and extinguished another way.

Little remains of Throckmorton's last years; our one notice of him — so like life — shows that good man in not a favourable

---

[1] Manning and Bray, *Surrey*, III. 40.

[2] Vivian, *Visitations*, 639 P.C.C. Administration Book, 1698, f. 95; Noel 13; Act Book, 1720, f. 125.

light. The rectory of Paulerspury was a valuable one, and in
the last year of his life Sir Arthur tried to impropriate it, *i.e.*
annex the fat rectorial tithes to himself and turn the living into
a donative, a curacy. Upon unpopular parson Pilkington's
death, some hanky-panky took place. In 1625 Throckmorton
presented Gerence James to the living, but there must have been
an improper understanding between them, for James held the
rectory of Tiffield and a curate, James Cary, was forked in to
serve Paulerspury.[1] This lasted Throckmorton's time and until
1631, when an interfering and not disinterested clergyman, one
Ezekiel Johnson, brought a charge of simony against James and
got the presentation to the living himself from the King. Throckmorton was now dead some years; Gerence James lived on
respectably at Tiffield to find a place under a slab in his chancel :
'an orthodox, pious and charitable minister, after many troublesome days in a time of wars, rested his feeble body here in peace'
— in 1645, aged eighty.

Throckmorton died at the end of July 1626, leaving a will
very true to him, 'all written with mine own hand and subscribed
with my name and sealed with my seal', and adding proudly
that he was the son of Sir Nicholas Throckmorton.[2] He wished
to be buried in the chapel on the north side of the chancel at
Paulerspury, 'the ancient chapel and burying place for the lord
of that manor, and my brother William and my son Wotton's
three little children laid there also by me'. He desired a tomb
to be made in remembrance of his father and mother, himself
and his wife and all his children. To his 'true loving and virtuous
dear wife' he left all his lands for life, afterwards to go to his
children according to the settlements made. The youngest
daughter remained 'yet with me and her mother unmarried and
unbestowed'; if she married with her mother's consent, she was
to have all the stock of cattle at Luffield on her mother's death ;
while at home unmarried £50 a year, and away £100 a year.
Alderminster had been settled on her. Sir Thomas Wotton was
to have the great gilt cup and cover engraved with the Throckmorton and Carew arms which Mary Stuart had given his father
in France, with his best horse, a mourning gown and hood and
the same to Wotton's wife. His friend Sir Henry Wotton was
left his next great gilt cup, the next horse and all his father's
papers relating to his embassies, with the wish that Sir Henry
would 'order and digest them in a book whereby to do my father

[1] Bridges, *Northamptonshire*, I. 272, 313 ; H.M.C., *App. Sixth Report*, 109.
[2] P.C.C. Hele 106.

right in many things he hatn been foully abused and wronged by spleen and malice, and by reports and by false flattering humourous books'. We do not know what these were, but Throckmorton's piety towards his father's memory was constant.

His nephew Carew Ralegh was left a mourning gown and hood — clearly he was expected to attend the funeral — and 'a gelding of my own breed'. Mr. Christopher Southerton, Nicholas Pey and Paul Ashton to have cloth cloaks, and the last £3.[1] His old servant Robert Pound got the parsonage of Thornborough for life; all his household servants mourning cloaks and gowns; seventy-one of his poorest tenants near by 6d. each, a piece of beef and a loaf. His lawyer, Serjeant Harvey was awarded a pear gilt cup and a gelding; Magdalen College all the books in the study after his wife had taken what English books she liked best.

Apparently his wife, who died three years later, liked all the English books, for it is those in foreign tongues that came to Magdalen. And a fine collection they make — though how much more valuable if it contained the original issues of Donne, Bacon, Andrewes, the quartos of Shakespeare and Ben Jonson among the playbooks, what not, that Throckmorton bought.

A man's books are a good index to his character of mind and his tastes. The books at Magdalen are not only those bought by Arthur Throckmorton but those he inherited from his father. We note the different inflexion of their interests: Sir Nicholas's almost exclusively politics and religion; to these Arthur adds literature, military arts, science, mainly astronomy and voyages. Where the father's books are chiefly French and secondarily Latin, the son's are dominantly Italian. This reflects their travels and interests abroad. Where Sir Nicholas underlines heavily and has forceful pointers to sentiments he agreed with in the margin, his son, a less forceful character, wrote moralistic sentiments on a title-page or the price of the book. He was a collector — we cannot be so sure that he read them all. To Sir Nicholas books were tools, to be used.

Sir Nicholas read his Machiavelli's *Prince* in the French translation of Guillaume Cappel, 1553. It is therefore of penetrating interest, in the somewhat theoretical discussion of Machiavelli's influence in Europe, to follow the sentiments that made a marked impression on the mind of this leading English statesman of his time. He scored and signposted such statements as these I translate: 'a prince should have no other end, take no other

---

[1] Paul had been churchwarden the year before, 1624–5, and from the Paulerspury register we find that he was married and having a family.

matter to heart, than the fact of war. . . . It is necessary to a
prince who wishes to maintain himself, to learn to be both good
and bad, and to use one and the other according to his needs.
. . . And if he is powerful in arms he will always have good
friends.' I think we may say that Sir Nicholas, like Ralegh, was
a Machiavellian; his son, a lesser man, who did not emerge in
that struggle for survival which is politics, was not. Much the
same disillusioned sentiments are approved in the French translation by Chomedey of Guicciardini read by Sir Nicholas. 'It
is not the office of a wise captain to make his dispositions according to the popular vote.' Wise doctors increase less important
maladies to diminish those more so. Affairs which depend on
several people do not succeed well. Nothing lasts so briefly as
the memory of benefits received. Men easily deceive themselves
about what they ardently desire — as Sir Nicholas had done, we
may remind his shade, as to the precise situation in France in
1562–3. Princes are more often led by what is of utility to them
then by considerations of honesty and decency. It might be the
voice of Ralegh speaking. Such were the conclusions Sir Nicholas
drew from experience; this is what he sadly thought.

His son's reflections are altogether less gripping; they serve
the purpose not of steeling himself for action, but of consoling
himself, perhaps for inaction. At the top of the title-page of the
second volume of Ramusio's *Navigationi et Viaggi*, he has written
and signed it:

> Par longues chemins et beaucoup de traverses
> Mille maux et fortunes diverses.

In the third volume he has inscribed, as in a number of others
when preparing for his end, *Ex dono Arthuri Throckmorton milit.*
1626. Once and again he encourages himself to action with such
a sentiment as *feriendo aut ferendo faciam* inscribed in his copy of
Ariosto, the Venice edition of 1584, which he bought in London
in 1589 for 20s.; or the inscription in a collection of Latin writers
De Re Rustica: *ex nihil agendo discas male agere.* A. Throck. But
more true to him are inscriptions like those in his Italian New
Testament (Lyons, 1556): *Patientia et Penitentia. Voluntas cum
virtute. Honos cum honestate. Recte vivetur religione.*

This is very different in tone from the sombre reflections his
statesman-father extracted from his reading of Commines: 'a
prince or any other man who was never deceived can be but a
beast, have no knowledge of good and evil, nor what difference
there is'. The *Histoires et Chroniques du Monde*, drawn from

337

Hebrew and Greek (Paris, 1561) was thoroughly read, perhaps during Sir Nicholas's captivity, for it has a detailed index to it in manuscript at the end, heavy underscoring with signposts to such encouraging sentiments as 'Exercise turns our thoughts from vice'. Or our attention is directed in the Memoirs of Martin du Bellay (Paris, 1569) to the thought 'who commands London commands the whole kingdom' — which must have turned Sir Nicholas's mind back to Wyatt's rebellion that so nearly captured London in 1554. His library was essentially that of a practising diplomat whose business was to know France thoroughly. Thus there are several histories of France, informative books on the French provinces — the Annals of Aquitaine, Anjou, Savoy; the Ordinances of the French kings, the military discipline of the kingdom; the customs of the duchy of Burgundy, the antiquities of Nîmes. One inscription brings back Sir Nicholas's envenomed dispute with his colleague Sir Thomas Smith: the French translation of Jewel's *Apology* has 'N. Throckmorton' on the outside cover, 'Thomas Smith' on the title-page within.

Arthur's books equally bring back the glad early days in Italy. His Italian translation of Josephus has notes at the end: *Vicenza fu edificata da Francesi Senonensi*, with remarks on the building and history of other Italian towns. More intimately, we come across a charming gift of a book, the *Concetti* of Hieronimo Garimberto and others (Venice, 1579): *Richardus Spencerus ornatissimo clarissimo domino Arthuro Throckmorton scripsit amicitiae ergo, Patavii 2° Augusti 1581*. There they were at Padua together forty-five years before the book fetched up on the shelves of the library at Magdalen. Or there is the humorous inscription in Ariosto's comedy *Cassaria* that belonged to another companion abroad, Thomas Cobham, who wrote his name in front with 'I hope the hapye daye', and at the end:

> I swere by hym that made Adam
> I am the boke of Thomas Cobham
> Which is so merye and pleasant
> Grete losse it wear that he shuld want
> ffor he dothe make me oft merye
> whoo ells full oft wolde be sorye.

We have noticed already some of Throckmorton's purchases in Italy, and there are others: the recently published *Historia Fiorentina* of Buoninsegni: 'Arthuro Throckmorton fiorenza Septem: 23: 1581. 8 libri'; and the same day the Supplement

to Jacopo Filippo's Universal Chronicles. A very few of the
books were not purchased : Giordano Bruno's *Dialogues* and an
Italian translation of Pomponius Mela, for example, had belonged
to Anthony Stokes. While a Spanish translation of Marcus
Aurelius (Antwerp, 1594) has 'T. Tresami et Amicorum' on the
title-page — perhaps Arthur brought that away with him from
Rushton when he searched the house at the time of Gunpowder
Plot ? Nor have we completed the spoils from Cadiz : a *Manuale
Confessoriorum* has at the foot of the title-page 'del Collegio de la
Compania de Jesus de Cadiz' ; while the *Reportorio de Todas las
Pragmaticas y Capitulos de Cortes* (Salamanca, 1566) would probably
have come from there. We do not have a full picture of Arthur
Throckmorton's interests unless we add the astronomical works
of Copernicus and Tycho Brahe, the *De Re Metallica* of Agricola,
the books on natural history. It is the collection of a curious
rather than a forceful mind, a sympathetic man of somewhat
diffuse but cultivated interests. Altogether some 250 to 300
volumes have come to rest at Magdalen, though some contain
more than one work bound together. The big heavy folios were
mostly Sir Nicholas's, the smaller books, mostly in their original
vellum covers, were bought by both, but more by the son. There
seems something appropriate in that.

The embellishment of the chapel at Paulerspury according to
Throckmorton's wish was set in hand : at the west end is an
extraordinary, a unique, monument in black and white marble,
of him and his spouse each reclining upon a tomb set lengthwise,
each propped up on elbow gazing fondly at the other in the
middle. I know no other of this design. He is in full armour —
and indeed his helmet, gauntlets and corselet have survived the
ages among the débris of the chapel where they lie. He wears
a skull-cap — or one of those night-caps he used to buy when he
went up to London — and shows a mild, inoffensive, contented
face with double chin, Caroline-upturned moustache and tiny
tuft below the lip. Anne has her hair bunched out beneath her
widow's hood, slashed sleeves and quilled ruff, a stronger countenance looking devotedly upon him.

Above them on the wall is a tablet summing up his qualities
and their life together : the heir to his great father's virtues,
*politis moribus, animi fortis, exculti ingenii, religiosae mentis, oeconomia
splendida, candidissimo pectore.*[1] It is just enough. We learn that
Anne was nearly sixty at her death and had been married forty

[1] Cf. Baker, *Northamptonshire*, II. 207.

years: so she was a girl of nineteen when he married her. They lived together forty years without a quarrel, the table says: we know better, thanks to the Diary. Nevertheless a happy marriage, as marriages go. In the medieval lancet-windows of the Paveleys before them — from whom Paulerspury got its name and of whom two wooden effigies remain — is set the heraldic glass of the four daughters. Catherine, the youngest, is given as unmarried and the books repeat that so she died. But if we take the trouble to call in at the church of Alderminster, where the manor was her inheritance, we find that a marriage was found for her the very next year. A tablet to her tells us that 'Edward Partherich [Partridge], late of Bridge in the county of Kent, hath erected this monument, to whom he was blestly married 30 August 1627'; that she had five children in five years, died in 1632 and was buried in the chancel of Hollingbourne in Kent.

The eldest daughter's Wotton marriage transferred her main interests to Kent, and to Boughton Malherbe where she went to live and whither her father's Diary went and was lost to view for so long. Her husband died, still young, in 1630, leaving her with four daughters, co-heiresses: so were families and their possessions broken up, redistributed.[1] We find Sir Henry Wotton, now elderly, paying a visit once a year to his old home, where his nephew's widow lived with her daughters, finding there 'a cure for all cares by the cheerful company, which he called the living furniture of that place, and a restoration of his strength by the connaturalness of that which he called his genial air'.[2] In 1639 we have a letter from Sir Henry promising his niece a visit and interesting himself in the negotiations for her second daughter's marriage with Baptist Noel, the second Lord Campden. The eldest daughter married the Earl of Chesterfield, through whom Boughton Malherbe descended to the Stanhopes, who allowed it to go to ruin and sold the fine Renaissance pannelling off to America.[3] It is a lucky accident that we have as much of the Diary as we have. Lady Wotton died in 1658 and was buried there beside her lord.

Paulerspury fell to the inheritance of the youngest daughter Anne, who married Sir Edward Hales, through whom it descended in the next century to Sir Benjamin Bathurst, Cofferer of the Household to Queen Anne. In the year of Trafalgar, 1805, it was purchased by an American Loyalist returning to

---

[1] G. E. C. *Complete Peerage*, XII, pt. II. 867.
[2] *q.* Pearsall Smith, *Wotton*, I. 212. [3] R. F. Jessup, *Kent*, 72.

SIR ARTHUR
THROCKMORTON
AND HIS WIFE

this country after the Revolution, who now has his place in the
ancient burying place of the manor along with the medieval
Paveleyes and Elizabethan Throckmortons: 'Robert Shedden,
esquire, of Paulerspury Park. . . . He married Agatha Wells,
daughter of John Goodrich esquire of Nansemond Plantation in
the Province of Virginia, where he was residing as a merchant
prior to the American Rebellion, in which country, adhering to
the cause of loyalty, his possessions were confiscated and his
flattering prospects in the colony sacrificed; but being blessed
with prudence and energy of character, on his return to Great
Britain he amply redeemed, during forty years of activity and
perseverance, the cost of loyalty and fidelity.'[1] Robert Shedden
was not alone in adhering to the King's cause, so did his father-
in-law, with whom he took refuge on board Lord Dunmore's
ships, the last royal governor of Virginia. Coming back to
England, Shedden made a second fortune and purchased several
estates, of which Paulerspury was one.

Paulerspury continued in this family several generations,
though Throckmorton's mansion — which the parish always
called the Great House — was deserted, became the poor-house
and then was pulled down before the middle of the last century.[2]
And now, though something of Ralegh remains in the nucleus
of the house he built at Sherborne, nothing remains of Throckmorton's efforts in building and shaping an estate at Paulerspury
but a windy bare slope. There remains, however, his Diary, for
three centuries and a half put by, as if asleep awaiting us, now
laid bare to bring back all that life — at home and abroad,
soldiering in the Netherlands, touring Germany, Austria, Italy
and France in the high Renaissance, Elizabethan London, the
road to Scotland, across the counties in Shakespeare's day from
Warwickshire to Devon, an intimate record of settled life in the
Northamptonshire of King James and Ralegh's years in the
Tower — once more, with a kind of clairvoyance, before our
eyes.

[1] Baker, II. 207-8.   [2] A. Goldberg, *A Short History of Paulerspury*, 7-8.

INDEX

PRINTED BY R. & R. CLARK, LTD., EDINBURGH